Law 4 Layman

Law 4 Layman

BY

Kush Kalra
&
Ayushi Gaur

Foreword by

Dr Kiran Bedi, IPS

Vij Books India Pvt Ltd

New Delhi (India)

Published by

Vij Books India Pvt Ltd
2/19, Ansari Road, Darya Ganj
New Delhi - 110002
Phones: 91-11- 43596460, 47340674
Fax: 91-11-47340674
e-mail : vijbooks@rediffmail.com
web : www.vijbooks.com

First Published : 2014

ISBN : 978-93-82652-32-8

Acknowledgements

My special thanks to Bhanu Tanwar (Student of Law, NLU Delhi), and Lalit Ajmani (Student of Law, RGNUL) for helping me in research work.

Contents

Foreword

Education is the most potent mechanism for the advancement of human beings. It enlarges, enriches and improves an individual's image of the future. It emancipates the human beings and leads to liberation from ignorance. A man without education is no more than an animal. It is said that in the twenty first century, 'a nation's ability to convert knowledge into wealth and social good through the process of innovation is going to determine its future,' accordingly twenty first century is termed as century of knowledge. The most important function of education is enriching the character. What we need today more than anything else is moral leadership- founded on courage, intellectual integrity and a sense of values. Your education has been in vain if it has not fostered in you the habit of clear, independent thinking.

Different people have different perceptions as to what law is. The law has to be therefore described rather than defined. Even the definition of law can have different angles, for example in terms of a judicial process in terms of its purpose or in terms of its social facts. As observed by Sabyasachi Mukherjee Judge in Pomal Kunji Govindji vs Vrajlal Karasandas Purohit law must respond and be responsible to the felt and desirable compulsions of circumstances that would be equitable, fair and just and unless there is anything contrary to the statute Court must take cognizance of the fact and act accordingly. A definition of law should have two aims. Firstly, to make precise the meaning of law and secondly, to call up in the mind of the reader a true picture of law and its operation.

There is a old maxim "Ignorance of Law is no Excuse". Every citizen of this country is expected to know the law of the land. Now come to the reality. Whether a common man, not been a student of law, have any convenient & handy source to acquaint with law? We know very well the use and importance of law in our daily life. It is essential to know at least the basic laws of the land. Knowing about laws helps citizens to enjoy the Freedom i.e. Freedom of speech and expression, Freedom to form associations, Freedom to assemble peacefully without arms as mentioned in constitution of India. Freedom is fundamental not only for expressing one's personality, but also for it's all round development. Development is not possible without opportunities. Freedom gives us opportunities to perform.

The Book "Law 4 Layman" is an attempt to provide a forum for discussion and debate on all kinds of legal and social issues that confront us today. In the first issue of the book varied subjects like Freedom of Speech and Expression, Right to Life, Free Legal Aid, Delay in Justice and Right to Education, PIL and Human Rights have been covered. This book shall help the Layman in his day to day life.

I wish the book the wide circulation which it deserves.

- Dr Kiran Bedi, IPS

All the troubles may be summed up in three lines (T.S. Eliot)

"Where is the Life we have lost in living?
Where is the wisdom we have lost in Knowledge?
Where is the knowledge we have lost in information?"

List of Abbreviations

AIR	-	All India Reporter
Bom	-	Bombay
D.B.	-	Division Bench
Govt.	-	Government
ILR	-	Indian Law Reporter
IPC	-	Indian Penal Code
Lah	-	Lahore
LJ	-	Law Journal
LR	-	Law Reporter
Mah	-	Maharashtra
M.P.	-	Madhya Pradesh
P&H	-	Punjab and Haryana
Sec	-	Section
SC	-	Supreme Court
SCC	-	Supreme Court Cases
SCR	-	Supreme Court Reporter

Freedom of Speech and Expression

Speech is God's gift to mankind. Through speech a human being conveys his thoughts, sentiments and feelings to others. Freedom of speech and expression is thus a natural right which a human being acquires on birth. It is, therefore, a basic human right. "Everyone has the right to freedom of opinion and expression; the right includes freedom to hold opinions without interference and to seek and receive and impart information and ideas through any media and regardless of frontiers" proclaims the Universal Declaration of Human Rights (1948). The People of India declared in the Preamble[1] of the Constitution which they gave unto themselves their resolve to secure to all citizens liberty of thought and expression. This resolve is reflected in Article 19(1)(a) which is one of the articles found in Part III[2] of the Constitution which enumerates the Fundamental Rights. That article reads as under:

19(1). All citizens shall have the right-

(a) to freedom of speech and expression;

The words 'freedom of speech and expression' must, therefore, be broadly construed to include the freedom to circulate one's views by words of mouth or in writing or through audio-visual instrumentalities. It,

---

1 **Preamble of the Constitution:**
WE, THE PEOPLE OF INDIA, having solemnly resolved to constitute India into a SOVEREIGN SOCIALIST SECULAR DEMOCRATIC REPUBLIC and to secure to all its citizens:
JUSTICE, social, economic and political;
LIBERTY, of thought, expression, belief, faith and worship;
EQUALITY of status and of opportunity;
and to promote among them all
FRATERNITY assuring the dignity of the individual and the unity and integrity of the Nation;
IN OUR CONSTITUENT ASSEMBLY this twenty-sixth day of November, 1949, DO HEREBY ADOPT, ENACT AND GIVE TO OURSELVES THIS CONSTITUTION.

2 '**Part III – Fundamental Rights'** is a charter of rights contained in the Constitution of India. It guarantees civil liberties such that all Indians can lead their lives in peace and harmony as citizens of India. These include individual rights common to most liberal democracies, such as equality before law, freedom of speech and expression, and peaceful assembly, freedom to practice religion, and the right to constitutional remedies for the protection of civil rights by means of writs such as habeas corpus. Violation of these rights result in punishments as prescribed in the Indian Penal Code or other special laws, subject to discretion of the judiciary. The Fundamental Rights are defined as basic human freedoms which every Indian citizen has the right to enjoy for a proper and harmonious development of personality. These rights universally apply to all citizens, irrespective of race, place of birth, religion, caste, creed, colour or gender. Aliens (persons who are not citizens) are also considered in matters like equality before law. They are enforceable by the courts, subject to certain restrictions. The Rights have their origins in many sources, including England's Bill of Rights, the United States Bill of Rights and France's Declaration of the Rights of Man.

therefore, includes the right to propagate one's views through the print media or through any other communication channel e.g. the radio and the television. Every citizen of this free country, therefore, has the right to air his or her views through the printing and/or the electronic media subject of course to permissible restrictions imposed under Article 19(2)[3] of the Constitution. The print media, the radio and the tiny screen play the role of public educators, so vital to the growth of a healthy democracy. Freedom to air one's views is the life line of any democratic institution and any attempt to stifle, suffocate or gag this right would sound a death-knell to democracy and would help usher in autocracy or dictatorship. It cannot be gainsaid that modern communication mediums advance public interest by informing the public of the events and developments that have taken place and thereby education the voters, a role considered significant for the vibrant functioning of a democracy. Therefore, in any set up, more so in a democratic set up like ours, dissemination of news and views for popular consumption is a must and any attempt to deny the same must be frowned upon unless it falls within the mischief of Article 19(2) of the Constitution. It follows that a citizen for propagation of his or her ideas has a right to publish for circulation his views in periodicals, magazines and journals or through the electronic media since it is well known that these communication channels are great purveyors of news and views and make considerable impact on the minds of the readers and viewers and arc known to mould public opinion on vital issues of national importance. Once it is conceded, and it cannot indeed be disputed, that freedom of speech and expression includes freedom of circulation and propagation of ideas, there can be no doubt that the right extends to the citizen being permitted to use the media to answer the criticism leveled against the view propagated by him. Every free citizen has an undoubted right to lay what sentiments he pleases before the public; to forbid this,

3 **Article 19 (2) in The Constitution Of India 1949**
19. Protection of certain rights regarding freedom of speech etc
(1) All citizens shall have the right
(a) to freedom of speech and expression;
(b) to assemble peaceably and without arms;
(c) to form associations or unions;
(d) to move freely throughout the territory of India;
(e) to reside and settle in any part of the territory of India; and
(f) omitted
(g) to practise any profession, or to carry on any occupation, trade or business
(2) Nothing in sub clause (a) of clause (1) shall affect the operation of any existing law, or prevent the State from making any law, in so far as such law imposes reasonable restrictions on the exercise of the right conferred by the said sub clause in the interests of the sovereignty and integrity of India, the security of the State, friendly relations with foreign States, public order, decency or morality or in relation to contempt of court, defamation or incitement to an offence

except to the extent permitted by Article 19(2), would be an inroad on his freedom. This freedom must, however, be exercised with circumspection and care must be taken not to trench on the rights of other citizens or to jeopardise public interest. It is manifest from Article 19(2) that the right conferred by Article 19(1)(a) is subject to imposition of reasonable restrictions in the interest of, amongst others, public order, decency or morality or in relation to defamation or incitement to an offence. It is, therefore, obvious that subject to reasonable restrictions placed under Article 19(2) a citizen has a right to publish, circulate and disseminate his views and any attempt to thwart or deny the same would offend Article 19(1)(a). History tells us that dissent in all walks of life contributes to the evolution of society. Those who question unquestioned assumptions contribute to the alteration of social norms. Democracy is founded upon respect for their courage. Any attempt by the State to clamp down on the free expression of opinion must hence be frowned upon.

1

Freedom of Speech and Expression[1]

Ratio Decidendi[2]: "Fertile imagination of anybody especially of minors should not be a matter that should be agitated in the Court of law."

Facts in Nutshell:

Petitioner[3], a lawyer by profession. Respondent[4] No. 1 - Union of India, respondent No. 2, a statutory body[5], respondent Nos. 3 & 4, leading national daily newspapers and respondent No. 5 & 6 - news agencies. Petition[6] involved a substantial question of law and public importance on the fundamental right of the citizens, regarding the Freedom of Speech and expression as enshrined under Article 19(1)(a)[7] of the Constitution of India. Petitioner's grievance was that the freedom of

---

1 Appellants: **Ajay Goswami Vs.** Respondent: **Union of India (UOI) and Ors.**
AIR2007SC493
Hon'ble Judges: Dr. AR. Lakshmanan and Tarun Chatterjee, JJ.

2 **Meaning of Ration Decidendi:** ***Ratio decidendi*** is a Latin phrase meaning "the reason" or "the rationale for the decision." The *ratio decidendi* is "the point in a case which determines the judgment" or "the principle which the case establishes."

3 **Meaning of Petitioner:** A person who presents a Petition. (**Meaning of Petition:** A formal message requesting something that is submitted to an authority)

4 **Meaning of Respondent:** A **respondent** is a person who is called upon to issue a response to a communication made by another. In legal usage, this specifically refers to the defendant in a legal proceeding commenced by a petition, or to an appellee, or the opposing party, in an appeal of a decision by an initial fact-finder.

5 **Meaning of Statutory Body:**
Statutory body is one created by an Act of Parliament or state Legislatures. Examples: Reserve Bank of India under the Reserve Bank of India Act, .State Bank of India under a similar Act. etc.

6 **Meaning of Petition**: A formal written application requesting a court for a specific judicial action

7 **Article 19(1) in The Constitution Of India 1949**
(1) All citizens shall have the right
(a) to freedom of speech and expression;
(b) to assemble peaceably and without arms;
(c) to form associations or unions;
(d) to move freely throughout the territory of India;
(e) to reside and settle in any part of the territory of India; and
(f) omitted
(g) to practise any profession, or to carry on any occupation, trade or business

speech and expression enjoyed by the newspaper industry is not keeping balance with the protection of children from harmful and disturbing materials. Article 19(1)(a) guarantees freedom of speech and expression of individual as well as press. It acknowledges that the press is free to express its ideas but on the same hand, individual also has right to their own space and right not to be exposed against their will to other's expressions of ideas and actions. Petitioner requested the Court to direct the authorities to strike a reasonable balance between the fundamental right of freedom of speech and expression enjoyed by the press and the duty of the Government, being signatory of United Nations Convention on the Rights of the Child, 1989 and Universal Declaration of Human Rights, to protect the vulnerable minors from abuse, exploitation and harmful effects of such expression. The petitioner requested the Court to direct the concerned authorities to provide for classification or introduction of a regulatory system for facilitating climate of reciprocal tolerance which may include:

(a) an acceptance of other people's rights to express and receive certain ideas and actions; and

(b) accepting that other people have the right not to be exposed against their will to one's expression of ideas and actions.

The purpose behind petition was that the nature and extent of the material having *sexual contents should not be exposed to the minors*[8] indiscriminately and without regard to the age of minor. The discretion in this regard should vest with parents, guardians, teachers or experts on sex education.

Right of Minor/Children:

The right of the minor flows from Article 19(1)(a), Article 21[9] read with Article 39(f)[10] of the Constitution of India and United Nation Convention

8 **Meaning of Minor:**
Someone under legal age, which is generally 18, except for certain purposes such as drinking alcoholic beverages.

9 **Article 21 in The Constitution Of India 1949**
21. Protection of life and personal liberty No person shall be deprived of his life or personal liberty except according to procedure established by law

10 **Article 39(f) in The Constitution Of India 1949**
Certain principles of policy to be followed by the State: The State shall, in particular, direct its policy towards securing
(f) that children are given opportunities and facilities to develop in a healthy manner and in conditions of freedom and dignity and that childhood and youth are protected against exploitation

on the Rights of the Child. In a judgment delivered by Supreme Court in the matter of ***Director General, Directorate General of Doordarshan and Ors. v. Anand Patwardhan and Anr.***[11], ***Dr. Justice AR. Lakshmanan,*** observed as under:

...one of the most controversial issue is balancing the need to protect society against the potential harm that may flow from obscene material, and the need to ensure respect for freedom of expression and to preserve a free flow of information and idea.

It was further observed by Supreme Court:

...The Indian Penal Code on obscenity grew out of the English Law, which made court the guardian of public morals. It is important that where bodies exercise discretion, which may interfere in the enjoyment of constitutional rights, that discretion must be subject to adequate law.

.The judge should thereafter place himself in the position of a reader of every age group in whose hands the book is likely to fall and should try to appreciate what kind of possible influence the book is likely to have in the minds of the readers.

It was observed by Supreme Court in the matter of *Lakshmikant Pandey v. Union of India*[12] as follows:

It is obvious that in a civilized society the importance of child welfare cannot be over-emphasized, because the welfare of the entire community, its growth and development, depend on the health and well-being of its children. Children are a "supremely important national asset" and the future well being of the nation depends on how its children grow and develop. The great poet Milton put it admirably when he said: "Child shows the man as morning shows the day" and the Study Team on Social Welfare said much to the same effect when it observed that "the physical and mental health of the nation is determined largely by the manner in which it is shaped in the early stages". The child is a soul with a being, a nature and capacities of its own, who must be helped to find them, to grow into their maturity, into fulness of physical and vital energy and the utmost breadth, depth and height of its emotional, intellectual and spiritual being; otherwise there cannot be a healthy growth of the

---

and against moral and material abandonment

11 (C.A. No. 613 of 2005)

12 [1984]2SCR795

nation. Now obviously children need special protection because of their tender age and physique mental immaturity and incapacity to look-after themselves. That is why there is a growing realisation in every part of the globe that children must be brought up in an atmosphere of love and affection and under the tender care and attention of parents so that they may be able to attain full emotional, intellectual and spiritual stability and maturity and acquire self-confidence and self-respect and a balanced view of life with full appreciation and realisation of the role which they have to play in the nation building process without which the nation cannot develop and attain real prosperity because a large segment of the society would then be left out of the developmental process. In India this consciousness is reflected in the provisions enacted in the Constitution. Clause (3) of Article 15[13] enables the State to make special provisions inter alia for children and Article 24[14] provides that no child below the age of fourteen years shall be employed to work in any factory or mine or engaged in any other hazardous employment. Clauses (e) and (f) of Article 39[15] provide that the State shall direct its policy towards securing

13 **Article 15 in The Constitution Of India 1949**

15. Prohibition of discrimination on grounds of religion, race, caste, sex or place of birth

(1) The State shall not discriminate against any citizen on grounds only of religion, race, caste, sex, place of birth or any of them

(2) No citizen shall, on grounds only of religion, race, caste, sex, place of birth or any of them, be subject to any disability, liability, restriction or condition with regard to

(a) access to shops, public restaurants, hotels and palaces of public entertainment; or

(b) the use of wells, tanks, bathing ghats, roads and places of public resort maintained wholly or partly out of State funds or dedicated to the use of the general public

(3) Nothing in this article shall prevent the State from making any special provision for women and children

(4) Nothing in this article or in clause (2) of Article 29 shall prevent the State from making any special provision for the advancement of any socially and educationally backward classes of citizens or for the Scheduled Castes and the Scheduled Tribes

14 **Article 24 in The Constitution Of India 1949**

24. Prohibition of employment of children in factories, etc No child below the age of fourteen years shall be employed to work in any factory or mine or engaged in any other hazardous employment Provided that nothing in this sub clause shall authorise the detention of any person beyond the maximum period prescribed by any law made by Parliament under sub clause (b) of clause (7); or such person is detained in accordance with the provisions of any law made by Parliament under sub clauses (a) and (b) of clause (7)

15 **Article 39 in The Constitution Of India 1949**

39. Certain principles of policy to be followed by the State: The State shall, in particular, direct its policy towards securing

(a) that the citizens, men and women equally, have the right to an adequate means to livelihood;

(b) that the ownership and control of the material resources of the community are so distributed as best to subserve the common good;

(c) that the operation of the economic system does not result in the concentration of wealth and means of production to the common detriment;

(d) that there is equal pay for equal work for both men and women;

(e) that the health and strength of workers, men and women, and the tender age of children are

inter alia that the tender age of children is not abused, that citizens are not forced by economic necessity to enter avocations unsuited to their age and strength and that children are given facility to develop in a healthy manner and in conditions of freedom and dignity and that childhood and youth are protected against exploitation and against moral and material abandonment. These constitutional provisions reflect the great anxiety of the constitution makers to protect and safeguard the interest and welfare of children in the country. The Government of India has also in pursuance of these constitutional provisions evolved a National Policy for the Welfare of Children. This Policy starts with a goal-oriented perambulatory introduction:

The nation's children are a supremely important asset. Their nurture and solicitude are our responsibility. Children's programme should find a prominent part in our national plans for the development of human resources, so that our children grow up to become robust citizens, physically fit, mentally alert and morally healthy, endowed with the skills and motivations needed by society. Equal opportunities for development to all children during the period of growth should be our aim, for this would serve our larger purpose of reducing inequality and ensuring social justice.

The National Policy sets out the measures which the Government of India proposes to adopt towards attainment of the objectives set out in the perambulatory introduction and they include measures designed to protect children against neglect, cruelty and exploitation and to strengthen family ties "so that full potentialities of growth of children are realised within the normal family neighbourhood and community environment.

Obscenity:

The definition of obscenity differs from culture to culture, between communities within a single culture, and also between individuals within those communities. Many cultures have produced laws to define what is considered to be obscene, and censorship is often used to try to suppress or control materials that are obscene under these definitions. The term

not abused and that citizens are not forced by economic necessity to enter avocations unsuited to their age or strength;

(f) that children are given opportunities and facilities to develop in a healthy manner and in conditions of freedom and dignity and that childhood and youth are protected against exploitation and against moral and material abandonment

obscenity is most often used in a legal context to describe expressions (words, images, actions) that offend the prevalent sexual morality. On the other hand the Constitution of India guarantees the right of freedom to speech and expression to every citizen. This right will encompass an individuals take on any issue. However, this right is not absolute, if such speech and expression is immensely gross and will badly violate the standards of morality of a society. Therefore, any expression is subject to reasonable restriction. Freedom of expression has contributed much to the development and well-being of our free society. This right conferred by the Constitution has triggered various issues. One of the most controversial issues is balancing the need to protect society against the potential harm that may flow from obscene material, and the need to ensure respect for freedom of expression and to preserve a free flow of information and idea.

In ***Shri Chandrakant Kalyandas Kakodkar v. The State of Maharashtra and Ors.***[16] , Supreme Court observed that:

The concept of obscenity would differ from country to country depending on the standards of morals of contemporary society. What is considered as a piece of literature in France may be obscene in England and what is considered in both countries as not harmful to public order and morals may be obscene in our country. But to insist that the standard should always be for the writer to see that the adolescent ought not to be brought into contact with sex or that if they read any references to sex in what is written whether that is the dominant theme or not they would be affected, would be to require authors to write books only for the adolescent and not for the adults.

Freedom of Speech and Expression:

Article 19(1)(a) deals with freedom of speech and expression. In the matter of ***Virendra v. State of Punjab and Anr.***[17] Court held:

It is certainly a serious encroachment on the valuable and cherished right to freedom of speech and expression if a newspaper is prevented from publishing its own views or the views of its correspondents relating to or concerning what may be the burning topic of the day. Our social interest ordinarily demands the free propagation and interchange of views but

16 1962 (2) SCC 687

17 [1958]1SCR308

circumstances may arise when the social interest in public order may require a reasonable subordination of the social interest in free speech and expression to the needs of our social interest in public order.

Our Constitution recognises this necessity and has attempted to strike a balance between the two social interests. It permits the imposition of reasonable restrictions on the freedom of speech and expression in the interest of public order and on the freedom of carrying on trade or business in the interest of the general public.

Therefore, the crucial question must always be : Are the restrictions imposed on the exercise of the rights under Arts. 19(1)(a) and 19(1)(g)[18] reasonable in view of all the surrounding circumstances ? In other words are the restrictions reasonably necessary in the interest of public order under Article 19(2)[19] or in the interest of the general public under Article 19(6)[20]?

Decision of the Supreme Court:

Court held that any steps to ban publishing of certain news pieces or pictures would fetter the independence of free press which is one of the hallmarks of our democratic setup. A culture of 'responsible reading' should be inculcated among the readers of any news article. No news item should be viewed or read in isolation. It is necessary that publication

18 **Article 19(1) in The Constitution Of India 1949**
(1) All citizens shall have the right
(g) to practise any profession, or to carry on any occupation, trade or business

19 **Article 19 (2) in The Constitution Of India 1949**
19. Protection of certain rights regarding freedom of speech etc
(2) Nothing in sub clause (a) of clause (1) shall affect the operation of any existing law, or prevent the State from making any law, in so far as such law imposes reasonable restrictions on the exercise of the right conferred by the said sub clause in the interests of the sovereignty and integrity of India, the security of the State, friendly relations with foreign States, public order, decency or morality or in relation to contempt of court, defamation or incitement to an offence

20 **Article 19 (6) in The Constitution Of India 1949**
19. Protection of certain rights regarding freedom of speech etc
(6) Nothing in sub clause (g) of the said clause shall affect the operation of any existing law in so far as it imposes, or prevent the State from making any law imposing, in the interests of the general public, reasonable restrictions on the exercise of the right conferred by the said sub clause, and, in particular, nothing in the said sub clause shall affect the operation of any existing law in so far as it relates to, or prevent the State from making any law relating to,
(i) the professional or technical qualifications necessary for practising any profession or carrying on any occupation, trade or business, or
(ii) the carrying on by the State, or by a corporation owned or controlled by the State, of any trade, business, industry or service, whether to the exclusion, complete or partial, of citizens or otherwise

must be judged as a whole and news items, advertisements or passages should not be read without the accompanying message that is purported to be conveyed to the public. Also the members of the public and readers should not look for meanings in a picture or written article, which is not conceived to be conveyed through the picture or the news item.

Court further held that the petitioner failed to establish his case clearly. The petitioner only stated that the pictures and the news items that were published by the respondents 3 and 4 'leave much for the thoughts of minors'. Therefore, court observed that fertile imagination of anybody especially of minors should not be a matter that should be agitated in the court of law. Court dismissed the writ petition[21].

21 **Meaning of Writ Petition:** Under the Indian legal system, jurisdiction to issue 'prerogative writs' is given to the Supreme Court, and to the High Courts of Judicature of all Indian states. Parts of the law relating to writs are set forth in the Constitution of India. The Supreme Court, the highest in the country, may issue writs under Article 32 of the Constitution for enforcement of Fundamental Rights and under Articles 139 for enforcement of rights other than Fundamental Rights, while High Courts, the superior courts of the States, may issue writs under Articles 226. 'Writ' is eminently designed by the makers of the Constitution, and in the same way it is developed very widely and efficiently by the courts in India. The Constitution broadly provides for five kinds of "prerogative" writs, namely, Habeas Corpus, Certiorari, Mandamus, Quo Warranto and Prohibition.

2

Refusal to telecast documentary film violates freedom of speech and expression[1]

Facts in Nutshell:

The question raised in petition[2] was whether the refusal of Doordarshan to telecast "In Memory of Friends", a documentary produced by the petitioner[3], violates his fundamental right of freedom of speech and expression. Petitioner a well-known documentary film maker. The documentary films made by the petitioner in the past were acclaimed at national and international level. The petitioner produced and directed the documentary film in question "In Memory of Friends" about the violence and terrorism in Punjab, about a group of Sikhs and Hindus, who at great personal risk were engaged in an attempt to recover the tolerance and communal harmony that once existed in Punjab. The memory of the legendary martyr Bhagat Singh plays a central role in the film. The film a 60 minute documentary which was completed in January 1990. It was screened in the London Film Festival, 1990 as well as in the non-feature section of the Indian Panorama at the Madras International Film Festival early in 1991. It has been selected as the best investigative documentary for the year 1990 and given award by the Government of India. The jury which selected it as the best investigative documentary said that the film treated the subject of violence and terrorism with courage, honesty and lucidity, Besides, the said film has won the Silver Couch at the First Bombay International Festival of documentary and short films and special jury prize at Mannheim in Germany.

---

1 Appellants: **Shri Anand Patwardhan Vs.** Respondent: **The Union of India (UOI) and Ors.**
MANU/MH/0444/1996
Hon'ble Judges: A.P. Shah, Judge

2 **Meaning of Petition**: A formal written application requesting a court for a specific judicial action

3 **Meaning of Petitioner:** A person who presents a Petition. (**Meaning of Petition:** A formal message requesting something that is submitted to an authority)

The petitioner submitted the film to the Doordarshan on 12th March, 1991 for screening on television. The Doordarshan chose not to reply to the petitioner. The petitioner was constrained to send a legal notice dated 29th April, 1991 in which he called upon Doordarshan to screen the film on T.V. In response to the said letter, Doordarshan sent reply to the petitioner dated 16th May, 1991 in which it was said that the copy of the film was not traceable. The petitioner delivered another copy of the film by hand on 17th July, 1991. The petitioner was informed by letter dated 3rd February, 1992, that the film was not found suitable for telecast over Doordarshan under national programmes. It was the case of the petitioner that the respondents[4] (Doordarshan) have unfairly and arbitrarily rejected the petitioner's film and deprived him of his right of expression guaranteed by Article 19(1)(a)[5] of the Constitution. The petitioner submitted that refusal of the respondents to have the said film telecast on Doordarshan deprives the Indian citizens of their right to be informed and enlightened about the situation in Punjab which was so vital to the composition and existence of the Indian State.

Freedom of Speech and Expression:

In *Odyssey Communications Pvt. Ltd. v. Lokvidayan Sanghatana*[6], a public interest litigation[7] was commenced under Article 226[8] of the Constitution

4 **Meaning of Respondent:** A **respondent** is a person who is called upon to issue a response to a communication made by another. In legal usage, this specifically refers to the defendant in a legal proceeding commenced by a petition, or to an appellee, or the opposing party, in an appeal of a decision by an initial fact-finder.

5 **Article 19(1) in The Constitution Of India 1949**
(1) All citizens shall have the right
(a) to freedom of speech and expression;
(b) to assemble peaceably and without arms;
(c) to form associations or unions;
(d) to move freely throughout the territory of India;
(e) to reside and settle in any part of the territory of India; and
(f) omitted
(g) to practise any profession, or to carry on any occupation, trade or business

6 AIR1988SC1642

7 **Meaning of Public Interest Litigation:**
Public-Interest Litigation is litigation for the protection of the public interest. In Indian law, **Article 32** of the Indian constitution contains a tool which directly joints the public with judiciary. PIL may be introduced in a court of law by the court itself (*suo motu*), rather than the aggrieved party or another third party. For the exercise of the court's jurisdiction, it is unnecessary for the victim of the violation of his or her rights to personally approach the court. In PIL, the right to file suit is given to a member of the public by the courts through judicial activism. The member of the public may be a non-governmental organization (NGO), an institution or an individual.

8 **Article 226 in The Constitution Of India 1949**
226. Power of High Courts to issue certain writs

to restrain the authorities from telecasting the serial 'Honi Anhony' on the plea that it was likely to spread false and blind beliefs and superstitions amongst the members of the public. The High Court by an interim injunction[9] restrained the authorities from telecasting the serial which led the producer thereof to approach the Supreme Court. The Supreme Court while allowing the appeal[10] held that the right of a citizen to exhibit films on Doordarshan subject to the conditions imposed by the Doordarshan being a part of the fundamental right of freedom of expression could be curtailed only under circumstances set out in Article 19(2)[11] and in no other manner. *The right to exhibit the film was similar to the right of a*

---

(1) Notwithstanding anything in Article 32 every High Court shall have powers, throughout the territories in relation to which it exercise jurisdiction, to issue to any person or authority, including in appropriate cases, any Government, within those territories directions, orders or writs, including writs in the nature of habeas corpus, mandamus, prohibitions, quo warranto and certiorari, or any of them, for the enforcement of any of the rights conferred by Part III and for any other purpose

(2) The power conferred by clause (1) to issue directions, orders or writs to any Government, authority or person may also be exercised by any High Court exercising jurisdiction in relation to the territories within which the cause of action, wholly or in part, arises for the exercise of such power, notwithstanding that the seat of such Government or authority or the residence of such person is not within those territories

(3) Where any party against whom an interim order, whether by way of injunction or stay or in any other manner, is made on, or in any proceedings relating to, a petition under clause (1), without

(a) furnishing to such party copies of such petition and all documents in support of the plea for such interim order; and

(b) giving such party an opportunity of being heard, makes an application to the High Court for the vacation of such order and furnishes a copy of such application to the party in whose favour such order has been made or the counsel of such party, the High Court shall dispose of the application within a period of two weeks from the date on which it is received or from the date on which the copy of such application is so furnished, whichever is later, or where the High Court is closed on the last day of that period, before the expiry of the next day afterwards on which the High Court is open; and if the application is not so disposed of, the interim order shall, on the expiry of that period, or, as the case may be, the expiry of the aid next day, stand vacated

(4) The power conferred on a High Court by this article shall not be in derogation of the power conferred on the Supreme court by clause (2) of Article 32

9 **Meaning of Interim Injunction:** An Injunction made by a court that prevents someone from doing something until there is a full trial to solve the disagreement.

10 **Meaning of Appeal:** In law, an **appeal** is a process for requesting a formal change to an official decision. Very broadly speaking there are appeals on the record and *de novo* appeals. In *de novo* appeals, a new decision maker re-hears the case without any reference to the prior decision maker. In appeals on the record, the decision of the prior decision maker is challenged by arguing that he or she misapplied the law, came to an incorrect factual finding, acted in excess of his jurisdiction, abused his powers, was biased, considered evidence which he should not have considered or failed to consider evidence that he should have considered.

11 **Article 19(2) in The Constitution Of India 1949**
19. Protection of certain rights regarding freedom of speech etc
(2) Nothing in sub clause (a) of clause (1) shall affect the operation of any existing law, or prevent the State from making any law, in so far as such law imposes reasonable restrictions on the exercise of the right conferred by the said sub clause in the interests of the sovereignty and integrity of India, the security of the State, friendly relations with foreign States, public order, decency or morality or in relation to contempt of court, defamation or incitement to an offence

citizen to publish his views through any other media such as newspapers, magazines, advertisement hoardings, etc.

In the case of *Life Insurance Corporation of India v. Manubhai D. Shah*[12], the Supreme Court was considering the question whether refusal of the Doordarshan to exhibit documentary based on "Bhopal Gas Disaster" on the ground that it was out dated and lost relevance was legal and proper. After noting the traits of the decisions of the Indian Courts, the Supreme Court observed in paragraph 8 of the judgment as under :

"The words 'freedom of speech and expression' must, therefore, be broadly construed to include the freedom to circulate one's views by words of mouth or in writing or through audio-visual instrumentalities. It, therefore, includes the right to propagate one's views through the print media or through any other communication channel e.g. the radio and the television. Every citizen of this free country, therefore, has the right to air his or her views through the printing and/or the electronic media subject of course to permissible restrictions imposed under Article 19(2) of the Constitution. The print media, the radio and the tiny screen play the role of public educators, so vital to the growth of a healthy democracy. Freedom to air one's views is the lifetime of any democratic institution and any attempt to stifle, suffocate or gag this right would sound a death-knell to democracy and would help usher in autocracy or dictatorship. It cannot be gainsaid that modern communication medium advances public interest by informing the public of the events and developments that have taken place and thereby educating the voters, a role considered significant for the vibrant functioning of a democracy. Therefore, in any set up, more so in a democratic set up like ours, dissemination of news and views for popular consumption is a must and any attempt to deny the same must be frowned upon unless it falls within the mischief of Article 19(2) of the Constitution. It follows that a citizen for propagation of his or her ideas has a right to publish for circulation his views in periodicals, magazines and journals or through the electronic media since it is well known that these communication channels are great purveyors of news and views and make considerable impact on the minds of the readers and viewers and are known to mould public opinion on vital issues of national importance. Once it is conceded, and it cannot indeed be disputed, that freedom of speech and expression includes freedom of circulation and propagation of ideas, there can be no doubt that the right extends to the citizen being permitted to use the media to answer the criticism levelled against the

12 [1992]3SCR595

view propagated by him. Every free citizen has an undoubted right to lay what sentiments he pleases before the public, to forbid this, except to the extent permitted by Article 19(2), would be an inroad on his freedom. This freedom must, however, be exercised with circumspection and care must be taken not to trench on the rights of other citizens or to jeopardise public interest. It is manifest from Article 19(2) that the right conferred by Article 19(1)(a)[13] to subject to imposition of reasonable restrictions in the interest of, amongst others, public order, decency or morality or in relation to defamation or incitement to an offence. It is, therefore, obvious that subject to reasonable restrictions placed under Article 19(2) a citizen has a right to publish, circulate and disseminate his views and any attempt to thwart or deny the same would offend Article 19(1)(a)."

The Supreme Court then proceeded to hold that a film maker has a fundamental right under Article 19(1)(a)to exhibit his films, and therefore, the onus lies on the party which claims that it would be entitled to refuse enforcement of this right by virtue of the law made under Article 19(2) to show that the film did not conform to the requirement of that law.

Decision of High Court:

Court directed doordarshan to exhibit documentary film.

13 **Article 19 in The Constitution Of India 1949**
19. Protection of certain rights regarding freedom of speech etc
(1) All citizens shall have the right
(a) to freedom of speech and expression

3

Restrictions on freedom of speech and freedom of assembly[1]

Facts in Nutshell:

Petition[2] under Article 32[3] of the Constitution for issuing an appropriate writ[4] to the respondents[5] not to enforce the provisions of section 144[6] of

---

1 Appellants: **Babulal Parate Vs.** Respondent: **State of Maharashtra and Ors.** AIR1961SC884
Hon'ble Judges: B. P. Sinha, C.J., A. K. Sarkar, J. R. Madholkar, N. Rajagopala Ayyangar and S. K. Das, JJ.

2 **Meaning of Petition:** A formal message requesting something that is submitted to an authority

3 **Article 32 in The Constitution Of India 1949**
32. Remedies for enforcement of rights conferred by this Part
(1) The right to move the Supreme Court by appropriate proceedings for the enforcement of the rights conferred by this Part is guaranteed
(2) The Supreme Court shall have power to issue directions or orders or writs, including writs in the nature of habeas corpus, mandamus, prohibition, quo warranto and certiorari, whichever may be appropriate, for the enforcement of any of the rights conferred by this Part
(3) Without prejudice to the powers conferred on the Supreme Court by clause (1) and (2), Parliament may by law empower any other court to exercise within the local limits of its jurisdiction all or any of the powers exercisable by the Supreme Court under clause (2)
(4) The right guaranteed by this article shall not be suspended except as otherwise provided for by this Constitution

4 **Meaning of Writ:** A written order of a judge requiring specific action by the person or entity to whom the writ is directed.

5 **Meaning of Respondent:** A **respondent** is a person who is called upon to issue a response to a communication made by another. In legal usage, this specifically refers to the defendant in a legal proceeding commenced by a petition, or to an appellee, or the opposing party, in an appeal of a decision by an initial fact-finder.

6 **Section 144, CrPc, 1973**
144. Power to issue order in urgent cases of nuisance or apprehended danger
(1) In cases where, in the opinion of a District Magistrate, a Sub-divisional Magistrate or any other Executive Magistrate specially empowered by the State Government in this behalf, there is sufficient ground for proceeding under this section and immediate prevention or speedy remedy is desirable, such Magistrate may, by a written order stating the material facts of the case and served in the manner provided by section 134, direct any person to abstain from a certain act or to take certain order with respect to certain property in his possession or under his management,
if such Magistrate considers that such direction is likely to prevent, or tends to prevent, obstruction, annoyance or injury to any person lawfully employed, or danger to human life, health or safety, or a disturbance of the public tranquillity, or a riot, or an affray

the Criminal Procedure Code or an appropriate writ forbidding respondent No. 4 from proceeding further with the prosecution of the petitioner[7] for offences under Sections 143[8] and 188[9] of the Indian Penal Code read

---

(2) An order under this section may, in cases of emergency or in cases where the circumstances do not admit of the serving in due time of a notice upon the person against whom the order is directed, be passed ex parte

(3) An order under this section may be directed to a particular individual, or to persons residing in a particular place or area, or to the public generally when frequenting or visiting a particular place or area

(4) No order under this section shall remain in force for more than two months from the making thereof:

Provided that, if the State Government considers it necessary so to do for preventing danger to human life, health or safety or for preventing a riot or any affray, it may, by notification, direct that an order made by a Magistrate under this section shall remain in force for such further period not exceeding six months from the date on which the order made by the Magistrate would have, but for such order, expired, as it may specify in the said notification

(5) Any Magistrate may, either on his own motion or on the application of any person aggrieved, rescind or alter any order made under this section, by himself or any Magistrate subordinate to him or by his predecessor-in-office

(6) The State Government may, either on its own motion or on the application of any person aggrieved, rescind or alter any order made by it under the proviso to sub- section (4)

(7) Where an application under sub-section (5), or sub-section (6) is received, the Magistrate, or the State Government, as the case may be, shall afford to the applicant an early opportunity of appearing before him or it, either in person or by pleader and showing cause against the order, and if the Magistrate or the State Government, as the case may be, rejects the application wholly or in part, he or it shall record in writing the reasons for so doing

7 **Meaning of Petitioner:** A person who presents a Petition. (**Meaning of Petition:** A formal message requesting something that is submitted to an authority)

8 **Section 143 in The Indian Penal Code, 1860**
143. Punishment.-- Whoever is a member of an unlawful assembly, shall be punished with imprisonment of either description for a term which may extend to six months, or with fine, or with both.

9 **Section 188 in The Indian Penal Code, 1860**
188. Disobedience to order duly promulgated by public servant.-- Whoever, knowing that, by an order promulgated by a public servant lawfully empowered to promulgate such order, he is directed to abstain from a certain act, or to take certain order with certain property in his possession or under his management. disobeys such direction, shall, if such disobedience causes or tends to cause obstruction, annoyance or injury, or risk of obstruction, annoyance or injury, to any persons lawfully employed, be punished with simple imprisonment for a term which may extend to one month or with fine which may extend to two hundred rupees, or with both: and if such disobedience causes or tends to cause danger to human life, health or safety, or causes or tends to cause a riot or affray, shall be punished with imprisonment of either description for a term which may extend to six months, or with fine which may extend to one thousand rupees, or with both. Explanation.- It is not necessary that the offender should intend to produce harm, or contemplate his disobedience as likely to produce harm. It is sufficient that he knows of the order which he disobeys, and that his disobedience produces, or is likely to produce, harm. Illustration An order is promulgated by a public servant lawfully empowered to promulgated such order, directing that a religious procession shall not pass down a certain street. A knowingly disobeys the order, and thereby causes danger of riot. A has committed the offence defined in this section.

with section 117[10] thereof, for quashing[11] the proceedings against the petitioner before respondent No. 4 and for the issue of a writ of habeas corpus[12] to respondents 1 to 3 directing them to produce or to cause to be produced the petitioner to be dealt with according to law and to set him at liberty.

There were two unions of textile workers in Nagpur, one known as the Rashtriya Mill Majdoor Sangh and the other as Nagpur Mill Majdoor Sangh. The former is a branch of the Indian National Trade Union Congress. The Rashtriya Mill Majdoor Sangh entered into an agreement with the management of the Empress Mills regarding the closure of Empress Mill No. 1 for rebuilding it and regarding the employment of workers who were employed therein in a third shift. This agreement was opposed by the Nagpur Mill Majdoor Sangh. On January 25, 1956, a group of workers belonging to the Nagpur Mill Majdoor Sangh went in a procession to Gujar's Wada, Mahal, Nagpur, where the office of the Rashtriya Mill Majdoor Sangh was located. It was said that a scuffle took place there between some members of the procession and some workers belonging to Rashtriya Mill Majdoor Sangh. Thereupon an offence under section 452[13] read with section 147[14] of the Indian Penal Code was registered by the police on January 27, 1956. A large procession consisting

10 **Section 117 in The Indian Penal Code, 1860**
117. Abetting commission of offence by the public or by more than ten persons.-- Whoever abets the commission of an offence by the public generally or by any number or class of persons exceeding ten, shall be punished with imprisonment of either description for a term which may extend to three years, or with fine, or with both.

11 **Meaning of Quash:** To annul or set aside. In law, a motion to quash asks the judge for an order setting aside or nullifying an action, such as "quashing" service of a summons when the wrong person was served.

12 **Meaning of Habeas Corpus:** A writ of ***habeas corpus*** is a writ (legal action) that requires a person under arrest to be brought before a judge or into court. The principle of habeas corpus ensures that a prisoner can be released from unlawful detention—that is, detention lacking sufficient cause or evidence. The remedy can be sought by the prisoner or by another person coming to the prisoner's aid. This right originated in the English legal system, and is now available in many nations. It has historically been an important legal instrument safeguarding individual freedom against arbitrary state action.

13 **Section 452 in The Indian Penal Code, 1860**
452. House- trespass alter preparation for hurt, assault or wrongful restraint.-- Whoever commits house- trespass, having made preparation for causing hurt to any person or for assaulting any person, or for wrongfully restraining any person, or for putting and person in fear of hurt, or of assault, or of wrongful restraint, shall be punished with imprisonment of either description for a term which may extend to seven years, and shall also be liable to fine.

14 **Section 147 in The Indian Penal Code, 1860**
147. Punishment for rioting.-- Whoever is guilty of rioting, shall be punished with imprisonment of either description for a term which may extend to two years, or with fine, or with both.

of the workers of the Nagpur Mill Majdoor Sangh was taken out. This procession marched through the city of Nagpur shouting slogans which, according to the District Magistrate, were provocative. On the same night a meeting was held at the Kasturchand Park in which it was alleged that the workers belonging to the Nagpur Mill Majdoor Sangh were instigated by the speakers who addressed the meeting to offer satyagraha in front of the Empress Mill No. 1 and also to take out a precession to the office of the Rashtriya Mill Majdoor Sangh. On January 28, 1956, the workers belonging to the Nagpur Mill Majdoor Sangh assembled in large numbers in Mahal Chowk and on Mahal road blocking the traffic on the road. It is said that these persons were squatting[15] on the road and as they refused to budge the District Magistrate passed an order at 4-00 a.m. on January 29, 1956, which came into force immediately and was to remain in force for a period of fifteen days prohibiting, among other things, the assembly of five or more persons in certain areas specified in the order.

The petitioner entertained the view that the order promulgated by the District Magistrate under section 144 of the Code of Criminal Procedure was an encroachment on the fundamental rights of the citizens to freedom of speech and expression and to assemble peaceably and without arms, guaranteed under Art.19(1)(a) and (b) of the Constitution and, therefore, he held a public meeting outside the area covered by the aforesaid order. It was alleged that at that meeting he criticised the District Magistrate and exhorted the workers to contravene his order and take out procession in the area covered by the order. Thereupon he was arrested by the Nagpur police for having committed the offences already referred to and produced before a magistrate. The magistrate remanded him to jail custody till February 15, 1956. The petitioner's application for bail[16] was rejected on the ground that the accusation against him related to a non-bailable offence. Thereupon the petitioner moved the High Court at Nagpur for his release on bail but his application was rejected on February 22, 1956. The petitioner then presented a petition before the High Court under for a writ of habeas corpus. That petition was dismissed by the High Court on May 9, 1956. The petitioner then moved the High Court for granting a certificate under Art. 132[17] of the Constitution. The High Court refused

15 **Meaning of Squatting:** To occupy a given piece of public land in order to acquire title to it.

16 **Meaning of Bail:** The money or bond put up to secure the release of a person who has been charged with a crime.

17 **Article 132 in The Constitution Of India 1949**

to grant the certificate on the ground that in its opinion the case did not involve any substantial question of law regarding the interpretation of the Constitution and was also not otherwise fit for grant of a certificate. On April 23, 1956, the petitioner presented the petition before Supreme Court. The petitioner also sought an ex parte[18] order for the stay of the proceedings before the respondent No. 4 till the decision on the petition.

Contentions of Petitioner's Counsel:

That section 144[19] of the Code of Criminal Procedure in so far as it relates to placing of restrictions on freedom of speech and freedom of assembly

---

132. Appellate jurisdiction of Supreme Court in appeals from High Courts in certain cases (1) An appeal shall lie to the Supreme Court from any judgment, decree or final order of a High Court in the territory of India, whether in a civil, criminal or other proceeding, if the High Court certifies under Article 134A that the case involves a substantial question of law as t the interpretation of this Constitution
(2) Omitted
(3) Where such a certificate is given, any party in the case may appeal to the Supreme Court on the ground that any such question as aforesaid has been wrongly decided Explanation For the purposes of this article, the expression final order includes an order declaring an issue which, if decided in favour of the appellant, would be sufficient for the final disposal of the case

18 **Meaning of Ex-Parte order: Ex parte** is a Latin legal term meaning "from (by or for) one party". An ex parte decision is one decided by a judge without requiring all of the parties to the controversy to be present.

19 **Section 144 of Code of Criminal Procedure, 1973:**
"(1) In cases where, in the opinion of District Magistrate, a Chief Presidency Magistrate, Sub-Divisional Magistrate, or of any other Magistrate (not being a Magistrate of the third class) specially empowered by the 'State Government' or the Chief Presidency Magistrate or the District Magistrate to act under this section there is sufficient ground for proceeding under this section and immediate prevention or speedy remedy is desirable,
such Magistrate may, by a written order stating the material facts of the case and served in manner provided by section 134, direct any person to abstain from a certain act or to take certain order with certain property in his possession or under his management, if such Magistrate considers that such direction is likely to prevent or tends to prevent, obstruction, annoyance or injury, or risk of obstruction, annoyance or injury to any person lawfully employed, or danger to human life, health or safety, or a disturbance of the public tranquilly or a riot, or an affray.
(2) An order under this section may, in cases of emergency or in cases where the circumstances do not admit of the serving in due time of a notice upon the person against whom the order is directed, be passed ex parte.
(3) An order under this section may be directed to a particular individual, or to the public generally when frequenting or visiting a particular place.
(4) Any Magistrate may, either on his own motion or on the application of any person aggrieved, rescind or alter any order made under this section by himself or any Magistrate subordinate to him, or by his predecessor in office.
(5) Where such an application is received, the Magistrate shall afford to the applicant an early opportunity of appearing before him either in person or by pleader and showing cause against the order; and if the Magistrate rejects the application wholly or in part, he shall record in writing his reasons for doing.
(6) No order under this section shall remain in force for more than two months from the making thereof; unless, in cases of danger to human life, health or safety, or a likelihood of a riot or an affray, the 'State Government' by notification in the Official Gazette, otherwise directs".

confers very wide powers on the District Magistrate and certain other magistrate and thus places unreasonable restrictions on the rights guaranteed under Art. 19(1)(a)[20] and (b)[21] of the Constitution.

It was contended that section 144 of the Code of Criminal Procedure confers very wide powers upon certain magistrates and that in exercise of those powers the magistrates can place very severe restrictions upon the rights of citizens to freedom of speech and expression and to assemble peaceably and without arms.

Provisions of Section 144 are attracted only in emergency:

It must be borne in mind that the provisions of section 144 are attracted only in an emergency. Thereunder, the initial judge of the emergency is, no doubt, the District Magistrate or the Chief Presidency Magistrate or the sub-divisional magistrate or any other magistrate specially empowered by the State Government. But then, the maintenance of law and order being the duty and function of the executive department of the State it is inevitable that the question of formation of the opinion as to whether there is an emergency or not must necessarily rest, in the first instance, with those persons through whom the executive exercises its functions and discharges its duties. It would be impracticable and even impossible to expect the State Government itself to exercise those duties and functions in each and every case. The provisions of the section therefore which commit the power in this regard to a magistrate belonging to any of the classes referred to therein cannot be regarded as unreasonable.

Decision of Supreme Court:

Court held that the order of the District Magistrate was not unconstitutional either because section 144 is itself violative of fundamental rights recognised in Article 19[22] or on the ground that it is vague and places

20 **Article 19(1) in The Constitution Of India 1949**
(1) All citizens shall have the right
(a) to freedom of speech and expression

21 **Article 19(1) in The Constitution Of India 1949**
(1) All citizens shall have the right
b) to assemble peaceably and without arms

22 **Article 19 in The Constitution Of India 1949**
19. Protection of certain rights regarding freedom of speech etc
(1) All citizens shall have the right
(a) to freedom of speech and expression;
(b) to assemble peaceably and without arms;

unreasonable restrictions on those fundamental rights.

(c) to form associations or unions;
(d) to move freely throughout the territory of India;
(e) to reside and settle in any part of the territory of India; and
(f) omitted
(g) to practise any profession, or to carry on any occupation, trade or business
(2) Nothing in sub clause (a) of clause (1) shall affect the operation of any existing law, or prevent the State from making any law, in so far as such law imposes reasonable restrictions on the exercise of the right conferred by the said sub clause in the interests of the sovereignty and integrity of India, the security of the State, friendly relations with foreign States, public order, decency or morality or in relation to contempt of court, defamation or incitement to an offence
(3) Nothing in sub clause (b) of the said clause shall affect the operation of any existing law in so far as it imposes, or prevent the State from making any law imposing, in the interests of the sovereignty and integrity of India or public order, reasonable restrictions on the exercise of the right conferred by the said sub clause
(4) Nothing in sub clause (c) of the said clause shall affect the operation of any existing law in so far as it imposes, or prevent the State from making any law imposing, in the interests of the sovereignty and integrity of India or public order or morality, reasonable restrictions on the exercise of the right conferred by the said sub clause
(5) Nothing in sub clauses (d) and (e) of the said clause shall affect the operation of any existing law in so far as it imposes, or prevent the State from making any law imposing, reasonable restrictions on the exercise of any of the rights conferred by the said sub clauses either in the interests of the general public or for the protection of the interests of any Scheduled Tribe
(6) Nothing in sub clause (g) of the said clause shall affect the operation of any existing law in so far as it imposes, or prevent the State from making any law imposing, in the interests of the general public, reasonable restrictions on the exercise of the right conferred by the said sub clause, and, in particular, nothing in the said sub clause shall affect the operation of any existing law in so far as it relates to, or prevent the State from making any law relating to,
(i) the professional or technical qualifications necessary for practising any profession or carrying on any occupation, trade or business, or
(ii) the carrying on by the State, or by a corporation owned or controlled by the State, of any trade, business, industry or service, whether to the exclusion, complete or partial, of citizens or otherwise

4

Expulsion from School and Freedom of Speech and Expression[1]

Ratio Decidendi[2]: *"Person shall be entitled for protection of fundamental right[3] if they are infringed by order of Court."*

Facts in Nutshell:

The three child appellants[4], Bijoe, Binu Mol and Bindu Emmanuel are the faithful of Jehovah's Witnesses. They attend school Daily, during the morning Assembly, when the National Anthem 'Jana Gana Mana' was sung, they stand respectfully but they do not sing. They do not sing because, according to them, it was against the tenets of their religious faith not the words or the thoughts of the Anthem but the singing of it. This they and before them their elder sisters who attended the same school earlier have done all these several years. No one bothered, No

1 Appellants: **Bijoe Emmanuel and Ors. Vs.** Respondent: **State of Kerala and Ors.** AIR1987SC748
Hon'ble Judges: M. M. Dutt and O. Chinnappa Reddy, JJ.

2 **Meaning of Ration Decidendi:** ***Ratio decidendi*** is a Latin phrase meaning "the reason" or "the rationale for the decision." The *ratio decidendi* is "the point in a case which determines the judgment" or "the principle which the case establishes."

3 **Meaning of Fundamental Right:** ***'Part III – Fundamental Rights'*** is a charter of rights contained in the Constitution of India. It guarantees civil liberties such that all Indians can lead their lives in peace and harmony as citizens of India. These include individual rights common to most liberal democracies, such as equality before law, freedom of speech and expression, and peaceful assembly, freedom to practice religion, and the right to constitutional remedies for the protection of civil rights by means of writs such as habeas corpus. Violation of these rights result in punishments as prescribed in the Indian Penal Code or other special laws, subject to discretion of the judiciary. The Fundamental Rights are defined as basic human freedoms which every Indian citizen has the right to enjoy for a proper and harmonious development of personality. These rights universally apply to all citizens, irrespective of race, place of birth, religion, caste, creed, colour or gender. Aliens (persons who are not citizens) are also considered in matters like equality before law. They are enforceable by the courts, subject to certain restrictions. The Rights have their origins in many sources, including England's Bill of Rights, the United States Bill of Rights and France's Declaration of the Rights of Man.

4 **Meaning of Appellant:** A person who, dissatisfied with the judgment rendered in a lawsuit decided in a lower court or the findings from a proceeding before an Administrative Agency, asks a superior court to review the decision.

one worried. No one thought it disrespectful or unpatriotic. The children were left in peace and to their beliefs. That was until July, 1985, when some patriotic gentleman took notice. The gentleman thought it was unpatriotic of the children not to sing the National Anthem. He happened to be a Member of the Legislative Assembly. So, he put a question in the Assembly. A Commission was appointed to enquire and report. Commission reported that the children are 'law-abiding' and that they showed no disrespect to the National Anthem. Indeed it was nobody's case that the children are other than well-behaved or that they have ever behaved disrespectfully when the National Anthem was sung. They have always stood up in respectful silence. But these matters of conscience, which though better left alone, are sensitive and emotionally evocative. So, under the instructions of Deputy Inspector of Schools, the Head Mistress expelled the children from the school from July 26, 1985. The father of the children made representations requesting that his children may be permitted to attend the school pending orders from the Government. The Head Mistress expressed her helplessness in the matter. Finally the children filed a Writ Petition[5] in the High Court seeking an order restraining the authorities from preventing them from attending School. First a learned single Judge and then a Division Bench rejected the prayer of the children. They approached Supreme Court by special leave under Article 136[6] of the Constitution. The objection of the petitioners was not to the language or the sentiments of the National Anthem.

Meaning of Jehovah's Witnesses

In 'The New Encyclopaedia Britannica' (Macropaedia) Vol. 10 page 538, after mentioning that Jehovah's Witnesses are "the adherents of the

5 **Meaning of Writ Petition:** Under the Indian legal system, jurisdiction to issue �prerogative writs� is given to the Supreme Court, and to the High Courts of Judicature of all Indian states. Parts of the law relating to writs are set forth in the Constitution of India. The Supreme Court, the highest in the country, may issue writs under Article 32 of the Constitution for enforcement of Fundamental Rights and under Articles 139 for enforcement of rights other than Fundamental Rights, while High Courts, the superior courts of the States, may issue writs under Articles 226. �Writ� is eminently designed by the makers of the Constitution, and in the same way it is developed very widely and efficiently by the courts in India. The Constitution broadly provides for five kinds of "prerogative" writs, namely, Habeas Corpus, Certiorari, Mandamus, Quo Warranto and Prohibition.

6 **Article 136 in The Constitution Of India 1949**
136. Special leave to appeal by the Supreme Court
(1) Notwithstanding anything in this Chapter, the Supreme Court may, in its discretion, grant special leave to appeal from any judgment, decree, determination, sentence or order in any cause or matter passed or made by any court or tribunal in the territory of India
(2) Nothing in clause (1) shall apply to any judgment, determination, sentence or order passed or made by any court or tribunal constituted by or under any law relating to the Armed Forces

apocalyptic sect organized by Charles Taze Russell in the early 1870", it is further mentioned, " They believe that the Watch Tower Bible and Tract Society, their legal agency and publishing arm, exemplifies the will of God and proclaims the truths of the Bible against the evil triumvirate of organized religion, the business world, and the state The Witnesses also stand apart from civil society, refusing to vote, run for public office, serve in any armed forces, salute the flag, stand for the national anthem, or recite the pledge of allegiance. Their religious stand have brought clashes with various governments, resulting in law suits, mob violence, imprisonment, torture, and death. At one time more than 6,000 Witnesses were inmates of Nazi concentration camps. Communist and Fascist states usually forbid Watch Tower activities. In the U.S. the society has taken 45 cases to the Supreme Court and has won significant victories for freedom of religion and speech. The Witnesses have been less successful in claiming exemptions as ministers from military service and in seeking to withhold blood transfusions from their children."

Freedom of speech and Expression:

Article 19(1)(a)[7] of the Constitution guarantees to all citizens freedom of speech and expression, but Article19(2)[8] provides that nothing in Article 19(1)(a) shall prevent a State from making any law, in so far as such law imposes reasonable restrictions on the exercise of the right conferred by the said sub-clause in the interests of the sovereignty and integrity of India, the security of the State, friendly relations with foreign States, public order, decency or morality, or in; relation to contempt of Court,

7 **Article 19(1)(a) in The Constitution Of India 1949**
(1) All citizens shall have the right
(a) to freedom of speech and expression

8 **Article 19 (2) in The Constitution Of India 1949**
19. Protection of certain rights regarding freedom of speech etc
(1) All citizens shall have the right
(a) to freedom of speech and expression;
(b) to assemble peaceably and without arms;
(c) to form associations or unions;
(d) to move freely throughout the territory of India;
(e) to reside and settle in any part of the territory of India; and
(f) omitted
(g) to practise any profession, or to carry on any occupation, trade or business
(2) Nothing in sub clause (a) of clause (1) shall affect the operation of any existing law, or prevent the State from making any law, in so far as such law imposes reasonable restrictions on the exercise of the right conferred by the said sub clause in the interests of the sovereignty and integrity of India, the security of the State, friendly relations with foreign States, public order, decency or morality or in relation to contempt of court, defamation or incitement to an offence

defamation or incitement to an offence. Article25(1)[9] guarantees to all persons freedom of conscience and the right freely to profess, practise and propagate religion, subject to public order, morality and health and to the other provisions of Part III[10] of the Constitution.

Question before the Supreme Court:

Whether the ban imposed by the Kerala Education Authorities against silence when the National Anthem was sung and expulsion of students from the school is consistent with the rights guaranteed by Articles 19(1)(a) and 25 of the Constitution.

Respect to National Anthem:

There is no provision of law which obliges anyone to sing the National Anthem nor it is disrespectful to the National Anthem if a person who stands up respectfully when the National Anthem is sung does not join the signing. It is true Article 51-A(a)[11] of the Constitution enjoins a duty

9 **Article 25 in The Constitution Of India 1949**
25. Freedom of conscience and free profession, practice and propagation of religion
(1) Subject to public order, morality and health and to the other provisions of this Part, all persons are equally entitled to freedom of conscience and the right freely to profess, practise and propagate religion
(2) Nothing in this article shall affect the operation of any existing law or prevent the State from making any law
(a) regulating or restricting any economic, financial, political or other secular activity which may be associated with religious practice;
(b) providing for social welfare and reform or the throwing open of Hindu religious institutions of a public character to all classes and sections of Hindus Explanation I The wearing and carrying of kirpans shall be deemed to be included in the profession of the Sikh religion Explanation II In sub clause (b) of clause reference to Hindus shall be construed as including a reference to persons professing the Sikh, Jaina or Buddhist religion, and the reference to Hindu religious institutions shall be construed accordingly

10 ***'Part III – Fundamental Rights'*** is a charter of rights contained in the Constitution of India. It guarantees civil liberties such that all Indians can lead their lives in peace and harmony as citizens of India. These include individual rights common to most liberal democracies, such asequality before law, freedom of speech and expression, and peaceful assembly, freedom to practice religion, and the right to constitutional remedies for the protection of civil rights by means of writs such as habeas corpus. Violation of these rights result in punishments as prescribed in the Indian Penal Code or other special laws, subject to discretion of the judiciary. The Fundamental Rights are defined as basichuman freedoms which every Indian citizen has the right to enjoy for a proper and harmonious development of personality. These rights universally apply to all citizens, irrespective of race, place of birth, religion, caste, creed, colour or gender. Aliens (persons who are not citizens) are also considered in matters like equality before law. They are enforceable by the courts, subject to certain restrictions. The Rights have their origins in many sources, including England's Bill of Rights, the United States Bill of Rights and France's Declaration of the Rights of Man.

11 **Article 51A in The Constitution Of India 1949**
51A. Fundamental duties It shall be the duty of every citizen of India (a) to abide by the Constitution and respect its ideals and institutions, the national Flag and the National Anthem;

on every citizen of India "to abide by the Constitution and respect its ideals and institutions, the National Flag and the National Anthem." Proper respect is shown to the National Anthem by standing up when the National Anthem is sung. It will not be right to say that disrespect is shown by not joining in the singing. Parliament has not been unmindful of 'National Honour'. The Prevention of Insults to National Honour Act was enacted in 1971. While Section 2[12] deals with insult to the Indian National Flag and the Constitution of India, Section 3 deals with the National Anthem and enacts,

Whoever, intentionally prevents the singing of the National Anthem or causes disturbance to any assembly engaged in such singing shall be punished with imprisonment for a term which may extend to three years, or with fine, or with both.

Standing up respectfully when the National Anthem is sung but not singing oneself clearly does not either prevent the singing of the National Anthem or cause disturbance to an assembly engaged in such singing so as to constitute the offence mentioned in Section 3 of the Prevention of Insults to National Honour Act.

Decision of the Supreme Court:

Court held that the expulsion of the three children from the school for the reason that because of their conscientiously held religious faith, they do not join the singing of the national anthem in the morning assembly though they do stand up respectfully when the anthem was sung, is a violation of their fundamental right 'to freedom of conscience and freely to profess, practise and propagate religion'.

Court further held that the Fundamental Rights of the appellants (Children) under Articles 19(1)(a) and 25(1) have been infringed and they were entitled to be protected. Court observed : our tradition teaches tolerance; our philosophy preaches tolerance; our Constitution practises tolerance; let us not dilute it.

---

12 **Section 2 of Prevention of Insults to National Honour Act was enacted in 1971**
2. INSULT TO INDIAN NATIONAL FLAG AND CONSTITUTION OF INDIA
Whoever in any public place or in any other place within public view burns, mutilates, defaces, defiles, disfigures, destroys, tramples upon or *otherwise shows disrespect to or brings into contempt (whether by words, either spoken or written, or by acts) the Indian National Flag or the Constitution of India or any part thereof, shall be punished with imprisonment for a term which may extend to three years, or with fine, or with both.

5

Free speech and expression is a value which is fundamental to the functioning of a democratic society[1]

Ratio Decidendi[2]: *Free speech and expression is a value which is fundamental to the functioning of a democratic society.*

Facts in Nutshell:

"Chand Bujh Gaya", a feature film produced by Faaiz Anwar. The film dwells on the travails of a young couple -a Hindu boy and a Muslim girl - whose friendship and lives were torn asunder in riots in the State of Gujarat. The Central Board of Film Certificate ('CBFC') refused to certify the film for exhibition. The Film Certification Appellate Tribunal affirmed that order. The producer proceeded before the High Court under Article 226[3] of the

---

1 Appellants: **F.A. Picture International Vs.** Respondent: **Central Board of Film Certification and Anr.**
AIR2005Bom145
Hon'ble Judges: Bhandari Dalveer, C.J. and Chandrachud D.Y., Judge

2 **Meaning of Ration Decidendi:** ***Ratio decidendi*** is a Latin phrase meaning "the reason" or "the rationale for the decision." The *ratio decidendi* is "the point in a case which determines the judgment" or "the principle which the case establishes."

3 **Article 226 in The Constitution Of India 1949**
226. Power of High Courts to issue certain writs
(1) Notwithstanding anything in Article 32 every High Court shall have powers, throughout the territories in relation to which it exercise jurisdiction, to issue to any person or authority, including in appropriate cases, any Government, within those territories directions, orders or writs, including writs in the nature of habeas corpus, mandamus, prohibitions, quo warranto and certiorari, or any of them, for the enforcement of any of the rights conferred by Part III and for any other purpose
(2) The power conferred by clause (1) to issue directions, orders or writs to any Government, authority or person may also be exercised by any High Court exercising jurisdiction in relation to the territories within which the cause of action, wholly or in part, arises for the exercise of such power, notwithstanding that the seat of such Government or authority or the residence of such person is not within those territories
(3) Where any party against whom an interim order, whether by way of injunction or stay or in any other manner, is made on, or in any proceedings relating to, a petition under clause (1), without
(a) furnishing to such party copies of such petition and all documents in support of the plea for such interim order; and
(b) giving such party an opportunity of being heard, makes an application to the High Court for the vacation of such order and furnishes a copy of such application to the party in whose favour such order has been made or the counsel of such party, the High Court shall dispose of the application

Constitution. Besides "Chand Bujh Gaya", Mr. Faaiz Anwar stated that he has been associated with the production of several films, among them "Dil Hai ke Manta Nahi", "Sajan" and "Vijay Path", "Chand Bujh Gaya" was produced under the banner of F.A. Picture International with an aggregate footage of 11602 feet comprised in 15 reels. On 22nd September, 2003 the petitioner[4] applied for certification of the film for public exhibition to the regional office of the CBFC at Calcutta. The film was examined by the Examination Committee. On 24th September, 2003 the petitioner received an intimation that the Committee recommended a refusal of certificate to the film for the following reason :

"The film from the end of Reel No. 8 contains visuals as well as dialogues, which may have the danger of inciting communal violence among the people. Besides, a large number of visuals are extremely terrifying and as such unsuitable for public exhibition."

The petitioner by a letter dated 16th October, 2003 communicated a willingness to change the contents of dialogues and visuals which could not be certified in the view of the Committee. Thereupon after discussions with the Examining Committee the petitioner carried out deletions and alterations after the eighth reel reducing the footage of the film to 10,966 feet. The revised footage was submitted on 8th December, 2003 to the first respondent[5] at Calcutta. On 12th December, 2003, the CBFC informed the petitioner that the Committee had recommended that the certificate be refused for the following reasons :

"The film from after Reel No. 7 has depicted the following :

1. Gruesome communal violence, which, it is felt will ferment communal disharmony.

---

within a period of two weeks from the date on which it is received or from the date on which the copy of such application is so furnished, whichever is later, or where the High Court is closed on the last day of that period, before the expiry of the next day afterwards on which the High Court is open; and if the application is not so disposed of, the interim order shall, on the expiry of that period, or, as the case may be, the expiry of the aid next day, stand vacated

(4) The power conferred on a High Court by this article shall not be in derogation of the power conferred on the Supreme court by clause (2) of Article 32

4 **Meaning of Petitioner:** A person who presents a Petition. (**Meaning of Petition:** A formal message requesting something that is submitted to an authority)

5 **Meaning of Respondent:** A **respondent** is a person who is called upon to issue a response to a communication made by another. In legal usage, this specifically refers to the defendant in a legal proceeding commenced by a petition, or to an appellee, or the opposing party, in an appeal of a decision by an initial fact-finder.

2. Certain characters and incidents which are clearly identifiable with actual personalities and individuals, the public exhibition of which may lead to public disharmony.

3. The Gujarat violence is a live issue and a scar on national sensitivity. Exhibition of the film will certainly aggravate the situation."

Petitioner contended before High Court that a serious encroachment of the right to free speech and expression guaranteed by Article 19(1)(a)[6] of the Constitution has been done due to the Act of CBFC.

Freedom of Speech and Expression:

Article 19(1)(a) of the Constitution guarantees to every citizen the fundamental right to the freedom of speech and expression. Films have always been regarded as constituting a powerful medium of expression. Succeeding generations bred on a diet of the electronic media may well cause a sense of spondaic to those who decry the loss of the habit of reading. The genius of a Somerset Maugham, the Universe of Wordsworth or closer home, the imagery of a P.L. Deshpande may well need adaptations in an age dominated by the electronic media. The form of the medium may change but the values which underlie the importance of expression are constant. They are values which a society founded on a commitment to individual freedom holds dear. In a democratic society every citizen has a right to speak as indeed, the right to know. Knowledge of the affairs of governance and the invocation of peaceful forms of dissent is a necessary precondition to the existence of a stable society formed of informed citizens. Nothing can be as destructive of the social fabric in a democratic society than the attempt of those who govern to prevent access to information to those whose security depends upon the preservation of order. As environment in which human rights are respected is nurtured by a vibrant flow of information and avenues for a critical assessment of governance.

Artists, writers, play rights and film makers are the eyes and the ears of a free society. They are the veritable lungs of a free society because the power of their medium imparts a breath of fresh air into the drudgery of daily existence. Their right to communicate ideas in a medium of their choosing is as fundamental as the right of any other citizen to speak. Our

6 **Article 19(1)(a) in The Constitution Of India 1949**
(1) All citizens shall have the right
(a) to freedom of speech and expression

constitutional democracy guarantees the right of free speech and that right is not conditional upon the expression of views which may be palatable to mainstream thought. Dissent is the quintessence of democracy. Hence, those who express views which are critical of prevailing social reality have a valued position in the constitutional order. History tells us that dissent in all walks of life contributes to the evolution of society. Those who question unquestioned assumptions contribute to the alteration of social norms. Democracy is founded upon respect for their courage. Any attempt by the State to clamp down on the free expression of opinion must hence be frowned upon. The regulatory power of the State when it comes into contract with the fundamental right to free speech must be confined within the boundaries that have been prescribed by Article 19(2)[7] of the Constitution. That sub-article contemplates the regulatory power of the State to impose by law reasonable restrictions on the fundamental right to free speech and expression; in the interests of (i) the sovereignty and integrity of India; (ii) the security of the State; (iii) friendly relations with Foreign States; (iv) public order, decency or morality; and (v) in relation to Contempt of Court, defamation or incitement to an offence.

Section 5B[8] of the Cinematograph Act, 1952 adopts the grounds which have been spelt out in sub-article (2) of Article 19[9] as constituting reasons

7 **Article 19 (2) in The Constitution Of India 1949**
19. Protection of certain rights regarding freedom of speech etc
(1) All citizens shall have the right
(a) to freedom of speech and expression;
(b) to assemble peaceably and without arms;
(c) to form associations or unions;
(d) to move freely throughout the territory of India;
(e) to reside and settle in any part of the territory of India; and
(f) omitted
(g) to practise any profession, or to carry on any occupation, trade or business
(2) Nothing in sub clause (a) of clause (1) shall affect the operation of any existing law, or prevent the State from making any law, in so far as such law imposes reasonable restrictions on the exercise of the right conferred by the said sub clause in the interests of the sovereignty and integrity of India, the security of the State, friendly relations with foreign States, public order, decency or morality or in relation to contempt of court, defamation or incitement to an offence

8 **Section 5B of the Cinematograph Act, 1952**
5-B. Principles for guidance in certifying films. – (1) A film shall not be certified for public exhibition if, in the opinion of the authority competent to grant the certificate, the film or any part of it is against the interests of [(Ins. by Act 49 of 1981 (w.e.f. 1-6-1983) the sovereignty and integrity of India] the security of the State, friendly relations with foreign States, public order, decency or morality, or involves defamation or contempt of court or is likely to incite the commission of any offence.
(2) Subject to the provisions contained in sub-section (1), the Central Government may issue such directions as it may think fit setting out the principles which shall guide the authority competent togrant certificates under this Act in sanctioning films for public exhibition.

9 **Article 19 in The Constitution Of India 1949**

on the basis of which a film shall not be certified for public exhibition. The validity of the decision of the certifying authority to decline certification of a film for public exhibition must, therefore, be assessed with reference to those grounds. There is no general residuary discretion in a certifying authority to invent grounds which lie outside the purview of the regulatory power conferred by Article 19(2) of the Constitution of section 5B of the Cinematograph Act, 1952. Censorship in a free society can be tolerated within the narrowest possible confines and strictly within the limits which are contemplated in a constitutional order.

Cases Referred:

In *Indian Express Newspapers v. Union of India*[10], the Supreme Court

---

19. Protection of certain rights regarding freedom of speech etc

(1) All citizens shall have the right

(a) to freedom of speech and expression;

(b) to assemble peaceably and without arms;

(c) to form associations or unions;

(d) to move freely throughout the territory of India;

(e) to reside and settle in any part of the territory of India; and

(f) omitted

(g) to practise any profession, or to carry on any occupation, trade or business

(2) Nothing in sub clause (a) of clause (1) shall affect the operation of any existing law, or prevent the State from making any law, in so far as such law imposes reasonable restrictions on the exercise of the right conferred by the said sub clause in the interests of the sovereignty and integrity of India, the security of the State, friendly relations with foreign States, public order, decency or morality or in relation to contempt of court, defamation or incitement to an offence

(3) Nothing in sub clause (b) of the said clause shall affect the operation of any existing law in so far as it imposes, or prevent the State from making any law imposing, in the interests of the sovereignty and integrity of India or public order, reasonable restrictions on the exercise of the right conferred by the said sub clause

(4) Nothing in sub clause (c) of the said clause shall affect the operation of any existing law in so far as it imposes, or prevent the State from making any law imposing, in the interests of the sovereignty and integrity of India or public order or morality, reasonable restrictions on the exercise of the right conferred by the said sub clause

(5) Nothing in sub clauses (d) and (e) of the said clause shall affect the operation of any existing law in so far as it imposes, or prevent the State from making any law imposing, reasonable restrictions on the exercise of any of the rights conferred by the said sub clauses either in the interests of the general public or for the protection of the interests of any Scheduled Tribe

(6) Nothing in sub clause (g) of the said clause shall affect the operation of any existing law in so far as it imposes, or prevent the State from making any law imposing, in the interests of the general public, reasonable restrictions on the exercise of the right conferred by the said sub clause, and, in particular, nothing in the said sub clause shall affect the operation of any existing law in so far as it relates to, or prevent the State from making any law relating to,

(i) the professional or technical qualifications necessary for practising any profession or carrying on any occupation, trade or business, or

(ii) the carrying on by the State, or by a corporation owned or controlled by the State, of any trade, business, industry or service, whether to the exclusion, complete or partial, of citizens or otherwise

10 A.I.R. 1986 S.C. 515

emphasised that in a democratic society people have a right to be informed of developments that take place in the democratic process. In *Odyssey Communications Pvt. Ltd. v. Lokvidayan Sanghatana*[11] the telecasting of the serial "Honi Anhonee" was sought to be restrained on the ground that it was likely to spread blind beliefs and superstitions. The Supreme Court vacated an injunction[12] which was granted by the High Court. The Supreme Court held that the right of a citizen to exhibit a film on Television would be curtailed only in the circumstances set out in Article19(2) of the Constitution. In *S. Rangarajan v. P. Jagjivan Ram* [13], the High Court had revoked a certificate for unrestricted public exhibition granted by the Censor Board to a film whose theme was the reservation policy. Reversing the decision, the Supreme Court held that films constitute a legitimate and important medium for the treatment of issues of general concern and it was open to a producer to project his own message even if it is not approved of by others. The State, it was held, cannot prevent open discussion and open expression, however, hateful it may be to its policies. Restrictions on the freedom of expression under Article 19(2) must be justified on the anvil of necessity and not in the quicksand of convenience of expediency. In *LIC v. Manubhai D. Shah*[14], the telecasting of a documentary film on the Bhopal Gas Disaster was in issue. Confirming the judgment of the High Court directing Doordarshan to telecast the documentary, the Supreme Court held that the print media, the radio and television are vital public educators in a democracy, the freedom to air one's views is the lifeline of every democratic institution and any attempt to stifle, suffocate or gag this right would be inconsistent with a democratic set up.

Decision of High Court:

Court held that the decision of the Central Board of Film Certification (CBFC) was one which no reasonable body of persons could have arrived at. Where the decision of the CBFC entrenches upon the fundamental right to the freedom of speech and expression, it is not merely the function but the duty and responsibility of the Court to intervene. Free speech and expression is a value which is fundamental to the functioning of a democratic society.

11 AIR1988SC1642

12 **Meaning of Injunction:** A court order by which an individual is required to perform, or is restrained from performing, a particular act.

13 [1989]2SCR204

14 [1992]3SCR595

6

Freedom of speech and expression is a natural right[1]

Facts in Nutshell:

The respondent[2], the executive trustee of the Consumer Education & Research center (CERC), Ahmedabad, after undertaking research into the working of the Life Insurance Corporation (LIC) published on 10th July, 1978 a study paper titled "A fraud on policy holders-a shocking story". This study paper portrayed the discriminatory practice adopted by the LIC which adversely affected the interest of a large number of policy holders. This study paper was widely circulated by the respondent. Mr. N.C. Krishnan, a member of the LIC prepared a counter to the respondent's study paper and published the same as an article in the "Hindu", a daily newspaper, challenging the conclusions reached by the respondent in his study paper. The respondent prepared a rejoinder[3] which was published in the same newspaper. The LIC publishes a magazine called the 'Yogakshema' for informing its members, staff and agents about its activities. It was the contention of the LIC that this magazine is an in-house magazine and is not put in the market for sale to the general public. Mr. Krishnan's article which was in the nature of a counter to the respondent's study paper was published in this magazine. The respondent thereupon requested the LIC to publish his rejoinder to the said article in the said magazine but his request was spurned. The respondent thereafter met the Chairman of the LIC and requested him to revise the decision and to publish the article in the magazine but to no avail. Thereupon he filed

1 Appellants:**Life Insurance Corporation of India and Union of India and another Vs.** Respondent: **Prof. Manubhai D. Shah and Cinemart Foundation**
AIR1993SC171
Hon'ble Judges: A. M. Ahmadii and M. M. Punchhi, JJ.

2 **Meaning of Respondent:** A **respondent** is a person who is called upon to issue a response to a communication made by another. In legal usage, this specifically refers to the defendant in a legal proceeding commenced by a petition, or to an appellee, or the opposing party, in an appeal of a decision by an initial fact-finder.

3 **Meaning of Rejoinder:** The answer made by a defendant to the claimant's reply

the petition[4] contending that the refusal to publish his rejoinder in the magazine violated his fundamental right under Articles 14[5] and 19(1)(a)[6] of the Constitution.

Decision of the High Court:

The High Court came to the conclusion that the LIC's stand that the magazine was an in-house magazine was untenable for two reasons, namely (1) it was available to anyone on payment of subscription; and (2) it invited articles for publication therein from members of the public. The High Court took the view that merely because the magazine finds it circulation among officers, employees and agents of the Corporation, it does not acquire the character of an in-house magazine since the same can be purchased by any member of the public on payment of subscription and members of the public are invited to contribute articles for publication in the said magazine. It further held that assuming that the magazine was an in-house magazine. as contended by the LIC, the Corporation cannot under the guise of publication of an in-house magazine violate the fundamental right of the respondent. Taking note of the fact that the LIC was a State within the meaning of Article 12[7] of the Constitution and the in-house magazine was published with the aid of public funds and public money, the High Court held that in the interest of democracy and free society the magazine should be available to both, an admirer and a critic, for dissemination of information. High Court concluded that the LIC had violated the respondent's fundamental right under Article 19(1)(a) of the Constitution by refusing to publish his rejoinder to Mr. Krishnan's counter to his study paper. It also concluded that the refusal of the LIC was arbitrary and violative of Article 14 of the Constitution as well. The High Court, therefore, directed the LIC to publish in the, immediate next issue of Yogakshema the respondent's rejoinder to Mr. Krishnan's reply to his study paper of 10th July, 1978. This view of the Gujarat High Court was

4 **Meaning of Petition:** A formal message requesting something that is submitted to an authority

5 **Article 14 in The Constitution Of India 1949**

14. Equality before law: The State shall not deny to any person equality before the law or the equal protection of the laws within the territory of India Prohibition of discrimination on grounds of religion, race, caste, sex or place of birth

6 **Article 19 in The Constitution Of India 1949**

19. Protection of certain rights regarding freedom of speech etc

(1) All citizens shall have the right

(a) to freedom of speech and expression

7 **Article 12 in The Constitution Of India 1949**

12. Definition In this part, unless the context otherwise requires, the State includes the Government and Parliament of India and the Government and the Legislature of each of the States and all local or other authorities within the territory of India or under the control of the Government of India

assailed[8] by the LIC in the first appeal[9].

Freedom of Speech and Expression:

Speech is God's gift to mankind. Through speech a human being conveys his thoughts, sentiments and feelings to others. Freedom of speech and expression is thus a natural right which a human being acquires on birth. It is, therefore, a basic human right. "Everyone has the right to freedom of opinion and expression; the right includes freedom to hold opinions without interference and to seek and receive and impart information and ideas through any media and regardless of frontiers" proclaims the Universal Declaration of Human Rights (1948). The People of India declared in the Preamble[10] of the Constitution which they gave unto themselves their resolve to secure to all citizens liberty of thought and expression. This resolve is reflected in Article 19(1)(a) which is one of the articles found in Part III[11] of the Constitution which enumerates the Fundamental Rights. That article reads as under:

---

8 **Meaning of Assailed:** To attack verbally, as with arguments, criticism, or abuse.

9 **Meaning of Appeal:** In law, an **appeal** is a process for requesting a formal change to an official decision. Very broadly speaking there are appeals on the record and *de novo* appeals. In *de novo* appeals, a new decision maker re-hears the case without any reference to the prior decision maker. In appeals on the record, the decision of the prior decision maker is challenged by arguing that he or she misapplied the law, came to an incorrect factual finding, acted in excess of his jurisdiction, abused his powers, was biased, considered evidence which he should not have considered or failed to consider evidence that he should have considered.

10 **Preamble of the Constitution:**
WE, THE PEOPLE OF INDIA, having solemnly resolved to constitute India into a SOVEREIGN SOCIALIST SECULAR DEMOCRATIC REPUBLIC and to secure to all its citizens:
JUSTICE, social, economic and political;
LIBERTY, of thought, expression, belief, faith and worship;
EQUALITY of status and of opportunity;
and to promote among them all
FRATERNITY assuring the dignity of the individual and the unity and integrity of the Nation;
IN OUR CONSTITUENT ASSEMBLY this twenty-sixth day of November, 1949, DO HEREBY ADOPT, ENACT AND GIVE TO OURSELVES THIS CONSTITUTION.

11 **'Part III – Fundamental Rights'** is a charter of rights contained in the Constitution of India. It guarantees civil liberties such that all Indians can lead their lives in peace and harmony as citizens of India. These include individual rights common to most liberal democracies, such asequality before law, freedom of speech and expression, and peaceful assembly, freedom to practice religion, and the right to constitutional remedies for the protection of civil rights by means of writs such as habeas corpus. Violation of these rights result in punishments as prescribed in the Indian Penal Code or other special laws, subject to discretion of the judiciary. The Fundamental Rights are defined as basic human freedoms which every Indian citizen has the right to enjoy for a proper and harmonious development of personality. These rights universally apply to all citizens, irrespective of race, place of birth, religion, caste, creed, colour or gender. Aliens (persons who are not citizens) are also considered in matters like equality before law. They are enforceable by the courts, subject to certain restrictions. The Rights have their origins in many sources, including England's Bill of Rights, the United States Bill of Rights and France's Declaration of the Rights of Man.

19(1). All citizens shall have the right-
(a) to freedom of speech and expression;
Article 19(2) which has relevance may also be reproduced:

19(2). Nothing in Sub-clause (a) of Clause (1) shall affect the operation of any existing law, or prevent the State from making any law, insofar as such law imposes reasonable restrictions on the exercise of the right conferred by the said Sub-clause in the interests of [the sovereignty arid integrity of India,] the security of the State, friendly relations with foreign States, public order, decency or morality or in relation to contempt of court, defamation or incitement to an offence.

The words 'freedom of speech and expression' must, therefore, be broadly construed to include the freedom to circulate one's views by words of mouth or in writing or through audio-visual instrumentalities. It, therefore, includes the right to propagate one's views through the print media or through any other communication channel e.g. the radio and the television. Every citizen of this free country, therefore, has the right to air his or her views through the printing and/or the electronic media subject of course to permissible restrictions imposed under Article 19(2) of the Constitution. The print media, the radio and the tiny screen play the role of public educators, so vital to the growth of a healthy democracy. Freedom to air one's views is the life line of any democratic institution and any attempt to stifle, suffocate or gag this right would sound a death-knell to democracy and would help usher in autocracy or dictatorship. It cannot be gainsaid that modern communication mediums advance public interest by informing the public of the events and developments that have taken place and thereby education the voters, a role considered significant for the vibrant functioning of a democracy. Therefore, in any set up, more so in a democratic set up like ours, dissemination of news and views for popular consumption is a must and any attempt to deny the same must be frowned upon unless it falls within the mischief of Article19(2) of the Constitution. It follows that a citizen for propagation of his or her ideas has a right to publish for circulation his views in periodicals, magazines and journals or through the electronic media since it is well known that these communication channels are great purveyors of news and views and make considerable impact on the minds of the readers and viewers and arc known to mould public opinion on vital issues of national importance. Once it is conceded, and it cannot indeed be disputed, that freedom of speech and expression includes freedom of circulation and propagation of ideas, there can be no doubt that the right extends to the citizen being permitted to use the media to answer the criticism leveled against the view propagated by him. Every free citizen has an undoubted right to lay what sentiments he pleases before the public; to forbid this, except to the extent permitted by Article 19(2), would be an inroad on his freedom. This freedom must, however, be exercised with circumspection and care must be taken not to trench on the rights of other citizens or to jeopardise public interest. It is manifest from Article 19(2) that the right conferred by Article 19(1)(a) is subject to imposition of reasonable restrictions in the interest of, amongst others, public order, decency or morality or in relation to defamation or incitement to an offence. It is, therefore, obvious that subject to reasonable restrictions placed under Article 19(2) a citizen has a right to publish, circulate and disseminate his views and any attempt to thwart or deny the same would offend Article 19(1)(a).

Cases Referred:

In *Romesh Tappar v. The State of Madras*[12] Supreme Court held that the freedom of speech and expression includes freedom of propagation of ideas and this freedom is ensured by the freedom of circulation. It pointed out that freedom of speech and expression are the foundation of all democratic organisations and are essential for the proper functioning of the processes of democracy. This view was reiterated in *Sakal Papers Pvt. Ltd.*[13] wherein Supreme Court observed that the freedom of speech and expression guaranteed by Article 19(1)(a) includes the freedom of the Press. For propagating his ideas a citizen had the right to publish them, to disseminate them and to circulate them, either by word of mouth or by writing.

Decision of the Supreme Court:

Court held that by refusing to print and publish the rejoinder the LIC had violated the respondent's fundamental right. A wrong doer cannot be heard to say that its persistent refusal to print and publish the article must yield the desired result, namely to frustrate the respondent. The Court must be careful to see that it does not, even unwittingly, aid the effort to defeat a party's right.

12 [1950] SCR 495

13 MANU/SC/0090/1961

7

Freedom of free expression is of cardinal value in a democratic Government[1]

Facts in Nutshell:

The petitioner[2], a well known activist and film maker. He was producer of documentary films and writes scripts for films. In 2003 the petitioner produced a documentary film in one reel (running time 18 minutes) called Aakrosh on communal riots that took place in Gujarat in the year 2002. The documentary makes a sincere attempt to give expression to the sufferings and woes of the survivors of the holocaust. This was done in a series of interviews. The documentary has deliberately avoided images of gruesome violence and dead bodies. It has limited itself to the expression of anguish by the victims who were trying to come to terms with the meaninglessness of it all. The petitioner's documentary was selected for screening at Hyderabad Film Festival organized by South Asian Forum and Film Festival organized by the Surabhi Foundation in collaboration with Film Division and Times Foundation. The petitioner applied to the Central Board of Film Certification on February 26, 2003 for a certificate under the Cinematograph Act, 1952 for U Certificate for unrestricted exhibition of the film. He received a letter (March 3, 2003) from the Regional Officer that the Examining Committee had come to the conclusion that the certificate cannot be granted to the petitioner for its exhibition. The said letter further informed the petitioner that he has a right to prefer appeal to the Revising Committee of the Board. The petitioner accordingly preferred appeal and received a letter (March 31, 2003) from the Board which communicated that the Revising Committee and the Board had come to the conclusion that the certificate cannot be granted for exhibition of petitioner's documentary. Aggrieved by the decisions of the

1 Appellants: **Ramesh Pimple Vs.** Respondent: **Central Board of Film Certification and Anr.** 2004(5)BomCR214

Hon'ble Judges: A.P. Shah and S.C. Dharmadhikari, JJ.

2 **Meaning of Petitioner:** A person who presents a Petition. (**Meaning of Petition:** A formal message requesting something that is submitted to an authority)

Examining Committee and Revising Committee, the petitioner preferred appeal to the Film Certification Appellate Tribunal under Section 5(c)[3] of the Cinematograph Act, 1952. The Appellate Tribunal, after hearing the petitioner confirmed the decision of the Board vide its decision dated August 11, 2003.

Decision of Tribunal:

The Tribunal observed that the film was one sided version of one particular community and if it was shown to masses, not only a selective crowd but anyone and everyone, is bound to provoke communal feeling and desire to retaliate and take revenge. The tribunal further observed that such a film endanger restoration of peace and tranquility and to quote the words of the tribunal "………these riots are now history, and therefore, be forgotten by public to avoid repetition of such cruel acts". Besides that the tribunal was of the opinion that some fact finding enquiry committee/ commissions are already examining the matter and collecting evidence and some judicial proceedings in Courts of law are also pending and, therefore, it would not be proper to exhibit such provocative documentary at this stage.

Provisions of the Cinematograph Act, 1952

The Act was enacted to provide for the certification of cinematograph films for exhibition and for regulating their exhibition. Section 3 of the Act empowers the Central Government to constitute a Board consisting of a Chairman, five whole time members and six honorary members, three of whom must be persons engaged or employed in the film industry, for the purpose of sanctioning films for public exhibition. Section 3B empowers the Board so constituted to constitute by special or general

---

3 **Cinematograph Act, 1952:**

5-C. Appeals. – (1) Any person applying for a certificate in respect of a film who is aggrieved by any order of the Board -

(a) Refusing to grant a certificate ; or

(b) Granting only an "A" certificate ; or

(c) Granting only a "S" certificate ; or

(d) Granting only a "UA" certificate ; or(e) Directing the applicant to carry out any excisions or modifications, may, within thirty days from the date of such order, prefer an appeal to the Tribunal :Provided that the Tribunal may, if it is satisfied that the appellant was prevented by sufficient cause from filing the appeal within the aforesaid period of thirty days, allow such appeal to be admitted within a further period of thirty days.

(2) Every appeal under this section shall be made by a petition in writing and shall be accompanied by a brief statement of the reasons for the order appealed against where such statement has been furnished to the appellant and by such fees, not exceeding rupees one thousand, as may be prescribed.

order an Examining Committee for the examination of any film or class of films, and a Revising Committee for re-considering, if necessary, the recommendations of Examining Committee. Any person desiring to exhibit any film has to make an application as provided by Section 4 to the Board in the prescribed manner for a certificate and the Board may after examination of the film sanction the film for unrestricted public exhibition or sanction the film for public exhibition restricted to adults or to direct the applicant to carry out such excisions and modifications in the film as it thinks necessary before sanctioning it for unrestricted public exhibition or for public exhibition restricted to adults or refuse to sanction the film for public exhibition. Section 4A provides for the examination of films by Examining Committee and in the case of difference of opinion amongst the members of the Examining Committee for further examination by the Revising Committee. Section 5A provides for certification of films. If after examination the Board considers that the film is suitable for unrestricted public exhibition or that although not suitable for such exhibition, it is suitable for public exhibition restricted to adults, it is required to issue a "U" certificate in the case of the former and an "A" certificate in the case of the latter. Section 5B provides for laying down principles for guidance in the matter of certification of films. This section to the extent relevant for our purpose reads as under :

"5B Principles for guidance in certifying films. -- (1) A film shall not be certified for public exhibition if, in the opinion of the authority competent to grant the certificate, the film or any part of it is against the interest of the sovereignty and integrity of India, the security of the State, friendly relations with foreign States, public order, decency or morality, or involve defamation or contempt of Court or is likely to incite the commission of any offence.

(2) Subject to the provisions contained in Sub-section (1)......... the Central Government may issue such directions as it may think fit setting out the principles which shall guide the authority competent to grant certificates under this Act in sanctioning films for public exhibition..."

Section 5C provides for the constitution of appellate tribunals, whereas Section 5D provides for appeals against the Board's decision refusing to grant the certificate or granting "A" certificate or directing the applicant to carry out any excisions or modifications. In addition thereto revisional powers have been conferred on the Central Government to call for the record of any proceeding in relation to any film at any stage where it is not made the subject matter of appeal to enquire into the matter and make such order in relation thereto as it thinks fit and where necessary give direction that the exhibition of the film should be suspended for a period not exceeding two months. Sub-section (5) of Section 6 lays down that the Central Government may, if satisfied in relation to any films in respect of which an order has been made by an appellate tribunal under Section 5B that it is necessary so to do in the interest of (i) the sovereignty and integrity of India or (ii) the security of the State or (iii) friendly relations with foreign States, or (iv) public order or decency or morality, make such enquiry into the matter as it deems necessary and pass such order in relation thereto as it thinks fit. Thereupon the Board must dispose of the matter in conformity with such order. Section 7 lays down the penalties for contravention of the requirement of Part II of the Act. Section 8 confers power to make rules and Section 9 empowers the Central Government to exempt the exhibition or export of a film or class of films from any of the provisions of the said part or of any rules made thereunder subject to such conditions and restrictions, if any, as it may impose. Part II of the Act deals with the regulation of exhibition by means of Cinematograph with which we are not concerned. This in brief is the scheme of the statute.

In exercise of power conferred by Sub-section (2) of Section 5B of the Act the Central Government has laid down the principles which should guide the authorities in sanctioning the films for public exhibition. These guidelines came to be revised in 1991 and Clause 1 thereof require the Board of Film Certification to ensure that :

"(a) the medium of film remains responsible and sensitive to the values and standards of society;

(b) artistic expression and creative freedom are not unduly curbed;

(c) certification is responsive to social change;

(d) the medium of film provides clean and healthy entertainment; and

(e) as far as possible, the film is of aesthetic value and cinematically of a good standard.

Clause (2) states that the Board of Film Censors shall ensure that :

"2.(vii) human sensibilities are not offended by vulgarity, obscenity or depravity;

(ix) scenes degrading or denigrating women in any manner are not presented;

(x) scenes involving sexual violence against women like attempt to rape, rape or any form of molestation or scenes of a similar nature are avoided and if any such incident is germane to the theme, they shall be reduced to the minimum and no details are shown."

In following these guidelines or principles the Board of Film Certification has been cautioned to ensure that the film is judged in its entirety from the point of view of its overall impact and is judged in the light of contemporary standards of the country and the people to which the film relates, provided that, the film does not deprave the morality of the audience.

Censorship is permitted mainly on social interests specified under Article 19(2)[4] of the Constitution with emphasis on maintenance of values and standards of society. Therefore, the censorship by prior restraint must necessarily be reasonable that could be saved by the well accepted principles of judicial review[5].

Cases Referred:

In *S. Rangarajan v. P. Jagjivan Ram*[6] the Court emphasized that the

4 **Article 19 in The Constitution Of India 1949**
19. Protection of certain rights regarding freedom of speech etc
(1) All citizens shall have the right
(a) to freedom of speech and expression;
(b) to assemble peaceably and without arms;
(c) to form associations or unions;
(d) to move freely throughout the territory of India;
(e) to reside and settle in any part of the territory of India; and
(f) omitted
(g) to practise any profession, or to carry on any occupation, trade or business
(2) Nothing in sub clause (a) of clause (1) shall affect the operation of any existing law, or prevent the State from making any law, in so far as such law imposes reasonable restrictions on the exercise of the right conferred by the said sub clause in the interests of the sovereignty and integrity of India, the security of the State, friendly relations with foreign States, public order, decency or morality or in relation to contempt of court, defamation or incitement to an offence

5 **Meaning of Judicial Review: Judicial review** is the doctrine under which legislative and executive actions are subject to review (and possible invalidation) by the judiciary. A specific court with judicial review power must annul the acts of the state when it finds them incompatible with a higher authority (such as the terms of a written constitution). Judicial review is an example of check and balances in a modern governmental system (where the judiciary checks the other branches of government). This principle is interpreted differently in different jurisdictions, which also have differing views on the different hierarchy of governmental norms. As a result, the procedure and scope of judicial review differs from country to country and state to state.

6 [1989]2SCR204

freedom of expression means the right to express one's opinion by words of mouth, writing, printing, picture or in any other manner. It would thus include the freedom of communication and the right to propagate or publish opinion.

In *Sakal Papers (P) Ltd. v. Union of India* [7], Mudholkar, Judge said :

> "......... The Courts must be ever vigilant in guarding perhaps the most precious of all the freedoms guaranteed by our Constitution. The reason for this is obvious. The freedom of speech and expression of opinion is of paramount importance under a democratic Constitution which envisages changes in the composition of legislatures and governments and must be preserved."

In Indian Express Newspapers (Bombay) Pvt. Ltd, v. Union of India[8], the Court pointed out that the constitutional guarantee of the freedom of speech and expression is not so much for the benefit of the press as it is for the benefit of the public. The people have a right to be informed of the developments that take place in a democratic process and the press plays a vital role in disseminating this information. Neither the Government nor any instrumentality of the Government or any public sector undertaking run with the help of public funds can shy away from articles which expose weaknesses in its functioning and which in given cases pose a threat to their power by attempting to create obstacles in the information percolating to the members of the community.

The freedom of free expression guaranteed by Article 19(1)(a) is of cardinal value in a democratic government. Tolerance of a diversity of view point and the acceptance of freedom of speech of those whose thinking may not accord a main stream, are the cardinal values, which lie at the very foundation of democratic form of government. Respect for and tolerance of a diversity of view point is what ultimately sustain a democratic society and government.

Decision of the High Court:

Court held that the tribunal was not right in observing that the movie would incite people and would lead to further violence. It was not correct to say that average people will not learn their mistakes of the past and perhaps will not commit same mistake again. The documentary creates

7 [1962]3SCR842

8 AIR 1986 SC 515

an impression of the message of peace and co-existence and compassion for the people who suffered in the riots. Therefore in court opinion the decision of the tribunal as well as the decisions of the Examining Committee and Revising Committee cannot be sustained. Court directed to grant appropriate certificate for the exhibition of the film "Aakrosh".

Free Legal Aid and Right to Life

Constitution and Fundamental Rights:

Our Constitution guarantees all the basic and fundamental human rights set out in the Universal Declaration of Human Rights, 1948, to its citizens and other persons. The chapter dealing with the Fundamental Rights is contained in Part III[1] of the Constitution. The purpose of this part is to safeguard the basic human rights from the vicissitudes[2] of political controversy and to place them beyond the reach of the political parties who, by virtue of their majority, may come to form the Govt. at the center or in the State.. The Fundamental Rights are available to all the "Citizens" of the country but a few of them are also available to "persons". While Article 14[3], which guarantees equality before law or the equal protection of laws within the territory of India, is applicable to "person" which would also include the "citizen" of the country and "non-citizen" both, Article 15[4] speaks only of "citizen" and it is specifically provided therein

1 ***'Part III – Fundamental Rights'*** is a charter of rights contained in the Constitution of India. It guarantees civil liberties such that all Indians can lead their lives in peace and harmony as citizens of India. These include individual rights common to most liberal democracies, such as equality before law, freedom of speech and expression, and peaceful assembly, freedom to practice religion, and the right to constitutional remedies for the protection of civil rights by means of writs such as habeas corpus. Violation of these rights result in punishments as prescribed in the Indian Penal Code or other special laws, subject to discretion of the judiciary. The Fundamental Rights are defined as basic human freedoms which every Indian citizen has the right to enjoy for a proper and harmonious development of personality. These rights universally apply to all citizens, irrespective of race, place of birth, religion, caste, creed, colour or gender. Aliens (persons who are not citizens) are also considered in matters like equality before law. They are enforceable by the courts, subject to certain restrictions. The Rights have their origins in many sources, including England's Bill of Rights, the United States Bill of Rights and France's Declaration of the Rights of Man.

2 **Meaning of vicissitudes: 1.** Regular change or succession of one state or thing to another. **2.** Change or variation; mutation; mutability

3 **Article 14 in The Constitution Of India 1949**
14. Equality before law: The State shall not deny to any person equality before the law or the equal protection of the laws within the territory of India Prohibition of discrimination on grounds of religion, race, caste, sex or place of birth

4 **Article 15 in The Constitution Of India 1949**
15. Prohibition of discrimination on grounds of religion, race, caste, sex or place of birth
(1) The State shall not discriminate against any citizen on grounds only of religion, race, caste, sex, place of birth or any of them
(2) No citizen shall, on grounds only of religion, race, caste, sex, place of birth or any of them, be

that there shall be no discrimination against any "citizen" on the ground only of religion, race, caste, sex, place of birth or any of them nor shall any citizen be subjected to any disability, liability, restriction or condition with regard to access to shops, public restaurants, hostel and places of public entertainment, or the use of wells, tanks, bathing ghats, roads and place of public resort on the aforesaid grounds. Fundamental Rights guaranteed under Article 15 is, therefore, restricted to "citizen". So also, Article 16[5] which guarantees equality of opportunity in matters of public employment is applicable only to "citizens". The Fundamental Rights contained in Article 19[6], which contains the right to "Basic Freedoms",

---

subject to any disability, liability, restriction or condition with regard to

(a) access to shops, public restaurants, hotels and palaces of public entertainment; or

(b) the use of wells, tanks, bathing ghats, roads and places of public resort maintained wholly or partly out of State funds or dedicated to the use of the general public

(3) Nothing in this article shall prevent the State from making any special provision for women and children

(4) Nothing in this article or in clause (2) of Article 29 shall prevent the State from making any special provision for the advancement of any socially and educationally backward classes of citizens or for the Scheduled Castes and the Scheduled Tribes

5 **Article 16 in The Constitution Of India 1949**

16. Equality of opportunity in matters of public employment

(1) There shall be equality of opportunity for all citizens in matters relating to employment or appointment to any office under the State

(2) No citizen shall, on grounds only of religion, race, caste, sex, descent, place of birth, residence or any of them, be ineligible for, or discriminated against in respect or, any employment or office under the State

(3) Nothing in this article shall prevent Parliament from making any law prescribing, in regard to a class or classes of employment or appointment to an office under the Government of, or any local or other authority within, a State or Union territory, any requirement as to residence within that State or Union territory prior to such employment or appointment

(4) Nothing in this article shall prevent the State from making any provision for the reservation of appointments or posts in favor of any backward class of citizens which, in the opinion of the State, is not adequately represented in the services under the State

(5) Nothing in this article shall affect the operation of any law which provides that the incumbent of an office in connection with the affairs of any religious or denominational institution or any member of the governing body thereof shall be a person professing a particular religion or belonging to a particular denomination

6 **Article 19 in The Constitution Of India 1949**

19. Protection of certain rights regarding freedom of speech etc

(1) All citizens shall have the right

(a) to freedom of speech and expression;

(b) to assemble peaceably and without arms;

(c) to form associations or unions;

(d) to move freely throughout the territory of India;

(e) to reside and settle in any part of the territory of India; and

(f) omitted

(g) to practise any profession, or to carry on any occupation, trade or business

(2) Nothing in sub clause (a) of clause (1) shall affect the operation of any existing law, or prevent the State from making any law, in so far as such law imposes reasonable restrictions on the exercise of the right conferred by the said sub clause in the interests of the sovereignty and

namely, freedom of speech and expression; freedom to assemble peaceably and without arms; freedom to form associations or unions; freedom to move freely throughout the territory of India; freedom to reside and settle in any part of the territory of India and freedom to practice any profession, or to carry on any occupation, trade or business, are available only to "citizens" of the country.

In *Anwar v. State of J. & K.*[7], it was held that the rights under Articles 20[8], 21 and 22[9] are available not only to "citizens" but also to

---

integrity of India, the security of the State, friendly relations with foreign States, public order, decency or morality or in relation to contempt of court, defamation or incitement to an offence

(3) Nothing in sub clause (b) of the said clause shall affect the operation of any existing law in so far as it imposes, or prevent the State from making any law imposing, in the interests of the sovereignty and integrity of India or public order, reasonable restrictions on the exercise of the right conferred by the said sub clause

(4) Nothing in sub clause (c) of the said clause shall affect the operation of any existing law in so far as it imposes, or prevent the State from making any law imposing, in the interests of the sovereignty and integrity of India or public order or morality, reasonable restrictions on the exercise of the right conferred by the said sub clause

(5) Nothing in sub clauses (d) and (e) of the said clause shall affect the operation of any existing law in so far as it imposes, or prevent the State from making any law imposing, reasonable restrictions on the exercise of any of the rights conferred by the said sub clauses either in the interests of the general public or for the protection of the interests of any Scheduled Tribe

(6) Nothing in sub clause (g) of the said clause shall affect the operation of any existing law in so far as it imposes, or prevent the State from making any law imposing, in the interests of the general public, reasonable restrictions on the exercise of the right conferred by the said sub clause, and, in particular, nothing in the said sub clause shall affect the operation of any existing law in so far as it relates to, or prevent the State from making any law relating to,

(i) the professional or technical qualifications necessary for practising any profession or carrying on any occupation, trade or business, or

(ii) the carrying on by the State, or by a corporation owned or controlled by the State, of any trade, business, industry or service, whether to the exclusion, complete or partial, of citizens or otherwise

7 [1971]1SCR637

8 **Article 20 in The Constitution Of India 1949**

20. Protection in respect of conviction for offences

(1) No person shall be convicted of any offence except for violation of the law in force at the time of the commission of the act charged as an offence, nor be subjected to a penalty greater than that which might have been inflicted under the law in force at the time of the commission of the offence

(2) No person shall be prosecuted and punished for the same offence more than once

(3) No person accused of any offence shall be compelled to be a witness against himself

9 **Article 22 in The Constitution Of India 1949**

22. Protection against arrest and detention in certain cases

(1) No person who is arrested shall be detained in custody without being informed, as soon as may be, of the grounds for such arrest nor shall he be denied the right to consult, and to be defended by, a legal practitioner of his choice

(2) Every person who is arrested and detained in custody shall be produced before the nearest magistrate within a period of twenty four hours of such arrest excluding the time necessary for the journey from the place of arrest to the court of the magistrate and no such person shall be detained in custody beyond the said period without the authority of a magistrate

"persons" which would include "non-citizens". Article 20 guarantees right to protection in respect of conviction for offences. Article 21 guarantees right to life and personal liberty while Article 22 guarantees right to protection against arbitrary arrest and detention. These are wholly in consonance with Article 3, Article 7 and Article 9 of the Universal Declaration of Human Rights, 1948.

The word "LIFE" has also been used prominently in the Universal Declaration of Human Rights, 1948. [See Article 3 UDHR, 1948]. The Fundamental Rights under the Constitution are almost in consonance with the Rights contained in the Universal Declaration of Human Rights as also the Declaration and the Covenants of Civil and Political Rights and the Covenants of Economic, Social and Cultural Rights, to which India is a party having ratified them. In *Kubic Darusz v. Union of India*[10], "LIFE" is also recognised as a basic human right in the Universal Declaration of Human Rights, 1948, it has to have the same meaning and interpretation as has been placed on that word by Supreme Court in its various decisions relating to Article 21 of the Constitution. The meaning of the word "life" cannot be narrowed down. According to the tenor of the language used in Article 21, **it will be available not only to every citizen of this Country, but also to a "person" who may not be a citizen of the country.**

---

(3) Nothing in clauses (1) and (2) shall apply (a) to any person who for the time being is an enemy alien; or (b) to any person who is arrested or detained under any law providing for preventive detention

(4) No law providing for preventive detention shall authorise the detention of a person for a longer period than three months unless (a) an Advisory Board consisting of persons who are, or have been, or are qualified to be appointed as, Judges of a High Court has reported before the expiration of the said period of three months that there is in its opinion sufficient cause for such detention:

(5) When any person is detained in pursuance of an order made under any law providing for preventive detention, the authority making the order shall, as soon as may be, communicate to such person the grounds on which the order has been made and shall afford him the earliest opportunity of making a representation against the order

(6) Nothing in clause (5) shall require the authority making any such order as is referred to in that clause to disclose facts which such authority considers to be against the public interest to disclose

(7) Parliament may by law prescribe

(a) the circumstances under which, and the class or classes of cases in which, a person may be detained for a period longer than three months under any law providing for preventive detention without obtaining the opinion of an Advisory Board in accordance with the provisions of sub clause (a) of clause (4);

(b) the maximum period for which any person may in any class or classes of cases be detained under any law providing for preventive detention; and

(c) the procedure to be followed by an Advisory Board in an inquiry under sub clause (a) of clause (4) Right against Exploitation

10 1990CriLJ796

Right to Life:

The word 'life' in Article 21 is very significant as it covers every facet of human existence. The word 'life' has not been defined in the Constitution but it does not mean nor can it be restricted only to the vegetative or animal life or mere existence from conception to death. Life does not merely connote a continued drudgery through life. The expression 'life' has a much wider meaning bringing within its sweep some of the finer graces of human civilisation which makes life worth living[11].

Life includes all such amenities and facilities which a person born in a free country is entitled to enjoy with dignity, legally and constitutionally. The amplitude of the word 'life' is so wide that the danger and encroachment complained of would impinge upon the fundamental rights of citizens as in the present case. The apex Court has interpreted Article 21 giving wide meaning to 'life' which includes the quality of life, adequate nutrition, clothing and shelter and cannot be restricted merely to physical existence. The word 'life' in the Constitution has not been used in a limited manner. A wide meaning should be given to the expression 'life' to enable a man not only to sustain life but to enjoy it in a full measure. The sweep of right to life conferred by Article 21 of the Constitution is wide and far-reaching so as to bring within its scope the right to pollution free air and the "right to decent environment[12]." Under our Constitutional set up the dignity of man and subject to law the privacy of home shall be inviolable. The Constitution through various Articles in Part III[13] and Part IV[14] guarantees

---

11 *Board of Trustees of the Port of Bombay v. D. R. Nadkarni*, AIR 1983 SC

12 *Shantistar Builders v. Narayan Khimalal Totame*, AIR 1990 SC 630

13 ***'Part III – Fundamental Rights'*** is a charter of rights contained in the Constitution of India. It guarantees civil liberties such that all Indians can lead their lives in peace and harmony as citizens of India. These include individual rights common to most liberal democracies, such asequality before law, freedom of speech and expression, and peaceful assembly, freedom to practice religion, and the right to constitutional remedies for the protection of civil rights by means of writs such as habeas corpus. Violation of these rights result in punishments as prescribed in the Indian Penal Code or other special laws, subject to discretion of the judiciary. The Fundamental Rights are defined as basichuman freedoms which every Indian citizen has the right to enjoy for a proper and harmonious development of personality. These rights universally apply to all citizens, irrespective of race, place of birth, religion, caste, creed, colour or gender. Aliens (persons who are not citizens) are also considered in matters like equality before law. They are enforceable by the courts, subject to certain restrictions. The Rights have their origins in many sources, including England's Bill of Rights, the United States Bill of Rights and France's Declaration of the Rights of Man.

14 The **Directive Principles of State Policy** are guidelines to the central and state governments of India, to be kept in mind while framing laws and policies. These provisions, contained in Part IV of the Constitution of India, are not enforceable by any court, but the principles laid down therein are considered fundamental in the governance of the country, making it the duty of the State to

the dignity of the individual and also right to life which if permitted to trample upon will result in negation of these rights and, dignity of human personality.

Constitutional and statutory provisions:

By the 42nd[15] Amendment to the Constitution, effected in 1977, Article 39-A was inserted. This Article provides for free legal aid by suitable legislation or schemes or in any other manner, to ensure that opportunities for securing justice are not denied to any citizen by reason of economic or other disabilities. Article 39-A of the Constitution reads as follows:

39A. Equal justice and free legal aid. - The State shall secure that the operation of the legal system promotes justice, on a basis of equal opportunity, and shall, in particular, provide free legal aid, by suitable legislation or schemes or in any other way, to ensure that opportunities for securing justice are not denied to any citizen by reason of economic or other disabilities.

Legal Services Authorities Act, 1987:

The Act provides for the constitution of a National Legal Services Authority, a Supreme Court Legal Services Committee, State Legal Services Authorities as well as Taluk Legal Services Committees. Section 12[16] of

---

apply these principles in making laws to establish a just society in the country. The principles have been inspired by the Directive Principles given in the Constitution of Ireland and also by the principles of Gandhism; and relate to social justice, economic welfare, foreign policy, and legal and administrative matters.

15 **42nd Amendment to the Constitution of India:** The **Forty-second Amendment** of the Constitution of India, enacted in 1976, attempted to reduce the power of the Indian Supreme Court andHigh Courts to pronounce upon the constitutional validity of laws. It also declared India to be a socialist and secular republic, and as securingfraternity assuring the unity "and integrity" of the Nation, by adding these words to the Preamble of the Constitution of India. It laid down theFundamental Duties of Indian citizens to the nation. This amendment brought about the most widespread changes to the Constitution until then, and is often called a "mini-Constitution" or the "Constitution of Indira"

16 **Section 12 of Legal Services Authorities Act, 1987:**

12. Criteria for giving legal services - Every person who has to file or defend a case shall be entitled to legal services under this Act if that person is--

(a) a member of a Scheduled Caste or Scheduled Tribe;

(b) a victim of trafficking in human beings or beggar as referred in article 23 of the Constitution;

(c) a woman or a child;

(d) a person with disability as defined in clause (i) of section 2 of the Persons with Disabilities (Equal pportunities, Protection of Rights and Full Participation) Act, 1995 (1 of 1996);]

(e) a person under circumstances of undeserved want such as being a victim of a mass disaster, ethnic violence, caste atrocity, flood, drought, earthquake or industrial disaster; or

the Act lays down the criteria for providing legal services. It provides, inter alia, that every person who has to file or defend a case shall be entitled to legal services, if he or she is in custody. Section 13 of the Act provides that persons meeting the criteria laid down in Section 12 of the Act will be entitled to legal services provided the concerned authority is satisfied that such person has a prima facie case to prosecute or defend.

It is important to note in this context that Sections 12 and 13[17] of the Act do not make any distinction between the trial stage and the appellate stage for providing legal services. In other words, an eligible person is entitled to legal services at any stage of the proceedings which he or she is prosecuting or defending. In fact the Supreme Court Legal Services Committee provides legal assistance to eligible persons in Supreme Court. This makes it abundantly clear that legal services shall be provided to an eligible person at all stages of the proceedings, trial as well as appellate. It is also important to note that in view of the constitutional mandate of Article 39-A, legal services or legal aid is provided to an eligible person free of cost.

(f) an industrial workman; or

(g) in custody, including custody in a protective home within the meaning of clause (g) of section 2 of the Immoral Traffic (Prevention) Act, 1956, or in a Juvenile home within the meaning of clause (j) of section 2 of the Juvenile Justice Act, 1986, or in a psychiatric hospital or psychiatric nursing home within the meaning of clause (g) of section 2 of the Mental Health Act, 1987; or

[(h) in receipt of annual income less than rupees nine thousand or such other higher amount as may be prescribed by the State Government, if the case is before a court other than the Supreme Court, and less than rupees twelve thousand or such other higher amount as may be prescribed by the Central Government, if the case is before the Supreme Court.

17 **Section 13 of Legal Services Authorities Act, 1987**

13. Entitlement to legal services - (1) Persons who satisfy or any of the criteria specified in section 12 shall be entitled to receive legal services provided that the concerned Authority is satisfied that such person has a prima-facie case to prosecute or to defend.

(2) An affidavit made by a person as to his income may be regarded as sufficient for making him eligible to the entitlement of legal services under this Act unless the concerned Authority has reason to disbelieve such affidavit.

8

Free Legal Service[1]

Ratio Decidendi[2]: ***"Right to free legal service is must for reasonable, fair and just procedure of law."***

Facts in Nutshell:

The appellants[3] and five other accused[4] were charged in the court of the Additional Deputy Commissioner, Dibang Valley, Anini, Arunachal Pradesh for an offence under Section 506[5] read with Section34[6] of the Indian Penal Code on the allegation that the appellants and the other five accused threatened Shri H.S. Kohli, Assistant Engineer, Central Public Works Department, Anini with a view to compelling him to cancel the transfer orders of the accused which had been passed by him. The case was tried as a warrant case[7] and at the trial 8 witnesses, on behalf of the

1 Appellants: **Suk Das Vs.** Respondent: **Union Territory of Arunachal Pradesh** AIR1986SC991
Hon'ble Judges/Coram: P. N. Bhagwati, C.J., D. P. Madon and G. L. Oza, JJ.

2 **Meaning of Ration Decidendi:** ***Ratio decidendi*** is a Latin phrase meaning "the reason" or "the rationale for the decision." The *ratio decidendi* is "the point in a case which determines the judgment" or "the principle which the case establishes."

3 **Meaning of Appellant:** A person who, dissatisfied with the judgment rendered in a lawsuit decided in a lower court or the findings from a proceeding before an Administrative Agency, asks a superior court to review the decision.

4 **Meaning of Accused:** A person charged with a criminal offense, or the state of being so charged

5 **Section 506 in The Indian Penal Code, 1860**
506. Punishment for criminal intimidation.-- Whoever commits the offence of criminal intimidation shall be punished with imprisonment of either description for a term which may extend to two years, or with fine, or with both; If threat be to cause death or grievous hurt, etc. If threat be to cause death or grievous hurt, etc.-- and if the threat be to cause death or grievous hurt, or to cause the destruction of any property by fire, or to cause an offence punishable with death or 3[imprisonment for life], of with imprisonment for a term which may extend to seven years, or to impute unchastity to a woman, shall be punished with imprisonment of either description for a term which may extend to seven years, or with fine, or with both.

6 **Section 34 in The Indian Penal Code, 1860**
34. [Acts done by several persons in futherance of common intention.-- When a criminal act is done by several persons in furtherance of the common intention of all, each of such persons is liable for that act in the same manner as if it were done by him alone.]

7 **Meaning of Warrant Case:**
Section 2 (x) CrPc, 1973
"warrant-case" means a case relating to an offence punishable with death, imprisonment for life

prosecution[8], were examined. The appellant was not represented by any lawyer since he was admittedly unable to afford legal representation on account of his poverty and the result was that he could not cross-examine[9] the witnesses[10] of the prosecution. The appellants wished to examine 7 witnesses in defence but out of them two could not be examined since they were staying far away and moreover, in the opinion of the court, they were not material witnesses. The remaining 5 witnesses were examined by the appellants without any legal assistance. The result was that at the end of the trial four of the other accused were acquitted[11] but the appellant and another accused were convicted of the offence under Section 506 of the Indian Penal Code and they were sentenced to undergo simple imprisonment for a period of two years.

The appellant thereupon preferred an appeal before the Gauhati High Court. The contention raised before High Court was that the appellant were not provided free legal aid for his defence and the trial was therefore vitiated[12].

High Court took the view that, though it was undoubtedly the right of the appellant to be provided free legal assistance, the appellant did no make any request to the learned Additional Deputy Commissioner praying for legal aid and since no application for legal aid was made by him, "it could not be said in the facts and circumstances of the case that failure to provide legal assistance vitiated the trial". The High Court in the circumstances confirmed the conviction of the appellant but in view of the fact that he was already in jail for a period of nearly 8 months, the High Court held that the ends of justice would be met if the sentence on the appellant was reduced to that already undergone by him. The appellant was accordingly ordered to be, set at liberty forthwith but since the order of conviction passed against him was sustained by the High

---

or imprisonment for a term exceeding two years

8 **Meaning of Prosecution:** The institution and conducting of legal proceedings against someone in respect of a criminal charge:

9 **Meaning of Cross-Examine:** Questioning of an accused or witness in a court to (1) test his or her knowledge or memory, (2) extract information favorable to one party and damaging to the other, (3) demonstrate bias, or (4) prove his or her previous statements as contradictory.

10 **Meaning of Witnesses: a.** One who is called on to testify before a court.
b. One who is called on to be present at a transaction in order to attest to what takes place.
c. One who signs one's name to a document for the purpose of attesting to its authenticity.

11 **Meaning of Acquittal:** In the common law tradition, an **acquittal** formally certifies that the accused is free from the charge of an offense, as far as the criminal law is concerned.

12 **Meaning of Vitiated: 1.** To reduce the value or impair the quality of.
2. To corrupt morally; debase.

Court, he preferred the Special Leave petition before Supreme Court.

Question before the Supreme Court:

Appeal[13] by special leave[14] in Supreme Court raised a question of considerable importance relating to the administration of criminal justice in the country. The question was whether an accused[15] who on account of his poverty was unable to afford legal representation for himself in a trial[16] involving possibility of imprisonment imperilling his personal liberty, is entitled to free legal aid at State cost and whether it is obligatory on him to make an application for free legal assistance or the Magistrate or the Sessions Judge trying him is bound to inform him that he is entitled to free legal aid and inquire from him whether he wishes to have a lawyer provided to him at State cost: if he is not so informed and in consequence he does not apply for free legal assistance and as a result he is not represented by any lawyer in the trial and is convicted[17], is the conviction vitiated and liable to be set aside? This question was extremely important because we have almost 50% population which is living below the poverty line and around 70% is illiterate and large sections of people just do not know that if they are unable to afford legal representation in a criminal trial, they are entitled to free legal assistance provided to them at State cost.

---

13 **Meaning of Appeal:** In law, an **appeal** is a process for requesting a formal change to an official decision. Very broadly speaking there are appeals on the record and *de novo* appeals. In *de novo* appeals, a new decision maker re-hears the case without any reference to the prior decision maker. In appeals on the record, the decision of the prior decision maker is challenged by arguing that he or she misapplied the law, came to an incorrect factual finding, acted in excess of his jurisdiction, abused his powers, was biased, considered evidence which he should not have considered or failed to consider evidence that he should have considered.

14 **Article 136 in The Constitution Of India 1949**

136. Special leave to appeal by the Supreme Court

(1) Notwithstanding anything in this Chapter, the Supreme Court may, in its discretion, grant special leave to appeal from any judgment, decree, determination, sentence or order in any cause or matter passed or made by any court or tribunal in the territory of India

(2) Nothing in clause (1) shall apply to any judgment, determination, sentence or order passed or made by any court or tribunal constituted by or under any law relating to the Armed Forces

15 **Meaning of Accused:** A person charged with a criminal offense, or the state of being so charged

16 **Meaning of Trial:**

a. The judicial examination of the issues in a civil or criminal cause by a competent tribunal and the determination of these issues in accordance with the law of the land

b. The determination of an accused person's guilt or innocence after hearing evidence for the prosecution and for the accused and the judicial examination of the issues involved

17 **Meaning of Convicted:** Someone guilty of an offense or crime, especially by the verdict of a court

Right to Free Legal Service:

It Hussainara Khatoon's case[18] it was held that "the right to free legal service is ...clearly an essential ingredient of reasonable, fair and just procedure for a person accused of an offence and it must be held to be implicit in the guarantee of Article 21[19]. This is a constitutional right of every accused person who is unable to engage a lawyer and secure legal services on account of reasons such as poverty, indigence or incommunicado situation and the State is under a mandate to provide a lawyer to an accused person if the circumstances of the case and the needs of justice so require, provided of course the accused person does not object to the provision of such lawyer". It is an essential ingredient of reasonable, fair and just procedure to prisoner who is to seek his liberation through the court's process that he should have legal service available to him.

In *M.H. Hoskot v. State of Maharashtra*[20] it was held that free legal assistance at State cost is a fundamental right of a person accused of an offence which may involved jeopardy to his life or personal liberty and this fundamental right is implicit in the requirement of reasonable, fair and just procedure prescribed by Article 21. Of course, it must be recognised that there may be cases involving offences, such as, economic offences or offences against law prohibiting prostitution or child abuse and the like, where social justice may require that free legal service may not be provided by the State. There can in the circumstances be no doubt that the appellant[21] was entitled to a free legal assistance at State cost when he was placed in peril of their personal liberty by reason of being accused of an offence which is proved would clearly entail imprisonment for a terra of two years.

In *Khatri and Ors. v. State of Bihar and Ors.*[22], it was ruled that the Magistrate or the Sessions Judge before whom an accused appears must be held to be under an obligation to inform the accused that if he is unable

18 1979CriLJ1045

19 **Article 21 in The Constitution Of India 1949**
21. Protection of life and personal liberty No person shall be deprived of his life or personal liberty except according to procedure established by law

20 1978CriLJ1678

21 **Meaning of Appellant:** A person who, dissatisfied with the judgment rendered in a lawsuit decided in a lower court or the findings from a proceeding before an Administrative Agency, asks a superior court to review the decision.

22 1981CriLJ597

to engage the services of a lawyer on account of poverty or indigence, he is entitled to obtain free legal services at the cost of the State.

Decision of the Supreme Court:

Court held that no fresh trial should be held against appellant and he should be reinstated in service but without back wages.

9

High Court is under an obligation to enquire from the Accused whether he requires legal assistance[1]

Ratio Decidendi[2]: ***"High Court is under an obligation to enquire from the Accused whether he requires legal assistance and if he does, it should have been provided to him at State expense."***

Facts in Nutshell:

On 06.12.1998, seven persons including Rajoo were alleged to have gang-raped 'G'. The Trial Court convicted[3] all of them for the offence and sentenced each of them to 10 years rigorous imprisonment and a fine of Rs. 500/-. In default thereof they were required to undergo rigorous imprisonment for a further period of 3 months. Appeals[4] were filed by all the convicted persons before the High Court. By its judgment and order dated 05.09.2006, the High Court set aside the conviction in respect of five of the convicts, but upheld the conviction in respect of Rajoo and Vijay. Vijay has accepted the judgment of the High Court. Only Rajoo has appealed against his conviction and sentence before Supreme Court.

Constitutional and statutory provisions:

By the 42nd[5] Amendment to the Constitution, effected in 1977,

1 Appellants: **Rajoo @ Ramakant Vs.** Respondent: **The State of Madhya Pradesh** AIR2012SC3034
Hon'ble Judges/Coram: A.K. Patnaik and Madan B. Lokur, JJ.

2 **Meaning of Ration Decidendi:** ***Ratio decidendi*** is a Latin phrase meaning "the reason" or "the rationale for the decision." The *ratio decidendi* is "the point in a case which determines the judgment" or "the principle which the case establishes."

3 **Meaning of Convicted: S**omeone guilty of an offense or crime, especially by the verdict of a court

4 **Meaning of Appeal:** In law, an **appeal** is a process for requesting a formal change to an official decision. Very broadly speaking there are appeals on the record and *de novo* appeals. In *de novo* appeals, a new decision maker re-hears the case without any reference to the prior decision maker. In appeals on the record, the decision of the prior decision maker is challenged by arguing that he or she misapplied the law, came to an incorrect factual finding, acted in excess of his jurisdiction, abused his powers, was biased, considered evidence which he should not have considered or failed to consider evidence that he should have considered.

5 **42nd Amendment to the Constitution of India:** The **Forty-second Amendment** of the Constitution of India, enacted in 1976, attempted to reduce the power of the Indian Supreme Court andHigh

Article 39-A was inserted. This Article provides for free legal aid by suitable legislation or schemes or in any other manner, to ensure that opportunities for securing justice are not denied to any citizen by reason of economic or other disabilities. Article 39-A of the Constitution reads as follows:

39A. Equal justice and free legal aid. - The State shall secure that the operation of the legal system promotes justice, on a basis of equal opportunity, and shall, in particular, provide free legal aid, by suitable legislation or schemes or in any other way, to ensure that opportunities for securing justice are not denied to any citizen by reason of economic or other disabilities.

Legal Services Authorities Act, 1987:

The Act provides for the constitution of a National Legal Services Authority, a Supreme Court Legal Services Committee, State Legal Services Authorities as well as Taluk Legal Services Committees. Section 12[6] of the Act lays down the criteria for providing legal services. It provides, inter alia, that every person who has to file or defend a case shall be entitled to legal services, if he or she is in custody. Section 13 of the Act provides that persons meeting the criteria laid down in Section 12 of the Act will

---

Courts to pronounce upon the constitutional validity of laws. It also declared India to be a socialist and secular republic, and as securingfraternity assuring the unity "and integrity" of the Nation, by adding these words to the Preamble of the Constitution of India. It laid down theFundamental Duties of Indian citizens to the nation. This amendment brought about the most widespread changes to the Constitution until then, and is often called a "mini-Constitution" or the "Constitution of Indira"

6 **Section 12 of Legal Services Authorities Act, 1987:**

12. Criteria for giving legal services - Every person who has to file or defend a case shall be entitled to legal services under this Act if that person is--

(a) a member of a Scheduled Caste or Scheduled Tribe;

(b) a victim of trafficking in human beings or beggar as referred in article 23 of the Constitution;

(c) a woman or a child;

(d) a person with disability as defined in clause (i) of section 2 of the Persons with Disabilities (Equal pportunities, Protection of Rights and Full Participation) Act, 1995 (1 of 1996);]

(e) a person under circumstances of undeserved want such as being a victim of a mass disaster, ethnic violence, caste atrocity, flood, drought, earthquake or industrial disaster; or

(f) an industrial workman; or

(g) in custody, including custody in a protective home within the meaning of clause (g) of section 2 of the Immoral Traffic (Prevention) Act, 1956, or in a Juvenile home within the meaning of clause (j) of section 2 of the Juvenile Justice Act, 1986, or in a psychiatric hospital or psychiatric nursing home within the meaning of clause (g) of section 2 of the Mental Health Act, 1987; or [(h) in receipt of annual income less than rupees nine thousand or such other higher amount as may be prescribed by the State Government, if the case is before a court other than the Supreme Court, and less than rupees twelve thousand or such other higher amount as may be prescribed by the Central Government, if the case is before the Supreme Court.

be entitled to legal services provided the concerned authority is satisfied that such person has a prima facie case to prosecute or defend.

It is important to note in this context that Sections 12 and 13[7] of the Act do not make any distinction between the trial stage and the appellate stage for providing legal services. In other words, an eligible person is entitled to legal services at any stage of the proceedings which he or she is prosecuting or defending. In fact the Supreme Court Legal Services Committee provides legal assistance to eligible persons in Supreme Court. This makes it abundantly clear that legal services shall be provided to an eligible person at all stages of the proceedings, trial as well as appellate. It is also important to note that in view of the constitutional mandate of Article 39-A, legal services or legal aid is provided to an eligible person free of cost.

Question before the Supreme Court:

The issue of providing free legal services or free legal aid or free legal representation (all terms being understood as synonymous) came up for consideration before Supreme Court.

Free Legal Aid, Cases Referred:

In ***Hussainara Khatoon (IV) v. Home Secretary, State of Bihar***[8] in that case, reference was made to Article 39-A of the Constitution and it was held that free legal service is an inalienable element of "reasonable, fair and just procedure for a person accused of an offence and it must be held implicit in the guarantee of Article 21[9] of the Constitution." It was noted that this is "a constitutional right of every accused person who is unable to engage a lawyer and secure free legal services on account of reasons such as poverty, indigence or incommunicado situation." It was held that the State is under a mandate to provide a lawyer to an accused person if the circumstances of the case and the needs of justice so require, subject

7 **Section 13 of Legal Services Authorities Act, 1987**

13. Entitlement to legal services - (1) Persons who satisfy or any of the criteria specified in section 12 shall be entitled to receive legal services provided that the concerned Authority is satisfied that such person has a prima-facie case to prosecute or to defend.

(2) An affidavit made by a person as to his income may be regarded as sufficient for making him eligible to the entitlement of legal services under this Act unless the concerned Authority has reason to disbelieve such affidavit.

8 (1980) 1 SCC 98

9 **Article 21 in The Constitution Of India 1949**

21. Protection of life and personal liberty: No person shall be deprived of his life or personal liberty except according to procedure established by law

of course to the accused person not objecting to the providing of a lawyer.

In ***Khatri (II) v. State of Bihar***[10] in that case, it was noted that the Judicial Magistrate did not provide legal representation to the accused persons because they did not ask for it. This was found to be unacceptable. Supreme Court went further and held that it was the obligation of the Judicial Magistrate before whom the accused were produced to inform them of their entitlement to legal representation at State cost. In this context, it was observed that the right to free legal services would be illusory unless the Magistrate or the Sessions Judge before whom the accused is produced informs him of this right. It would also make a mockery of legal aid if it were to be left to a poor, ignorant and illiterate accused to ask for free legal services thereby rendering the constitutional mandate a mere paper promise.

In. ***Suk Das v. Union Territory of Arunachal Pradesh***[11] reiterated the requirement of providing free and adequate legal representation to an indigent person and a person accused of an offence. In that case, it was reiterated that an accused need not ask for legal assistance - the Court dealing with the case is obliged to inform him or her of the entitlement to free legal aid. Supreme Court observed that it was now "settled law that free legal assistance at State cost is a fundamental right of a person accused of an offence which may involve jeopardy to his life or personal liberty and this fundamental right is implicit in the requirement of reasonable, fair and just procedure prescribed by Article 21 of the Constitution."

Decision of the Supreme Court:

Court was of the opinion that neither the Constitution nor the Legal Services Authorities Act makes any distinction between a trial and an appeal for the purposes of providing free legal aid to an accused or a person in custody. Court further held that the High Court was under an obligation to enquire from Rajoo whether he required legal assistance and if he did, it should have been provided to him at State expense.

10 (1981) 1 SCC 627

11 (1986) 2 SCC 401

10

Offence of rape is violation of Fundamental Right to Life[1]

Facts in Nutshell:

Mrs. Chandrima Das, a practicing advocate of the Calcutta High Court, filed petition[2] under Article 226[3] of the Constitution against the Chairman, Railway Board; General Manager, Eastern Railway; Divisional Railway Manager, Howrah Division; Chief Commercial Manager, Eastern Railway;

1 Appellants: **The Chairman, Railway Board & Ors. Vs.**Respondent: **Mrs. Chandrima Das & Ors.**
AIR2000SC988
Hon'ble Judges/Coram: S. Saghir Ahmad and R. P. Sethi, JJ.

2 **Meaning of Petition:** A formal written application requesting a court for a specific judicial action

3 **Article 226 in The Constitution Of India 1949**
226. Power of High Courts to issue certain writs
(1) Notwithstanding anything in Article 32 every High Court shall have powers, throughout the territories in relation to which it exercise jurisdiction, to issue to any person or authority, including in appropriate cases, any Government, within those territories directions, orders or writs, including writs in the nature of habeas corpus, mandamus, prohibitions, quo warranto and certiorari, or any of them, for the enforcement of any of the rights conferred by Part III and for any other purpose
(2) The power conferred by clause (1) to issue directions, orders or writs to any Government, authority or person may also be exercised by any High Court exercising jurisdiction in relation to the territories within which the cause of action, wholly or in part, arises for the exercise of such power, notwithstanding that the seat of such Government or authority or the residence of such person is not within those territories
(3) Where any party against whom an interim order, whether by way of injunction or stay or in any other manner, is made on, or in any proceedings relating to, a petition under clause (1), without
(a) furnishing to such party copies of such petition and all documents in support of the plea for such interim order; and
(b) giving such party an opportunity of being heard, makes an application to the High Court for the vacation of such order and furnishes a copy of such application to the party in whose favour such order has been made or the counsel of such party, the High Court shall dispose of the application within a period of two weeks from the date on which it is received or from the date on which the copy of such application is so furnished, whichever is later, or where the High Court is closed on the last day of that period, before the expiry of the next day afterwards on which the High Court is open; and if the application is not so disposed of, the interim order shall, on the expiry of that period, or, as the case may be, the expiry of the aid next day, stand vacated
(4) The power conferred on a High Court by this article shall not be in derogation of the power conferred on the Supreme court by clause (2) of Article 32

State of West Bengal through the Chief Secretary, Home Secretary Government of West Bengal, Superintendent of Police (Railways), Howrah; Superintendent of Police, Howrah; Director General of Police, West Bengal and many other Officers including the Deputy High Commissioner, Republic of Bangladesh; claiming compensation for the victim[4], Smt. Hanuffa Khatoon, a Bangladeshi national who was gang-raped by many including employees of the Railways in a room at Yatri Niwas at Howrah Station of the Eastern Railway regarding which G.R.P.S. Case No. 19/98 was registered on 27th February, 1998. Mrs. Chandrima Das also claimed several other reliefs including a direction to the respondents[5] to eradicate anti-social and criminal activities at Howrah Railway Station.

Hanufa came from Bangladesh. She at the relevant time was the elected representative of the Union Board. She arrived at Howrah Railway Station on 26th February, 1998 to avail Jodhpur Express at 23.00 hours for paying a visit to Ajmer Sharif. With that intent in mind, she arrived at Calcutta on 24th February, 1998 and stayed at a hotel. She had a wait listed ticket and so she approached a Train Ticket Examiner at the Station for confirmation of berth against her ticket. The Train Ticket Examiner asked" her to wait in the Ladies Waiting room. She accordingly came to the ladies waiting room and rested there.

On 26th February, 1998 two unknown persons (later identified as one Ashoka Singh, a tout[6] who posed himself as a very influential person of the Railway and Siya Ram Singh a railway ticket broker having good acquaintance with some of the Railway Staff of Howrah Station) approached her, took her ticket and returned the same after confirming reservation in Coach No. S-3 (Berth No. 17) of Jodhpur Express. At about 20.00 hours Siya Ram Singh came again to her with a boy named Kashi and told her to accompany the boy to a restaurant if she wanted to have food for the night. Accordingly at about 21.00 hours she went to a nearby eating house with Kashi and had her meal there. Soon after she had taken her meal, she vomitted and came back to the Ladies Waiting room. At about 21.00 hours Ashoke Singh along with Rafl Ahmed a Parcel

4 **Meaning of Victim: 1.** a person who suffers from a destructive or injurious action or agency **2.** a person who is deceived or cheated

5 **Meaning of Respondent:** A **respondent** is a person who is called upon to issue a response to a communication made by another. In legal usage, this specifically refers to the defendant in a legal proceeding commenced by a petition, or to an appellee, or the opposing party, in an appeal of a decision by an initial fact-finder.

6 **Meaning of Tout:** Also called **ticket tout** a person who sells tickets unofficially for a heavily booked sporting event, concert, etc., at greatly inflated prices

Supervisor at Howrah Station came to the Ladies Niwas before boarding the train. She appeared to have some doubt initially but on being certified by the lady attendants engaged on duty at the Ladies Waiting Room about their credentials she accompanied them to Yatri Niwas. Sitaram Singh, a Khalasi of Electric Department of Howrah Station joined them on way to Yatri Niwas. She was taken to room No. 102 on the first floor of Yatri Niwas. The room was booked in the name of Ashoke Singh against Railway Card Pass. In room No. 102 two other persons viz. one Lalan Singh, Parcel Clerk of Howrah Railway Station and Awdesh Singh, Parcel Clearing Agent were waiting. Hanufa Khatun suspected something amiss when Ashoke Singh forced her into the room. Awdesh Singh bolted the room from outside and stood on guard outside the room. The remaining four persons viz. Ashoke, Lalan, Raft and Sitaram took liquor inside the room and also forcibly compelled her to consume liquor. When she could recover she managed to escape from the room of Yatri Niwas and came back to the platform where again she met Siya Ram Singh and found him talking to Ashoke Singh. Seeing her plight Siya Ram Singh pretended to be her savior and also abused and slapped Ashoke Singh. Since it was well past midnight and Jodhpur Express had already departed, Siya Ram requested Hanufa Khatoon to accompany him to his residence to rest for the night with his wife and children. He assured her to help entrain Poorva Express on the following morning. Thereafter Siyaram accompanied by Ram Samiram Sharma, a friend of Siyaram took her to the rented fiat of Ram Samiram Sharma at 66, Pathuriaghata Street, Police Station Jorabagan, Calcutta. There Siyaram raped Hanufa and when she protested and resisted violently Siyaram and Ram Samiran Sharma gagged her mouth and nostrils intending to kill her as a result Hanufa bled profusely. On being informed by the landlord of the building following the hue and cry raised by Hanufa Khatun she was rescued by Jorabagan Police.

Decision of the High Court:

High Court awarded a sum of Rs, 10 lacs as compensation for Smt. Hanuffa Khatoon as the High Court was of the opinion that the rape was committed at the building (Rail Yatri Niwas) belonging to the Railways and was perpetrated by the Railway employees.

Question before the Supreme Court:

The only question was that the Railways would not be liable to pay compensation to Smt. Hanuffa Khatoon who was a foreigner and was not an Indian national.

Rape is a Crime against whole Society:

In *Bodhisattwa v. Ms. Subhra Chakraborty* [7] it was held that "rape" is an offence which is violative of the Fundamental Right of a person guaranteed under Article 21[8] of the Constitution. The Court observed as under (Para 10 of AIR):

Rape is a crime not only against the person of a woman, it is a crime against the entire society. It destroys the entire psychology of a woman and pushes her into deep emotional crisis. Rape is therefore the most hated crime. It is a crime against basic human rights and is violative of the victims most cherished right, namely, right to life which includes right to live with human dignity contained in Article 21.

Universal Declaration of Human Rights, 1948:

Article 1- All human beings are born free and equal in dignity and rights. They are endowed with reason and conscience and should act towards one another in a spirit of brotherhood.

Article 2.- Every one is entitled to all the rights and freedoms set forth in this Declaration, without distinction of any kind, such as race, colour, sex, language, religion, political or other opinion, NATIONAL OR SOCIAL ORIGIN, PROPERTY, BIRTH OR OTHER STATUS.

Furthermore, NO DISTINCTION SHALL BE MADE ON THE BASIS OF THE POLITICAL, JURISDICTIONAL OR INTERNATIONAL STATUS OF THE COUNTRY OR TERRITORY to which a person belongs, whether it be independent, trust, non-self governing or under any other limitation of sovereignty.

Article 3- Everyone has the right to life, liberty and security of person.

Article 5- No one shall be subjected to torture or to cruel, inhuman or degrading treatment or punishment.

Article 7- All are equal before the law and are entitled without any discrimination to equal protection of the law. All are entitled to equal protection against any discrimination in violation of this Declaration and against any incitement to such discrimination.

---

7 AIR1996SC922

8 **Article 21 in The Constitution Of India 1949**
21. Protection of life and personal liberty: No person shall be deprived of his life or personal liberty except according to procedure established by law

Article 9- No one shall be subjected to arbitrary arrest, detention or exile.

Declaration on the Elimination of Violence against Women by its Resolution dated 20th December, 1993 observed in

Article 1 that, "violence against women" means any act of gender-based violence that results in, or is likely to result in, physical, sexual or psychological harm or suffering to women, including threats of such acts, coercion or arbitrary deprivation of liberty, whether occurring in public or in private life.

In Article 2, it was specified that, violence against women shall be understood to encompass, but not be limited to:

(a) Physical, sexual and psychological violence occurring in the family including battering, sexual abuse of female children in the household, dowry-related violence, marital rape, female genital mutilation and other traditional practices harmful to women, non-spousal violence and violence related Lo exploitation;

(b) Physical, sexual and psychological violence occurring within the general community, including rape, sexual abuse, sexual harassment and intimidation at work, in educational institutions and elsewhere, trafficking in women and forced prostitution;

(c) Physical, sexual and psychological violence perpetrated or condoned by the State, wherever it occurs.

In Article 3, it was specified that "women are entitled to the equal enjoyment and protection of all human rights, which would include, inter alia:

(a) the right to life,

(b) the right to equality, and

(c) the right to liberty and security of person,

Constitution and Fundamental Rights:

Our Constitution guarantees all the basic and fundamental human rights set out in the Universal Declaration of Human Rights, 1948, to its citizens and other persons. The chapter dealing with the Fundamental Rights is contained in Part III[9] of the Constitution. The purpose of this part is to safeguard the basic human rights from the vicissitudes[10] of political controversy and to place them beyond the reach of the political parties who, by virtue of their majority, may come to form the Govt. at the center or in the State.. The Fundamental Rights are available to all the "Citizens" of the country but a few of them are also available to "persons". While Article 14[11], which guarantees equality before law or the equal protection of laws within the territory of India, is applicable to "person" which would also include the "citizen" of the country and "non-citizen" both, Article 15[12] speaks only of "citizen" and it is specifically provided therein that there shall be no discrimination against any "citizen" on the ground only of religion, race, caste, sex, place of birth or any of them nor shall any citizen be subjected to any disability, liability, restriction or condition with regard to access to shops, public restaurants, hostel and places of public entertainment, or the use of wells, tanks, bathing ghats, roads

9 ***'Part III – Fundamental Rights'*** is a charter of rights contained in the Constitution of India. It guarantees civil liberties such that all Indians can lead their lives in peace and harmony as citizens of India. These include individual rights common to most liberal democracies, such asequality before law, freedom of speech and expression, and peaceful assembly, freedom to practice religion, and the right to constitutional remedies for the protection of civil rights by means of writs such as habeas corpus. Violation of these rights result in punishments as prescribed in the Indian Penal Code or other special laws, subject to discretion of the judiciary. The Fundamental Rights are defined as basichuman freedoms which every Indian citizen has the right to enjoy for a proper and harmonious development of personality. These rights universally apply to all citizens, irrespective of race, place of birth, religion, caste, creed, colour or gender. Aliens (persons who are not citizens) are also considered in matters like equality before law. They are enforceable by the courts, subject to certain restrictions. The Rights have their origins in many sources, including England's Bill of Rights, the United States Bill of Rights and France's Declaration of the Rights of Man.

10 **Meaning of vicissitudes: 1.** Regular change or succession of one state or thing to another. **2.** Change or variation; mutation; mutability

11 **Article 14 in The Constitution Of India 1949**
14. Equality before law: The State shall not deny to any person equality before the law or the equal protection of the laws within the territory of India Prohibition of discrimination on grounds of religion, race, caste, sex or place of birth

12 **Article 15 in The Constitution Of India 1949**
15. Prohibition of discrimination on grounds of religion, race, caste, sex or place of birth
(1) The State shall not discriminate against any citizen on grounds only of religion, race, caste, sex, place of birth or any of them
(2) No citizen shall, on grounds only of religion, race, caste, sex, place of birth or any of them, be subject to any disability, liability, restriction or condition with regard to
(a) access to shops, public restaurants, hotels and palaces of public entertainment; or
(b) the use of wells, tanks, bathing ghats, roads and places of public resort maintained wholly or partly out of State funds or dedicated to the use of the general public
(3) Nothing in this article shall prevent the State from making any special provision for women and children
(4) Nothing in this article or in clause (2) of Article 29 shall prevent the State from making any special provision for the advancement of any socially and educationally backward classes of citizens or for the Scheduled Castes and the Scheduled Tribes

and place of public resort on the aforesaid grounds. Fundamental Rights guaranteed under Article 15 is, therefore, restricted to "citizen". So also, Article 16[13] which guarantees equality of opportunity in matters of public employment is applicable only to "citizens". The Fundamental Rights contained in Article 19[14], which contains the right to "Basic Freedoms",

13 **Article 16 in The Constitution Of India 1949**

16. Equality of opportunity in matters of public employment

(1) There shall be equality of opportunity for all citizens in matters relating to employment or appointment to any office under the State

(2) No citizen shall, on grounds only of religion, race, caste, sex, descent, place of birth, residence or any of them, be ineligible for, or discriminated against in respect or, any employment or office under the State

(3) Nothing in this article shall prevent Parliament from making any law prescribing, in regard to a class or classes of employment or appointment to an office under the Government of, or any local or other authority within, a State or Union territory, any requirement as to residence within that State or Union territory prior to such employment or appointment

(4) Nothing in this article shall prevent the State from making any provision for the reservation of appointments or posts in favor of any backward class of citizens which, in the opinion of the State, is not adequately represented in the services under the State

(5) Nothing in this article shall affect the operation of any law which provides that the incumbent of an office in connection with the affairs of any religious or denominational institution or any member of the governing body thereof shall be a person professing a particular religion or belonging to a particular denomination

14 **Article 19 in The Constitution Of India 1949**

19. Protection of certain rights regarding freedom of speech etc

(1) All citizens shall have the right

(a) to freedom of speech and expression;

(b) to assemble peaceably and without arms;

(c) to form associations or unions;

(d) to move freely throughout the territory of India;

(e) to reside and settle in any part of the territory of India; and

(f) omitted

(g) to practise any profession, or to carry on any occupation, trade or business

(2) Nothing in sub clause (a) of clause (1) shall affect the operation of any existing law, or prevent the State from making any law, in so far as such law imposes reasonable restrictions on the exercise of the right conferred by the said sub clause in the interests of the sovereignty and integrity of India, the security of the State, friendly relations with foreign States, public order, decency or morality or in relation to contempt of court, defamation or incitement to an offence

(3) Nothing in sub clause (b) of the said clause shall affect the operation of any existing law in so far as it imposes, or prevent the State from making any law imposing, in the interests of the sovereignty and integrity of India or public order, reasonable restrictions on the exercise of the right conferred by the said sub clause

(4) Nothing in sub clause (c) of the said clause shall affect the operation of any existing law in so far as it imposes, or prevent the State from making any law imposing, in the interests of the sovereignty and integrity of India or public order or morality, reasonable restrictions on the exercise of the right conferred by the said sub clause

(5) Nothing in sub clauses (d) and (e) of the said clause shall affect the operation of any existing law in so far as it imposes, or prevent the State from making any law imposing, reasonable restrictions on the exercise of any of the rights conferred by the said sub clauses either in the interests of the general public or for the protection of the interests of any Scheduled Tribe

(6) Nothing in sub clause (g) of the said clause shall affect the operation of any existing law in so far as it imposes, or prevent the State from making any law imposing, in the interests of the general public, reasonable restrictions on the exercise of the right conferred by the said sub clause, and,

namely, freedom of speech and expression; freedom to assemble peaceably and without arms; freedom to form associations or unions; freedom to move freely throughout the territory of India; freedom to reside and settle in any part of the territory of India and freedom to practice any profession, or to carry on any occupation, trade or business, are available only to "citizens" of the country,

In *Anwar v. State of J. & K.*[15], it was held that the rights under Articles 20[16], 21 and 22[17] are available not only to "citizens" but also to

---

in particular, nothing in the said sub clause shall affect the operation of any existing law in so far as it relates to, or prevent the State from making any law relating to,

(i) the professional or technical qualifications necessary for practising any profession or carrying on any occupation, trade or business, or

(ii) the carrying on by the State, or by a corporation owned or controlled by the State, of any trade, business, industry or service, whether to the exclusion, complete or partial, of citizens or otherwise

15 [1971]1SCR637

16 **Article 20 in The Constitution Of India 1949**

20. Protection in respect of conviction for offences

(1) No person shall be convicted of any offence except for violation of the law in force at the time of the commission of the act charged as an offence, nor be subjected to a penalty greater than that which might have been inflicted under the law in force at the time of the commission of the offence

(2) No person shall be prosecuted and punished for the same offence more than once

(3) No person accused of any offence shall be compelled to be a witness against himself

17 **Article 22 in The Constitution Of India 1949**

22. Protection against arrest and detention in certain cases

(1) No person who is arrested shall be detained in custody without being informed, as soon as may be, of the grounds for such arrest nor shall he be denied the right to consult, and to be defended by, a legal practitioner of his choice

(2) Every person who is arrested and detained in custody shall be produced before the nearest magistrate within a period of twenty four hours of such arrest excluding the time necessary for the journey from the place of arrest to the court of the magistrate and no such person shall be detained in custody beyond the said period without the authority of a magistrate

(3) Nothing in clauses (1) and (2) shall apply (a) to any person who for the time being is an enemy alien; or (b) to any person who is arrested or detained under any law providing for preventive detention

(4) No law providing for preventive detention shall authorise the detention of a person for a longer period than three months unless (a) an Advisory Board consisting of persons who are, or have been, or are qualified to be appointed as, Judges of a High Court has reported before the expiration of the said period of three months that there is in its opinion sufficient cause for such detention:

(5) When any person is detained in pursuance of an order made under any law providing for preventive detention, the authority making the order shall, as soon as may be, communicate to such person the grounds on which the order has been made and shall afford him the earliest opportunity of making a representation against the order

(6) Nothing in clause (5) shall require the authority making any such order as is referred to in that clause to disclose facts which such authority considers to be against the public interest to disclose

(7) Parliament may by law prescribe

(a) the circumstances under which, and the class or classes of cases in which, a person may

"persons" which would include "non-citizens". Article 20 guarantees right to protection in respect of conviction for offences. Article 21 guarantees right to life and personal liberty while Article 22 guarantees right to protection against arbitrary arrest and detention. These are wholly in consonance with Article 3, Article 7 and Article 9 of the Universal Declaration of Human Rights, 1948.

The word "LIFE" has also been used prominently in the Universal Declaration of Human Rights, 1948. [See Article 3 UDHR, 1948]. The Fundamental Rights under the Constitution are almost in consonance with the Rights contained in the Universal Declaration of Human Rights as also the Declaration and the Covenants of Civil and Political Rights and the Covenants of Economic, Social and Cultural Rights, to which India is a party having ratified them. In *Kubic Darusz v. Union of India*[18], "LIFE" is also recognised as a basic human right in the Universal Declaration of Human Rights, 1948, it has to have the same meaning and interpretation as has been placed on that word by Supreme Court in its various decisions relating to Article 21 of the Constitution. The meaning of the word "life" cannot be narrowed down. According to the tenor of the language used in Article 21, **it will be available not only to every citizen of this Country, but also to a "person" who may not be a citizen of the country.**

Decision of the Supreme Court:

Court held that Smt. Hanuffa Khatoon, who was not the citizen of this country (India) but came here as a citizen of Bangladesh was, nevertheless, entitled to all the constitutional rights available to a citizen so far as "Right to Life" was concerned. She was entitled to be treated with dignity and was also entitled to the protection of her person as guaranteed under Article 21 of the Constitution. As a national of another country, she could not be subjected to a treatment which was below dignity nor could she be subjected to physical violence at the hands of Govt. employees who outraged her modesty. The right available to her under Article 21 was thus violated. Consequently, the State was under the Constitutional liability to pay compensation to her. The judgment passed by the Calcutta

be detained for a period longer than three months under any law providing for preventive detention without obtaining the opinion of an Advisory Board in accordance with the provisions of sub clause (a) of clause (4);

(b) the maximum period for which any person may in any class or classes of cases be detained under any law providing for preventive detention; and

(c) the procedure to be followed by an Advisory Board in an inquiry under sub clause (a) of clause (4) Right against Exploitation

18 1990CriLJ796

High Court, therefore, allowing compensation to her for having been gang raped, cannot be said to suffer from any infirmity.

Court also referred the case of State of Rajasthan v. Mst. Vidhyawati[19] wherein it was held that the Govt. will be vicariously liable for the tortious act of its employees. This was a case where a claim for damages was made by the heirs of a person who died in an accident caused by the negligence of the driver of a Govt. vehicle.

Running of Railways is a commercial activity. Establishing Yatri Niwas at various Railway Stations to provide lodging and boarding facilities to passengers on payment of charges is a part of the commercial activity of the Union of India and this activity cannot be equated with the exercise of Sovereign power. The employees of the Union of India who are deputed to run the Railways and to manage the establishment, including the Railway Stations and Yatri Niwas, are essential components of the Govt. machinery which carriage on the commercial activity. If any of such employees commits an act of tort, the Union Govt., of which they are the employees, can, subject to other legal requirements being satisfied, be held vicariously liable in damages to the person wronged by those employees.

19 AIR1962SC933

11

Clean drinking water and Right to Life[1]

Facts in Nutshell:

On December 23, 1997, Anshu Sharma, a student of M.C.D. Primary School, New Delhi, aged about 7 years, was crushed to death by a vehicle while crossing the road in front of the school. He had gone outside the school during school hours to fetch drinking water for himself as potable hygienic water was not available in the school. Public interest writ petition[2] was filed by All India Lawyers Union, a voluntary organisation, for various directions in that matter.

Water and Right to Life:

Water sustains life. To deny water is to deny adequate sustenance. The State, under Article 39(f)[3] of the Constitution, is required to secure opportunities and facilities to children to develop in a healthy manner. When even water cannot be provided to children in a school, the question of their development in a healthy manner would be a far cry. Provision for wholesome potable water in schools is part of right to life enshrined under Article 21[4] of the Constitution. All schools must provide clean

---

1 Appellants: **All India Lawyers Union Vs.** Respondent: **Union Of India & Ors.**
AIR1999Delhi120
Hon'ble Judges/Coram: Anil Dev Singh and Mukul Mudgal, JJ.

2 **Meaning of Writ Petition:** Under the Indian legal system, jurisdiction to issue 'prerogative writs' is given to the Supreme Court, and to the High Courts of Judicature of all Indian states. Parts of the law relating to writs are set forth in the Constitution of India. The Supreme Court, the highest in the country, may issue writs under Article 32 of the Constitution for enforcement of Fundamental Rights and under Articles 139 for enforcement of rights other than Fundamental Rights, while High Courts, the superior courts of the States, may issue writs under Articles 226. 'Writ' is eminently designed by the makers of the Constitution, and in the same way it is developed very widely and efficiently by the courts in India. The Constitution broadly provides for five kinds of "prerogative" writs, namely, Habeas Corpus, Certiorari, Mandamus, Quo Warranto and Prohibition.

3 **Article 39 (f) in The Constitution Of India 1949**
39(f) Certain principles of policy to be followed by the State: The State shall, in particular, direct its policy towards securing
(f) that children are given opportunities and facilities to develop in a healthy manner and in conditions of freedom and dignity and that childhood and youth are protected against exploitation and against moral and material abandonment

4 **Article 21 in The Constitution Of India 1949**
21. Protection of life and personal liberty: No person shall be deprived of his life or personal

drinking water to the children.

Decision of the High Court:

Court held that the school authorities owe a duty to provide adequate security to the children to prevent chances of injury to them. That duty has not been performed by the authorities. Therefore, respondent[5] No. 5, which runs the school was held liable to pay compensation to the parents of the deceased child.

liberty except according to procedure established by law

5 **Meaning of Respondent:** A **respondent** is a person who is called upon to issue a response to a communication made by another. In legal usage, this specifically refers to the defendant in a legal proceeding commenced by a petition, or to an appellee, or the opposing party, in an appeal of a decision by an initial fact-finder.

12

Cigarette Smoking and Right to Life[1]

Facts in Nutshell:

Petition[2] was filed highlighting the public health issue of the dangers of passive smoking and in which prayers were made to declare that smoking of tobacco in any form, whether in the form of cigarette, cigar, beedies or otherwise in public places was illegal, unconstitutional and violative of Article 21[3] of the Constitution of India.

Cigarette Smoking:

One million Indians die every year from tobacco-related diseases. This is more than the number of deaths due to motor accidents, AIDS, alcohol and drug abuse put together, say the Indian Medical Association (IMA) and the Indian Academy of Paediatrics (IAP), quoting studies. Cigarette smoking is the major preventable cause of death in America, contributing to an estimated 350000 deaths annually. Epidemiologic and experimental evidence has identified cigarette smoking as the primary cause of lung cancer and chronic obstructive pulmonary diseases (COPD) and as a major risk factor for coronary heart disease. Smoking has been associated with other cancers, cerebrovascular[4] and peripheral vascular diseases[5], and peptic ulcer disease. Smokers also suffer more acute respiratory illness. Cigarette smoke, consisting of particles dispersed in a gas phase, is a complex mixture of thousands of compounds produced by the incomplete combustion of the tobacco leaf. Smoke constituents strongly implicated in causing disease are nicotine and tar in the particulate

1 Appellants: **K. Ramakrishnan and Anr. Vs.** Respondent: **State of Kerala and Ors.** AIR1999Ker385
Hon'ble Judges/Coram: A.R. Lakshmanan, Ag. C.J. and K. Narayana Kurup, Judge

2 **Meaning of Petition:** A formal message requesting something that is submitted to an authority

3 **Article 21 in The Constitution Of India 1949**
21. Protection of life and personal liberty No person shall be deprived of his life or personal liberty except according to procedure established by law

4 **Meaning of Cerebrovascular:** Pertaining to the cerebrum and its associated blood vessels.

5 **Meaning of Vascular Diseases: Vascular Disease** includes any condition that affects your circulatory system, such as peripheral artery disease. This ranges from diseases of your arteries, veins and lymph vessels to blood disorders that affect circulation.

phase and carbon monoxide in the gas phase. Smokers have a 70 per cent higher mortality rate than non smokers. The risk of dying increases with the amount and duration of smoking and is higher in smokers who inhale. Coronary heart disease is the chief contributor to the excess mortality among cigarette smokers, followed by lung cancer and chronic obstructive pulmonary disease (COPD). Life expectancy is significantly shortened by smoking cigarettes. Tobacco smoke also gets dissolved in the saliva and is swallowed, exposing the upper gastrointestinal tract to carcinogens. A strong association between smoking and lung cancer has been demonstrated in multiple prospective and retrospective epidemiologic studies, and corroborated by autopsy evidence. Lung cancer has been the leading cause of cancer death in men since the 1950s, and it surpassed breast cancer as a leading cause of cancer death in women in 1985. Male smokers have a tenfold higher risk of developing lung cancer, and the risk increases with the number of cigarettes smoked. There is also strong evidence that smoking is a major cause of cancers of the larynx, oral cavity anoesophagus. The risk of these cancers increases with the intensity of exposure to cigarette smoke either active or passive. Epidemiologic studies show an association between smoking and cancers of the bladder, pancreas stomach, and u terine cervix.

Cigarette smoking is a major independent risk factor for coronary artery disease. Retrospective and prospective epidemiologic studies have demonstrated a strong relationship between smoking and coronary morbidity and mortality in both men and women. The coronary disease death rate in smokers is 70% higher than in nonsmokers, and the risk increases with the amount of cigarette exposure. The risk of sudden death is two to four times higher in smokers. Smoking is also a risk factor for cardiac arrest and severe malignant arrythmias. In addition to increased coronary mortality, smokers have a higher risk of non fatal myocardial infraction or unstable angina. Patients with angina lower their exercise tolerance if they smoke. Women who smoke and use oral contraceptives or pot-menopausal estrogen replacement greatly increase their risk of myocardial infarction.

Autopsy studies demonstrate more atheromatous changes in smokers than nonsmokers. Carbon monoxide in cigarette smoke decreases oxygen delivery to endothelial tissues. In addition, smoking may trigger acute ischemia. Carbon monoxide decreases myocardial oxygen supply, while nicotine increases myocardial demand by releasing catecholamines that raise blood pressure, heart rate, and conractility. Carbon monoxide and nicotine also induce platelet aggregation that may cause occulision of narrowed vessels. Cigarette smoking is the most important risk factor for peripheral vascular disease. In patients with intermittent claudication, smoking lowers exercise tolerance and may shorten graft survival after vascular surgery. Smokers have more aortic atherosclerosis and an increased risk of dying from a ruptured aortic aneurysm. Smokers under the age of 65 have a higher risk of dying from cerebrovascular disease and women who smoke have a greater risk of subarachnoid haemorrhage, especially if they also use oral contraceptives.

Smoking and Pulmonary Disease:

Cigarette smoking is the primary cause of chronic bronchitis and emphysema. Smokers have a higher prevalence of respiratory symptoms than non smokers. Studies of pulmonary function indicate that impairment exists in asymptomatic as well as symptomatic smokers. Smokers have a higher risk of acute as well as chronic pulmonary disease. Inhaling cigarette smoke impairs pulmonary clearance mechanisms by paralyzing ciliary transport. This may explain the susceptibility to viral respiratory infections, including influenza. Smokers who develop acute respiratory infections have longer and more severe courses, with a more prolonged cough.

Other Health Consequences:

Smokers have a higher prevalence of peptic ulcer disease and a higher case fatality rate. Smoking has been associated with increased osteoporosis in men and post-menopausal women. Female smokers weigh less than non smokers and have an earlier age of menopause; both of these factors are associated with osteoporosis and may contribute to the relationship between smoking and osteoporosis. Moreover, smoking depresses serum estrogen levels in post-menopausal women taking estrogen replacement therapy.

Passive Smoking (Environmental Smoke Exposure):

Nonsmokers involuntarily inhale the smoke of nearby smokers, a phenomenon known as passive smoking. Wives, children and friends of smokers are a highly risk-prone group. Inhalation of sidestream smoke by a non-smoker is definitely more harmful to him than to the actual smoker as he inhales more toxins. This is because sidestream smoke contains three times more nicotine, three times more tar and about 50 times more ammonia. Passive smoking (because of smoking by their fathers) could lead to severe complications in babies aged below two. It is pointed out that in India hospital admission rates are 28 per cent higher among the children of smokers. These children have acute lower respiratory infection, decreased lung function, increased eczema and asthma and increased cot deaths. Also children of heavy smokers tend to be shorter.

Passive smoking is associated with an overall 23 per cent increase in risk of coronary heart disease (CHD) among men and women who had never smoked. The following data shows just how heavy is cigarette smoking's toll on non-smokers. A new "meta-analysis" of data from 14 studies involving 6,166 individuals with coronoary heart disease (CHD) finds that passive smoking was associated with an overall 23 per cent increase in the risk of CHD among men and women who had never smoked. It is estimated that 35,000 to 40,000 non-smokers' deaths each year in the United States can be attributed to passive smoking. This underscores the need to eliminate passive smoking as an important strategy to reduce the societal burden of CHD. The United Nations health agency insisted that passive smoking caused lung cancer and that an environmental tobacco smoke poses a positive health hazard. Research on the subject has found an estimated 16 per cent increase in the risk of developing lung cancer among nonsmoking spouses of smokers and an estimated 17 per cent rise in risk for work place exposure. The public is left high and dry over the risks of "second-hand smoke." For non-smokers, the major source of carbon monoxide is from passively inhaled cigarette smoke. Environmental tobacco smoke (ETS) has been shown to reduce rung function in children. Its irritant effect could not be ignored as this is the reason why most people object to being the victims of passive smoking. Patients with asthma find this irritant effect will worsen symptoms. The most remarkable effect of environmental tobacco smoke (ETS) is the development of lung cancer in passively exposed non-smokers as shown by reports from Japan and Greece. Large number of controlled studies have confirmed a relative risk of developing lung cancer in passively exposed subjects. Estimates from the United States have suggested that 3000 to 5000 deaths per year from lung cancer can be attributed to passive smoking.

Maternal smoking during pregnancy increases risks to foetus and non-smokers chronically exposed to tobacco smoke will suffer health hazards. Maternal smoking during pregnancy contributes to fetal growth retardation. Infants born to mothers who smoke weigh an average of 200 gm less but have no shorter gestations than infants of non-smoking mothers. Carbon monoxide in smoke may decrease oxygen availability to the fetus and account for the growth retardation. Smoking during pregnancy has also been linked with higher rates of spontaneous abortion, fetal death, and neonatal death.

When smoking occurs in enclosed areas with poor ventilation, such as in buses, bars, and conference rooms, high levels of smoke exposure can occur. Acute exposure to smoke-contaminated air decreases exercise capacity in healthy non-smokers and can worsen symptoms in individuals with angina, chronic obstructive pulmonary disease (COPD) or asthma. Chronic exposure to smoky air occurs in the workplace and in the homes of smokers. Non-smokers in smoky workplaces develop small-airways dysfunction similar to that observed in tight smokers. Compared to the children of non-smokers, children whose parents smoke have more respiratory infections throughout childhood, a higher risk of asthma, and alternations in pulmonary function tests. In recent studies of non-smoking women, those married to smokers had higher lung cancer rates than those married to non-smokers. Chronic smoke exposure may be associated with increased incidence of cardiopulmonary disease in nonsmokers.

Environmental tobacco smoke (ETS) also contributes to respiratory morbidity of children. Increased platelet aggregation also occurs when a nonsmoker smokes or is passively exposed to smoke. Although environmental tobacco smoke (ETS) differs from "mainstream smoke" in several ways, it contains many of the same toxic substances. Infants and toddlers may be especially at risk when exposed to environmental tobacco smoke (ETS). Considering the substantial morbidity, and even modality of acute respiratory illness in childhood, a doubling in risk attributable to passive smoking clearly represents a serious paediatric health problem. Exposure to environmental tobacco smoke (ETS) has been associated with increased asthma-related trips to the emergency room of hospitals. There is now sufficient evidence to conclude that passive smoking is associated with additional episodes and increased severity of asthma in children who already have the disease. Exposure to passive smoking may alter children's intelligence and behaviour and passive smoke exposure in childhood may be a risk factor for developing lung cancer as an adult. Environmetal tobacco smoke (ETS) contains more than 4000 chemicals and at least 40 known carcinogens. Nicotine, the addictive drug contained in tobacco leads to acute increase in heart rate and blood pressure. ETS also increases platelet aggregation, or blood clotting. It also damages the endothelium, the layer of cells that line all blood vessels, including the coronary arteries. In addition, nonsmokers who have high blood pressure or high blood cholesterol are at even greater risk of developing heart diseases from ETS exposure". An investigation in Bristol has found that the children of smokers have high levels of cotinine, a metabolite of nicotine, in their saliva. The results indicated that children who had two smoking parents were breathing in as much nicotine as if they themselves were smoking 80 cigarettes a year. A study published in the "New England Journal of Medicine" found that the children of smoking mothers were less efficient at breathing.

Thus, it can be safely concluded that the dangers of passive smoking are real, broader than once believed and parallel those of direct smoke. It has long been established that smoking harms the health of those who smoke. Now, new epide- miological studies and reviews are strengthening the evidence that it also harms the health of other people nearby who inhale the toxic fumes generated by the smoker, particularly from the burning end of the cigarette. Such indirect, or second-hand, smoking causes death not only by lung cancer but even more by heart attack, the studies show. The studies on passive smoking, as it is often called, also strenthen the link between parental smoking and respiratory damage in children. According to experts, there was little question that passive smoking is a major health hazard.

"Mainstream smoke" is inhaled and consists of large particles deposited in the larger airways of the lung. "Sidestream smoke" is generated from the burning end of cigarettes, cigars and pipes during the smouldering between puffs. It may come from someone else's tobacco or from one's own and in the major source of environmental tobacco smoke (ETS). It is a mixture of irritating gasses and carcinogenic tar particles that reach deeper into the lungs because they, are small. According to scientists, because of incomplete combustion from the lower temperatures of a smouldering cigarette, sidestream smoke is dirtier and chemically different from, mainstream smoke. Scientists have found a 30 per cent increase in risk of death from heart attacks among nonsmokers living with smokers due to passive smoking. Researchers have found that passive smoking makes platelets the tiny fragments in the blood that help it clot, stickier. Platelets can form clots on plaques in fat-clogged arteries to cause heart attacks and they may also play a role in promoting arteriosclerosis, the underlying cause of most heart attacks. Researchers have also shown that passive smoking affects heart function, decreasing the ability of people with and without heart disease to exercise. It has been pointed out that passive smoking increases the demand on the heart during exercise and reduces the heart's capacity to speed up. For people with heart disease, the decreased function can precipitate chest pains from angina. The children exposed to passive smoke since birth, had increased amounts of cholesterol and lower levels of HDL, a protein in blood that is believed to provide protection against heart attacks'. The researchers found that the greater the exposure to passive smoke, the greater were the biochemical changes.

Every year, 1 million tobacco-related deaths take place in India. An estimated 65 per cent of men use tobacco and in some parts a large proportion of women chew tobacco and bidies. About 33 per cent of all cancers are caused by tobacco. About 50 per cent of all cancers among men and 25 per cent among women are tobacco-related. The number of cases of avoidable tobacco-related cancers of the upper alimentary and respiratory tracts, coronary heart disease and chronic obstructive pulmonary disease (COPD) has been estimated as 2,00,000 every year. Many still-births, low birth infants, and pre-natal mortality have been reported among female chewers.

Tobacco kills 50 per cent of its regular users within 40 years. Apart from these direct health implications of tobacco use, the hazards faced by those engaged in the plucking and curing of tobacco leaves have been highlighted by researchers of the Ahmedabad-based National Institute of Occupational Health. The hands of the workers get affected by the chemicals in tobacco and sickness is caused when nicotine gets absorbed into the body through the skin. The symptoms are head-ache, nausea and vomitting. All these well-documented findings are available with the State but if it has not taken any effective action it can only be attributed to the clout which the lethal leaf enjoys in the corridors of power. One of the pet contentions of the protagonists of tobacco is that it makes a significant contribution to the exchequer by way of taxes and hence should not be disturbed. Also a large number of tobacco farmers will be hit if consumption is curbed. Both these have been countered by WHO forcefully. Several studies have brought out that the cost of healthcare of those affected by tobacco-related ailments, which is met from the Government exchequer, is much more than what the Government garners by way of taxes. Thus, there is a net drain on the Government resources. Illness or the premature death of the tobacco-users would cast a heavy economic burden on their families, perpetuating the cycle of poverty. As regards the possible impact of any curb on tobacco use on tobacco farmers, studies by the Rajahmundry-based Tobacco Research Institute of the ICAR have brought out equally remunerative alternative to tobacco cultivation, besides use of tobacco for purposes other than smoking and chewing.

Right to Life:

The word 'life' in Article 21 is very significant as it covers every facet of human existence. The word 'life' has not been defined in the Constitution but it does not mean nor can it be restricted only to the vegetative or animal life or mere existence from conception to death. Life does not merely connote a continued drudgery through life. The expression 'life' has a much wider meaning bringing within its sweep some of the finer graces of human civilisation which makes life worth living[6].

Life includes all such amenities and facilities which a person born in a free country is entitled to enjoy with dignity, legally and constitutionally. The amplitude of the word 'life' is so wide that the danger and encroachment complained of would impinge upon the fundamental rights of citizens as in the present case. The apex Court has interpreted Article 21 giving wide meaning to 'life' which includes the quality of life, adequate nutrition, clothing and shelter and cannot be restricted merely to physical existence. The word 'life' in the Constitution has not been used in a limited manner. A wide meaning should be given to the expression 'life' to enable a man not only to sustain life but to enjoy it in a full measure. The sweep of right to life conferred by Article 21 of the Constitution is wide and far-reaching so as to bring within its scope the right to pollution free air and the "right to decent environment[7]." Under our Constitutional set up the dignity of man and subject to law the privacy of home shall be inviolable. The Constitution through various Articles in Part III and Part IV[8] guarantees the dignity of the individual and also right to life which if permitted to trample upon will result in negation of these rights and, dignity of human personality.

6 *Board of Trustees of the Port of Bombay v. D. R. Nadkarni*, AIR 1983 SC

7 *Shantistar Builders v. Narayan Khimalal Totame*, AIR 1990 SC 630

8 The **Directive Principles of State Policy** are guidelines to the central and state governments of India, to be kept in mind while framing laws and policies. These provisions, contained in Part IV of the Constitution of India, are not enforceable by any court, but the principles laid down therein are considered fundamental in the governance of the country, making it the duty of the State to apply these principles in making laws to establish a just society in the country. The principles have been inspired by the Directive Principles given in the Constitution of Ireland and also by the principles of Gandhism; and relate to social justice, economic welfare, foreign policy, and legal and administrative matters.

Decision of the High Court:

Court held that Maintenance of health and environment falls within the purview of Article 21 of the Constitution as it adversely affects the life of the citizens by slow and insidious poisoning thereby reducing the very life span itself. Exposing unsuspecting individuals to environmental tobacco smoke (ETS) with ominous consequences amounts to taking away their life, not by execution of death sentence but by a slow and gradual process by robbing him of all his qualities and graces, a process which is much more cruel than sending a man to gallows. To convert human existence into animal existence no doubt amounts to taking away human life, because a man lives not by his physical existence or by bread alone but by his human existence[9]. Smokers dig not only their own graves prematurely but also pose a serious threat to the lives of lakhs of innocent nonsmokers who get themselves exposed to ETS thereby violating their right to life guaranteed under Article 21 of the Constitution of India. A healthy body is the very foundation for all human activities. In a welfare State it is the obligation of the State to ensure the creation and the sustaining of conditions congenial to good health.

Court further held that Public smoking of tobacco in any form whether in the form of cigarettes, cigars, beedies or otherwise is illegal, unconstitutional and violative of Article 21 of the Constitution of India.

9 *Sankar Banerjee v. Durgapur Projects Ltd.* (AIR 1988 Calcutta 136)

13

Use of black films upon vehicles and Right to Life[1]

Facts in Nutshell:

Alarming rise in heinous crimes like kidnapping, sexual assault on women and dacoity have impinged upon the right to life and the right to live in a safe environment which are within the contours of Article 21[2] of the Constitution of India. *One of the contributory factors to such increase is use of black films on windows/windshields of four-wheeled vehicles.* The Petitioner[3], a public spirited person, invoked the extra-ordinary jurisdiction of Supreme Court under Article 32[4] of the Constitution in the public interest litigation[5], praying for certain directions to stop this

---

1 Appellants: **Avishek Goenka Vs.** Respondent: **Union of India (UOI) and Anr.** (2012)5SCC321
Hon'ble Judges/Coram: S.H. Kapadia, C.J.I., A.K. Patnaik and Swatanter Kumar, JJ.

2 **Article 21 in The Constitution Of India 1949**
21. Protection of life and personal liberty No person shall be deprived of his life or personal liberty except according to procedure established by law

3 **Meaning of Petitioner:** A person who presents a Petition. (**Meaning of Petition:** A formal message requesting something that is submitted to an authority)

4 **Article 32 in The Constitution Of India 1949**
32. Remedies for enforcement of rights conferred by this Part
(1) The right to move the Supreme Court by appropriate proceedings for the enforcement of the rights conferred by this Part is guaranteed
(2) The Supreme Court shall have power to issue directions or orders or writs, including writs in the nature of habeas corpus, mandamus, prohibition, quo warranto and certiorari, whichever may be appropriate, for the enforcement of any of the rights conferred by this Part
(3) Without prejudice to the powers conferred on the Supreme Court by clause (1) and (2), Parliament may by law empower any other court to exercise within the local limits of its jurisdiction all or any of the powers exercisable by the Supreme Court under clause (2)
(4) The right guaranteed by this article shall not be suspended except as otherwise provided for by this Constitution

5 **Meaning of Public Interest Litigation: Public-Interest Litigation** is litigation for the protection of the public interest. In Indian law, **Article 32** of the Indian constitution contains a tool which directly joints the public with judiciary. PIL may be introduced in a court of law by the court itself (*suo motu*), rather than the aggrieved party or another third party. For the exercise of the court's jurisdiction, it is unnecessary for the victim of the violation of his or her rights to personally approach the court. In PIL, the right to file suit is given to a member of the public by the courts through judicial activism. The member of the public may be a non-governmental organization (NGO), an institution or an individual. The Supreme Court of India, rejecting the criticism of judicial activism, has stated

menace. According to the Petitioner, Supreme Court should issue a writ[6] or direction requiring use of such safety glasses on the windows/ windshields in vehicles having 100 per cent Visual Light Transmission (for short 'VLT') only and, to that extent, the Petitioner challenged the correctness of Rule 100 of the Motor Vehicles Rules, 1989 (for short "the Rules"). He further prays for prohibition on use of black films on the glasses of the vehicles, proper implementation of law in that behalf and finally, for taking stringent actions against the offenders, using vehicles with black filmed glasses. He also prays that a larger police force should be deputed to monitor such offences.

Side- Effects of Black Films:

The use of black films upon the vehicles gives immunity to the violators in committing a crime and is used as a tool of criminality, considerably increasing criminal activities. At times, heinous crimes like dacoity, rape, murder and even terrorist acts are committed in or with the aid of vehicles having black films pasted on the side windows and on the screens of the vehicles. It was stated that because of non- observance of the norms, Regulations and guidelines relating to the specifications for the front and rear windscreens and the side windows of the vehicles, the offenders can move undetected in such vehicles and commit crimes without hesitation.

The word 'tinted' means shade or hue as per the dictionary. The rear and front and side glasses of vehicles are provided with such shade or tint, and therefore, they are widely referred to as 'tinted glasses', which is different from 'black films'. The glasses of the vehicles having a coating of black films cannot be termed as 'tinted glasses' because they are not manufactured as such. Besides aiding in commission of crimes, black films on the vehicles are also at times positively correlated with motor accidents on the roads. It is for the reason that the comparative visibility to that through normal/tinted glasses which are manufactured as such is much lesser and the persons driving at high speed, especially on highways, meet with accidents because of use of black filmed glasses.

The use of black films also prevents the traffic police from seeing the activity in the car and communicating with the driver of the vehicle. The

---

that the judiciary has stepped in to give direction due to executive inaction; laws enacted by Parliament and the state legislatures for the poor since independence have not been properly implemented.

6 **Meaning of Writ:** A written order issued by a court, commanding the party to whom it is addressed to perform or cease performing a specified act.

Petitioner also cites that the number of fatal accidents of vehicles having black films is much higher in India than in other parts of the world. The black filmed vehicles have lower visibility and therefore, the chances of accident are increased by 18 per cent to 38 per cent due to low visibility.

Black filmed glasses help in commission of crime as well as hiding the criminals even during vehicle checks at 'Naka' points. The Petitioner also stated that the use of black films is not prevalent in developed and/or developing countries all over the world. In fact, in some of the countries, it is specifically banned. In Afghanistan, Belarus, Nigeria, Uganda and even in Pakistan, use of black films on the vehicle glasses is banned. Use of black films is not prevalent in United States of America, United Kingdom, Germany and other countries as well.

Right to Life:

The citizens at large have a right to life i.e. to live with dignity, freedom and safety. This right emerges from Article 21 of the Constitution of India.

The Motor Vehicle Act, 1939:

The Motor Vehicle Act, 1939 was enacted to consolidate and amend the laws relating to motor vehicles. This Act was subjected to various amendments. Finally, the Motor Vehicles Act, 1988 (for short 'the Act') was enacted, inter alia, with the object and reason being, to provide for quality standards for pollution control devices, provisions for issuing fitness certificate of the vehicle and effective ways of tracking down traffic offenders. Section 190 of the Act provides that any person who drives or causes or allows to be driven in any public place a motor vehicle or a trailer which has any defect, or violates the standards prescribed in relation to road safety, or violates the provisions of the Act or the Rules made therein, is punishable as per the provisions of the Act. In other words, alteration to the conditions of the vehicle in a manner contravening the Act is not permissible in law. Section 52 of the Act declares that no owner of a motor vehicle shall so alter the vehicle that the particulars contained in the certificate of registration are at variance with those originally specified by the manufacturer. However, certain changes are permissible in terms of the proviso to this Section and that too with the approval of the Central Government/competent authority. In terms of Section 53 of the Act, if any registering authority or other prescribed authority has reason to believe that any motor vehicle within its jurisdiction is in such a condition that its use in a public place would constitute a danger to the public, or that it fails to comply with the requirements of the Act or the Rules made thereunder, whether due to alteration of vehicle violative of Section 52 of the Act or otherwise, the Authority may, after giving opportunity of hearing, suspend the registration certificate for the period required for rectification of such defect, and if the defect is still not removed, for cancellation of registration. In exercise of its power, under various provisions of the Act, the Central Government has framed the Rules. Chapter V of the Rules deals with construction, equipment and maintenance of motor vehicles. Rule 92 mandates that no person shall use or cause or allow to be used in any public place any motor vehicle which does not comply with the provisions of this Chapter. There are different Rules which deals with various aspects of construction and maintenance of vehicles including lights, brakes, gears and other aspects including overall dimensions of the vehicles. Rule 100 of the Rules concerns itself with the glass of windscreen and VLT of light of such glass windscreen. It specifically provides for fixation of glasses made of laminated safety glass conforming to Indian standards IS: 2553-Part 2 -1992 and even for the kind of windscreen wipers required to be fixed on the front screen of the vehicle.

Relevant part of Rule 100, with which we are concerned, reads as under:

100. Safety glass.-(1) The glass of windscreens and the windows of every motor vehicle 188[other than agricultural tractors] shall be of safety glass:

Provided that in the case of three-wheelers and vehicles with hood and side covers, the windows may be of 189[acrylic or plastic transparent sheet.]

Explanation.-For the purpose of this rule,-

(i) safety glass" means glass conforming to the specifications of the Bureau of Indian Standards or any International Standards and so manufactured or treated that if fractured, it does not fly or break into fragments capable of causing severe cuts;

(ii) any windscreen or window at the front of the vehicle, the inner surface of which is at an angle more than thirty degrees to the longitudinal axis of the vehicle shall be deemed to face to the front.

[(2) The glass of the windscreen and rear window of every motor vehicle shall be such and shall be maintained in such a condition that the visual transmission of light is not less than 70%. The glasses used for side windows are such and shall be maintained in such condition that the visual transmission of light is not less than 50%, and shall conform to Indian Standards [IS: 2553- Part 2-1992];

(3) The glass of the front windscreen of every motor vehicle [other than two wheelers and agricultural tractors] manufactured after three years from the coming into force of the Central Motor Vehicles (Amendment) Rules, 1993 shall be made of laminated safety glass: Provided that on and from three months after the commencement of the Central Motor Vehicles (Amendment) Rules, 1999, the glass of the front windscreen of every motor vehicle other than two-wheelers and agricultural tractors shall be made of laminated safety glass conforming to the Indian Standards IS: 2553-Part 2-1992.

Explanation.-For the purpose of these sub-rules "laminated safety glass" shall mean two or more pieces of glass held together by an intervening layer or layers of plastic materials. The laminated safety glass will crack and break under sufficient impact, but the pieces of the glass tend to adhere to the plastic material and do not fly, and if a hole is produced, the edges would be less jagged than they would be in the case of an ordinary glass.

From the above provisions, it is clear that the Rules deal with every minute detail of construction and maintenance of a vehicle.

Decision of the Supreme Court:

Court held that the use of black films or any other material upon safety glass, windscreen and side windows is impermissible.

14

Manual Scavenging and Right to Life[1]

Facts in Nutshell:

Writ petition[2] was filed in public interest by one G. Narayanan, who appeared in person, with a prayer for issuance of a writ of Mandamus[3] directing the respondents[4] to discontinue the employment of human being in cleaning manholes and sewerage lines and septic tanks in the State of Tamil Nadu and with a further direction to direct the respondents to adequately rehabilitate those who were currently employed in cleaning manholes and sewerage lines.

Employment of manual scavengers has already been declared illegal under the Employment of Manual Scavengers & Construction of Dry Latrines (Prohibition) Act, 1993. It has been stated in the petition that the sanitary workers in the State were made to literally go down the drains every day and without safety precautions and supervision and without any

1 Appellants: **A. Narayanan Vs.** Respondent: **The Chief Secretary, Government of Tamil Nadu and Ors.** MANU/TN/1331/2008
Hon'ble Judges/Coram: A.K. Ganguly, C.J. and F.M. Ibrahim Kalifulla, Judge

2 **Meaning of Writ Petition:** Under the Indian legal system, jurisdiction to issue ⍰prerogative writs⍰ is given to the Supreme Court, and to the High Courts of Judicature of all Indian states. Parts of the law relating to writs are set forth in the Constitution of India. The Supreme Court, the highest in the country, may issue writs under Article 32 of the Constitution for enforcement of Fundamental Rights and under Articles 139 for enforcement of rights other than Fundamental Rights, while High Courts, the superior courts of the States, may issue writs under Articles 226. ⍰Writ⍰ is eminently designed by the makers of the Constitution, and in the same way it is developed very widely and efficiently by the courts in India. The Constitution broadly provides for five kinds of "prerogative" writs, namely, Habeas Corpus, Certiorari, Mandamus, Quo Warranto and Prohibition.

3 **Meaning of Writ of Mandamus: Mandamus** is a judicial remedy — in the form of an order from a superior court, to any government subordinate court, corporation, orpublic authority — to do (or forbear from doing) some specific act which that body is obliged under law to do (or refrain from doing) — and which is in the nature of public duty, and in certain cases one of a statutory duty. It cannot be issued to compel an authority to do something against statutory provision. For example, it cannot be used to force a lower court to reject or authorize applications that have been made, but if the court refuses to rule one way or the other then a mandamus can be used to order the court to rule on the applications.

4 **Meaning of Respondent**: A **respondent** is a person who is called upon to issue a response to a communication made by another. In legal usage, this specifically refers to the defendant in a legal proceeding commenced by a petition, or to an appellee, or the opposing party, in an appeal of a decision by an initial fact-finder.

emergency medical support, and therefore, they were subjected to these inhuman treatment. It has also been urged that various news papers have highlighted this problem by reporting such incidents of engaging human beings by asking them to work inside the drain for clearing sewerage blocks and septic tanks. It has been widely reported in the newspapers and it is also an open secret that these workers die frequently due to asphyxia and even though when they die in harness, the concerned authority like Chennai Metro Water Supply and Sewerage Board (herein after referred to as 'CMWSS Board') refuses to pay any compensation citing rules that the workers were contract labourers. It has been alleged that such stand on behalf of the CMWSS Board was not only unfair, but also violative of the fundamental rights[5] of the workers. Such workers die without getting any compensation and the CMWSS Board gets away by showing unethical labour practice.

With the abolition of Manual Scavenging[6] all workers were used for cleaning manholes and septic tanks. It has been further alleged that though CMWSS Board claims that they have procured safety equipments, but the number of machines and safety accessories procured were grossly inadequate to the enormous task of sewer maintenance, and the exploitation of asking workers to go inside the drains still continues. It was said that the common practice is asking them to consume alcohol before getting into the drains as without that they cannot stand the stench of poisonous gas with combination of Hydrogen Sulphide and Methane, and many workers die in the process of cleaning the lines, and even if they do not die, they develop respiratory problems and various diseases

5 ***'Part III – Fundamental Rights'*** is a charter of rights contained in the Constitution of India. It guarantees civil liberties such that all Indians can lead their lives in peace and harmony as citizens of India. These include individual rights common to most liberal democracies, such as equality before law, freedom of speech and expression, and peaceful assembly, freedom to practice religion, and the right to constitutional remedies for the protection of civil rights by means of writs such as habeas corpus. Violation of these rights result in punishments as prescribed in the Indian Penal Code or other special laws, subject to discretion of the judiciary. The Fundamental Rights are defined as basic human freedoms which every Indian citizen has the right to enjoy for a proper and harmonious development of personality. These rights universally apply to all citizens, irrespective of race, place of birth, religion, caste, creed, colour or gender. Aliens (persons who are not citizens) are also considered in matters like equality before law. They are enforceable by the courts, subject to certain restrictions. The Rights have their origins in many sources, including England's Bill of Rights, the United States Bill of Rights and France's Declaration of the Rights of Man.

6 **Manual scavenging** refers to the removal of human waste/excreta from unsanitary, "dry" toilets, which are not connected to a sewer system. The practice is primarily conducted in South Asia. In 1993 legislation was passed in India to ban manual scavenging, but has not been widely implemented. In February 2013 Delhi announced that it was the first state to ban manual scavenging and require construction of sanitary latrines.

which were beyond any remedy. According to the petitioner[7], such employment of workers was violative of Articles 21[8], 14[9], 17[10] & 23[11] of the Constitution. As such certain directions were prayed from High Court to stop illegal and inhuman practice.

Directions of the High Court:

Court passed the following order:

(i) It directed that entry of sanitary workers into the sewerage system under the guise of removing the blocks should be prohibited, except under exceptional circumstances. Such exceptional circumstances may be for the following:

(a) For the removal of concrete/FRP manhole door which gets damaged due to the heavy vehicular traffic and often falls inside the manhole causing obstructions/blocks in the sewer and which results in the blockage of sewerage system, and where mechanical equipments cannot be put into operation.

(b) For the purpose of inter-linking the newly laid sewer main with the existing sewer main, where it will be wholly necessary to block the main sewer main in the servicing manhole. Entry of sanitary workers on such occasions has to be necessarily permitted, inasmuch as it is stated that large size sewer i.e., where the dia is more than 300 mm, blocking the sewer main from the top of the manhole is not possible and only the

7 **Meaning of Petitioner:** A person who presents a Petition. (**Meaning of Petition:** A formal message requesting something that is submitted to an authority)

8 **Article 21 in The Constitution Of India 1949**
21. Protection of life and personal liberty No person shall be deprived of his life or personal liberty except according to procedure established by law

9 **Article 14 in The Constitution Of India 1949**
14. Equality before law The State shall not deny to any person equality before the law or the equal protection of the laws within the territory of India Prohibition of discrimination on grounds of religion, race, caste, sex or place of birth

10 **Article 17 in The Constitution Of India 1949**
17. Abolition of Untouchability Untouchability is abolished and its practice in any form is forbidden The enforcement of any disability arising out of Untouchability shall be an offence punishable in accordance with law

11 **Article 23 in The Constitution Of India 1949**
23. Prohibition of traffic in human beings and forced labour
(1) Traffic in human beings and begar and other similar forms of forced labour are prohibited and any contravention of this provision shall be an offence punishable in accordance with law
(2) Nothing in this article shall prevent the State from imposing compulsory service for public purpose, and in imposing such service the State shall not make any discrimination on grounds only of religion, race, caste or class or any of them

sanitary worker has to enter the main hole and that too with necessary safety gadgets for blocking the sewer temporarily.

(c) For the removal of submersible pump sets fixed at the bottom of the suction wells, which goes out of order, for which the sanitary worker has to enter the well again with necessary safety gadgets after emptying the sewage from the well in order to remove the pump set. It was made clear that before allowing any sanitary worker to enter on such occasions, steps should be taken to see that the sewage is totally emptied and thereby further ensure that no poisonous gas remains in the sewage line.

(d) For the reconstruction of the man hole or rectification of the sewer main due to any damage caused by sinking of man hole covers/sewer line when the sewage pipe line gets blocked or gets obstructed, which results in the system getting surcharged. Here again, before allowing any sanitary worker to enter the sewer line, it is essential that sewage line is emptied by blocking the main holes in the system on either side of the sinking man holes/damaged man holes.

Poverty

Article 21[1] of the Constitution and Right to Free Legal Service[2] to accused on Account of Poverty

Article 21 of the Constitution, as interpreted in the decision in Suk Das's case[3] wherein the court held that the petitioner's had a fundamental right to free legal service and the learned Magistrate was under an obligation towards them to inform them regarding the availability of such aid at State cost and as this was not done, there has been violation of their fundamental right and the trials held against them are vitiated due to fatal constitutional infirmity.

Court in Hussainara Khatoon's case[4] held that 'the right to free legal service is...clearly an essential ingredient of reasonable, fair and just procedure for a person accused of an offence and it must be held to be constitutional right of every accused person, who is unable to engage a lawyer and secure legal services on account of reasons such as **POVERTY**, indigence or incommunicado situation and the State is under a mandate to provide lawyer to an accused person if the circumstances of the case and the needs of justice so require, provided, of course, the accused person does not object to the provision of such lawyer.'

It is now settled law that free legal assistance at State cost is a fundamental right of a person accused of an offence, which may involve jeopardy to his life or personal liberty and this fundamental right is implicit in the requirement of reasonable, fair and just procedure prescribed by Article 21.

1 **Article 21 in The Constitution Of India 1949**
21. Protection of life and personal liberty No person shall be deprived of his life or personal liberty except according to procedure established by law

2 **Article 39 A Constitution of India, 1950**
Equal Justice and Free Legal Aid
39A. The State shall secure that the operation of the legal system promotes justice, on a basis of equal opportunity, and shall, in particular, provide free legal aid, by suitable legislation or schemes or in any other way, to ensure that opportunities for securing justice are not denied to any citizen by reason of economic or other disabilities.

3 1986CriLJ1084

4 1979CriLJ1045

Of course, it must be recognized that there may be cases involving offences, such as economic offences or offences against law prohibiting prostitution or child abuse and the like, where social justice may require that free legal service may not be provided by the State. There can, in the circumstances, be no doubt that the appellants[5] were entitled to free legal assistance at State cost when they were placed in peril of their personal liberty by reason of being accused of an of fence, which if proved, would clearly entail imprisonment for a term of two years.

In *Khatri v. State of Bihar*[6] court ruled that the Magistrate or the Sessions Judge, before whom an accused appears must be held to be under an obligation to inform the accused that if he is unable to engage the service of a lawyer on account of **POVERTY** or indigence, he is entitled to obtain free legal services at the cost of the State. It is clear that the obligation on the part of the Presiding Officers to inform the accused of his fundamental right of free legal assistance at State cost in case he is unable to engage the service of a lawyer on account of **POVERTY** or indigence, is absolute and is not conditioned upon the accused himself applying for such legal assistance.

Due to Poverty Most People Can't approach the Court

The origin and evolution of Public Interest Litigation in India emanated from realization of constitutional obligation by the Judiciary towards the vast sections of the society-the poor and the marginalized sections of the society. This jurisdiction has been created and carved out by the judicial creativity and craftsmanship. In *M.C. Mehta and Anr. v. Union of India* and[7], Court observed that Article 32 of the constitution[8] does not merely confer

5 **Meaning of Appellant:** A person who, dissatisfied with the judgment rendered in a lawsuit decided in a lower court or the findings from a proceeding before an Administrative Agency, asks a superior court to review the decision.

6 1981CriLJ597

7 AIR 1987 SC 1086

8 **Article 32 in The Constitution Of India 1949**
32. Remedies for enforcement of rights conferred by this Part
(1) The right to move the Supreme Court by appropriate proceedings for the enforcement of the rights conferred by this Part is guaranteed
(2) The Supreme Court shall have power to issue directions or orders or writs, including writs in the nature of habeas corpus, mandamus, prohibition, quo warranto and certiorari, whichever may be appropriate, for the enforcement of any of the rights conferred by this Part
(3) Without prejudice to the powers conferred on the Supreme Court by clause (1) and (2), Parliament may by law empower any other court to exercise within the local limits of its jurisdiction all or any of the powers exercisable by the Supreme Court under clause (2)
(4) The right guaranteed by this article shall not be suspended except as otherwise provided for

power on Court to issue direction, order or writ for the enforcement of fundamental rights. Instead, it also lays a constitutional obligation on this Court to protect the fundamental rights of the people. The Court asserted that, in realization of this constitutional obligation, "it has all incidental and ancillary powers including the power to forge new remedies and fashion new strategies designed to enforce the fundamental rights". The Court realized that because of extreme **POVERTY**, a large number of sections of society cannot approach the Court. The fundamental rights have no meaning for them and in order to preserve and protect the fundamental rights of the marginalized section of society by judicial innovation, the Courts by judicial innovation and creativity started giving necessary directions and passing orders in the public interest.

---

by this Constitution

15

No appeal was filed by Accused due to Poverty[1]

Facts in Nutshell:

Appeal[2] was filed by the appellant[3] from jail under Section 19[4] of the Terrorists and Distributive Activities (Prevention) Act, 1987 (hereinafter referred to as TADA).

Prosecution[5] Story:

Suresh being accompanied by his brother Subhash was going on a scooter to village. Both the said accused suddenly appeared armed with pistol and they made an attempt to stop the scooter, but his brother Subhash did not allow to do so. The accused[6] however caught hold of

---

1 Appellants: **Ajit Singh Vs.** Respondent: **State of Haryana** 1996(20)ACR362(SC)
Hon'ble Judges: G. N. Ray and N. P. Singh, JJ.

2 **Meaning of Appeal:** In law, an **appeal** is a process for requesting a formal change to an official decision. Very broadly speaking there are appeals on the record and *de novo* appeals. In *de novo* appeals, a new decision maker re-hears the case without any reference to the prior decision maker. In appeals on the record, the decision of the prior decision maker is challenged by arguing that he or she misapplied the law, came to an incorrect factual finding, acted in excess of his jurisdiction, abused his powers, was biased, considered evidence which he should not have considered or failed to consider evidence that he should have considered.

3 **Meaning of Appellant:** A person who, dissatisfied with the judgment rendered in a lawsuit decided in a lower court or the findings from a proceeding before an Administrative Agency, asks a superior court to review the decision.

4 **Section 19 of the Terrorist and Distributive Activities Act, 1987:**
19. Appeal- (1) Notwithstanding anything contained in the Code, an appeal shall lie as a matter of right from any judgment, sentence or order, not being an interlocutory order, of a Designated Court to the Supreme Court both on facts and on law.
(2) Except as aforesaid, no appeal or revision shall lie to any court from any judgment, sentence or order including an interlocutory order of a Designated Court.
(3) Every appeal under this section shall be preferred within a period of thirty days from the date of the judgment; sentence or order appealed from:
Provided that the Supreme Court may entertain an appeal after the expiry of the said period of thirty days if it is satisfied that the appellant had sufficient cause for not preferring the appeal within the period of thirty days.

5 **Meaning of Prosecution:**
a. the institution and conduct of legal proceedings against a person
b. the proceedings brought in the name of the Crown to put an accused on trial

6 **Meaning of Accused:** A person charged with a criminal offense, or the state of being so charged

the scooter by its handle and pointed pistol on the back of Suresh urging him to handover whatever valuable was in his possession. Out of fear, Suresh handed over a purse containing Rs. 1775/- and his wrist watch and the wrist watch of his brother Subhash was also removed by the other accused (Rajpal) forcibly. Both the accused were arrested and at the instance of the accused, the wrist watches snatched from were recovered.

Decision of the Lower Court

Court convicted both the accused for offences under Section 392[7] read with Section 397[8] IPC and also under Section 394[9] IPC passed a sentence of 10 years rigorous imprisonment against both the accused and also a fine of Rs. 250/- under Section 394 in default of making payment of fine, to undergo further rigorous imprisonment for three months. Both the said accused were also sentenced to undergo rigorous imprisonment for seven years for offences under Section 392 read with Section 397 IPC.

Decision by Supreme Court:

Court reduced the sentence for both accused for five years after appeal was filed by one of them in court. One Co-accused who has not filed appeal, Court directed to reduce his sentence.[10] Court has indicated that if any of the accused fails to prefer an appeal **DUE TO POVERTY** or otherwise, he will be entitled to the benefit of the modification of Sentence passed against the other accused in similar circumstances by Court. Court presumed that the co-accused has failed to prefer any appeal before Court not out of his own accord but **DUE TO POVERTY.**

7 **Section 392 in The Indian Penal Code, 1860**
392. Punishment for robbery-- Whoever commits robbery shall be punished with rigorous imprisonment for a term which may extend to ten years, and shall also be liable to fine; and, if the robbery be committed on the highway between sunset and sunrise, the imprisonment may be extended to fourteen years.

8 **Section 397 in The Indian Penal Code, 1860**
397. Robbery or dacoity, with attempt to cause death or grievous hurt-- If, at the time of committing robbery or dacoity, the offender uses any deadly weapon, or causes grievous hurt to any person, so attempts to cause death or grievous hurt to any person, the imprisonment with which such offender shall be punished shall not be less than seven years.

9 **Section 394 in The Indian Penal Code, 1860**
394. Voluntarily causing hurt in committing robbery- If any person, in committing or in attempting to commit robbery, voluntarily causes hurt, such person, and any other person jointly concerned in committing or attempting to commit such robbery, shall be punished with [imprisonment for life], or with rigorous imprisonment for a term which may extend to ten years, and shall also be liable to fine.

10 1992 Suppl. (3) SCC 45

16

Obligation of Judge to Provide Lawyer to Accused on account of Poverty[1]

Ratio Decidendi: *"Court shall convict Accused if guilt of Accused proved by congent and corroborative evidences on record."*

Facts in Nutshell:

The Appellant[2], Mohammed Ajmal Mohammad Amir Kasab @ Abu Mujahid (hereinafter referred to as 'the Appellant' or as 'Kasab'), who is a Pakistani national, has earned for himself five death penalties and an equal number of life terms in prison for committing multiple crimes of a horrendous kind in India. Some of the major charges against him were: conspiracy to wage war against the Government of India; collecting arms with the intention of waging war against the Government of India; waging and abetting the waging of war against the Government of India; commission of terrorist acts; criminal conspiracy to commit murder; criminal conspiracy, common intention and abetment to commit murder; committing murder of a number of persons; attempt to murder with common intention; criminal conspiracy and abetment; abduction for murder; robbery/dacoity with an attempt to cause death or grievous hurt; and causing explosions punishable under the Explosive Substance Act, 1908. He was found guilty of all these charges besides many others and was awarded the death sentence on five counts, life-sentence on five other counts, as well as a number of relatively lighter sentences of imprisonment for the other offences by the High Court. Kasab Filed a appeal in Supreme Court against death sentence and court appointed a senior lawyer to assist him.

---

1 Appellants: **Mohammed Ajmal Mohammad Amir Kasab @ Abu Mujahid Vs.** Respondent: **State of Maharashtra AND** Appellants: **State of Maharashtra Vs.** Respondent: **Fahim Harshad Mohammad Yusuf Ansari and Anr. AND** Appellants: **Radhakant Yadav Vs.** Respondent: **Union of India (UOI) and Ors.**
AIR2012SC3565
Hon'ble Judges: Aftab Alam and Chandramauli Kumar Prasad, JJ.

2 **Meaning of Appellant:** A person who, dissatisfied with the judgment rendered in a lawsuit decided in a lower court or the findings from a proceeding before an Administrative Agency, asks a superior court to review the decision.

Right to Fair Trail (Submissions by Counsel of Kasab)

Right to fair trial is an integral part of the right to life and personal liberty guaranteed under Article 21 of the Constitution of India[3], and that the fundamental right under Article 21 was inalienable and there can be no question of any waiver of the right by any person.

Proceeding from the premise that fair trial is an inalienable right of every person the Counsel for Kasab submitted that Kasab was not made aware of his Constitutional right to counsel under Article 22(1) of the Constitution[4] at the time of his arrest and production before the Judicial Magistrate in remand proceedings. Counsel submitted that a mere offer of legal aid is not the same as being made aware that one has the Constitutional right to consult, and to be defended by, a legal practitioner, and that simply the offer of legal aid does not satisfy the Constitutional requirement. Counsel also submitted that the omission to make the Appellant aware of his Constitutional right to consult, and be defended by, a legal practitioner resulted in the denial of protection against self-incrimination guaranteed under Article 20(3) of the Constitution[5].

Self Incrimination[6]

Court in *State of Bombay v. Kathi Kalu Oghad* [7], in which an eleven-Judge Bench of Court examined the true import of Article 20(3) and held that "an accused person cannot be said to have been compelled to be a witness against himself simply because he made a statement while in police

3 **Article 21 in The Constitution Of India 1949**
21. Protection of life and personal liberty No person shall be deprived of his life or personal liberty except according to procedure established by law

4 **Article 22 (1) in The Constitution Of India 1949**
22. Protection against arrest and detention in certain cases
(1) No person who is arrested shall be detained in custody without being informed, as soon as may be, of the grounds for such arrest nor shall he be denied the right to consult, and to be defended by, a legal practitioner of his choice

5 **Article 20 in The Constitution Of India 1949**
20. Protection in respect of conviction for offences
(1) No person shall be convicted of any offence except for violation of the law in force at the time of the commission of the act charged as an offence, nor be subjected to a penalty greater than that which might have been inflicted under the law in force at the time of the commission of the offence
(2) No person shall be prosecuted and punished for the same offence more than once
(3) No person accused of any offence shall be compelled to be a witness against himself

6 **Meaning of Self Incrimination:** Making statements or producing evidence which tends to prove that one is guilty of a crime.

7 (1962) 3 SCR 10

custody without anything more"; and that "the mere questioning of an accused person by a police officer, resulting in a voluntary statement, which may ultimately turn out to be incriminatory, is not 'compulsion'". Voluntary statements are not proscribed by Article20(3) and do not amount to violation of the privilege against self-incrimination.

Guidelines by Court:

(a) Under Article 22(1) of the Constitution, the right to consult an advocate of his choice shall not be denied to any person who is arrested. If however an accused expresses the wish to have his lawyer by his side at the time of examination, this facility shall not be denied, because, by denying the facility, the police will be exposed to the serious reproof that they are trying to secure in secrecy and by coercing the will an involuntary self-incrimination. It is not as if a lawyer's presence is a panacea for all problems of self-incrimination, because, he cannot supply answers or whisper hints or otherwise interfere with the course of questioning except to intercept where intimidatory tactics are tried and to caution his client where incrimination is attempted and to insist on questions and answers being noted where objections are not otherwise fully appreciated. The lawyer cannot harangue the police, but may help his client and complain on his behalf. The police also need not wait for more than a reasonable time for the advocate's arrival.

(b) Where a lawyer of his choice is not available, after the examination of the accused, the police officer must take him to a magistrate, a doctor or other willing and responsible non-partisan official or non-official and allow a secluded audience where he may unburden himself beyond the view of the police and tell whether he has suffered duress, in which case he should be transferred to judicial or other custody where the police cannot reach him. The collocutor communicate the relevant conversation to the nearest magistrate.

The object of the criminal law process is to find out the truth and not to shield the accused from the consequences of his wrongdoing. A defense lawyer has to conduct the trial on the basis of the materials lawfully collected in the course of investigation.

Obligation of Judge to Provide Lawyer to Accused on account of Poverty

The right to free legal services is, therefore, clearly an essential ingredient of "reasonable, fair and just", procedure for a person accused of an offence and it must be held implicit in the guarantee of Article 21. This is a constitutional right of every accused person who is unable to engage a lawyer and secure legal services on account of reasons such as POVERTY, indigence or incommunicado situation and the State is under a mandate to provide a lawyer to an accused person if the circumstances of the case and the needs of justice so require, provided of course the accused person does not object to the provision of such lawyer. When the under-trial prisoners, charged with bailable offences, are produced before the Magistrates, the State Government should provide them a lawyer at its own cost for the purpose of making an application for bail, provided that no objection is raised to such lawyer on behalf of such under-trial prisoners and if any application for bail is made, the Magistrates should dispose of the same in accordance with the broad outlines set out.

Moreover, this constitutional obligation to provide free legal services to an indigent accused[8] does not arise only when the trial commences but also attaches when the accused is for the first time produced before the magistrate. It is elementary that the jeopardy to his personal liberty arises as soon as a person is arrested and produced before a magistrate, for it is at that stage that he gets the first opportunity to apply for bail and obtain his release as also to resist remand to police or jail custody. That is the stage at which an accused person needs competent legal advice and representation and no procedure can be said to be reasonable, fair and just which denies legal advice and representation to him at this stage. State is under a constitutional obligation to provide free legal services to an indigent accused not only at the stage of trial but also at the stage when he is first produced before the magistrate as also when he is remanded from time to time.

But even this right to free legal services would be illusory for an indigent accused unless the Magistrate or the Sessions Judge before whom he is produced informs him of such right....

...The Magistrate or the Sessions Judge before whom the accused appears must be held to be under an obligation to inform the accused that if he is unable to engage the services of a lawyer on account of POVERTY or indigence, he is entitled to obtain free legal services at the cost of the State....

8 **Meaning of Accused:** A person charged with a criminal offense, or the state of being so charged

Rarest of Rare Cases (Constitutional Validity of Death Penalty)[9] :

The kind of cases in which protection to life may be withdrawn and there may be the demand for death penalty were enumerated in the following paragraphs:

... It may do so "in rarest of rare cases" when its collective conscience is so shocked that it will expect the holders of the judicial power centre to inflict death penalty irrespective of their personal opinion as regards desirability or otherwise of retaining death penalty. The community may entertain such a sentiment when the crime is viewed from the platform of the motive for, or the manner of commission of the crime, or the anti-social or abhorrent nature of the crime, such as for instance:

1. Manner of commission of murder

When the murder is committed in an extremely brutal, grotesque, diabolical, revolting or dastardly manner so as to arouse intense and extreme indignation of the community. For instance,

(i) when the house of the victim is set aflame with the end in view to roast him alive in the house.

(ii) when the victim is subjected to inhuman acts of torture or cruelty in order to bring about his or her death.

(iii) when the body of the victim is cut into pieces or his body is dismembered in a fiendish manner.

II. Motive for commission of murder

When the murder is committed for a motive which evinces total depravity and meanness. For instance when (a) a hired assassin commits murder for the sake of money or reward (b) a cold-blooded murder is committed with a deliberate design in order to inherit property or to gain control over property of a ward or a person under the control of the murderer or vis-à-vis whom the murderer is in a dominating position or in a position of trust, or (c) a murder is committed in the course for betrayal of the motherland.

III. Anti-social or socially abhorrent nature of the crime

(a) When murder of a member of a Scheduled Caste or minority community,

9 *Bachan Singh v. State of Punjab* (1980) 2 SCC 684

etc., is committed not for personal reasons but in circumstances which arouse social wrath. For instance when such a crime is committed in order to terrorise such persons and frighten them into fleeing from a place or in order to deprive them of, or make them surrender, lands or benefits conferred on them with a view to reverse past injustices and in order to restore the social balance.

(b) In cases of "bride burning" and what are known as "dowry deaths" or when murder is committed in order to remarry for the sake of extracting dowry once again or to marry another woman on account of infatuation.

IV. Magnitude of crime

When the crime is enormous in proportion. For instance when multiple murders say of all or almost all the members of a family or a large number of persons of a particular caste, community, or locality, are committed.

V. Personality of victim of murder

When the victim of murder is (a) an innocent child who could not have or has not provided even an excuse, much less a provocation, for murder (b) a helpless woman or a person rendered helpless by old age or infirmity (c) when the victim is a person vis-à-vis whom the murderer is in a position of domination or trust (d) when the victim is a public figure generally loved and respected by the community for the services rendered by him and the murder is committed for political or similar reasons other than personal reasons.

The above principles are generally regarded by Court as the broad guidelines for imposition of death sentence and have been followed by the Court in many subsequent decisions.

Decision by Court:

Court held that the right to access to legal aid, to consult and to be defended by a legal practitioner, arises when a person arrested in connection with a cognizable offence is first produced before a magistrate. It is the duty and obligation of the magistrate before whom a person accused of committing a cognizable offence is first produced to make him fully aware that it is his right to consult and be defended by a legal practitioner and, in case he has no means (POVERTY) to engage a lawyer of his choice, that one would be provided to him from legal aid at the expense of the State. The right flows from Articles 21 and 22(1) of the Constitution and needs to be strictly enforced.

Court also held that this case has element of waging war against the Government of India and the magnitude of the war is of a degree as in no other case and the Appellant is convicted on the charge, among others, of waging war against the Government of India. The case has shocked the collective conscience of the Indian people as few other cases have. The offences committed by the Appellant (Kasab) show a degree of cruelty, brutality and depravity as in very few other cases.

In short, this is a case of terrorist attack from across the border. It has a magnitude of unprecedented enormity on all scales. The conspiracy behind the attack was as deep and large as it was vicious. The preparation and training for the execution was as thorough as the execution was ruthless. In terms of loss of life and property, and more importantly in its traumatizing effect, this case stands alone, or it is at least the very rarest of rare to come before this Court since the birth of the Republic. Therefore, it should also attract the rarest of rare punishment. Putting the matter once again quite simply, in this country death as a penalty has been held be be Constitutionally valid, though it is indeed to be awarded in the "rarest of rare cases when the alternative option (of life sentence) is unquestionably foreclosed". Now, as long as the death penalty remains on the statute book as punishment for certain offences, including "waging war" and murder, it logically follows that there must be some cases, howsoever rare or one in a million, that would call for inflicting that penalty. Court awarded Death penalty to Appellant (Kasab).

17

Under trial Prisoners in Jails due to Poverty[1]

Facts in Nutshell:

Public interest litigation[2] filed by member of the A.P. Legislative Assembly seeking for issue of habeas corpus[3] directing the State to forthwith set at liberty the undertrial prisoners in the State of A.P. The petitioner both as a citizen and as a public servant is concerned about the human tragedy and misery of unfortunate persons who are languishing in prison for the past several years. They exceed more than 6000 unfortunate helpless innocent poor people. These undertrial prisoners have already undergone imprisonment which is more than the maximum punishment that a law Court can inflict upon them any further detention these people in prisons is utterly unconstitutional, devoid of legality, totally unjustifiable, constitutionally immoral, statutorily indefensible and highly barbarous. The State unfortunately has become immunized and is impervious to either constitutional niceties or legal imperatives which constitute utter negation of rule of law and basic tenets of a civilised constitutionalism apart from violating the constitutional guarantees and

1 Appellants: **Nallapareddy Prasanna Kumar Reddy Vs.**Respondent: **State of Andhra Pradesh and Ors.**
1994CriLJ2016
Hon'ble Judges: M.N. Rao and P. Ramakrishnam Raju, JJ.

2 **Public-Interest Litigation** is litigation for the protection of the public interest. In Indian law, **Article 32** of the Indian constitution contains a tool which directly joints the public with judiciary. PIL may be introduced in a court of law by the court itself (*suo motu*), rather than the aggrieved party or another third party. For the exercise of the court's jurisdiction, it is unnecessary for the victim of the violation of his or her rights to personally approach the court. In PIL, the right to file suit is given to a member of the public by the courts through judicial activism. The member of the public may be a non-governmental organization (NGO), an institution or an individual. The Supreme Court of India, rejecting the criticism of judicial activism, has stated that the judiciary has stepped in to give direction due to executive inaction; laws enacted by Parliament and the state legislatures for the poor since independence have not been properly implemented.

3 A writ of ***habeas corpus*** is a writ (legal action) that requires a person under arrest to be brought before a judge or into court. The principle of habeas corpus ensures that a prisoner can be released from unlawful detention—that is, detention lacking sufficient cause or evidence. The remedy can be sought by the prisoner or by another person coming to the prisoner's aid. This right originated in the English legal system, and is now available in many nations. It has historically been an important legal instrument safeguarding individual freedom against arbitrary state action.

mandate contained in Articles 14[4], 19[5] and 21 of the Constitution of India[6].

Arrest and Custody

Article 21 of Constitution guarantees personal liberty and nobody shall be deprived of the same except in accordance with the procedure established by law. Criminal Civil Procedure Code is the main procedure Code for arrest and custody. The procedure prescribed by the Criminal

4 **Article 14 in The Constitution Of India 1949**
14. Equality before law The State shall not deny to any person equality before the law or the equal protection of the laws within the territory of India Prohibition of discrimination on grounds of religion, race, caste, sex or place of birth

5 **Article 19 in The Constitution Of India 1949**
19. Protection of certain rights regarding freedom of speech etc
(1) All citizens shall have the right
(a) to freedom of speech and expression;
(b) to assemble peaceably and without arms;
(c) to form associations or unions;
(d) to move freely throughout the territory of India;
(e) to reside and settle in any part of the territory of India; and
(f) omitted
(g) to practise any profession, or to carry on any occupation, trade or business
(2) Nothing in sub clause (a) of clause (1) shall affect the operation of any existing law, or prevent the State from making any law, in so far as such law imposes reasonable restrictions on the exercise of the right conferred by the said sub clause in the interests of the sovereignty and integrity of India, the security of the State, friendly relations with foreign States, public order, decency or morality or in relation to contempt of court, defamation or incitement to an offence
(3) Nothing in sub clause (b) of the said clause shall affect the operation of any existing law in so far as it imposes, or prevent the State from making any law imposing, in the interests of the sovereignty and integrity of India or public order, reasonable restrictions on the exercise of the right conferred by the said sub clause
(4) Nothing in sub clause (c) of the said clause shall affect the operation of any existing law in so far as it imposes, or prevent the State from making any law imposing, in the interests of the sovereignty and integrity of India or public order or morality, reasonable restrictions on the exercise of the right conferred by the said sub clause
(5) Nothing in sub clauses (d) and (e) of the said clause shall affect the operation of any existing law in so far as it imposes, or prevent the State from making any law imposing, reasonable restrictions on the exercise of any of the rights conferred by the said sub clauses either in the interests of the general public or for the protection of the interests of any Scheduled Tribe
(6) Nothing in sub clause (g) of the said clause shall affect the operation of any existing law in so far as it imposes, or prevent the State from making any law imposing, in the interests of the general public, reasonable restrictions on the exercise of the right conferred by the said sub clause, and, in particular, nothing in the said sub clause shall affect the operation of any existing law in so far as it relates to, or prevent the State from making any law relating to,
(i) the professional or technical qualifications necessary for practising any profession or carrying on any occupation, trade or business, or
(ii) the carrying on by the State, or by a corporation owned or controlled by the State, of any trade, business, industry or service, whether to the exclusion, complete or partial, of citizens or otherwise

6 **Article 21 in The Constitution Of India 1949**
21. Protection of life and personal liberty No person shall be deprived of his life or personal liberty except according to procedure established by law

Procedure Code has to be tested on the bed rock of Constitution and as long as the said procedure is not unconstitutional, it has to be followed without exception. So it has to be seen whether the provisions of Criminal Procedure Code with reference to arrest and custody are fair, just and reasonable. Section 57, Cr.P.C.[7] contemplates that any person accused of an offence shall be produced before the nearest Magistrate within 24 hours of his arrest. This procedure is prescribed in accordance with the mandate contained in Article 22 of the Constitution of India[8]. When the investigation could not be completed within the period of 24 hours as fixed by Section 57, Cr.P.C., the Magistrate may authorise the detention of the accused in such custody for a term not exceeding 15 days whether

7 **Section 57, CrPc, 1973:**
57. Person arrested not to be detained more than twenty-four hours
No police officer shall detain in custody a person arrested without warrant for a longer period than under all the circumstances of the case is reasonable, and such period shall not, in the absence of a special order of a Magistrate under section 167, exceed twenty-four hours exclusive of the time necessary for the journey from the place of arrest to the Magistrate's Court

8 **Article 22 in The Constitution Of India 1949**
22. Protection against arrest and detention in certain cases
(1) No person who is arrested shall be detained in custody without being informed, as soon as may be, of the grounds for such arrest nor shall he be denied the right to consult, and to be defended by, a legal practitioner of his choice
(2) Every person who is arrested and detained in custody shall be produced before the nearest magistrate within a period of twenty four hours of such arrest excluding the time necessary for the journey from the place of arrest to the court of the magistrate and no such person shall be detained in custody beyond the said period without the authority of a magistrate
(3) Nothing in clauses (1) and (2) shall apply (a) to any person who for the time being is an enemy alien; or (b) to any person who is arrested or detained under any law providing for preventive detention
(4) No law providing for preventive detention shall authorise the detention of a person for a longer period than three months unless (a) an Advisory Board consisting of persons who are, or have been, or are qualified to be appointed as, Judges of a High Court has reported before the expiration of the said period of three months that there is in its opinion sufficient cause for such detention:
(5) When any person is detained in pursuance of an order made under any law providing for preventive detention, the authority making the order shall, as soon as may be, communicate to such person the grounds on which the order has been made and shall afford him the earliest opportunity of making a representation against the order
(6) Nothing in clause (5) shall require the authority making any such order as is referred to in that clause to disclose facts which such authority considers to be against the public interest to disclose
(7) Parliament may by law prescribe
(a) the circumstances under which, and the class or classes of cases in which, a person may be detained for a period longer than three months under any law providing for preventive detention without obtaining the opinion of an Advisory Board in accordance with the provisions of sub clause (a) of clause (4);
(b) the maximum period for which any person may in any class or classes of cases be detained under any law providing for preventive detention; and
(c) the procedure to be followed by an Advisory Board in an inquiry under sub clause (a) of clause (4) Right against Exploitation

he has jurisdiction to try the case or not as per Section 167, Cr.P.C[9]. He may authorise the detention of the accused beyond the period of 15 days if he is satisfied that adequate grounds exist for doing so but he shall not authorise the detention of the accused for a total period exceeding 90 days, where the investigation relates to an offence punishable with death, imprisonment for life or imprisonment for a term not less than 10 years and 60 days where the investigation relates to any other offence. The Criminal Procedure Code is silent as to the period within which the trial of a case or a particular class of cases should be closed or completed presumably it is not possible to fix up any time frame for any case or class of cases as it would depend upon several circumstances.

Under trial Prisoners in Jails due to Poverty should be released

In *Hussainara Khatoon v. State of Bihar*[10] the Supreme Court gave guidelines for release of the accused from custody. Newspaper report published in "Indian Express" was the basis for the decision. The report showed several hundreds of prisoners are languishing in Bihar jails. The State has not filed counter-affidavit denying the allegations. The Court, therefore, had treated the allegations as true and decided the case on that basis. While considering this question the Supreme Court laid down the principle that speedy trial is an essential part of Article 21 of the Constitution. In appropriate cases, the Court observed that the undertrial prisoners languishing in jails for long period should be released on taking personal bonds. The factors that should be taken into consideration by the Court for granting such released are also mentioned by the Court. Accordingly the Supreme Court gave directions to Bihar Government to scrutinise the cases of undertrial prisoners charged with

9 **Section 167, CrPc, 1973:**

167. Procedure when investigation cannot be completed in twenty-four hours

(1) Whenever any person is arrested and detained in custody, and it appears that the investigation cannot be completed within the period of twenty-four hours fixed by section 57, and there are grounds for believing that the accusation or information is well-founded, the officer in charge of the police station or the police officer making the
investigation, if he is not below the rank of sub-inspector, shall forthwith transmit to the nearest Judicial Magistrate a copy of the entries in the diary hereinafter prescribed relating to the case, and shall at the same time forward the accused to such Magistrate

(2) The Magistrate to whom an accused person is forwarded under this section may, whether he has or has not jurisdiction to try the case, from time to time, authorise the detention of the accused in such custody as such Magistrate thinks fit, a term not exceeding fifteen days in the whole; and if he has no jurisdiction to try the case or commit it for trial, and considers further detention unnecessary, he may order the accused to be forwarded to a Magistrate having such jurisdiction

10 1979CriLJ1036

offences of punishable with fine only or punishable with imprisonment for a term not exceeding one year or punishable with imprisonment for a term exceeding one year but not exceeding three years and release such of them who are not liable to be proceeded against by reason of period of limitation being expired. The Supreme Court further directed that this exercise shall be carried out within a period of six weeks from the date of receipt of the order. Therefore, where the undertrial prisoners have been in jail for longer periods than the maximum term they would have been sentenced if convicted, their detention in jail is violative of Article 21 and therefore, they have to be released forthwith.

The undertrial prisoners who are in jail for periods longer than the term of the imprisonment for which they could be sentenced if convicted, could not apply for bail **DUE TO POVERT** and if the Court in those cases is of the opinion that they are entitled to bail in the normal circumstances, their applications for bail should not be opposed and they should be released. A duty is cast as per the Supreme Court on the Magistrate when an under trial prisoner is produced for remand under section 167, Cr.P.C. before making an order to further remand, he should inform the undertrial prisoner that he is entitled to be released on bail.

Decision of the Court

Court directed the state to release under trial prisoners who are languishing in jails because they have no means to apply for Bail.

18

Due to Poverty most people can't approach the Court[1]

Ratio Decidendi[2] : "Rule of locus standi[3] in field of public interest litigation[4] does not give any right to busybody or meddlesome interloper[5] to approach Court under guise of public interest litigation."

Facts in Nutshell:

The petitioner[6] filed the writ petition[7] styled as "Public Interest Litigation", assailing the appointment of the respondent[8] as AYUSH Doctors on the

---

1 Appellants: **Shri Yunman Lokendro Singh Vs.** Respondent: **State of Manipur and Ors.** 2010(2)GLD74
Hon'ble Judges: T. NK. Singh and B.K. Singh, JJ.

2 **Meaning of Ration Decidendi:** ***Ratio decidendi*** is a Latin phrase meaning "the reason" or "the rationale for the decision." The *ratio decidendi* is "the point in a case which determines the judgment" or "the principle which the case establishes."

3 **Meaning of Locus Standi:** The right of a party to appear and be heard before a court

4 **Public-Interest Litigation** is litigation for the protection of the public interest. In Indian law, **Article 32** of the Indian constitution contains a tool which directly joints the public with judiciary. PIL may be introduced in a court of law by the court itself (*suo motu*), rather than the aggrieved party or another third party. For the exercise of the court's jurisdiction, it is unnecessary for the victim of the violation of his or her rights to personally approach the court. In PIL, the right to file suit is given to a member of the public by the courts through judicial activism. The member of the public may be a non-governmental organization (NGO), an institution or an individual. The Supreme Court of India, rejecting the criticism of judicial activism, has stated that the judiciary has stepped in to give direction due to executive inaction; laws enacted by Parliament and the state legislatures for the poor since independence have not been properly implemented.

5 **Meaning of Interloper:** One that interferes with the affairs of others, often for selfish reasons; a meddler.

6 **Meaning of Petitioner:** A person who presents a Petition. (**Meaning of Petition:** A formal message requesting something that is submitted to an authority)

7 **Meaning of Writ Petition:** Under the Indian legal system, jurisdiction to issue prerogative writs is given to the Supreme Court, and to the High Courts of Judicature of all Indian states. Parts of the law relating to writs are set forth in the Constitution of India. The Supreme Court, the highest in the country, may issue writs under Article 32 of the Constitution for enforcement of Fundamental Rights and under Articles 139 for enforcement of rights other than Fundamental Rights, while High Courts, the superior courts of the States, may issue writs under Articles 226. 'Writ' is eminently designed by the makers of the Constitution, and in the same way it is developed very widely and efficiently by the courts in India. The Constitution broadly provides for five kinds of "prerogative" writs, namely, Habeas Corpus, Certiorari, Mandamus, Quo Warranto and Prohibition.

8 **Meaning of Respondent:**
A **respondent** is a person who is called upon to issue a response to a communication made by

grounds that the respondent have not fulfilled the requisite qualifications inasmuch as they have not completed the compulsory rotating internship of one year after passing the final BHMS examination.

Question before the Court

The question, which falls for consideration, is whether or not the writ petition, styled as 'Public Interest Litigation', filed by the petitioner assailing the appointment of the respondent as AYUSH Doctors by the respondent is a 'Public Interest Litigation'.

Guidelines to be followed for entertaining letters/petitions received in Court as public interest litigation.

No petition involving individual/personal matter shall be entertained as a PIL matter except as indicated hereinafter. Letters/Petitions falling under the following categories alone will originally be entertained as Public Interest Litigation:

1. Bonded Labour matters.
2. Neglected children.
3. Non-payment of minimum wages to workers and exploitation of casual workers and complaints of violation of Labour Laws (except in individual cases).
4. Petitions from Jails complaining of harassment, for premature release and seeking release after having completed 14 years in Jail, death in Jail, release on personal bond, speedy trial as a right.
5. Petitions against police for refusing to register a case, harassment by police and death in police custody.
6. Petitions against atrocities on women, in particular harassment of bride, bride-burning, rape, murder, kidnapping etc.
7. Petitions complaining of harassment or torture of villagers by co-villagers or by police from persons belonging to Scheduled Castes and Scheduled Tribes and economically backward classes.

---

another. In legal usage, this specifically refers to the defendant in a legal proceeding commenced by a petition, or to an appellee, or the opposing party, in an appeal of a decision by an initial fact-finder.

8. Petitions pertaining to environment pollution, disturbances of ecological balance, drugs and food adulteration, maintenance of heritage and culture, antiques, forest and wild life and other matters of public importance.

9. Petitions from plot-victims.

10. Family pension.

Cases falling under the following categories will not be entertained as public interest litigation and these may be returned to the petitioner or filed in the PIL Cell. As the case may be:

1) Landlord-Tenant matters.

2) Service matter and those pertaining to pension and Gratuity.

3) Complaints against Central/State Government Deptts. and local Bodies except those relating to item Nos. (1) to (10) above.

4) Admission to medical and other educational institution.

5) Petitions for early hearing of cases pending in High Courts and Subordinate Courts.

In regard to the petitions concerning maintenance' of the wife, children and parents, the petitioner may be asked to file petition under Section 125, Code of Criminal Procedure or a suit in the Court of competent jurisdiction and for that purpose to approach the nearest Legal Aid Committee for legal aid and advice.

Public Interest Litigation

Public interest litigation is not in the nature of adversary litigation but it is a challenge and an opportunity to the government and its officers to make basic human rights meaningful to the deprived and vulnerable sections of the community and to assure them social and economic justice which is the signature tune of our Constitution. The Government and its officers must welcome public interest litigation because it would provide them an occasion to examine whether the poor and the down-trodden are getting their social and economic entitlements or whether they are continuing to remain victims of deception and exploitation at the hands of strong and powerful sections of the community and whether social and economic justice has become a meaningful reality for them or it has remained merely a teasing allusion and a promise of unreality, so that in case the complaint in the public interest litigation is found to be true, they can in discharge of their constitutional obligation root out exploitation and injustice and ensure to the; weaker sections their rights and entitlements.

Before admitting the PIL, the Court has to be satisfied about : (a) the credentials of the applicant; (b) the prima facie correctness or nature of information given by him; and (c) the information being not vague and indefinite. The information should show the gravity and seriousness involved. There must be real and genuine public interest involved in the litigation and concrete or credible basis for maintaining a cause before Court and not merely an adventure of knight errant borne out of wishful thinking and the credibility of such claims or litigations should be adjudged on the creditworthiness of the materials averred and not even on the credentials claimed of the person moving the Courts in such cases. Further, in admitting the PIL, the Court has to strike a balance between two conflicting interests.

In *Dattaraj Nathuji Thaware v. State of Maharashtra and Ors.*[9], observed that when there is material to show that a petition styled as public interest litigation is nothing but a camouflage to foster personal disputes, the said petition is to be thrown out. Public interest litigation which has now come to occupy an important field in the administration of law should not be "publicity interest litigation" or "private interest litigation" or "politics interest litigation", or the latest trend "paisa income litigation."

Due to Poverty Most People Can't approach the Court

The origin and evolution of Public Interest Litigation in India emanated from realization of constitutional obligation by the Judiciary towards the vast sections of the society-the poor and the marginalized sections of the society. This jurisdiction has been created and carved out by the judicial creativity and craftsmanship. In *M.C. Mehta and Anr. v. Union of India* and[10], Court observed that Article 32 of the constitution[11] does not

9 2005 (1) SCC 590

10 AIR 1987 SC 1086

11 **Article 32 in The Constitution Of India 1949**
32. Remedies for enforcement of rights conferred by this Part
(1) The right to move the Supreme Court by appropriate proceedings for the enforcement of the rights conferred by this Part is guaranteed
(2) The Supreme Court shall have power to issue directions or orders or writs, including writs in the nature of habeas corpus, mandamus, prohibition, quo warranto and certiorari, whichever may be appropriate, for the enforcement of any of the rights conferred by this Part

merely confer power on Court to issue direction, order or writ for the enforcement of fundamental rights. Instead, it also lays a constitutional obligation on this Court to protect the fundamental rights of the people. The Court asserted that, in realization of this constitutional obligation, "it has all incidental and ancillary powers including the power to forge new remedies and fashion new strategies designed to enforce the fundamental rights". The Court realized that because of extreme **POVERTY**, a large number of sections of society cannot approach the Court. The fundamental rights have no meaning for them and in order to preserve and protect the fundamental rights of the marginalized section of society by judicial innovation, the Courts by judicial innovation and creativity started giving necessary directions and passing orders in the public interest.

Directions of the Court to preserve the purity and sanctity of PIL:

(1) The Courts must encourage genuine and bona fide PIL and effectively discourage and curb the PIL filed for extraneous considerations.

(2) Instead of every individual Judge devising his own procedure for dealing with the public interest litigation, it would be appropriate for each High Court to properly formulate rules for encouraging the genuine PIL and discouraging the PIL filed with oblique motives. Consequently, we request that the High Courts who have not yet framed the rules, should frame the rules within three months. The Registrar General of each High Court is directed to ensure that a copy of the Rules prepared by the High Court is sent to the Secretary General of this Court immediately thereafter.

(3) The Courts should prima facie verify the credentials of the petitioner before entertaining a PIL.

(4) The Court should be prima facie satisfied regarding the correctness of the contents of the petition before entertaining a PIL.

(5) The Court should be fully satisfied that substantial public interest is involved before entertaining the petition.

---

(3) Without prejudice to the powers conferred on the Supreme Court by clause (1) and (2), Parliament may by law empower any other court to exercise within the local limits of its jurisdiction all or any of the powers exercisable by the Supreme Court under clause (2)

(4) The right guaranteed by this article shall not be suspended except as otherwise provided for by this Constitution

(6) The Court should ensure that the petition which involves larger public interest, gravity and urgency must be given priority over other petitions.

(7) The Courts before entertaining the PIL should ensure that the PIL is aimed at redressal of genuine public harm or public injury. The Court should also ensure that there is no personal gain, private motive or oblique motive behind filing the public interest litigation.

(8) The Court should also ensure that the petitions filed by busybodies for extraneous and ulterior motives must be discouraged by imposing exemplary costs or by adopting similar novel methods to curb frivolous petitions and the petitions filed for extraneous considerations.

Decision of the Court:

Court held that the petition, falling under 'service matters', cannot be treated as 'public interest litigation' and imposed exemplary costs of Rs 2,000 on the petitioner.

19

Free Copy of Judgment to accused on Account of Poverty[1]

Facts in Nutshell:

Application filed by Anil Kumar Biswas for a copy of judgment of acquittal[2] passed by Court in exercise of its criminal revisional jurisdiction. The applicant was convicted under Section 409, I. P. C.[3] and his conviction was upheld on appeal[4]. On revision[5] however that conviction was set aside and the applicant was acquitted.

Section 371 of the Code of Criminal Procedure

"Under the provisions of Section 371 of the Code of Criminal Procedure the accused is entitled to the copy free of cost." In view of Sections 424

---

1 Appellants: **Anil Kumar Biswas Vs.** Respondent: **The State**
AIR1954Cal29
Hon'ble Judges: Guha Ray and Debabrata Mookerjee, JJ.

2 **Meaning of Acquittal:** In the common law tradition, an **acquittal** formally certifies that the accused is free from the charge of an offense, as far as the criminal law is concerned.

3 **Section 409 in The Indian Penal Code, 1860**
409. Criminal breach of trust by public servant, or by banker, merchant or agent.-- Whoever, being in any manner entrusted with property, or with any dominion over property in his capacity of a public servant or in the way of his business as a banker, merchant, factor, broker, attorney or agent, commits criminal breach of trust in respect of that property, shall be punished with [imprisonment for life], or with imprisonment of either description for a term which may extend to ten years, and shall also be liable to fine.

4 **Meaning of Appeal:** In law, an **appeal** is a process for requesting a formal change to an official decision. Very broadly speaking there are appeals on the record and *de novo* appeals. In *de novo* appeals, a new decision maker re-hears the case without any reference to the prior decision maker. In appeals on the record, the decision of the prior decision maker is challenged by arguing that he or she misapplied the law, came to an incorrect factual finding, acted in excess of his jurisdiction, abused his powers, was biased, considered evidence which he should not have considered or failed to consider evidence that he should have considered.

5 **Section 115 CPC, 1908**
Revision
The High Court may call for the record of an case which has been decided by any Court subordinate to such High Court and in which no appeal lies thereto and if such subordinate Court appears
(a) to have exercised a jurisdiction not vested in it by law, or
(b) to have failed to exercise a jurisdiction so vested, or
(c) to have acted in the exercise of its jurisdiction illegally or with material irregularity, the High Court may make such order in the case as it thinks fit

and 371, Cr. P. C. the accused was not entitled as a matter of right to a free copy but Section 548 entitled the court to allow a copy free of cost at its own discretion and in that case a copy was allowed free of cost.

Section 548 of the Code Criminal Procedure

Section 548 Cr.PC provides a complete answer. Section 548, is much wider in its scope than either 371 or 424; because, in the first place, it entitles any person affected by a judgment or order passed by a criminal court which includes, of course, the accused in a criminal case, to have a copy of the judgment, charge to the jury or of any order or deposition or other part of the record of which he wants to have a copy. Thus Section 548 entitled any such party to have a copy of not merely the judgment but also of other parts of the record including any other order or deposition.

Decision of the Court (Free Copy of Judgment to accused on account of Poverty):

Court held that Section 548 Cr.P.C gives the court enough discretion in the matter to grant a copy free of costs whenever it thinks fit to do so for any reasons specially to be recorded. The applicant Said the cost of the copy is likely to be pretty heavy and in any event it is too heavy for him because he is poor. That he is too poor to be able to pay for a copy, Court readily believed, because he was under suspension for a long time and then discharged. Court under Section 548, Cr. P. C. allowed a free copy to be granted to the applicant on the ground of his poverty.

20

Free Legal assistance to accused if he cannot hire a lawyer on account of Poverty[1]

Ratio Decidendi[2]: "Judicial authority has obligation to inform accused of his fundamental right[3] of free legal assistance if he cannot hire lawyer."

Facts in Nutshell:

Traffic Superintendent of the Flying Squad of the Madhya Pradesh State Road Transport Corporation, Bhopal checked the bus bearing registration No. CPF 9128 when it was on its way to Dhar. He found that the petitioner[4] was the conductor in the bus and he had collected fare to the tune of Rs. 17/- from the passengers and despite having covered a distance of 10 Kilometres he had not issued tickets to them. He, therefore, filed a complaint before the Special Magistrate, who was holding mobile Court. On his plea of guilty, the petitioner was convicted and sentenced

1 Appellants: **Hiralal Gopilal Rathore Vs.** Respondent: **M.P. State and Anr.** 1988CriLJ457
Hon'ble Judges: K.L. Shrivastava, Judge

2 **Meaning of Ration Decidendi:** ***Ratio decidendi*** is a Latin phrase meaning "the reason" or "the rationale for the decision." The *ratio decidendi* is "the point in a case which determines the judgment" or "the principle which the case establishes."

3 ***'Part III – Fundamental Rights'*** is a charter of rights contained in the Constitution of India. It guarantees civil liberties such that all Indians can lead their lives in peace and harmony as citizens of India. These include individual rights common to most liberal democracies, such asequality before law, freedom of speech and expression, and peaceful assembly, freedom to practice religion, and the right to constitutional remedies for the protection of civil rights by means of writs such as habeas corpus. Violation of these rights result in punishments as prescribed in the Indian Penal Code or other special laws, subject to discretion of the judiciary. The Fundamental Rights are defined as basichuman freedoms which every Indian citizen has the right to enjoy for a proper and harmonious development of personality. These rights universally apply to all citizens, irrespective of race, place of birth, religion, caste, creed, colour or gender. Aliens (persons who are not citizens) are also considered in matters like equality before law. They are enforceable by the courts, subject to certain restrictions. The Rights have their origins in many sources, including England's Bill of Rights, the United States Bill of Rights and France's Declaration of the Rights of Man.

4 **Meaning of Petitioner:** A person who presents a Petition. (**Meaning of Petition:** A formal message requesting something that is submitted to an authority)

by the learned Magistrate. The petitioner made a revision petition[5] to the Sessions Judge, Indore, who negatived the various contentions by the petitioner's learned Counsel and ultimately, dismissed the revision petition.

In other petition by Mehmood Khan, another conductor in the employment of the M.P. State Road Transport Corporation, his bus was checked he too was found to have committed an offence under the same penal provision and on his plea of guilty was convicted by the Judicial Magistrate First Class, Indore, in a summary trial and was sentenced to pay a fine of Rs. 100/-. The revision petition preferred by him was also dismissed.

Article 21 of the Constitution and Right to Free Legal Service[6] to accused on Account of Poverty

Article 21 of the Constitution, as interpreted in the decision in Suk Das's case[7] , the petitioner's had a fundamental right to free legal service and the learned Magistrate was under an obligation towards them to inform them regarding the availability of such aid at State cost and as this was not done, there has been violation of their fundamental right and the trials held against them are vitiated due to fatal constitutional infirmity.

Court in Hussainara Khatoon's case[8] held that 'the right to free legal service is...clearly an essential ingredient of reasonable, fair and just procedure for a person accused of an offence and it must be held to be constitutional right of every accused person, who is unable to engage a lawyer and secure legal services on account of reasons such as **POVERTY**, indigence or incommunicado situation and the State is under a mandate to provide lawyer to an accused person if the circumstances of the case and the needs of justice so require, provided, of course, the accused person does not object to the provision of such lawyer.'

It is now settled law that free legal assistance at State cost is a fundamental right of a person accused of an offence, which may involve jeopardy to

5 **Meaning of Petition:** A formal message requesting something that is submitted to an authority

6 **Article 39 A Constitution of India, 1950**
Equal Justice and Free Legal Aid
39A. The State shall secure that the operation of the legal system promotes justice, on a basis of equal opportunity, and shall, in particular, provide free legal aid, by suitable legislation or schemes or in any other way, to ensure that opportunities for securing justice are not denied to any citizen by reason of economic or other disabilities.

7 1986CriLJ1084

8 1979CriLJ1045

his life or personal liberty and this fundamental right is implicit in the requirement of reasonable, fair and just procedure prescribed by Article 21. Of course, it must be recognized that there may be cases involving offences, such as economic offences or offences against law prohibiting prostitution or child abuse and the like, where social justice may require that free legal service may not be provided by the State. There can, in the circumstances, be no doubt that the appellants[9] were entitled to free legal assistance at State cost when they were placed in peril of their personal liberty by reason of being accused of an of fence, which if proved, would clearly entail imprisonment for a term of two years.

In *Khatri v. State of Bihar*[10] court ruled that the Magistrate or the Sessions Judge, before whom an accused appears must be held to be under an obligation to inform the accused that if he is unable to engage the service of a lawyer on account of **POVERTY** or indigence, he is entitled to obtain free legal services at the cost of the State.

It is clear that the obligation on the part of the Presiding Officers to inform the accused of his fundamental right of free legal assistance at State cost in case he is unable to engage the service of a lawyer on account of **POVERTY** or indigence, is absolute and is not conditioned upon the accused himself applying for such legal assistance.

Decision of the Court:

Court held that there was a clear case of contravention of the fundamental right under Article 21 of the Constitution. The conviction and sentence of each of the petitioners were set aside. The cases are remanded to the trial court for disposal according to law

9 **Meaning of Appellant:** A person who, dissatisfied with the judgment rendered in a lawsuit decided in a lower court or the findings from a proceeding before an Administrative Agency, asks a superior court to review the decision.

10 1981CriLJ597

21

Poor People Telegram to court will be treated as Public Interest Litigation[1]

Facts in Nutshell:

Petition[2] was registered on a telegram received by the Chief Justice issued by a Advocate. The contains of the telegram are that Vaiyapuri, son of Govindaswamy, aged 18 years was forcibly taken by the Inspector of Police. It was stated that the life of the petitioner is in stake and relatives are not allowed to feed him. The Chief Justice was requested to intervene and save life of the petitioner.

Telegrams treated as Public Interest Litigations[3]

It was seen that the telegrams are treated as Public Interest Litigations by the P.I.L. Cell of the High Courts and registered as writ petitioners[4] by the Registry of the High Court. On such registration, the Legal Aid Centre is requested to nominate a lawyer for conducting the case on behalf of the petitioner if the telegrams have been sent by persons other than lawyers. If the senders of the telegrams are advocates, they are themselves treated as counsel in the case and their names are printed in the cause list.

---

1 Appellants: **M.G. Shivaraj Vs.** Respondent: **Inspector of Police, Thuraipakkam Police Station** 1994CriLJ1770
Hon'ble Judge: M. Srinivasan and Thangamani, JJ.

2 **Meaning of Petition**: A formal written application requesting a court for a specific judicial action

3 **Public-Interest Litigation** is litigation for the protection of the public interest. In Indian law, **Article 32** of the Indian constitution contains a tool which directly joints the public with judiciary. PIL may be introduced in a court of law by the court itself (*suo motu*), rather than the aggrieved party or another third party. For the exercise of the court's jurisdiction, it is unnecessary for the victim of the violation of his or her rights to personally approach the court. In PIL, the right to file suit is given to a member of the public by the courts through judicial activism. The member of the public may be a non-governmental organization (NGO), an institution or an individual. The Supreme Court of India, rejecting the criticism of judicial activism, has stated that the judiciary has stepped in to give direction due to executive inaction; laws enacted by Parliament and the state legislatures for the poor since independence have not been properly implemented.

4 **Meaning of Petitioner:** A person who presents a Petition. (**Meaning of Petition:** A formal message requesting something that is submitted to an authority)

Characteristics of Public Interest Litigations Cases

In *Janata Dal v. H. S. Chowdhary*[5], the Supreme Court warned against frivolous litigations in the garb of public interest litigation and said :-

"It is thus clear that only a person acting bona fide and having sufficient interest in the proceedings of PIL will alone have a locus standi[6] and can approach the Court to wipe out the tears of the **Poor** and needy, suffering from violation of their fundamental rights, but not a person for personal gain or private profit or political motive or any oblique consideration. A vexatious petition under the colour of PIL brought before the Court for vindicating any personal grievance, deserves rejection at the threshold.

In the words of Bhagwati, Judge "the Courts must be careful in entertaining public interest litigations" .

Guidelines of the Court

(1) A telegram should not be registered as Public Interest Litigation/Writ Petition unless it contains the following particulars :-

(a) the connection or relationship between the sender of the telegram and the persons who are said to have been taken into custody and illegally detained;

(b) full particulars of the sender.

(2) A telegram sent by an advocate on behalf of a party should not be registered as PIL/Writ Petition. No advocate should indulge in sending a telegram to the Chief Justice and requesting the latter to treat it as a writ petition. It is the duty of an advocate to advise the party appropriately and file a proper petition before the Court. The procedure of sending telegram and registering it as writ petition is intended only for **POOR PEOPLE** who cannot afford to engage advocates.

Decision of the Court:

Court dismissed the petition of person on ground that only telegram by **POOR PEOPLE** will be treated as PIL/Writ Petition.

---

5 1993CriLJ600

6 **Meaning of Locus Standi:** The right of a party to appear and be heard before a court

22

Courts must become the Courts for the Poor[1]

Facts in Nutshell:

Writ petition[2] was filed by **POOR** starving petitioner Smt. Sayari Devi widow of late Shri Mangi Lal. for issuing a mandamus[3] for payment of General Provident Fund, State Insurance amounts and Family Pension on the ground that her deceased husband late Shri Mangi Lal was serving in the office of Public Works Department Jodhpur. Learned Single Judge of High Court issued notice to show cause to the respondents[4] as to why the petition should not be admitted and allowed.

Preamble of the Constitution and Social Security Measures

Preamble of the Constitution directs the centres of powers, legislative, executive and judiciary to set up a socialist state making effective provisions for securing right to work, to education and to public assistance in cases

1 Appellants: **Sayari Devi Vs.** Respondent: **State of Rajasthan**
(1996)IIILLJ1181Raj
Hon'ble Judges: R.R. Yadav, Judge

2 **Meaning of Writ Petition:** Under the Indian legal system, jurisdiction to issue prerogative writs is given to the Supreme Court, and to the High Courts of Judicature of all Indian states. Parts of the law relating to writs are set forth in the Constitution of India. The Supreme Court, the highest in the country, may issue writs under Article 32 of the Constitution for enforcement of Fundamental Rights and under Articles 139 for enforcement of rights other than Fundamental Rights, while High Courts, the superior courts of the States, may issue writs under Articles 226. 'Writ' is eminently designed by the makers of the Constitution, and in the same way it is developed very widely and efficiently by the courts in India. The Constitution broadly provides for five kinds of "prerogative" writs, namely, Habeas Corpus, Certiorari, Mandamus, Quo Warranto and Prohibition.

3 **Mandamus** is a judicial remedy — in the form of an order from a superior court, to any government subordinate court, corporation, orpublic authority — to do (or forbear from doing) some specific act which that body is obliged under law to do (or refrain from doing) — and which is in the nature of public duty, and in certain cases one of a statutory duty. It cannot be issued to compel an authority to do something against statutory provision. For example, it cannot be used to force a lower court to reject or authorize applications that have been made, but if the court refuses to rule one way or the other then a mandamus can be used to order the court to rule on the applications.

4 **Meaning of Respondent:** A **respondent** is a person who is called upon to issue a response to a communication made by another. In legal usage, this specifically refers to the defendant in a legal proceeding commenced by a petition, or to an appellee, or the opposing party, in an appeal of a decision by an initial fact-finder.

of unemployment, old age, sickness and disablement and in other cases of undeserved want. It is well to remember that the old age has to come in the life of every one, as has come to the **POOR** starving petitioner, who is running from pillar to post to obtain family pension after death of her husband Shri Mangi Lal. In the case of *Randhir Singh v. Union of India* [5] wherein Court observed;

The under-Privileged also are clamouring for their rights and are seeking the intervention of the Court with touching faith and confidence in the Court. The judges of the Court have a duty to redeem their constitutional oath and do justice no less to the pavement dweller than to the guest of the Five Star Hotel.

In the case of *People's Union of Democratic Right v. Union of India* [6] wherein the Court observed....."The time has now come when the Courts must become the Courts for the **POOR** and struggling masses of this Country. They must shed their character as upholder of the established order and the status quo. They must be sensitised to the need of doing justice to the large masses of people to whom justice has been denied by a cruel and heartless society for generation..........."

Decision of the Court:

Court held that the rule of law does not mean that protection of law must be available only to fortunate few guest of Five State Hotel but it should also be awarded to **POOR** starving people who are illiterate, socially educationally and economically are in disadvantaged position having no knowledge and awareness where to go for redressal of their grievances with empty hand. Courts cannot afford to open its gate only for affluent wealthy people of the State to unlock the door of justice with promptitude having large influence and economic power.

Entertainment of the writ petition by letter is of a recent origin which for the first time opened the gate of justice to the **POOR** struggling down-trodden ignorant illiterate masses having no knowledge where to go for redressal of their grievance with empty hand. Writ petition was allowed and the respondents were directed to treat deceased Mangi Lal as permanent employee of Public Works Department. Since, he was a permanent Government Servant and he died in service, therefore, the petitioner was entitled to family pension in accordance with the Rules.

5 MANU/SC/0234/1982

6 MANU/SC/0038/1982

23

Poverty and Equal Wealth Distribution[1]

Facts in Nutshell:

The Writ Petitions[2] portray the plight of lakhs of persons who live on pavements and in slums in the city of Bombay. They constitute nearly half the population of the city. The first group of petitions relates to pavement dwellers while the second group relates to both pavement and Basti or Slum dwellers. Those who have made pavements their homes exist in the midst of filth and squalor, which has to be seen to be believed. Rabid dogs in search of stinking meat and cats in search of hungry rats keep them company. They cook and sleep where they ease, for no conveniences are available to them. Their daughters, come of age, bathe under the nosy gaze of passers by, unmindful of the feminine sense of bashfulness. The cooking and washing over, women pick lice from each other's hair. The boys beg. Menfolk, without occupation, snatch chains with the connivance of the defenders of law and order; when caught, if at all, they say : "Who doesn't commit crimes in this city?"

It is these men and women who have come to the Court to ask for a judgment that they cannot be evicted from their squalid shelters without being offered alternative accommodation. They rely for their rights on Article 21 of the Constitution[3] which guarantees that no person shall

1 Appellants: **Olga Tellis and Ors. Vs.** Respondent: **Bombay Municipal Corporation and Ors. AND** Appellants: **Vayyapuri Kuppusami and Ors. Vs.** Respondent: **State of Maharashtra and Ors.** AIR1986SC180
Hon'ble Judges/Coram: Y. V. Chandrachud, C.J., A. V. Varadarajan, O. Chinnappa Reddy, S. Murtaza Fazal Ali and V. D. Tulzapurkar, JJ.

2 **Meaning of Writ Petition:** Under the Indian legal system, jurisdiction to issue prerogative writs is given to the Supreme Court, and to the High Courts of Judicature of all Indian states. Parts of the law relating to writs are set forth in the Constitution of India. The Supreme Court, the highest in the country, may issue writs under Article 32 of the Constitution for enforcement of Fundamental Rights and under Articles 139 for enforcement of rights other than Fundamental Rights, while High Courts, the superior courts of the States, may issue writs under Articles 226. Writ is eminently designed by the makers of the Constitution, and in the same way it is developed very widely and efficiently by the courts in India. The Constitution broadly provides for five kinds of "prerogative" writs, namely, Habeas Corpus, Certiorari, Mandamus, Quo Warranto and Prohibition.

3 **Article 21 in The Constitution Of India 1949**
21. Protection of life and personal liberty No person shall be deprived of his life or personal liberty except according to procedure established by law

be deprived of his life except according to procedure established by law. They do not contend that they have a right to Live on the pavements. Their contention is that they have a right to live, a right which cannot be exercised without the means of livelihood. They have no option but to flock to big cities like Bombay, which provide the means of bare subsistence. They only choose a pavement or a slum which is nearest to their place of work. In a word, their plea is that the right to life is illusory without a right to the protection of the means by which alone life can be Lived. And, the right to life can only be taken away or abridged by a procedure established by law, which has to be fair and reasonable, not fanciful or arbitrary such as is prescribed by the Bombay Municipal Corporation Act or the Bombay Police Act. They also rely upon their right to reside and settle in any part of the country which is guaranteed by Article19(1)(e)[4].

Violation of Article 19 & 21 of Constitution

The decision of the respondents (state) to demolish the huts is challenged by the petitioners[5] on the ground that it is violative of Articles 19[6] and 21 of

4 **Article 19(1)(e) in The Constitution Of India 1949**
19. Protection of certain rights regarding freedom of speech etc
(1) All citizens shall have the right
(e) to reside and settle in any part of the territory of India

5 **Meaning of Petitioner:** A person who presents a Petition. (**Meaning of Petition:** A formal message requesting something that is submitted to an authority)

6 **Article 19 in The Constitution Of India 1949**
19. Protection of certain rights regarding freedom of speech etc
(1) All citizens shall have the right
(a) to freedom of speech and expression;
(b) to assemble peaceably and without arms;
(c) to form associations or unions;
(d) to move freely throughout the territory of India;
(e) to reside and settle in any part of the territory of India; and
(f) omitted
(g) to practise any profession, or to carry on any occupation, trade or business
(2) Nothing in sub clause (a) of clause (1) shall affect the operation of any existing law, or prevent the State from making any law, in so far as such law imposes reasonable restrictions on the exercise of the right conferred by the said sub clause in the interests of the sovereignty and integrity of India, the security of the State, friendly relations with foreign States, public order, decency or morality or in relation to contempt of court, defamation or incitement to an offence
(3) Nothing in sub clause (b) of the said clause shall affect the operation of any existing law in so far as it imposes, or prevent the State from making any law imposing, in the interests of the sovereignty and integrity of India or public order, reasonable restrictions on the exercise of the right conferred by the said sub clause
(4) Nothing in sub clause (c) of the said clause shall affect the operation of any existing law in so far as it imposes, or prevent the State from making any law imposing, in the interests of the sovereignty and integrity of India or public order or morality, reasonable restrictions on the exercise of the right conferred by the said sub clause
(5) Nothing in sub clauses (d) and (e) of the said clause shall affect the operation of any existing

the Constitution. The reliefs asked for in the two groups of writ petitions are that the respondents[7] should be directed to withdraw the decision to demolish the pavement dwellings and the slum hutments and, where they are already demolished, to restore possession of the sites to the former occupants.

Main thrust of the petitioners' case is that evicting a pavement dweller or slum dweller from his habitat amounts to depriving of his right to livelihood, which is comprehended in the right guaranteed by Article 21 of the Constitution that no person shall be deprived of his life except according to procedure established by law. Counsel for the petitioners contended that the Court must determine in these petitions the content of the right to life, the function of property in a welfare state, the dimension and true meaning of the constitutional mandate that property must subserve common good, the sweep of the right to reside and settle in any part of the territory of India which is guaranteed by Article 19(1)(e) and the right to carry on any occupation, trade or business which is guaranteed by Article 19(1)(g)[8], the competing claims of pavement dwellers on the one hand and of the pedestrians on the other and, the larger question of ensuring equality before the law. It was contended that it is the responsibility of the courts to reduce inequalities and social imbalances by striking down statutes which perpetuate them.

---

law in so far as it imposes, or prevent the State from making any law imposing, reasonable restrictions on the exercise of any of the rights conferred by the said sub clauses either in the interests of the general public or for the protection of the interests of any Scheduled Tribe

(6) Nothing in sub clause (g) of the said clause shall affect the operation of any existing law in so far as it imposes, or prevent the State from making any law imposing, in the interests of the general public, reasonable restrictions on the exercise of the right conferred by the said sub clause, and, in particular, nothing in the said sub clause shall affect the operation of any existing law in so far as it relates to, or prevent the State from making any law relating to,

(i) the professional or technical qualifications necessary for practising any profession or carrying on any occupation, trade or business, or

(ii) the carrying on by the State, or by a corporation owned or controlled by the State, of any trade, business, industry or service, whether to the exclusion, complete or partial, of citizens or otherwise

7 **Meaning of Respondent:** A **respondent** is a person who is called upon to issue a response to a communication made by another. In legal usage, this specifically refers to the defendant in a legal proceeding commenced by a petition, or to an appellee, or the opposing party, in an appeal of a decision by an initial fact-finder.

8 **Article 19(1)(g) in The Constitution Of India 1949**
19. Protection of certain rights regarding freedom of speech etc
(1) All citizens shall have the right
(g) to practise any profession, or to carry on any occupation, trade or business

Trespassers (Section 441 IPC[9])

It was urged by the petitioners that it was constitutionally impermissible to characterise the pavement dwellers as "trespassers" because, their occupation of pavements arises from economic compulsions. The State is under an obligation to provide to the citizens the necessities of life and, in appropriate cases, the courts have the power to issue order directing the State, by affirmative action, to promote and protect the right to life. The instant situation is one of crisis, which compels the use of public property for the purpose of survival and sustenance. Social commitment is the quintessence of our Constitution which defines the conditions under which liberty has to be enjoyed and justice has to be administered. Therefore, Directive Principles, which are fundamental in the governance of the country, must serve as a beacon light to the interpretation of the Constitutional provisions. Viewed in this context, it is urged, the impugned action of the State Government and the Bombay Municipal Corporation is violative of the provisions contained in Articles 19(1)(e), 19(1)(g) and 21 of the Constitution. The paucity of financial resources of the State is no excuse for defeating the fundamental rights of the citizens.

They live in Bombay because they are employed in Bombay and they live on pavements because there is no other place where they can live. This is the factual context in which the petitioners claim the right under Articles 19(1)(e) and (g) and Article 21 of the Constitution.

Directive Principle of State Policy[10]

Article 39(a) of the Constitution[11], which is a Directive Principle of State

9 **Section 441 in The Indian Penal Code, 1860**
441. Criminal trespass.-- Whoever enters into or upon property in the possession of another with intent to commit an offence or to intimidate, insult or annoy any person in possession of such property, or having lawfully entered into or upon such property, unlawfully remains there with intent thereby to intimidate, insult or annoy any such person, or with intent to commit an offence, is said to commit" criminal trespass".

10 The **Directive Principles of State Policy** are guidelines to the central and state governments of India, to be kept in mind while framing laws and policies. These provisions, contained in Part IV of the Constitution of India, are not enforceable by any court, but the principles laid down therein are considered fundamental in the governance of the country, making it the duty of the State to apply these principles in making laws to establish a just society in the country. The principles have been inspired by the Directive Principles given in the Constitution of Ireland and also by the principles of Gandhism; and relate to social justice, economic welfare, foreign policy, and legal and administrative matters.

11 **Article 39 (a) in The Constitution Of India 1949**
39. Certain principles of policy to be followed by the State: The State shall, in particular, direct its policy towards securing

Policy, provides that the State shall, in particular, direct its policy towards securing that the citizens, men and women equally, have the right to an adequate means of livelihood. Article 41[12], which is another Directive Principle, provides, inter alia, that the State shall, within the limits of its economic capacity and development, make effective provision for securing the right to work in cases of unemployment and of undeserved want. Article 37[13] provides that the Directive Principles, though not enforceable by any court, are nevertheless fundamental in the governance of the country. The Principles contained in Articles 39(a) and 41 must be regarded as equally fundamental in the understanding and interpretation of the meaning and content of fundamental rights. If there is an obligation upon the State to secure to the citizens an adequate means of livelihood and the right to work, it would be sheer pedantry to exclude the right to livelihood from the content of the right to life. The State may not, by affirmative action, be compellable to provide adequate means of livelihood or work to the citizens. But, any person, who is deprived of his right to livelihood except according to just and fair procedure established by law, can challenge the deprivation as offending the right to life conferred by Article 21.

Poverty and Labourers

The phenomenon of poverty which is common to all developing countries has to be tackled on an All-India basis by making the gains of development available to all sections of the society through a policy of equitable distribution of income and wealth. Urbanisation is a major problem facing the entire country, the migration of people from the rural to the urban areas being a reflection of the colossal poverty existing in the rural areas. The rural poverty cannot, however, be eliminated by increasing the pressure of population on metropolitan cities like Bombay. The problem of poverty has to be tackled by changing the structure of the society in which there will be a more equitable distribution of income and greater

---

(a) that the citizens, men and women equally, have the right to an adequate means to livelihood

12 **Article 41 in The Constitution Of India 1949**
41. Right to work, to education and to public assistance in certain cases The State shall, within the limits of its economic capacity and development, make effective provision for securing the right to work, to education and to public assistance in cases of unemployment, old age, sickness and disablement, and in other cases of undeserved want

13 **Article 37 in The Constitution Of India 1949**
37. Application of the principles contained in this Part The provisions contained in this Part shall not be enforceable by any court, but the principles therein laid down are nevertheless fundamental in the governance of the country and it shall be the duty of the State to apply these principles in making laws

generation of wealth.

A publication dated January 1982 of the Planning Commission, Government of India, namely, 'The Report of the Expert Group of Programmes for the Alleviation of Poverty', is relied on as showing the high incidence of poverty in India. That Report shows that in 1977-78, 48% of the population lived below the poverty line, which means that out of a population of 303 million who lived below the poverty line, 252 million belonged to the rural areas. In 1979-80 another 8 million people from the rural areas were found to live below the poverty line.

One of the major causes of the persistent rural poverty of landless labourers, marginal farmers, shepherds, physically handicapped persons and others is the extremely narrow base of production available to the majority of the rural population. Landless labourers have no resource base at all and they constitute the hardcore of poverty. Due to economic pressures and lack of employment opportunities, the rural population is forced to migrate to urban areas in search of employment.

Decision of the Court

Court held that no person has the right to encroach, by erecting a structure or otherwise, on footpaths, pavements or any other place reserved or ear-marked for a public purpose like, for example, a garden or a playground. Slums which have been in existence for a long time, say for twenty years or more, and which have been improved and developed will not be removed unless the land on which they stand or the appurtenant land, is required for a public purposes, in which case, alternate sites or accommodation will be provided to them, the 'Low Income Scheme Shelter Programme' which is proposed to be undertaken with the aid of the World Bank will be pursued earnestly; and, the Slum Upgradation Programme (SUP)' under which basic amenities are to be given to slum dwellers will be implemented without delay.

Compensation by State

Right to Life:

When dealing with Article 21[14] of the Constitution of India, which enshrines

14 **Article 21 in The Constitution Of India 1949**

21. Protection of life and personal liberty No person shall be deprived of his life or personal liberty except according to procedure established by law

right to life, the Hon'ble Supreme Court in *Chameli Singh v. State of U.P.*[15] has held that right to live as a human being is not ensured by meeting only the animal needs of man, in the following words:

In any organized society, right to live as a human being is not ensured by meeting only the animal needs of man. It is secured only when he is assured of all facilities to develop himself and is freed from restrictions which inhibit his growth. All human rights are designed to achieve this object. Right to live guaranteed in any civil society implies the right to food, water, decent environment, education, medical care and shelter. These are basic human rights known to any civilised society. The civil, political, social and cultural rights enshrined in the Universal Declaration of Human Rights and Convention or under the Constitution of India, cannot be exercised without these basic human rights.

In *Ajab Singh v. State of U.P.*[16], the Hon'ble Supreme Court, while considering about the compensation in respect of custodial death[17] of a person who was remanded to judicial custody and while in jail, he was removed to hospital where he died and on consideration of post-mortem report It was stated that he died due to shock and hemorrhage due to ante-mortem injuries, while ordering payment of compensation by refusing to accept the defence of the State Government, held that when such deaths occur, it is not only to the public at large that those holding custody are responsible, they are responsible also to the Courts under whose orders they hold such custody.

Issue of compensation:

In a case of custodial death, the Supreme Court relying upon *D.K. Basu v. State of West Bengal,*[18] held the State of Uttar Pradesh responsible in public law to compensate for the death of the victim. Even more recently, the Supreme Court laid down the law on the subject after exhaustively dealing with a large number of precedents. It was held in *Sube Singh v. State of Haryana,*[19]:

15 AIR1996SC1051

16 2000CriLJ1809

17 **Meaning of Custodial Death:** A **death in custody** is a death of a person in the custody of the police, prison service or other authorities. Death in custody remains a controversial subject, with the authorities often being accused of abuse, neglect, racism and cover-ups of the causes of these deaths.

18 (1997) 1 SCC 416: (1997 Cri LJ 743)

19 (2006) 3 SCC 178: (2006 Cri LJ 1242)

In cases where custodial death or custodial torture or other violation of the rights guaranteed under Article 21 is established, the Courts may award compensation in a proceeding under Article 32 [20]or 226[21] of Constitution. However, before awarding compensation, the Court will have to pose to itself the following questions:

(a) whether the violation of Article 21 is patent and incontrovertible,

(b) whether the violation is gross and of a magnitude to shock the conscience of the Court,

---

20 **Article 32 in The Constitution Of India 1949**

32. Remedies for enforcement of rights conferred by this Part

(1) The right to move the Supreme Court by appropriate proceedings for the enforcement of the rights conferred by this Part is guaranteed

(2) The Supreme Court shall have power to issue directions or orders or writs, including writs in the nature of habeas corpus, mandamus, prohibition, quo warranto and certiorari, whichever may be appropriate, for the enforcement of any of the rights conferred by this Part

(3) Without prejudice to the powers conferred on the Supreme Court by clause (1) and (2), Parliament may by law empower any other court to exercise within the local limits of its jurisdiction all or any of the powers exercisable by the Supreme Court under clause (2)

(4) The right guaranteed by this article shall not be suspended except as otherwise provided for by this Constitution

21 **Article 226 in The Constitution Of India 1949**

226. Power of High Courts to issue certain writs

(1) Notwithstanding anything in Article 32 every High Court shall have powers, throughout the territories in relation to which it exercise jurisdiction, to issue to any person or authority, including in appropriate cases, any Government, within those territories directions, orders or writs, including writs in the nature of habeas corpus, mandamus, prohibitions, quo warranto and certiorari, or any of them, for the enforcement of any of the rights conferred by Part III and for any other purpose

(2) The power conferred by clause (1) to issue directions, orders or writs to any Government, authority or person may also be exercised by any High Court exercising jurisdiction in relation to the territories within which the cause of action, wholly or in part, arises for the exercise of such power, notwithstanding that the seat of such Government or authority or the residence of such person is not within those territories

(3) Where any party against whom an interim order, whether by way of injunction or stay or in any other manner, is made on, or in any proceedings relating to, a petition under clause (1), without

(a) furnishing to such party copies of such petition and all documents in support of the plea for such interim order; and

(b) giving such party an opportunity of being heard, makes an application to the High Court for the vacation of such order and furnishes a copy of such application to the party in whose favour such order has been made or the counsel of such party, the High Court shall dispose of the application within a period of two weeks from the date on which it is received or from the date on which the copy of such application is so furnished, whichever is later, or where the High Court is closed on the last day of that period, before the expiry of the next day afterwards on which the High Court is open; and if the application is not so disposed of, the interim order shall, on the expiry of that period, or, as the case may be, the expiry of the aid next day, stand vacated

(4) The power conferred on a High Court by this article shall not be in derogation of the power conferred on the Supreme court by clause (2) of Article 32

(c) whether the custodial torture alleged has resulted in death or whether custodial torture is supported by medical report or visible marks or scars or disability. Where there is no evidence of custodial torture of a person except his own statement, and where such allegation is not supported by any medical report or other corroborative evidence, or where there are clear indications that the allegations are false or exaggerated fully or in part, the Courts may not award compensation as a public law remedy under Article 32 or 226, but relegate the aggrieved party to the traditional remedies by way of appropriate civil/criminal action.

Compensation in cases of Police Encounter:

While dealing with the claim of compensation in death cases during encounter with police in *Malkiat Singh v. State of U.P.*[22], under Article 32[23] of the Constitution of India the Hon'ble Supreme Court has granted compensation of Rs. 5,00,000

22 (1998)9SCC351

23 **Article 32 in The Constitution Of India 1949**

32. Remedies for enforcement of rights conferred by this Part

(1) The right to move the Supreme Court by appropriate proceedings for the enforcement of the rights conferred by this Part is guaranteed

(2) The Supreme Court shall have power to issue directions or orders or writs, including writs in the nature of habeas corpus, mandamus, prohibition, quo warranto and certiorari, whichever may be appropriate, for the enforcement of any of the rights conferred by this Part

(3) Without prejudice to the powers conferred on the Supreme Court by clause (1) and (2), Parliament may by law empower any other court to exercise within the local limits of its jurisdiction all or any of the powers exercisable by the Supreme Court under clause (2)

(4) The right guaranteed by this article shall not be suspended except as otherwise provided for by this Constitution

24

State shall be liable to pay compensation for wrongful act of its servant[1]

Ratio Decidendi[2]: ***"State shall be liable to pay compensation for wrongful act of its servant during course of his employment."***

Facts in Nutshell:

Writ petitions[3] were filed by the Women's and Civil Rights Organization known as SAHELI, a Women's Resources center on behalf of two women Maya Devi and Kamlesh Kumari who have been residing in one room tenatment each on the ground floor of house No. 408/5/AL Gali No. 29, Anand Parbat and were severely beaten up by the alleged landlord.

Kamlesh Kumari and her husband Inder Singh moved into the house No. 408/5/A L, Gali No. 29, Anand Parbat in 1974. They had three children, Saroj 13 years old girl, Naresh 9 years old boy and Suresh seven years old boy. They were living in one room on the ground floor of the said house which is a double storey. The other lady, Maya Devi has also been living in another room of the said house on the ground floor with her husband and children. The husbands of both Kamlesh Kumari and Maya Devi were truck drivers and they often remain away from their home. There was

1 Appellants: **Saheli, A Women's Resources center, Through Ms Nalini Bhanot and Ors. Vs.** Respondent: **Commissioner of Police Delhi Police Headquarters and Ors.**
AIR1990SC513
Hon'ble Judges: B. C. Ray and S. Ratnavel Pandian, JJ.

2 **Meaning of Ration Decidendi:** ***Ratio decidendi*** is a Latin phrase meaning "the reason" or "the rationale for the decision." The *ratio decidendi* is "the point in a case which determines the judgment" or "the principle which the case establishes."

3 **Meaning of Writ Petition:** Under the Indian legal system, jurisdiction to issue ?prerogative writs? is given to the Supreme Court, and to the High Courts of Judicature of all Indian states. Parts of the law relating to writs are set forth in the Constitution of India. The Supreme Court, the highest in the country, may issue writs under Article 32 of the Constitution for enforcement of Fundamental Rights and under Articles 139 for enforcement of rights other than Fundamental Rights, while High Courts, the superior courts of the States, may issue writs under Articles 226. ?Writ? is eminently designed by the makers of the Constitution, and in the same way it is developed very widely and efficiently by the courts in India. The Constitution broadly provides for five kinds of "prerogative" writs, namely, Habeas Corpus, Certiorari, Mandamus, Quo Warranto and Prohibition.

a dispute over the ownership of the house. In or about 1984, the old landlord, one Tajinder Singh left the house and one Manohar Lal claimed to be the new landlord. At the time of Dispute, one Puran Chand and his two sons Shambu Dayal and Prakash Chand claimed to have bought the said property from Manohar Lal and they have been illegally evicting all the tenants[4] from the said premises. In their attempt they succeeded in evicting all the tenants except the two tenants named Kamlesh Kumari and Maya Devi. It was because of these illegal threats of eviction, Kamlesh Kumari obtained an order of stay from the Court against her forceful eviction and that said order was in force. Some time in October, 1987 the so-called landlords cut off the water and electricity supply to Kamlesh Kumari's room. On November 2, 1987 the S.H.O. of Anand Parbat Police Station, Lal Singh called for Kamlesh Kumari and told her to vacate the room. On November 4, 1987, the said S.H.O. again called for Kamlesh Kumari and when she arrived at the police station she found that the so-called landlords were already present there. In the presence of Shambu Dayal and others, Lal Singh told Kamlesh Kumari to take some money and leave the room whereon Kamlesh Kumari said that she should be given some time especially because her children were studying in schools. On November 12, 1987, the said S.H.O. once again called Kamlesh Kumari and this time he threatened to lock her up if she refused to vacate the room. On November 13, 1987, Kamlesh Kumari went to Tis Hazari Court to consult her lawyer. On coming back she found her children missing and Maya Devi was standing outside, all her belongings thrown out. Maya Devi told Kamlesh Kumari that the Sub-Inspector of Police K.L. Nanda of Anand Parbat Police Station had come and had taken away her children and had thrown away Maya Devi from her room. Kamlesh Kumari immediately went to the Police Station and met the S.H.O., Lal Singh and asked him about her children. The S.H.O. said that her children had been kept locked up and she would not be allowed to see her children unless she vacated the room. Kamlesh Kumari then went to Tis Hazari Court to see her lawyer. The lawyer phoned the Police control room and rushed back to Anand Parbat Police Station. With great difficulty the lawyer got the three children released from the police station.

On the same day, i.e. November 13, 1987, after Kamlesh Kumari and her children had just taken their dinner, Shambu Dayal trespassed[5] into her

4 **Meaning of Tenant:** One who holds or possesses lands, tenements, or sometimes personal property by any kind of title.

5 **Meaning of Trespass:** To commit an unlawful injury to the person, property, or rights of another, with actual or implied force or violence, especially to enter onto another's land wrongfully.

room and hit Kamlesh Kumari on the forehead with a brick. She rushed to the police station and reported the matter to the police. The police had her medically examined but refused to take any action against the assailants[6].

On November 14, 1987, Kamlesh Kumari was attacked by Shambu Dayal, his brother Prakash Chand accompanied by Lal Singh in civilian clothes and Sham Lal, Sub-Inspector in uniform accompanied by two others. They beat Kamlesh Kumari, tore her clothes and molested her. Her nine years old son clung to his mother to protect her when Lal Singh took him away and forcibly threw him on the floor. Lal Singh also asked Shambu Dayal to beat Naresh. Kamlesh Kumari was dragged away to the police station and a criminal case was imposed upon her of trespass. She was sent to Tihar Jail and her lawyer got her released on November 16, 1987. Kamlesh Kumari on her release came back and found that her child, Naresh was in a very bad condition. The children took shelter at a neighbour's house and the neighbours had got local doctors to look after Naresh. On the advice of the doctors, Naresh was admitted to Ram Manohar Lohia Hospital.

As such the writ petitions were moved before Supreme Court praying amongst others the issuance of a writ for directions directing the respondents[7] to pay Kamlesh Kumari exemplary damages for the death of her son, Naresh.

Decision by Supreme Court:

Court held that an action for damages lies for bodily harm which includes battery[8], assault[9], false imprisonment, physical injuries and death. In cases of assault, battery and false imprisonment the damages are at large and represent a solatium for the mental pain, distress, indignity, loss of liberty and death. Son of Kamlesh Kumari aged 9 years died due to beating and assault by the S.H.O., Lal Singh and as such she was entitled to get the damages for the death of her son. It is well settled now that the State is

6 **Meaning of Assailant:** A person who attacks another.

7 **Meaning of Respondent:** A **respondent** is a person who is called upon to issue a response to a communication made by another. In legal usage, this specifically refers to the defendant in a legal proceeding commenced by a petition, or to an appellee, or the opposing party, in an appeal of a decision by an initial fact-finder.

8 **Meaning of Battery:** A battery is the unlawful touching the person of another by the aggressor himself, or any other substance put in motion by him.

9 **Meaning of Assault:**
a. An unlawful threat or attempt to do bodily injury to another.
b. The act or an instance of unlawfully threatening or attempting to injure another.

responsible for the tortious[10] acts of its employees. The respondent No. 2. Delhi Administration was held liable for payment of compensation (Sum of Rs. 75,000/-) to Smt. Kamlesh Kumari for the death of her son due to beating by the S.H.O. of Anand Parbat Police Station, Shri Lal Singh.

Court referred following cases while delivering the Judgment:

Joginder Kaur v. The Punjab State and Ors.[11] wherein it has been observed that :

In the matter of liability of the State for the torts committed by its employees, it is now the settled law that the State is liable for tortious acts committed by its employees in the course of their employment.

In *Peoples' Union for Democratic Rights through its Secretary and Anr. v. Police Commissioner, Delhi Police Headquarters and Anr.*[12] where one of the labourers who was taken to the police station for doing some work and on demand for wages was severely beaten and ultimately succumbed to the injuries. It was held that the State was liable to pay compensation and accordingly directed that the family of the deceased[13] labourer will be paid Rs. 75,000/- as compensation.

10 **Meaning of Tortious:** In order to establish that a particular act was tortious, a plaintiff must prove that an actionable wrong existed and that damages ensued from that wrong.

11 1969 ACJ 28

12 Writ Petition (Crl.) Nos. 401-402 of 1988

13 **Meaning of Deceased:** A dead person

25

Compensation by State on Ground of Poverty[1]

Ratio Decidendi[2] "Court shall play vital role for awarding compensation in case of custodial death if it shocks conscience of Court."

Facts in Nutshell:

Writ petition[3] was filed by the mother of a 16 years old juvenile[4] who was lodged in jail and died in custody (custodial death). Petitioner prayed for compensation for the custodial death of the juvenile of Rs. 1,50,000/- . In the writ petition it was stated that the doctor who conducted the post-mortem examination of the juvenile opined that death was due to exhaustion and chronic bilateral pulmonary tuberculosis. The Petitioner said that the juvenile was the only earning member of the family and he worked as an embroidery tailor earning Rs. 7,500/-per month.

Poverty of the Juvenile Parents:

The juvenile was unable to avail of the bail granted to him by Court. Juvenile's father was unable to get him released on bail due to **POVERTY** fact that the juvenile remained in custody for almost sixty (60) days after bail was granted by Court confirms his **POVERTY.** Therefore, even though

---

1 Appellants: **Naisul Khatun Vs.** Respondent: **State of Assam and Ors.**
2011CriLJ326
Hon'ble Judges: Madan B. Lokur, C.J. and B.P. Katakey, Judge

2 **Meaning of Ration Decidendi:** ***Ratio decidendi*** is a Latin phrase meaning "the reason" or "the rationale for the decision." The *ratio decidendi* is "the point in a case which determines the judgment" or "the principle which the case establishes."

3 **Meaning of Writ Petition:** Under the Indian legal system, jurisdiction to issue ⍰prerogative writs⍰ is given to the Supreme Court, and to the High Courts of Judicature of all Indian states. Parts of the law relating to writs are set forth in the Constitution of India. The Supreme Court, the highest in the country, may issue writs under Article 32 of the Constitution for enforcement of Fundamental Rights and under Articles 139 for enforcement of rights other than Fundamental Rights, while High Courts, the superior courts of the States, may issue writs under Articles 226. ⍰Writ⍰ is eminently designed by the makers of the Constitution, and in the same way it is developed very widely and efficiently by the courts in India. The Constitution broadly provides for five kinds of "prerogative" writs, namely, Habeas Corpus, Certiorari, Mandamus, Quo Warranto and Prohibition.

4 **Section 2(k) of the Juvenile Justice Act, 2000:**
2(k) "juvenile" or "child" means a person who has not completed eighteenth year of age

in a sense the custody of the juvenile was unobjectionable (the custody having been ordered by the Juvenile Justice Board) yet its continuance was constitutionally invalid because the juvenile remained incarcerated despite a bail order in his favour only because of his **Poverty**. And he remained so until his unfortunate death. A custodial death occurred is bad enough but what certainly makes it gross is that the death was of a juvenile, who was accused not of a heinous crime, but of burglary.

Right to Life and Human Dignity:

In *D. Bhuvan Mohan Patnaik v. State of A. P.*[5] it was observed: "Even a convict is entitled to the precious right guaranteed by Article 21 of the Constitution[6] that he shall not be deprived of his life or personal liberty except according to procedure established by law.

In *Francis Coralie Mullin v. Administrator,*[7] it was held that right to live with human dignity enshrined in Article 21of the Constitution derives its life breath from the Directive Principles of State Policy and particularly Clauses (e) and (f) of Article 39[8] and Articles 41[9] and 42[10] and therefore,

5 (1975) 3 SCC 185: (1975 Cri LJ 556)

6 **Article 21 in The Constitution Of India 1949**
21. Protection of life and personal liberty No person shall be deprived of his life or personal liberty except according to procedure established by law

7 (1981) 1 SCC 608): (1981 Cri LJ 306)

8 **Article 39 in The Constitution Of India 1949**
39. Certain principles of policy to be followed by the State: The State shall, in particular, direct its policy towards securing
(a) that the citizens, men and women equally, have the right to an adequate means to livelihood;
(b) that the ownership and control of the material resources of the community are so distributed as best to subserve the common good;
(c) that the operation of the economic system does not result in the concentration of wealth and means of production to the common detriment;
(d) that there is equal pay for equal work for both men and women;
(e) that the health and strength of workers, men and women, and the tender age of children are not abused and that citizens are not forced by economic necessity to enter avocations unsuited to their age or strength;
(f) that children are given opportunities and facilities to develop in a healthy manner and in conditions of freedom and dignity and that childhood and youth are protected against exploitation and against moral and material abandonment

9 **Article 41 in The Constitution Of India 1949**
41. Right to work, to education and to public assistance in certain cases The State shall, within the limits of its economic capacity and development, make effective provision for securing the right to work, to education and to public assistance in cases of unemployment, old age, sickness and disablement, and in other cases of undeserved want

10 **Article 42 in The Constitution Of India 1949**
42. Provision for just and humane conditions of work and maternity relief --The State shall make provision for securing just and humane conditions of work and for maternity relief

it must include protection of the health and strength of workers, men and women, and of the tender age of children against abuse, opportunities and facilities for children to develop in a healthy manner and in conditions of freedom and dignity, educational facilities, just and humane conditions of work and maternity relief. These are the minimum requirements which must exist in order to enable a person to live with human dignity and no State -- neither the Central Government nor any State Government -- has the right to take any action which will deprive a person of the enjoyment of these basic essentials.

Issue of compensation:

In a case of custodial death, the Supreme Court relying upon *D.K. Basu v. State of West Bengal,*[11] held the State of Uttar Pradesh responsible in public law to compensate for the death of the victim. Even more recently, the Supreme Court laid down the law on the subject after exhaustively dealing with a large number of precedents. It was held in *Sube Singh v. State of Haryana,*[12]:

In cases where custodial death or custodial torture or other violation of the rights guaranteed under Article 21 is established, the Courts may award compensation in a proceeding under Article 32 or 226[13] of Constitution.

11 (1997) 1 SCC 416: (1997 Cri LJ 743)

12 (2006) 3 SCC 178: (2006 Cri LJ 1242)

13 **Article 226 in The Constitution Of India 1949**
226. Power of High Courts to issue certain writs
(1) Notwithstanding anything in Article 32 every High Court shall have powers, throughout the territories in relation to which it exercise jurisdiction, to issue to any person or authority, including in appropriate cases, any Government, within those territories directions, orders or writs, including writs in the nature of habeas corpus, mandamus, prohibitions, quo warranto and certiorari, or any of them, for the enforcement of any of the rights conferred by Part III and for any other purpose
(2) The power conferred by clause (1) to issue directions, orders or writs to any Government, authority or person may also be exercised by any High Court exercising jurisdiction in relation to the territories within which the cause of action, wholly or in part, arises for the exercise of such power, notwithstanding that the seat of such Government or authority or the residence of such person is not within those territories
(3) Where any party against whom an interim order, whether by way of injunction or stay or in any other manner, is made on, or in any proceedings relating to, a petition under clause (1), without
(a) furnishing to such party copies of such petition and all documents in support of the plea for such interim order; and
(b) giving such party an opportunity of being heard, makes an application to the High Court for the vacation of such order and furnishes a copy of such application to the party in whose favour such order has been made or the counsel of such party, the High Court shall dispose of the application within a period of two weeks from the date on which it is received or from the date on which the copy of such application is so furnished, whichever is later, or where the High

However, before awarding compensation, the Court will have to pose to itself the following questions:

(a) whether the violation of Article 21 is patent and incontrovertible,

(b) whether the violation is gross and of a magnitude to shock the conscience of the Court,

(c) whether the custodial torture alleged has resulted in death or whether custodial torture is supported by medical report or visible marks or scars or disability. Where there is no evidence of custodial torture of a person except his own statement, and where such allegation is not supported by any medical report or other corroborative evidence, or where there are clear indications that the allegations are false or exaggerated fully or in part, the Courts may not award compensation as a public law remedy under Article 32 or 226, but relegate the aggrieved party to the traditional remedies by way of appropriate civil/criminal action.

Decision of the Court:

Court held that due to Poverty the parents of the Juvenile were unable to provide him medical assistance and Bail. Court directed the state to compensate the Petitioner[14](Mother of Juvenile) with an amount of Rs. 1,50,000/-for the custodial death of her son.

Court is closed on the last day of that period, before the expiry of the next day afterwards on which the High Court is open; and if the application is not so disposed of, the interim order shall, on the expiry of that period, or, as the case may be, the expiry of the aid next day, stand vacated

(4) The power conferred on a High Court by this article shall not be in derogation of the power conferred on the Supreme court by clause (2) of Article 32

14 **Meaning of Petitioner:** A person who presents a Petition. (**Meaning of Petition:** A formal message requesting something that is submitted to an authority)

26

Detention in Jail and Compensation by State[1]

Facts in Nutshell:

The petitioner[2] was acquitted[3] by the Court of Sessions, Muzaffarpur, Bihar, on June 3, 1968 but he was released from the jail on October 16, 1982, that is to say, more than 14 years after he was acquitted. By Habeas Corpus[4] petition[5] in Supreme Court, the petitioner asks for his release on the ground that his detention[6] in the jail was unlawful.

Decision of the Supreme Court:

Court held that Article 21[7] which guarantees the right to life and liberty will be denuded of its significant content if the power of Supreme Court were limited to passing orders to release from illegal detention. One of the telling ways in which the violation of that right can reasonably be prevented and due compliance with the mandate of Article 21 secured, is to mulct its violaters in the payment of monetary compensation. Administrative sclerosis leading to flagrant infringements of fundamental

1 Appellants: **Rudul Sah Vs.** Respondent: **State of Bihar and Anr.**
AIR1983SC1086
Hon'ble Judges: Y. V. Chandrachud, C.J. Ranganath Misra and A. N. Sen, JJ

2 **Meaning of Petitioner:** A person who presents a Petition. (**Meaning of Petition:** A formal message requesting something that is submitted to an authority)

3 **Meaning of Acquittal:** In the common law tradition, an **acquittal** formally certifies that the accused is free from the charge of an offense, as far as the criminal law is concerned.

4 A writ of ***habeas corpus*** is a writ (legal action) that requires a person under arrest to be brought before a judge or into court. The principle of habeas corpus ensures that a prisoner can be released from unlawful detention—that is, detention lacking sufficient cause or evidence. The remedy can be sought by the prisoner or by another person coming to the prisoner's aid. This right originated in the English legal system, and is now available in many nations. It has historically been an important legal instrument safeguarding individual freedom against arbitrary state action.

5 **Meaning of Petition:** A formal message requesting something that is submitted to an authority

6 **Meaning of Detention:** Custody or confinement, esp of a suspect awaiting trial

7 **Article 21 in The Constitution Of India 1949**
21. Protection of life and personal liberty No person shall be deprived of his life or personal liberty except according to procedure established by law

rights[8] cannot be corrected by any other method open to the judiciary to adopt. The right to compensation is some palliative for the unlawful acts of instrumentalities which act in the name of public interest and which present for their protection the powers of the State as a shield. If civilisation is not to perish in this country, it is necessary to educate ourselves into accepting that, *respect for the rights of individuals is the true bastion of democracy*. Therefore, the State must repair the damage done by its officers to the petitioner's rights.

Court further held that taking into consideration the great harm done to the petitioner by the Government of Bihar, Court ordered the State must pay to the petitioner a further sum of Rs. 30,000 (Rupees thirty-thousand) in addition to the sum of Rs. 5,000 (Rupees five thousand) already paid by it.

8 ***'Part III – Fundamental Rights'*** is a charter of rights contained in the Constitution of India. It guarantees civil liberties such that all Indians can lead their lives in peace and harmony as citizens of India. These include individual rights common to most liberal democracies, such asequality before law, freedom of speech and expression, and peaceful assembly, freedom to practice religion, and the right to constitutional remedies for the protection of civil rights by means of writs such as habeas corpus. Violation of these rights result in punishments as prescribed in the Indian Penal Code or other special laws, subject to discretion of the judiciary. The Fundamental Rights are defined as basichuman freedoms which every Indian citizen has the right to enjoy for a proper and harmonious development of personality. These rights universally apply to all citizens, irrespective of race, place of birth, religion, caste, creed, colour or gender. Aliens (persons who are not citizens) are also considered in matters like equality before law. They are enforceable by the courts, subject to certain restrictions. The Rights have their origins in many sources, including England's Bill of Rights, the United States Bill of Rights and France's Declaration of the Rights of Man.

27

Compensation for Murder of Prisoner in Jail[1]

Ratio decidendi[2]**:** *A claim against unconstitutional deprivation of life and liberty as guaranteed under Article 21*[3] *of Constitution of India is claim based on strict liability and is in addition to any claim available in private law for damages*

Facts in Nutshell:

According to the petitioner[4], her husband was implicated as an accused[5] for an alleged offence under Section 302[6] of Indian Penal Code. The petitioner's husband was arrested and remanded to judicial custody during 1996 pending investigation. He was confined in the Sub Jail, Nagercoil as trial prisoner. The application for bail[7] filed for the petitioner's husband was dismissed and therefore, he was in the Sub Jail, Nagercoil pending investigation. The husband of the petitioner, who was detained in the Cell, was murdered in the Sub Jail, Nagercoil and the crime was registered in Nesamony Nagar Police Station .

The petitioner's husband was aged about 36 years at the time of his

---

1 Appellants: **Tmt. Rohini Lingam Vs.** Respondent: **State represented by the Secretary to Government, (Dept. of Prisons), The Inspector General of Prisons and The Superintendent, Sub Jail** (2008)5MLJ822
Hon'ble Judges: P. Jyothimani, Judge

2 **Meaning of Ration Decidendi:** ***Ratio decidendi*** is a Latin phrase meaning "the reason" or "the rationale for the decision." The *ratio decidendi* is "the point in a case which determines the judgment" or "the principle which the case establishes."

3 **Article 21 in The Constitution Of India 1949**
21. Protection of life and personal liberty No person shall be deprived of his life or personal liberty except according to procedure established by law

4 **Meaning of Petitioner:** A person who presents a Petition. (**Meaning of Petition:** A formal message requesting something that is submitted to an authority)

5 **Meaning of Accused:** A person charged with a criminal offense, or the state of being so charged

6 **Section 302, IPC 1860**
Punishment for murder
302. Punishment for murder.--Whoever commits murder shall be punished with death, or [imprisonment for life], and shall also be liable to fine

7 **Meaning of Bail: 1.** To secure the release of by providing security.
2. To release (a person) for whom security has been paid

murder and he had left behind him the petitioner being his wife and two minor children and his aged parents. The respondents[8] (Police Officials) have the legal duty to keep the petitioner's husband, being an accused facing investigation, with proper safety and due to their negligence in not taking proper steps, the petitioner's husband was killed. In view of the same, the petitioner filed the writ petition, claiming an amount of Rs. 10,00,000/- as compensation.

Prison Act, 1894:

Under the Prisons Act, 1894 the term 'prison' is defined under Section 3(1), which is as follows:

Section 3(1) "Prison" means any jail or place used permanently or temporarily under the general or special orders of a State Government for the detention of prisoners, and includes all lands and buildings appurtenant thereto, but does not include-

(a) any place for the confinement of prisoners who are exclusively in the custody of the police;

(b) any place specially appointed by the State Government under Section 541 of the Code of Criminal Procedure, 1882; or

(c) any place which has been declared by the State Government, by general or special order, to be a subsidiary jail;

Section 4 of the Act which deals about the accommodation for prisoners envisages a duty on the part of the State Government to give accommodation which is as follows:

Section 4. Accommodation for Prisoners:- The State Government shall provide, for the prisoners in the territories under such Government, accommodation in prisons constructed and regulated in such manner as to comply with the requirements of this Act in respect of the separation of prisoners.

Section 19 mandates a jailer to be present at night, which is as follows:

Section 19. Jailer to be present at night:- The Jailer shall not be absent

8 **Meaning of Respondent:** A **respondent** is a person who is called upon to issue a response to a communication made by another. In legal usage, this specifically refers to the defendant in a legal proceeding commenced by a petition, or to an appellee, or the opposing party, in an appeal of a decision by an initial fact-finder.

from the prison for a night without permission in writing from the Superintendent; but, if absent without leave for a night from unavoidable necessity, he shall immediately report the fact and the cause of it to the Superintendent.

Section 20 also makes it clear that every Deputy Jailer or Assistant Jailer be competent to perform the duties of the Jailer.

Section 20. Powers of Deputy and Assistant Jailers:- Where a Deputy Jailer or Assistant Jailer is appointed to a prison, he shall, subject to the orders of the Superintendent, be competent to perform any of the duties, and be subject to all the responsibilities of a Jailer under this Act or any rule thereunder.

Right to Life:

When dealing with Article 21 of the Constitution of India, which enshrines right to life, the Hon'ble Supreme Court in *Chameli Singh v. State of U.P.*[9] has held that right to live as a human being is not ensured by meeting only the animal needs of man, in the following words:

In any organized society, right to live as a human being is not ensured by meeting only the animal needs of man. It is secured only when he is assured of all facilities to develop himself and is freed from restrictions which inhibit his growth. All human rights are designed to achieve this object. Right to live guaranteed in any civil society implies the right to food, water, decent environment, education, medical care and shelter. These are basic human rights known to any civilised society. The civil, political, social and cultural rights enshrined in the Universal Declaration of Human Rights and Convention or under the Constitution of India, cannot be exercised without these basic human rights.

In *Ajab Singh v. State of U.P.*[10], the Hon'ble Supreme Court, while considering about the compensation in respect of custodial death[11] of a person who was remanded to judicial custody and while in jail, he was removed to hospital where he died and on consideration of post-mortem report it stated that he died due to shock and hemorrhage due to ante-

9 AIR1996SC1051

10 2000CriLJ1809

11 **Meaning of Custodial Death:** A **death in custody** is a death of a person in the custody of the police, prison service or other authorities. Death in custody remains a controversial subject, with the authorities often being accused of abuse, neglect, racism and cover-ups of the causes of these deaths.

mortem injuries, while ordering payment of compensation by refusing to accept the defence of the State Government, held that when such deaths occur, it is not only to the public at large that those holding custody are responsible, they are responsible also to the Courts under whose orders they hold such custody.

Compensation in cases of Police Encounter:

While dealing with the claim of compensation in death cases during encounter with police in *Malkiat Singh v. State of U.P.*[12], under Article 32[13] of the Constitution of India the Hon'ble Supreme Court has granted compensation of Rs. 5,00,000

Decision of the High Court:

Court held that ends of justice would be served if an amount of compensation of Rs. 6,00,000/- is awarded to the petitioner and her minor daughters.

---

12 (1998)9SCC351

13 **Article 32 in The Constitution Of India 1949**

32. Remedies for enforcement of rights conferred by this Part

(1) The right to move the Supreme Court by appropriate proceedings for the enforcement of the rights conferred by this Part is guaranteed

(2) The Supreme Court shall have power to issue directions or orders or writs, including writs in the nature of habeas corpus, mandamus, prohibition, quo warranto and certiorari, whichever may be appropriate, for the enforcement of any of the rights conferred by this Part

(3) Without prejudice to the powers conferred on the Supreme Court by clause (1) and (2), Parliament may by law empower any other court to exercise within the local limits of its jurisdiction all or any of the powers exercisable by the Supreme Court under clause (2)

(4) The right guaranteed by this article shall not be suspended except as otherwise provided for by this Constitution

28

Compensation for Negligence to Maintain Public Roads and Streets[1]

Facts in Nutshell:

In writ[2] proceeding under Article 226[3] of the Constitution of India, the petitioner[4] seeks directions to the Govt. of N.C.T. of Delhi (first respondent[5], hereafter "GNCTD") and Municipal Corporation of Delhi

1 Appellants: **Shakuntala Vs.** Respondent: **Govt. of NCT of Delhi and Anr.** 162(2009)DLT264
Hon'ble Judges/Coram: S. Ravindra Bhat, Judge

2 **Meaning of Writ:** A written order issued by a court, commanding the party to whom it is addressed to perform or cease performing a specified act

3 **Article 226 in The Constitution Of India 1949**
226. Power of High Courts to issue certain writs
(1) Notwithstanding anything in Article 32 every High Court shall have powers, throughout the territories in relation to which it exercise jurisdiction, to issue to any person or authority, including in appropriate cases, any Government, within those territories directions, orders or writs, including writs in the nature of habeas corpus, mandamus, prohibitions, quo warranto and certiorari, or any of them, for the enforcement of any of the rights conferred by Part III and for any other purpose
(2) The power conferred by clause (1) to issue directions, orders or writs to any Government, authority or person may also be exercised by any High Court exercising jurisdiction in relation to the territories within which the cause of action, wholly or in part, arises for the exercise of such power, notwithstanding that the seat of such Government or authority or the residence of such person is not within those territories
(3) Where any party against whom an interim order, whether by way of injunction or stay or in any other manner, is made on, or in any proceedings relating to, a petition under clause (1), without
(a) furnishing to such party copies of such petition and all documents in support of the plea for such interim order; and
(b) giving such party an opportunity of being heard, makes an application to the High Court for the vacation of such order and furnishes a copy of such application to the party in whose favour such order has been made or the counsel of such party, the High Court shall dispose of the application within a period of two weeks from the date on which it is received or from the date on which the copy of such application is so furnished, whichever is later, or where the High Court is closed on the last day of that period, before the expiry of the next day afterwards on which the High Court is open; and if the application is not so disposed of, the interim order shall, on the expiry of that period, or, as the case may be, the expiry of the aid next day, stand vacated
(4) The power conferred on a High Court by this article shall not be in derogation of the power conferred on the Supreme court by clause (2) of Article 32

4 **Meaning of Petitioner:** A person who presents a Petition. (**Meaning of Petition:** A formal message requesting something that is submitted to an authority)

5 **Meaning of Respondent:** A **respondent** is a person who is called upon to issue a response to a communication made by another. In legal usage, this specifically refers to the defendant in

(second respondent, hereafter "MCD") for the payment of compensation of Rs. 10,00,000/-, alleging that negligence and dereliction of public duty on their part resulted in untimely death of her husband, Sh. Sita Ram (hereafter "the deceased[6]").

The brief facts are that the deceased, a fruit vendor, carried on his trade from a roadside "Redi/" "Thela" (hand-cart). On the fateful day the deceased was selling fruits when two fighting bulls came by. In the ensuing melee he fell, was entangled between the fighting bulls and was badly mauled. He was immediately shifted to the GTB Hospital where he remained under treatment till 23.1.05, when he finally succumbed to his injuries and breathed his last. The postmortem report revealed that the cause of death was shock due to cranio-cerebral injuries produced by blunt force impact. All injuries are and possible by assault by bull.

The petitioner stated that the untimely demise of her husband who was the sole earning member, has left the family, consisting of herself (aged 39 years) and her five minor children (two sons aged 17 and 12 years and three daughters aged between 13 to 16 years) and parents of the deceased (aged 70 and 68 years), in grave financial distress and to fend for themselves. It was stated that the deceased was earning around Rs. 5,000/- per month. The petitioner alleged dereliction of duty on part of the respondents and stated that the MCD should have taken appropriate steps to ensure that stray bulls did not roam the public streets. Petitioner urged that the deceased, an Indian Citizen, lost his life due to negligence of the respondents, thus his fundamental right[7], guaranteed under Article 21[8], stood violated. The petitioner placed

---

a legal proceeding commenced by a petition, or to an appellee, or the opposing party, in an appeal of a decision by an initial fact-finder.

6 **Meaning of Deceased:** A dead person

7 ***'Part III – Fundamental Rights'*** is a charter of rights contained in the Constitution of India. It guarantees civil liberties such that all Indians can lead their lives in peace and harmony as citizens of India. These include individual rights common to most liberal democracies, such asequality before law, freedom of speech and expression, and peaceful assembly, freedom to practice religion, and the right to constitutional remedies for the protection of civil rights by means of writs such as habeas corpus. Violation of these rights result in punishments as prescribed in the Indian Penal Code or other special laws, subject to discretion of the judiciary. The Fundamental Rights are defined as basichuman freedoms which every Indian citizen has the right to enjoy for a proper and harmonious development of personality. These rights universally apply to all citizens, irrespective of race, place of birth, religion, caste, creed, colour or gender. Aliens (persons who are not citizens) are also considered in matters like equality before law. They are enforceable by the courts, subject to certain restrictions. The Rights have their origins in many sources, including England's Bill of Rights, the United States Bill of Rights and France's Declaration of the Rights of Man.

8 **Article 21 in The Constitution Of India 1949**

reliance on *D.K. Basu v. State of West Bengal*[9] that in case of violation of any fundamental rights compensation can be awarded under public law.

A Division Bench of High Court of Delhi in *Shyama Devi and Ors. v. National Capital Territory of Delhi*[10] also awarded compensation under Article 226 of the Constitution in a case where there was negligence in not defusing a rocket, resulting in the death of a Constable.

Right to Life:

It has been established now for nearly three decades, that the right to life enshrined in Article 21 is not a right to mere vegetative ("animal") existence, but to a life with dignity and a decent standard of living. The injury, suffered due to the state's or its agencies' neglect in the performance, or the wrongful performance of its duties, is as actionable in public law, as in tort. In this background the failure of the State to prevent the occurrence of negligent acts by its employees, or those who are accountable to it, within premises under its control, or in respect of zones of activities falling within their jurisdiction strikes at the root of the right to life, guaranteed under Article 21 of the Constitution of India.

Cases Referred:

In *Delhi Jal Board v. Raj Kumar and Ors.*[11]; the petitioner, who while riding a scooter drove over a manhole, that was three inches below the regular road surface and met with an accident. The Court held the Jal Board liable and observed that when power is given to do some act, it is often coupled with the duty to do that act properly. Therefore, the principle of strict liability[12] was applicable against the State also. The court further held that in cases where the principle of strict liability applies, the defendant has to pay damages for injury caused to the plaintiff[13], even though the defendants may not have been at any fault.

---

21. Protection of life and personal liberty No person shall be deprived of his life or personal liberty except according to procedure established by law

9 1997CriLJ743

10 AIR1999Delhi264

11 2005 VIII AD Delhi 533

12 Strict liability, sometimes called absolute liability, is the legal responsibility for damages, or injury, even if the person found strictly liable was not at fault or negligent. Strict liability has been applied to certain activities in TORT, such as holding an employer absolutely liable for the torts of her employees, but today it is most commonly associated with defectively manufactured products.

13 **Meaning of Plaintiff:** The party that institutes a suit in a court

In *Chand (Shri) and Anr. v. Chief Secretary and Ors.*[14]; the petitioner's son suffered a tragic death when a concrete slab from the water tank fell on his head at the UTSC complex, PWD (E) Delhi. The Court held that it was undoubtedly the duty of the respondents (Chief Secretary, NCTD and Chief Engineer, PWD zone, NCTD) to maintain the water tank and other amenities in the building in a manner so as not to endanger the lives of the passersby or those using such facilities. The court held the respondents guilty of negligence and awarded compensation.

Decision of the High Court:

Court held that the MCD (Municipal corporation of Delhi) was liable to pay compensation to the petitioner. Court directed the respondent, i.e. MCD to pay Rs. 10,00,000/- (Rupees ten lakhs only).

14 2004 IV AD Del 29

29

State held liable to compensate petitioners for damage done to their child[1]

Facts in Nutshell:

The petitioner[2] Jasbir Kaur, mother of the unfortunate child is shown to have been admitted in Shri Guru Teg Bahadur Hospital, Amritsar, on 24th June, 1993, allegedly in a serious condition of leakage. She was subjected to Sonography[3] and after caesarean operation on 25th June, 1993, a healthy normal male child is stated to have been born to her. The operation is stated to have been conducted by Dr. Harinder Kaur. It was submitted that no arrangements are made for any cradle for separately keeping the children born through caesarean operation for the people belonging to lower strata, termed as poor. The parents of the child and the relations were told that the mother and child should not sleep together on one bed because of the fear of infection. Under these circumstances, the child was kept with the relative of the petitioners on the intervening night of 25th-26th June, 1993. The electric light is alleged to have gone off suddenly in the maternity ward and the attendant sleeping with the child found the child missing from her side. Hue and cry was raised and search was made in the hospital premises, resulting in the discovery of the child in a profusely bleeding condition, with one eye totally gouged out along with the eyeball. The child in such a condition was found near the wash basin of the bathroom. The matter was brought to the notice of the authorities for holding an inquiry as the parents genuinely and bonafidely believed that their child had been replaced with a damaged eye child. As no action was taken, Smt. Vimla Dang, M.L.A., from Amritsar, was approached who thereafter made inquiries and wrote letters to the authorities for taking action in the matter. Despite registration and investigation of the

1 Appellants: **Jasbir Kaur and another Vs.** Respondent: **State of Punjab and others** AIR1995P&H278
Hon'ble Judges: R.P. Sethi and S.S. Sudhalkar, JJ.

2 **Meaning of Petitioner:** A person who presents a Petition. (**Meaning of Petition:** A formal message requesting something that is submitted to an authority)

3 **Meaning of Sonography:** Using the reflections of high-frequency sound waves to construct an image of a body organ (a sonogram); commonly used to observe fetal growth or study bodily organs

case, no action was taken by any of the authorities, of the respondent[4]-State, forcing the petitioners to approach High Court for the grant of relief by handing over the case to the Central Bureau of Investigation, an independent agency, for investigating the case in which the child of the petitioners was allegedly replaced or exchanged with another child or to ascertain the circumstances in which the child is stated to have been lifted by a cat and his one eyeball was gouged out. It was further prayed that the hospital authorities be directed to make proper arrangements and ensure proper working in the hospital and not to play with the lives of the human children by exposing them to be wasted at the hands of the animals like cats. It was alternatively prayed that the petitioners be awarded a compensation to the extent of rupees ten lakhs for negligence, callousness and carelessness of the respondents.

Decision of the High Court:

Court held that article 21[5] of the Constitution of India provides that no person shall be deprived of his life and property except according to the procedure established by law. The term "life" used in Article 21 is not only restricted to the mere nominal existence but extends to the inhibition against its deprivation to all those limits and faculties by which life is enjoyed. This Article is wide and of far reaching consequences. As and when life in any form or to any extent is taken away or endangered by any functionary of the State, a duty is cast upon the State representing the will of the people to compensate the victim by granting adequate compensation. The monarchial rule has to be distinguished from democratic set up and the State cannot shirk its responsibility to protect the life, liberty and property of the citizens. The maintenance of law and order and providing adequate facilities in the Government Hospitals is the responsibility of the Government who cannot abdicate its functions and allow the life and liberty of citizens to be in jeopardy on technical pleas and false pretexts. Therefore, respondent State was held liable to compensate the petitioners for the damage done to their child on account of the negligence of the staff of the hospital owned and managed by the respondent State. Court awarded rupees one lakh as damages to the petitioners.

4 **Meaning of Respondent:** A **respondent** is a person who is called upon to issue a response to a communication made by another. In legal usage, this specifically refers to the defendant in a legal proceeding commenced by a petition, or to an appellee, or the opposing party, in an appeal of a decision by an initial fact-finder.

5 **Article 21 in The Constitution Of India 1949**
21. Protection of life and personal liberty No person shall be deprived of his life or personal liberty except according to procedure established by law

30

Compensation by State on Ground of Illegal Arrest[1]

Facts in Nutshell:

On August 17, 1985, the opening day of the Budget Session of the Legislative Assembly, Shri Bhim Singh was suspended from the Assembly. He questioned the suspension in the High Court of Jammu & Kashmir. The order of suspension was stayed by the High Court on 9th September, 1985. On the intervening night of 9th-10th September, 1985, he was proceeding from Jammu to Srinagar. En route, at about 3.00 AM (on 10th), he was arrested at a place called Qazi Kund about 70 kms. from Srinagar. He was taken away by the police. As it was not known where he had been taken away and as the efforts to trace him proved futile, his wife Smt. Jayamala, acting on his behalf, filed the application for the issue of a writ[2] in Supreme Court to direct the respondents[3] to produce Shri Bhim Singh before the court, to declare his detention illegal and to set him at liberty. She impleaded the State of Jammu & Kashmir through the Chief Secretary as the first respondent, the Chief Minister, the Deputy Chief Minister and the Inspector General of Police, Jammu & Kashmir as respondents 2, 3 and 4.

On September 13, 1985, Supreme Court directed notice to be issued to the respondents and also directed the Inspector General of Police to inform Smt. Jayamala where Shri Bhim Singh was kept in custody. On September 16,1985, Shri Bhim Singh was released on bail[4] by the learned Additional

1 Appellants: **Bhim Singh, MLA Vs.** Respondent: **State of J & K and Ors.** AIR1986SC494
Hon'ble Judges: O. Chinnappa Reddy and V. Khalid, JJ.

2 **Meaning of Writ:** A written order issued by a court, commanding the party to whom it is addressed to perform or cease performing a specified act

3 **Meaning of Respondent:** A **respondent** is a person who is called upon to issue a response to a communication made by another. In legal usage, this specifically refers to the defendant in a legal proceeding commenced by a petition, or to an appellee, or the opposing party, in an appeal of a decision by an initial fact-finder.

4 **Meaning of Bail:** Security, usually a sum of money, exchanged for the release of an

Sessions Judge of Jammu before whom he was produced. Shri Bhim Singh categorically asserted that he was kept in police lock up from 10th to 14lh and that he was produced before a Magistrate for the first time only on the 14th.

Decision of the Supreme Court:

Court held that there was a gross violation of Shri Bhim Singh's constitutional rights under Articles 21[5] and 22(2)[6] of Constitution of India. Court awarded monetary compensation by way of exemplary costs as established by the decisions of Supreme court in *Rudul Shah v. State of Bihar and Anr.*[7] and *Sebestian M. Hongray v. Union of India*[8]. When a person comes to court with the complaint that he has been arrested and imprisoned with mischievous or malicious intent and that his constitutional and legal rights were invaded, the mischief or malice and the invasion may not be washed away or wished away by his being set free. In appropriate cases Court have the jurisdiction to compensate the victim by awarding suitable monetary compensation. Court directed the first respondent, the State of Jammu and Kashmir to pay to Shri Bhim Singh a sum of Rs. 50,000.

---

arrested person as a guarantee of that person's appearance for trial.

5 **Article 21 in The Constitution Of India 1949**
21. Protection of life and personal liberty No person shall be deprived of his life or personal liberty except according to procedure established by law

6 **Article 22 in The Constitution Of India 1949**
22. Protection against arrest and detention in certain cases
(1) No person who is arrested shall be detained in custody without being informed, as soon as may be, of the grounds for such arrest nor shall he be denied the right to consult, and to be defended by, a legal practitioner of his choice
(2) Every person who is arrested and detained in custody shall be produced before the nearest magistrate within a period of twenty four hours of such arrest excluding the time necessary for the journey from the place of arrest to the court of the magistrate and no such person shall be detained in custody beyond the said period without the authority of a magistrate

7 1983CriLJ1644

8 AIR1984 SC 1026

31

Medical facilities and Compensation by State[1]

Facts in Nutshell:

Petition[2] filed under Article 32[3] of the Constitution raises issue in the context of availability of facilities in Government hospitals for treatment of persons sustaining serious injuries. Hakim Seikh (petitioner[4] No. 2), a member of Paschim Banga Khet Mazdoor Samity (petitioner No. 1), an organisation of agricultural labourers, fell off a train at Mathurapur Station in West Bengal on July 8, 1992. As a result of the said fall Hakim Seikh suffered serious head injuries and brain haemorrhage. He was taken to the Primary Health center at Mathurapur. Since necessary facilities for treatment were not available at the Primary Health center, the medical officer in charge of the center referred him to the Diamond Harbour Sub-Divisional Hospital or any other State hospital for better treatment. Hakim Seikh was taken to N.R.S. Medical College Hospital near Sealdah Railway Station, Calcutta on July 8, 1992. The Emergency Medical Officer in the said Hospital, after examining him and after taking two X-ray prints

1 Appellants:**Paschim Banga Khet Mazdoor Samity and others Vs.** Respondent: **State of West Bengal and another**
AIR1996SC2426
Hon'ble Judges: S. C. Agrawal and G. T. Nanavati, JJ.

2 **Meaning of Petition:** A formal message requesting something that is submitted to an authority

3 **Article 32 in The Constitution Of India 1949**
32. Remedies for enforcement of rights conferred by this Part
(1) The right to move the Supreme Court by appropriate proceedings for the enforcement of the rights conferred by this Part is guaranteed
(2) The Supreme Court shall have power to issue directions or orders or writs, including writs in the nature of habeas corpus, mandamus, prohibition, quo warranto and certiorari, whichever may be appropriate, for the enforcement of any of the rights conferred by this Part
(3) Without prejudice to the powers conferred on the Supreme Court by clause (1) and (2), Parliament may by law empower any other court to exercise within the local limits of its jurisdiction all or any of the powers exercisable by the Supreme Court under clause (2)
(4) The right guaranteed by this article shall not be suspended except as otherwise provided for by this Constitution

4 **Meaning of Petitioner:** A person who presents a Petition. (**Meaning of Petition:** A formal message requesting something that is submitted to an authority)

of his skull recommended immediate admission for further treatment. But Hakim Seikh could not be admitted in the said hospital as no vacant bed was available in the Surgical Emergency ward and the regular Surgery Ward was also full. He was thereafter taken to Calcutta Medical College Hospital on July 9, 1992 but there also he was not admitted on the ground that no vacant bed was available. He was then taken to Shambhu Nath Pandit Hospital at about 1.00 A.M. on July 9, 1992. He was not admitted in that hospital and referred to a teaching hospital in the ENT, Neuro Surgeon Department on the ground that the hospital has no ENT Emergency or Neuro Emergency Department. At about 2.00 A.M. on July 9, 1992 he was taken to the Calcutta National Medical College Hospital but there also he was not admitted on account of non-availability of bed. At about 8.00 A.M. on July 9, 1992 he was taken to the Bangur Institute of Neurology but on seeing the CT Scan (which was got done at a private hospital on payment of Rs. 1310) it was found that there was haemorrhage condition in the frontal region of the head and that it was an emergency case which could not be handled in the said Institute. At about 10.00 A.M. on July 9, 1992 he was taken to SSKM Hospital but there also he was not admitted on the ground that the hospital has no facility of neuro surgery. Ultimately he was admitted in Calcutta Medical Research Institute, a private hospital, where he received treatment as an indoor patient from July 9, 1992 to July 22, 1992 and he had incurred an expenditure of approximately Rs. 17,000 in his treatment. Feeling aggrieved by the indifferent and callous attitude on the part of the medical authorities at the various State run hospitals in Calcutta in providing treatment for the serious injuries sustained by Hakim Seikh, the petitioners filed writ petition in Supreme Court.

Immediate Medical aid to Injured Persons:

In *Pt. Paramanand Katara v. Union of India and Ors.*[5], Supreme Court in the context of medico-legal cases, has emphasised the need for rendering immediate medical aid to injured persons to preserve life and the obligations of the State as well as doctors in that regard.

Right to Life:

The Constitution envisages the establishment of a welfare state at the federal level as well as at the state level. In a welfare state the primary duty of the Government is to secure the welfare to the people. Providing adequate medical facilities for the people is an essential part

5 1990CriLJ671

of the obligations undertaken by the Government in a welfare state. The Government discharges this obligation by running hospitals and health centers which provide medical care to the person seeking to avail those facilities. Article 21[6] imposes an obligation on the State to safeguard the right to life of every person. Preservation of human life is thus of paramount importance. The Government hospitals run by the State and the medical officers employed therein are duty bound to extend medical assistance for preserving human life. Failure on the part of the Government hospital to provide timely medical treatment to a person in need of such treatment results in violation of his right to life guaranteed under Article 21.

Decision by Supreme Court:

Court held that there was breach of the said right of Hakim Seikh guaranteed under Article 21 when he was denied treatment at the various Government hospitals which were approached even though his condition was very serious at that time and he was in need of immediate medical attention. Since the said denial of the right of Hakim Seikh guaranteed under Article 21 was by officers of the State in hospitals run by the State the State cannot avoid its responsibility for such denial of the constitutional right of Hakim Seikh. In respect of deprivation of the constitutional rights guaranteed under Part-III[7] of the Constitution the position is well settled that adequate compensation can be awarded by the court for such violation by way of redress in proceedings under

6 **Article 21 in The Constitution Of India 1949**
21. Protection of life and personal liberty No person shall be deprived of his life or personal liberty except according to procedure established by law

7 ***'Part III – Fundamental Rights'*** is a charter of rights contained in the Constitution of India. It guarantees civil liberties such that all Indians can lead their lives in peace and harmony as citizens of India. These include individual rights common to most liberal democracies, such asequality before law, freedom of speech and expression, and peaceful assembly, freedom to practice religion, and the right to constitutional remedies for the protection of civil rights by means of writs such as habeas corpus. Violation of these rights result in punishments as prescribed in the Indian Penal Code or other special laws, subject to discretion of the judiciary. The Fundamental Rights are defined as basichuman freedoms which every Indian citizen has the right to enjoy for a proper and harmonious development of personality. These rights universally apply to all citizens, irrespective of race, place of birth, religion, caste, creed, colour or gender. Aliens (persons who are not citizens) are also considered in matters like equality before law. They are enforceable by the courts, subject to certain restrictions. The Rights have their origins in many sources, including England's Bill of Rights, the United States Bill of Rights and France's Declaration of the Rights of Man.

Articles 32 and 226[8] of the Constitution. (See: *Rudal Sah v. State of Bihar*[9]; *Nilabati Behare v. State of Orissa*[10] and *Consumer Education and Research center v. Union of India*[11]). Court held that Hakim Seikh should, therefore, be suitably compensated for the breach of his right guaranteed under Article 21 of the Constitution. Having regard to the facts and circumstances of the case, court fixed the amount of such compensation at Rs. 25,000.

---

8 **Article 226 in The Constitution Of India 1949**

226. Power of High Courts to issue certain writs

(1) Notwithstanding anything in Article 32 every High Court shall have powers, throughout the territories in relation to which it exercise jurisdiction, to issue to any person or authority, including in appropriate cases, any Government, within those territories directions, orders or writs, including writs in the nature of habeas corpus, mandamus, prohibitions, quo warranto and certiorari, or any of them, for the enforcement of any of the rights conferred by Part III and for any other purpose

(2) The power conferred by clause (1) to issue directions, orders or writs to any Government, authority or person may also be exercised by any High Court exercising jurisdiction in relation to the territories within which the cause of action, wholly or in part, arises for the exercise of such power, notwithstanding that the seat of such Government or authority or the residence of such person is not within those territories

(3) Where any party against whom an interim order, whether by way of injunction or stay or in any other manner, is made on, or in any proceedings relating to, a petition under clause (1), without

(a) furnishing to such party copies of such petition and all documents in support of the plea for such interim order; and

(b) giving such party an opportunity of being heard, makes an application to the High Court for the vacation of such order and furnishes a copy of such application to the party in whose favour such order has been made or the counsel of such party, the High Court shall dispose of the application within a period of two weeks from the date on which it is received or from the date on which the copy of such application is so furnished, whichever is later, or where the High Court is closed on the last day of that period, before the expiry of the next day afterwards on which the High Court is open; and if the application is not so disposed of, the interim order shall, on the expiry of that period, or, as the case may be, the expiry of the aid next day, stand vacated

(4) The power conferred on a High Court by this article shall not be in derogation of the power conferred on the Supreme court by clause (2) of Article 32

9 1983CriLJ1644

10 1993CriLJ2899

11 (1995)IILLJ768SC

Right to Education

Right to Education and Right to Life[1]

Right to life is the compendious expression for all those rights which the courts must enforce because they are basic to the dignified enjoyment of life. It extends to the full range of conduct which the individual is free to pursue. The right to education flows directly from right to life. The right to life under Article 21[2] and the dignity of an individual cannot be assured unless it is accompanied by the right to education. The State Government is under an obligation to make endeavour to provide educational facilities at all levels to its citizens.

Right to Free and Compulsory Education:

It may be pertinent to mention that the right of children to free and compulsory education has been made a fundamental right under Article 21A[3] of the Constitution. Now every child of the age of 6 to 14 years has right to have free education in neighbourhood school till elementary education.

---

1 *Mohini Jain Vs State of Karnataka and ors.*1992 AIR 1858

2 **Article 21 in The Constitution Of India 1949**
21. Protection of life and personal liberty No person shall be deprived of his life or personal liberty except according to procedure established by law

3 **Article 21 A of Constitution of India:**
Right to education.-
"21A. The State shall provide free and compulsory education to all children of the age of six to fourteen years in such manner as the State may, by law, determine."

32

Right of children to free and compulsory education[1]

Ratio Decidendi[2]: *No child shall be deprived of his fundamental rights guaranteed under Constitution of India and bring to child traffic and abuse*

Facts in Nutshell:

Petition has been filed in public interest under Article 32[3] of the Constitution in the wake of serious violations and abuse of children who were forcefully detained in circuses, in many instances, without any access to their families under extreme inhuman conditions. There were instances of sexual abuse on a daily basis, physical abuse as well as emotional abuse. The children were deprived of basic human needs of food and water. It was stated in the petition[4] that the Petitioner[5] has filed the petition following a series of incidents where the Petitioner came in contact with many children who were trafficked into performing in circuses. The Petitioner found that circus is one of the ancient forms of

1 Appellants: **Bachpan Bachao Andolan Vs.** Respondent: **Union of India (UOI) and Ors.** AIR2011SC3361
Hon'ble Judges: Dalveer Bhandari and A. K. Patnaik, JJ.

2 **Meaning of Ration Decidendi:** ***Ratio decidendi*** is a Latin phrase meaning "the reason" or "the rationale for the decision." The *ratio decidendi* is "the point in a case which determines the judgment" or "the principle which the case establishes."

3 **Article 32 in The Constitution Of India 1949**
32. Remedies for enforcement of rights conferred by this Part
(1) The right to move the Supreme Court by appropriate proceedings for the enforcement of the rights conferred by this Part is guaranteed
(2) The Supreme Court shall have power to issue directions or orders or writs, including writs in the nature of habeas corpus, mandamus, prohibition, quo warranto and certiorari, whichever may be appropriate, for the enforcement of any of the rights conferred by this Part
(3) Without prejudice to the powers conferred on the Supreme Court by clause (1) and (2), Parliament may by law empower any other court to exercise within the local limits of its jurisdiction all or any of the powers exercisable by the Supreme Court under clause (2)
(4) The right guaranteed by this article shall not be suspended except as otherwise provided for by this Constitution

4 **Meaning of Petition**: A formal written application requesting a court for a specific judicial action

5 **Meaning of Petitioner:** A person who presents a Petition. (**Meaning of Petition:** A formal message requesting something that is submitted to an authority)

indigenous entertainment in the world, with humans having a major role to play. However, the activities that were undertaken in these circuses deprive the artists especially children of their basic fundamental rights. Most of them are trafficked from some poverty-stricken areas of Nepal as well as from backward districts of India. The outside world has no meaning for them. There is no life beyond the circus campus. Once they enter into the circuses, they are confined to the circus arena, with no freedom of mobility and choice. They are entrapped into the world of circuses for the rest of their lives, leading a vagrant tunneled existence away from the hub of society, which is tiresome, claustrophobic and dependent on vicissitudes.

It was submitted that the Petitioner is engaged in a social movement for the emancipation of children in exploitative labour, bondage and servitude. Bachpan Bachao Andolan has been able to liberate thousands of children with the help of the judiciary and the executive as well as through persuasion, social mobilization and education.

Trafficking in Human Beings:

Trafficking in human beings is not a new phenomenon. Women, children and men have been captured, bought and sold in market places for centuries. Human trafficking is one of the most lucrative criminal activities. Estimates of the United Nations state that 1 to 4 million people are trafficked worldwide each year. Trafficking in women and children is an operation which is worth more than $ 10 billion annually. The NHRC Committee on Missing Children has the following statistics to offer:

a. 12.6 million (Governmental sources) to 100 million (unofficial sources) stated to be child labour;

b. 44,000 children are reported missing annually, of which 11,000 get traced;

c. About 200 girls and women enter prostitution daily, of which 20% are below 15 years of age.

International conventions exist to punish and suppress trafficking especially women and children[6]. Trafficking is now defined as an organized crime and a crime against humanity. The convention being an

6 (Refer: UN Protocol to Prevent, Suppress and Punish Trafficking in Persons also referred as the PALERMO Protocol on Trafficking)

international convention is limited to cross border trafficking but does not address trafficking within the country. The definition of trafficking is significant:

...The recruitment, transportation, transfer, harboring or receipt of persons by means of threat or use of force or other forms of coercion, of abduction, of fraud, of deception, of the abuse of power or of a position of vulnerability or of the giving or receiving of payments or benefits to achieve the consent of a person having control over another person, for the purpose of exploitation....

Exploitation shall include at a minimum, the exploitation of the prostitutes of others or other forms of sexual exploitation, forced labour or service, slavery or practices similar to slavery, servitude or the removal of organs.

Three significant elements constitute trafficking:

a. The action involving recruitment and transportation;

b. The means employed such as force, coercion, fraud or deception including abuse of power and bribes; and

c. The purpose being exploitation including prostitution.

Internationally, there is a working definition of child trafficking. The working definition is clear because it incorporates the above three elements. In June 2001, India has adopted the PALERMO Protocol to evolve its working definition of child trafficking.

The forms and purposes of child trafficking may be:

a. Bonded labour;

b. Domestic work;

c. Agricultural labour;

d. Employment in construction activity;

e. Carpet industry;

f. Garment industry g. Fish/Shrimp Export;

h. Other sites of work in the formal and informal economy.

Trafficking can also be for illegal activities such as:

a. Begging;

b. Organ trade;

c. Drug peddling and smuggling;

Trafficking can be for sexual exploitation, i.e.

a. Forced prostitution;

b. Socially and religiously sanctified forms of prostitution;

c. Sex tourism;

d. Pornography;

Child trafficking can be to aid entertainment in sports:

a. Circus/dance troupes;

b. Camel jockeying

Articles 23[7], 39[8], 14[9] and 21[10] of the Constitution of India guarantee

7 **Article 23 in The Constitution Of India 1949**
23. Prohibition of traffic in human beings and forced labour
(1) Traffic in human beings and begar and other similar forms of forced labour are prohibited and any contravention of this provision shall be an offence punishable in accordance with law
(2) Nothing in this article shall prevent the State from imposing compulsory service for public purpose, and in imposing such service the State shall not make any discrimination on grounds only of religion, race, caste or class or any of them

8 **Article 39 in The Constitution Of India 1949**
39. Certain principles of policy to be followed by the State: The State shall, in particular, direct its policy towards securing
(a) that the citizens, men and women equally, have the right to an adequate means to livelihood;
(b) that the ownership and control of the material resources of the community are so distributed as best to subserve the common good;
(c) that the operation of the economic system does not result in the concentration of wealth and means of production to the common detriment;
(d) that there is equal pay for equal work for both men and women;
(e) that the health and strength of workers, men and women, and the tender age of children are not abused and that citizens are not forced by economic necessity to enter avocations unsuited to their age or strength;
(f) that children are given opportunities and facilities to develop in a healthy manner and in conditions of freedom and dignity and that childhood and youth are protected against exploitation and against moral and material abandonment

9 **Article 14 in The Constitution Of India 1949**
14. Equality before law The State shall not deny to any person equality before the law or the equal protection of the laws within the territory of India Prohibition of discrimination on grounds of religion, race, caste, sex or place of birth

10 **Article 21 in The Constitution Of India 1949**
21. Protection of life and personal liberty No person shall be deprived of his life or personal liberty except according to procedure established by law

every child to be freed from exploitation of any form. Article 23 prohibits trafficking in human beings, 'beggar' and other forms of forced labour. Trafficking in women and children has become an increasingly lucrative business especially since the risk of being prosecuted is very low. Women and children do not usually come to the brothels[11] on their own will, but are brought through highly systematic, organized and illegal trafficking networks run by experienced individuals who buy, transport and sell children into prostitution. Traffickers tend to work in groups and children being trafficked often change hands to ensure that neither the trafficker nor the child gets caught during transit. Different groups of traffickers include gang members, police, pimps and even politicians, all working as a nexus. Trafficking networks are well organized and have linkages both within the country and in the neighbouring countries. Most traffickers are men. The role of women in this business is restricted to recruitment at the brothels.

Right to Free and Compulsory Education:

It may be pertinent to mention that the right of children to free and compulsory education has been made a fundamental right under Article 21A[12] of the Constitution. Now every child of the age of 6 to 14 years has right to have free education in neighbourhood school till elementary education.

Directions of the Supreme Court:

(i) In order to implement the fundamental right of the children under Article 21A it is imperative that the Central Government must issue suitable notifications prohibiting the employment of children in circuses.

(ii) The Respondents[13] (Union of India) were directed to conduct simultaneous raids in all the circuses to liberate the children and check the violation of fundamental rights of the children. The rescued children

11 **Meaning of Brothel:** A house of prostitution

12 **Article 21 A of Constitution of India:**
Right to education.-
"21A. The State shall provide free and compulsory education to all children of the age of six to fourteen years in such manner as the State may, by law, determine."

13 **Meaning of Respondent:** A **respondent** is a person who is called upon to issue a response to a communication made by another. In legal usage, this specifically refers to the defendant in a legal proceeding commenced by a petition, or to an appellee, or the opposing party, in an appeal of a decision by an initial fact-finder.

be kept in the Care and Protective Homes till they attain the age of 18 years.

(iii) The Respondents were also directed to talk to the parents of the children and in case they are willing to take their children back to their homes, they may be directed to do so after proper verification.

(iv) The Respondents were directed to frame proper scheme of rehabilitation of rescued children from circuses.

33

Fundamental Right to Education[1]

Facts in Nutshell:

The writ petitions filed by private educational institutions engaged in or proposing to engage in imparting medical and engineering education - the correctness of the decision rendered by a Division Bench comprising Kuldip Singh and R.M. Sahai, JJ. in Miss *Mohini Jain v. State of Karnataka and Ors*[2]. is called in question. The petitioners, running medical/engineering colleges in the States of Andhra Pradesh, Karnataka, Maharashtra and Tamil Nadu, say that if Mohini Jain is correct and is followed and implemented by the respective State Governments as indeed they are bound to they will have to close down; no other option is left to them.

Question before the Court:

1. Whether a citizen has a Fundamental Right to education for a medical, engineering or other professional degree.

2. Whether the Constitution of India guarantees a fundamental right to education to its citizens?

3. Whether there is a fundamental right to establish an educational institution under Article 19(1)(g)[3]?

Right to Life

The Court Interpreted in *Bandhua Mukti Morcha v. Union of India* □: It is the fundamental right of everyone in this country, assured under

1 Appellants: **Unni Krishnan, J.P. and others etc. etc. Vs.** Respondent: **State of Andhra Pradesh and others etc. etc.**
AIR1993SC2178
Hon'ble Judges: L. M. Sharma, C.J., S. Ratnavel Pandian, S. Mohan, B.P. Jeevan Reddy and S. P. Bharucha,

2 1992 AIR 1858

3 **Article 19(1)(g) in The Constitution Of India 1949**
(g) to practise any profession, or to carry on any occupation, trade or business

the interpretation given Article 21[4] by the Court in Francis Mullin's case, to live with human dignity, free from citation. This right to live with human dignity enshrined in Article 21 derives its life breath the Directive Principles of State Policy and particularly Clauses (e) and (f) of Article 39[5] Articles 41[6] and 42[7] and at the least, therefore, it must include protection of the health and strength of workers, men and women, and of the tender age of children against abuse, unities and facilities for children to develop in a healthy manner and in conditions of freedom and dignity, educational facilities, just and humane conditions of work and maternity relief. These are the minimum requirements which must exist in order to enable a person to (with human dignity and no State - neither the Central Government nor any State eminent has the right to take any action which will deprive a person of the enjoyment basic essentials. Since the Directive Principles of State Policy contained in Clauses (e) and (f) of Article 39, Articles 41 and 42 are not enforceable in a court of law, it may not be possible to compel the State through the judicial process to make provision by statutory enactment or executive fiat for ensuring these basic essentials which go to make up a life of dignity but where legislation is already enacted by the State providing these basic requirements to the workmen and thus investing their right to live with basic human dignity, concrete reality and content, the State can certainly be obligated to ensure observance of legislation for inaction on the part of the State in securing implementation of such Nation would amount to denial of the right to live with human dignity enshrined in Article 21, more so in the context of Article 256 which provides that the executive power of every State so exercised as to ensure compliance with the laws made by Parliament and any 's which apply in that State.

4 **Article 21 in The Constitution Of India 1949**
21. Protection of life and personal liberty No person shall be deprived of his life or personal liberty except according to procedure established by law

5 Article 39 **Certain principles of policy to be followed by the State.**
(e) That the health and strength of workers, men and women, and the tender age of children are not abused and that citizens are not forced by economic necessity to enter avocations unsuited to their age or strength
[(f) That children are given opportunities and facilities to develop in a healthy manner and in conditions of freedom and dignity and that childhood and youth are protected against exploitation and against moral and material abandonment.]

6 Article 41 - Right to work, to education and to public assistance in certain cases.
The State shall, within the limits of its economic capacity and development, make effective provision for securing the right to work, to education and to public assistance in cases of unemployment, old age, sickness and disablement, and in other cases of undeserved want.

7 Article 42 – provision for just and humane conditions of work and maternity relief
The State shall make provision for securing just and humane conditions of work and for maternity relief

In Bandhua Mukti Morcha Court held that the right to life guaranteed by Article 21 does take in "educational facilities".

Right to Education and Right to Life[8]

Right to life is the compendious expression for all those rights which the courts must enforce because they are basic to the dignified enjoyment of life. It extends to the full range of conduct which the individual is free to pursue. The right to education flows directly from right to life. The right to life under Article 21 and the dignity of an individual cannot be assured unless it is accompanied by the right to education. The State Government is under an obligation to make endeavor to provide educational facilities at all levels to its citizens.

Right to education after the child/citizen completes the age of 14 years.

The right to free education is available only to children until they complete the age of 14 years. Thereafter, the obligation of the State to provide education is subject to the limits of its economic capacity and development[9].

The expression 'professional colleges' in the scheme includes:

(i) medical colleges, dental colleges and other institutions and colleges imparting Nursing, Pharmacy and other courses allied to Medicine, established and/or run by private education institutions,

(ii) colleges of engineering and colleges and institutions imparting technical education including electronics, computer sciences, established and/or run by private education institutions, and

(iii) such other colleges to which this scheme is made applicable by the Government, recognising and/or affiliating authority.

Whether there is a fundamental right to establish an educational institution. Article 19(1)(g). That reads as follows: To practice any profession, or to carry on any occupation, trade or business,

The question before the court was: what is the meaning to be attributed to the words "profession", "occupation", "trade" or "business".

8 *Mohini Jain Vs State of Karnataka and ors.*1992 AIR 1858

9 *Francis C. Mullin Administrator vs Union Territory of* Delhi 1981CriLJ306

In P. Ramanatha Aiyar's Law Lexicon Reprint Edition 1987 at page 897 "Occupation" means:

The principal business of one's life, vocation, calling, trade, the business which a man follows to procure a living or obtain wealth: that which occupies or engages one's time or attention, vocation, employment, calling, trade; the business in which a man is usually engaged, to the knowledge of his neighbour.

According to Black's Law Dictionary Fifth Edition at page 973 "Occupation" means:

Possession; control; tenure; use. The act or process by which real property is possessed and enjoyed. Where a person exercises physical control over land.

That which principally takes up one's time thought, and energies, especially, one's regular business or employment; also, whatever one follows as the means of making a livelihood. Particular business, profession, trade, or calling which engages individual's time and efforts; employment in which one regularly engages or vocation of his life.

In *P.V.G. Raju v. Commissioner of Expenditure*[10] it is observed thus:

The activity termed as "Occupation", if of wider import than vocation or profession. It is also distinct from a hobby which can be resorted to only in leisure hours for the purpose of killing time. Occupation, therefore, is that with which a person occupies himself either temporarily or permanently or for a considerable period with continuity of activity. It is analogous to a business, calling or pursuit. A person may have more than one occupation in a previous year. The Occupations may be seasonal or for the whole year.

The meaning of "business' can be gathered from Law Lexicon Edition 1987 by Ramnath Iyer:

Business is that which engages the time, talent and interest of a man" and is what a man proposes to himself. There may be a "Business" without pecuniary profit being at all contemplated.

In *State of Andhra Pradesh -vs- Abdul Bakshi*[11]

10 36 ITR . 267

11 [1964]7SCR664

The expression "business" though extensively used as a word of indefinite import, in taxing statutes it is used in the sense of an occupation, or profession which occupies the time, attention and labour of a person, normally with the object of making profit. To regard an activity as business there must be a course of dealings, either actually continued or contemplated to be continued with a profit motive, and no for sport of pleasure.

The expression "Business" includes every Trade, occupation, or profession. Section 2(b) of the Indian Partnership Act, 1932[12] also defines "Business" thus: Business includes every trade, occupation and profession.

In ***Ahmedabad St. Xaviers College Society*** v. ***State of Gujarat*** [13] it was observed:

The right to establish and administer educational institutions of their choice has been conferred on religious and linguistic minorities so that the majority who can always have their right by having proper legislation do not pass a legislation prohibiting minorities to establish and administer educational institutions of their choice. If the scope of Article 30(1)[14] is made an extension of the right under Article 29(1)[15] as the right to establish and administer educational institutions for giving religious instruction or for imparting education in their religious teachings or tenets the fundamental right of minorities to establish and administer educational institution of their choice will be taken away.

In *R.M.D.C. v. State till Bombay* [16], it was held that imparting education cannot be treated as trade or business. Education cannot be allowed to be converted into commerce nor can the petitioners seek to obtain the said result by relying upon the wider meaning of "occupation". The content

12 **Section 2(b) in The Indian Partnership Act, 1932**
(b) " business" includes every trade, occupation and profession;

13 [1975]1SCR173

14 Article 30- Right of minorities to establish and administer education institutions.
Article 30(1) All minorities, whether based on religion or language, shall have the right to establish and administer educational institutions of their choice.

15 Article 29- Protection of Interests of Minorities
(1) Any section of the citizens residing in the territory of India or any part thereof having a distinct language, script or culture of its own shall have the right to conserve the same.
(2) No citizen shall be denied admission into any educational institution maintained by the State or receiving aid out of State funds on grounds only of religion, race, caste, language or any of them.

16 [1957]1SCR874

of the ' expression "occupation" has to be ascertained keeping in mind the fact that Clause (g) employs all the four expressions viz., profession, occupation, trade and business.

It is significant to notice the words "to practice any profession".[17] Establishing educational institutions can by no stretch of imagination be treated as "practicing any profession". Teaching may be as profession but establishing an institution, employing teaching and non-teaching staff, procuring the necessary intrastate for running a school or college is not 'practising profession'. It may be anything but not practising a profession.

Case Referred-- *Mohini Jain vs State of Karnataka and Ors*[18]

Miss Mohini Jain, a non-Karnataka student (she was from Meerut in Uttar Pradesh) applied for admission in M.B.B.S. course in one of the private medical colleges in Karnataka. She was informed by the college that if she pays Rs. 60,000/- towards the first year's tuition fee and furnishes a Bank guarantee for the fees payable for the remaining years of the M.B.B.S. course, she will be admitted. Her parents were not in a position to pay the same and hence she could not be admitted. Her further case, which was denied by the Management of the college, was that she was asked to pay a capitation fee of Rs. 4,50,000/- as a condition of admission. She approached the Court under Article 32[19] challenging the aforesaid notification of the Karnataka Government and asking for a direction to be admitted on payment of the same fee as was payable by the Karnataka students admitted against the "Government Seats".

Questions before the Court in Mohini Jain Case:

Is there a 'right to education' guaranteed to the people of India under the Constitution? If so, does the concept of 'capitation fee' infarct the same?

17 *Employees v. Industrial Tribunal* A.I.R. 1962 S.C. 1085.

18 1992 AIR 1858

19 **Article 32- Remedies for enforcement of rights conferred by this part**

(1) The right to move the Supreme Court by appropriate proceedings for the enforcement of the rights conferred by this Part is guaranteed.

(2) The Supreme Court shall have power to issue directions or orders or writs, including writs in the nature of habeas corpus, mandamus, prohibition, quo warranto and certiorari, whichever may be appropriate, for the enforcement of any of

(3) Without prejudice to the powers conferred on the Supreme Court by clauses (1) and (2), Parliament may by law empower any other court to exercise within the local limits of its jurisdiction all or any of the powers exercisable by the Supreme Court under clause (2).

(4) The right guaranteed by this article shall not be suspended except as otherwise provided for by this Constitution.

(ii) Whether the charging of capitation fee in consideration of admission to educational institutions is arbitrary, unfair, unjust and as such violates the equality clause contained in Article 14 of the Constitution[20]?

(iii) Whether the impugned notification permits the Private Medical Colleges to charge capitation fee in the guise of regulating fees under the Act? And

(iv) Whether the notification is violative of the provisions of the Act which in specific terms prohibits the charging of capitation fee by any educational institution in the State of Karnataka?

Decision of Court in Mohini Jain Case

On the first question, the Bench held, on a consideration of Articles 21[21], 38[22], 39(a)[23] and (f)[24], 41[25] and 45[26] of the constitution:

(a) the framers of the Constitution made it obligatory for the State to

---

20 Article 14- **Equality before Law**
The State shall not deny to any person equality before the law or the equal protection of the laws within the territory of India.

21 Article 21- **Protection of Life and Personal Liberty**
No person shall be deprived of his life or personal liberty except according to procedure established by law.

22 Article 38- State to secure a social order for the promotion of welfare of the people
[(1)] The State shall strive to promote the welfare of the people by securing and protecting as effectively as it may a social order in which justice, social, economic and political, shall inform all the institutions of the national life.
[(2) The State shall, in particular, strive to minimise the inequalities in income, and endeavour to eliminate inequalities in status, facilities and opportunities, not only amongst individuals but also amongst groups of people residing in different areas or engaged in different vocations.]

23 Article 39 –Certain principles of policy to be followed by state
39 (a) That the citizens, men and women equally, have the right to an adequate means of livelihood;

24 Article 39- Certain principles of policy to be followed by state
39 (f) That children are given opportunities and facilities to develop in a healthy manner and in conditions of freedom and dignity and that childhood and youth are protected against exploitation and against moral and material abandonment

25 **Article 41- Right to work, to education and to public assistance in certain cases.**
The State shall, within the limits of its economic capacity and development, make effective provision for securing the right to work, to education and to public assistance in cases of unemployment, old age, sickness and disablement, and in other cases of undeserved want.

26 **Article-45 Provision for early childhood care and education to children below the age of six years**
Provision for early childhood care and education to children below the age of six years.
The State shall endeavours to provide early childhood care and education for all children until they complete the age of six years.

provide education for citizens";

(b) the objectives set forth in the preamble to the Constitution cannot be achieved unless education is provided to the citizens of this country;

(c) the preamble also assures dignity of the individual. Without education, dignity of the individual cannot be assured;

(d) Parts III and IV of the Constitution are supplementary to each other. Unless the 'right to education' mentioned in Article41 is made a reality, the fundamental rights in part III will remain beyond the reach of the illiterate majority;

(e) Article 21 has been interpreted by this Court to include the right to live with human dignity and all that goes along with it. The "right to education' flows directly from right to life." In other words, 'right to education' is concomitant to the fundamental rights enshrined in part II the Constitution. The State is under a constitutional mandate to provide educational Institutions at all levels for the benefit of citizens." The benefit of education cannot be confined to richer classes.

(f) Capitation fee is nothing but a consideration for admission. The concept of "teaching hops" is alien to our Constitutional scheme. Education in India has never been a commodity for sale.

(g) "Court held that every citizen has a "right to education' under the Constitution.

The State is under an obligation to establish educational institutions to enable the citizens to enjoy the said right. The State may discharge its obligation through state-owned for state-recognized educational institutions. When the State Government grants recognition to the private educational institutions it creates an agency to fulfill its obligation under the Constitution. The students are given admission to the educational institutions - whether state-owned or state-recognised - in recognition of their "right to education' under the Constitution. Charging capitation fee in consideration of admission to educational institutions, is a patent denial of citizen's right to education under the Constitution.

On the second question, the bench held that "the State action in permitting capitation fee be charged by state-recognised educational institutions is wholly arbitrary and as such violative of Article 14 of the Constitution of India.... The Capitation fee brings to the fore a clear class bias." Admission of no meritorious students by charging capitation fees - in any form whatsoever strikes at the very root of the constitutional scheme and our educational system. D.P. Joshi does not come to the rescue of the private institutions.

On the third question, the Bench held that having regard to the scheme of the Act, charging of Rs. 60,000/- for admission is "nothing but a capitation fee". The private medical colleges have further been given a free hand in the matter of admission of non-Karnataka students irrespective merit. It held further: "if the State Government fixes Rs. 2000 per annum as the tuition fee in government colleges and for "Government Seats" in private medical colleges then it is the state responsibility to see that any private college which has been set up with Government permission being run with Government recognition is prohibited from charging more than Rs. 2000 from any student who may be resident of any part of India. When the State Government permits private medical college to be set up and recognises its curriculum and degrees then the said college is performing a function which under the Constitution has been assigned to the State Government. Court held that Rs. 60,000 per annum permitted to be charged from Indian students from outside Karnataka in Para 1 (d) of the notification is not tuition fee but in fact a capitation fee and as such cannot be sustained and is liable to be struck down."

Decision of the Court with regard to Fundamental Right to Education:

1. The citizens of this country have a fundamental right to education. The said right flows from Article 21. This right is, however, not an absolute right. Its content and para meters have to be determined in the light of Articles 45 and 41. In other words every child/citizen of this country has a right to free education until he completes the age of fourteen years. Thereafter his right to education is subject to the limits of economic capacity and development of the State

2. The obligations created by Articles 41, 45 and 46 of the Constitution can be discharged by the State either by establishing institutions of its own or by aiding, recognising and/or granting affiliation to private educational institutions. Where aid is not granted to private educational institutions and merely recognition or affiliation is granted it may not be insisted that the private education institution shall charge only that fee as is charged for similar courses in governmental institutions. The private educational

institutions have to and are entitled to charge a higher fee, not exceeding the ceiling fixed in that behalf. The admission of students and the charging of fee in these private educational institutions shall be governed by the scheme evolved herein - set out in Part-III of this Judgment.

3. A citizen of this country may have a right to establish an educational institution but no citizen, person or institution has a right much less a fundamental right, to affiliation or recognition or to grant-in-aid from the State. The recognition and/or affiliation shall be given by the State subject only to the conditions set out in, and only accordance with the scheme continued in Part-III of this Judgment. No Government/University or authority shall be competent to grant recognition or affiliation except in accordance with the said scheme. The said scheme shall constitute a condition of such recognition or affiliation, as the case may be, in addition to such other conditions and terms which such Government, University or other authority may choose to impose. Those receiving aid shall, however, be subject to all such terms and conditions, as the aid giving authority may impose in the interest of general public.

34

Right to Education and Capitation Fees[1]

Facts in Nutshell:

Miss Mohini Jain a resident of Meerut was informed by the Management of Sri Siddhartha Medical College, in the State of Karnataka that she could be admitted to the MBBS course in the session. According to the management she was asked to deposit Rs. 60,000/- as the tuition fee for the first year and furnish a bank guarantee in respect of the fee for the remaining years of the MBBS course. The petitioner's father informed the management that it was beyond there means to pay the exorbitant annual fee of Rs. 60,000/- and as a consequence she was denied admission to the medical college. Mohini Jain had alleged that the management demanded a further capitation fee[2] of rupees four and a half lakhs.

Therefore Mohini Jain filed a petition under Article 32 of the Constitution[3] of India challenging the notification of the Karnataka Government permitting the Private Medical Colleges in the State of Karnataka to charge exorbitant tuition fees from the students other than those admitted to the "Government seats".

Arguments on behalf of the Counsel:

Counsel appearing for the medical college contended that the students from whom higher tuition fee is charged belong to a different class.

1 Appellants: **Miss. Mohini Jain Vs.**Respondent: **State of Karnataka and others**
AIR1992SC1858
Hon'ble Judges: Kuldip Singh and R.M. Sahai, JJ.

2 Capitation fee" means any amount, by whatever name called, paid or collected directly or indirectly in excess of the fee prescribed

3 **Article 32. Remedies for enforcement of rights conferred by this Part**
(1) The right to move the Supreme Court by appropriate proceedings for the enforcement of the rights conferred by this Part is guaranteed
(2) The Supreme Court shall have power to issue directions or orders or writs, including writs in the nature of habeas corpus, mandamus, prohibition, quo warranto and certiorari, whichever may be appropriate, for the enforcement of any of the rights conferred by this Part
(3) Without prejudice to the powers conferred on the Supreme Court by clause (1) and (2), Parliament may by law empower any other court to exercise within the local limits of its jurisdiction all or any of the powers exercisable by the Supreme Court under clause (2)
(4) The right guaranteed by this article shall not be suspended except as otherwise provided for by this Constitution

According to him those who are admitted to the "Government seats" are meritorious and the remaining non-meritorious. He states that classification of candidates into those who possess merit and these who do not possess merits a valid classification and as such the college-management is within its right to charge more fee from those who do not possess merit. He also stated that the object sought to be achieved by the said classification is to collect money to meet the expenses incurred by the college in providing medical education to the students.

Points of Consideration before the Court:

(1) Is there a 'right to education' guaranteed to the people of India under the Constitution? If so, does the concept of 'capitation fee' infracts the same?

(2) Whether the charging of capitation fee in consideration of admissions to educational institutions is arbitrary, unfair, unjust and as such violates the equality clause contained in Article 14 of the Constitution[4]?

Right to Education

It is correct that "right to education" as such has not been guaranteed as fundamental right under Part III of the Constitution[5] but reading Constitution provisions[6] cumulatively it becomes clear that the framers of the Constitution made it obligatory for the State to provide education for its citizens.

The "right to education", therefore, is concomitant to the fundamental rights enshrined under Part III of the Constitution. The State is under a constitutional-mandate to provide educational institutions at all levels for the benefit of the citizens. The educational institutions must function

4 **Article 14 in The Constitution Of India 1949**
14. Equality before law The State shall not deny to any person equality before the law or the equal protection of the laws within the territory of India Prohibition of discrimination on grounds of religion, race, caste, sex or place of birth

5 http://en.wikisource.org/wiki/Constitution_of_India/Part_III

6 **Article 41 Right to work, to education and to public assistance in certain cases.** - The State shall, within the limits of its economic capacity and development, make effective provision for securing the right to work, to education and to public assistance in cases of unemployment, old age, sickness and disablement, and in other cases of undeserved want.
Article 45. Provision for free and compulsory education for children. - The State shall endeavour to provide, within a period of ten years from the commencement of this Constitution, for free and compulsory education for ah children until they complete the age of fourteen years.

to the best advantage of the citizens. Opportunity to acquire education cannot be confined to the richer section of the society. Increasing demand for medical education has led to the opening of large number of medical colleges by private persons, groups and trusts with the permission and recognition of State Governments.

This Court in *E.P. Royappa v. State of Tamil Nadu and Anr.* [7] gave new dimension to Article 14 of the Constitution in the following words:

The capitation fee brings to the fore a clear class bias, It enables the rich to take admission whereas the poor has to withdraw due to financial inability. A poor student with better merit cannot get admission because he has no money whereas the rich can purchase the admission. Such a treatment is patently unreasonable, unfair and unjust. There is, threfore, no escape from the conclusion that charging of capitation fee in consideration of admissions to educational institutions is wholly arbitrary and as such infracts Article 14 of the Constitution.

Decision of the Court:

Court held that every citizen has a 'right to education' under the Constitution. The State is under an obligation to establish educational institutions to enable the citizens to enjoy the said right. The State may discharge its obligation through State-owned or State-recognised educational institutions. When the State Government grants recognition to the private educational institutions it creates an agency to fulfill its obligation under the Constitution. The students are given admission to the educational institutions - whether State owned or State recognised in recognition of their 'right to education' under the Constitution. *Charging capitation fee in consideration of admission to educational institutions, is a patent denial of a citizen's right to education under the Constitution.*

Capitation fee makes the availability of education beyond the reach of the poor. The State action in permitting capitation fee to be charged by State-recognised educational institutions is wholly arbitrary and as such violative of Article 14 of the Constitution of India. Court also held that charging of capitation fee by the private educational institutions as a consideration for admission is wholly illegal and cannot be permitted.

7 (1974)ILLJ172SC

Public Interest Litigation

In Stroud's Judicial Dictionary, Volume 4 (IV Edition), 'Public Interest' is defined thus:

"Public Interest a matter of public or general interest does not mean that which is interesting as gratifying curiosity or a love of information or amusement but that in which a class of the community have a pecuniary interest, or some interest by which their legal rights or liabilities are affected."

In Black's Law Dictionary (Sixth Edition), "public interest" is defined as follows:

"Public Interest something in which the public, or some interest by which their legal rights or liabilities are affected. It does not mean any thing the particular localities, which may be affected by the matters in question. Interest shared by national government...."

Therefore, lexically the expression "PIL" means the legal action initiated in a Court of law for the enforcement of public interest or general interest in which the public or a class of the community have pecuniary interest or some interest by which their legal rights or liabilities are affected. It is thus clear that only a person acting bona fide and having sufficient interest in the proceeding of PIL will alone have as locus standi and can approach the Court to wipe out the tears of the poor and needy, suffering from violation of their fundamental rights, but not a person for personal gain or private profit or political motive or any oblique consideration. Similarly a vexatious petition under the colour of PIL, brought before the Court for vindicating any personal grievance, deserves rejection at the threshold.

Public interest litigation is a weapon which has to be used with great care and circumspection and the judiciary has to be extremely careful to see that behind the beautiful veil of public interest an ugly private malice, vested interest and/or publicity seeking is not lurking. It is to be used as an effective weapon in the armory of law for delivering social justice to the citizens. The attractive brand name of public interest litigation should not be used for suspicious products of mischief. It should be aimed at redressal of genuine public wrong or public injury and not publicity oriented or founded on personal vendetta. Court must be careful to see that a body of persons or member of public, who approaches the court is acting bona fide and not for personal gain or private motive or political motivation or other oblique considerations. The Court must not allow its process to be abused for oblique considerations by masked phantoms who monitor at times from behind. Some persons with vested interest indulge in the pastime of meddling with judicial process either by force of habit or from improper motives, and try to bargain for a good deal as well to enrich themselves. Often they are actuated by a desire to win notoriety or cheap popularity. The petitions of such busy bodies deserve to be thrown out by rejection at the threshold, and in appropriate cases with exemplary costs[1]. The Council for Public Interest Law set up by the Ford Foundation in USA defined the "public interest litigation" in its report of Public Interest Law, USA, 1976 as follows:

"Public Interest Law is the name that has recently been given to efforts provide legal representation to previously unrepresented groups and interests. Such efforts have been undertaken in the recognition that ordinary market place for legal services fails to provide such services to significant segments of the population and to significant interests. Such groups and interests include the proper environmentalists, consumers, racial and ethnic minorities and others."

Public interest litigation has been devised as a means to provide easy access to weaker sections of society to combat exploitation and injustice, and in order to secure to the under-privileged segments of the society their social and economic entitlements and to rescue persons, who are unable to approach the Court on their own for justice and is not meant to be abused or misused for selfish ends. The claimant in the writ petition must have some representative capacity at least, though not individual or personal grievance or interest. The opinion rendered by V. Khalid, Judge of the Supreme Court in the decision reported in *Shri Sechidanand Pandey v. State of W. B.*[2] may be usefully referred to in this regard (at p. 1136):

"It is only when Courts are apprised of gross violation of fundamental

1 **Exemplary Costs:** Often called punitive damages, these are damages requested and/or awarded in a lawsuit when the defendant's willful acts were malicious, violent, oppressive, fraudulent, wanton, or grossly reckless. Examples of acts warranting exemplary damages: publishing that someone had committed murders when the publisher knew it was not true but hated the person; an ex-husband trashes his former wife's auto and threatens further property damage

2 [1987]2SCR223

rights[3] by a group or a class action or when basic human rights are invaded or when there are complaints of such acts as shock the judicial conscience that the Courts, especially Supreme Court, should leave aside procedural shackles and hear such petitions and extend its jurisdiction under all available provisions for remedying the hardships and miseries of the needy, the underdog and the neglected. I will be second to none in extending help when such help is required. But this does not mean that the doors of this Court are always open for anyone to walk in. It is necessary to have some self imposed restraint, on public interest litigants. Otherwise, it would amount to permitting busy bodies masquerading in the role of Saviours indulge in actions besmirching the character of others creating unnecessary fuss more for the sake of publicity than in real public interest."

3 ***'Part III – Fundamental Rights'*** is a charter of rights contained in the Constitution of India. It guarantees civil liberties such that all Indians can lead their lives in peace and harmony as citizens of India. These include individual rights common to most liberal democracies, such asequality before law, freedom of speech and expression, and peaceful assembly, freedom to practice religion, and the right to constitutional remedies for the protection of civil rights by means of writs such as habeas corpus. Violation of these rights result in punishments as prescribed in the Indian Penal Code or other special laws, subject to discretion of the judiciary. The Fundamental Rights are defined as basichuman freedoms which every Indian citizen has the right to enjoy for a proper and harmonious development of personality. These rights universally apply to all citizens, irrespective of race, place of birth, religion, caste, creed, colour or gender. Aliens (persons who are not citizens) are also considered in matters like equality before law. They are enforceable by the courts, subject to certain restrictions. The Rights have their origins in many sources, including England's Bill of Rights, the United States Bill of Rights and France's Declaration of the Rights of Man.

35

Public Interest Litigation (PIL) must be real and genuine[1]

Facts in Nutshell:

Petitioner[2] filed a petition[3] styled as "Public Interest Litigation"[4] before the Nagpur Bench of the Bombay High Court. By the judgment, the High Court dismissed it holding that there was no public interest involved and in fact the petitioner(Person from Legal Profession) had resorted to black mailing respondent[5] Nos. 6 and 7 and was caught red handed accepting "black mailing" money. Cost of Rs. 25,000/- (Rupees twenty five thousand only) which was levied, was directed to be paid to the affected respondent Nos. 6 and 7 before the High Court. The matter was further taken to Supreme Court.

Public Interest Litigation:

When there is material to show that a petition styled as a public interest litigation is nothing but a camouflage to foster personal disputes, said

1 Appellants: Dattaraj **Nathuji Thaware Vs.** Respondent: **State of Maharashtra and Ors.** AIR2005SC540
Hon'ble Judges/Coram: Dr. Arijit Pasayat and S. H. Kapadia , JJ.

2 **Meaning of Petitioner:** A person who presents a Petition. (**Meaning of Petition:** A formal message requesting something that is submitted to an authority)

3 **Meaning of Petition:** A formal message requesting something that is submitted to an authority

4 **Public-Interest Litigation** is litigation for the protection of the public interest. In Indian law, **Article 32** of the Indian constitution contains a tool which directly joints the public with judiciary. PIL may be introduced in a court of law by the court itself (*suo motu*), rather than the aggrieved party or another third party. For the exercise of the court's jurisdiction, it is unnecessary for the victim of the violation of his or her rights to personally approach the court. In PIL, the right to file suit is given to a member of the public by the courts through judicial activism. The member of the public may be a non-governmental organization (NGO), an institution or an individual. The Supreme Court of India, rejecting the criticism of judicial activism, has stated that the judiciary has stepped in to give direction due to executive inaction; laws enacted by Parliament and the state legislatures for the poor since independence have not been properly implemented.

5 **Meaning of Respondent:** A **respondent** is a person who is called upon to issue a response to a communication made by another. In legal usage, this specifically refers to the defendant in a legal proceeding commenced by a petition, or to an appellee, or the opposing party, in an appeal of a decision by an initial fact-finder.

petition is to be thrown out. Public Interest Litigation which has now come to occupy an important field in the administration of law should not be "publicity interest litigation" or "private interest litigation" or "politics interest litigation" or the latest trend "paise income litigation". If not properly regulated and abuse averted, PIL becomes also a tool in unscrupulous hands to release vendetta and wreck vengeance, as well. There must be real and genuine public interest involved in the litigation and not merely an adventure of knight errant borne out of wishful thinking. It cannot also be invoked by a person or a body of persons to further his or their personal causes or satisfy his or their personal grudge and enmity. Courts of justice should not be all owed to be polluted by unscrupulous litigants by resorting to the extraordinary jurisdiction. A person acting bona fide and having sufficient interest in the proceeding of public interest litigation will alone have a locus standi[6] and can approach the Court to wipe out violation of fundamental rights and genuine infraction of statutory provisions, but not for personal gain or private profit or political motive or any oblique consideration[7].

In Stroud's Judicial Dictionary, Volume 4 (IV Edition), 'Public Interest' is defined thus:

"Public Interest a matter of public or general interest does not mean that which is interesting as gratifying curiosity or a love of information or amusement but that in which a class of the community have a pecuniary interest, or some interest by which their legal rights or liabilities are affected."

In Black's Law Dictionary (Sixth Edition), "public interest" is defined as follows:

"Public Interest something in which the public, or some interest by which their legal rights or liabilities are affected. It does not mean any thing the particular localities, which may be affected by the matters in question. Interest shared by national government...."

Therefore, lexically the expression "PIL" means the legal action initiated in a Court of law for the enforcement of public interest or general interest in which the public or a class of the community have pecuniary interest or some interest by which their legal rights or liabilities are affected. It is thus

6 **Meaning of Locus Standi:** The right of a party to appear and be heard before a court

7 These aspects were highlighted by this Court in *The Janta Dal v. H.S. Chowdhary,* 1993CriLJ600 and *Kazi Lhendup Dorji v. Central Bureau of Investigation,* (1992)ILLJ922SC.

clear that only a person acting bona fide and having sufficient interest in the proceeding of PIL will alone have as locus standi and can approach the Court to wipe out the tears of the poor and needy, suffering from violation of their fundamental rights, but not a person for personal gain or private profit or political motive or any oblique consideration. Similarly a vexatious petition under the colour of PIL, brought before the Court for vindicating any personal grievance, deserves rejection at the threshold.

Public interest litigation is a weapon which has to be used with great care and circumspection and the judiciary has to be extremely careful to see that behind the beautiful veil of public interest an ugly private malice, vested interest and/or publicity seeking is not lurking. It is to be used as an effective weapon in the armory of law for delivering social justice to the citizens. The attractive brand name of public interest litigation should not be used for suspicious products of mischief. It should be aimed at redressal of genuine public wrong or public injury and not publicity oriented or founded on personal vendetta. Court must be careful to see that a body of persons or member of public, who approaches the court is acting bona fide and not for personal gain or private motive or political motivation or other oblique considerations. The Court must not allow its process to be abused for oblique considerations by masked phantoms who monitor at times from behind. Some persons with vested interest indulge in the pastime of meddling with judicial process either by force of habit or from improper motives, and try to bargain for a good deal as well to enrich themselves. Often they are actuated by a desire to win notoriety or cheap popularity. The petitions of such busy bodies deserve to be thrown out by rejection at the threshold, and in appropriate cases with exemplary costs[8]. The Council for Public Interest Law set up by the Ford Foundation in USA defined the "public interest litigation" in its report of Public Interest Law, USA, 1976 as follows:

"Public Interest Law is the name that has recently been given to efforts provide legal representation to previously unrepresented groups and interests. Such efforts have been undertaken in the recognition that ordinary market place for legal services fails to provide such services to significant segments of the population and to significant interests. Such groups and interests include the proper environmentalists, consumers,

8 **Exemplary Costs:** Often called punitive damages, these are damages requested and/or awarded in a lawsuit when the defendant's willful acts were malicious, violent, oppressive, fraudulent, wanton, or grossly reckless. Examples of acts warranting exemplary damages: publishing that someone had committed murders when the publisher knew it was not true but hated the person; an ex-husband trashes his former wife's auto and threatens further property damage

racial and ethnic minorities and others."

Decision of the Supreme Court:

Court held that it is disturbing feature which needs immediate remedial measure by the Bar Councils and the Bar Association to see that the process of law is not abused and polluted by its member. It is high time that the Bar Councils and the Bar Associations ensure that no member of the Bar becomes party as petitioner or in aiding and/or abetting files frivolous petitions carrying the attractive brand name of "Public Interest Litigation". That will be keeping in line with the high traditions of the Bar. No one should be permitted to bring disgrace to the noble profession.

36

Public interest litigation (PIL) cannot be invoked by a person to satisfy his personal grudge[1]

Facts in Nutshell:

Petition[2] under Article 32[3] of the Constitution of India, 1950 (in short 'the Constitution') has been filed purportedly in public interest. The prayer in the writ petition[4] is to the effect that the death sentence imposed on one Dhananjay Chatterjee @ Dhana (hereinafter referred to as 'the accused[5]') by the Sessions Court, Alipur, West Bengal, affirmed by the Calcutta High Court and Supreme Court, needs to be converted to a life sentence because there has been no execution of the death sentence for a long

1 Appellants: **Ashok Kumar Pandey Vs.** Respondent: **The State of West Bengal and Ors.** AIR2004SC280
Hon'ble Judges/Coram: Doraiswamy Raju and Dr. Arijit Pasayat, JJ.

2 **Meaning of Petition:** A formal message requesting something that is submitted to an authority

3 **Article 32 in The Constitution Of India 1949**
32. Remedies for enforcement of rights conferred by this Part
(1) The right to move the Supreme Court by appropriate proceedings for the enforcement of the rights conferred by this Part is guaranteed
(2) The Supreme Court shall have power to issue directions or orders or writs, including writs in the nature of habeas corpus, mandamus, prohibition, quo warranto and certiorari, whichever may be appropriate, for the enforcement of any of the rights conferred by this Part
(3) Without prejudice to the powers conferred on the Supreme Court by clause (1) and (2), Parliament may by law empower any other court to exercise within the local limits of its jurisdiction all or any of the powers exercisable by the Supreme Court under clause (2)
(4) The right guaranteed by this article shall not be suspended except as otherwise provided for by this Constitution

4 **Meaning of Writ Petition:**
Under the Indian legal system, jurisdiction to issue prerogative writs is given to the Supreme Court, and to the High Courts of Judicature of all Indian states. Parts of the law relating to writs are set forth in the Constitution of India. The Supreme Court, the highest in the country, may issue writs under Article 32 of the Constitution for enforcement of Fundamental Rights and under Articles 139 for enforcement of rights other than Fundamental Rights, while High Courts, the superior courts of the States, may issue writs under Articles 226. Writ is eminently designed by the makers of the Constitution, and in the same way it is developed very widely and efficiently by the courts in India. The Constitution broadly provides for five kinds of "prerogative" writs, namely, Habeas Corpus, Certiorari, Mandamus, Quo Warranto and Prohibition.

5 **Meaning of Accused:** A person charged with a criminal offense, or the state of being so charged

time. According to the petitioner[6], he saw a news item in a TV channel wherein it was shown that the authorities were unaware about the non-execution of the death sentence and, therefore, condemned prisoner, the accused has suffered a great degree of mental torture and that itself is a ground for conversion of his death sentence to a life sentence on the basis of ratio in *Smt. Triveniben v. State of Gujarat*[7]. The prayer for conversion of death sentence to life sentence has already been turned down by the Governor of West Bengal and the President of India in February 1994 and June 1994 respectively as stated in the petition.

Public Interest Litigation:

When there is material to show that a petition styled as a public interest litigation is nothing but a camouflage to foster personal disputes, said petition is to be thrown out. Public Interest Litigation which has now come to occupy an important field in the administration of law should not be "publicity interest litigation" or "private interest litigation" or "politics interest litigation" or the latest trend "paise income litigation". There must be real and genuine public interest involved in the litigation and not merely an adventure of knight errant or poke ones into for a probe. It cannot also be invoked by a person or a body of persons to further his or their personal causes or satisfy his or their personal grudge and enmity. Courts of justice should not be allowed to be polluted by unscrupulous litigants by resorting to the extraordinary jurisdiction. A person acting *bonafide* and having sufficient interest in the proceeding of public interest litigation will alone have a *locus standi* and can approach the Court to wipe out violation of fundamental rights and genuine infraction of statutory provisions, but not for personal gain or private profit or political motive or any oblique consideration. A writ[8] petitioner who comes to the Court for relief in public interest must come not only with clean hands like any other writ petitioner but also with a clean heart, clean mind and clean objective[9].

In Strouds Judicial Dictionary, Volume 4 (IV Edition), 'Public Interest' is defined thus:

6 **Meaning of Petitioner:** A person who presents a Petition. (**Meaning of Petition:** A formal message requesting something that is submitted to an authority)

7 1990CriLJ1810

8 **Meaning of Writ:** A written order issued by a court, commanding the party to whom it is addressed to perform or cease performing a specified act.

9 See *Ramjas Foundation v. Union of India, AIR1993SC852 and K.R. Srinivas v. R.M. Premchand, (1994)6SCC620*.

"Public Interest a matter of public or general interest does not mean that which is interesting as gratifying curiosity or a love of information or amusement but that in which a class of the community have a pecuniary interest, or some interest by which their legal rights or liabilities are affected."

In Black's Law Dictionary (Sixth Edition), "public interest" is defined as follows :

"Public Interest something in which the public, or some interest by which their legal rights or liabilities are affected. It does not mean anything the particular localities, which may be affected by the matters in question. Interest shared by national government...."

Therefore, lexically the expression "PIL" means the legal action initiated in a Court of law for the enforcement of public interest or general interest in which the public or a class of the community have pecuniary interest or some interest by which their legal rights or liabilities are affected.

Public interest litigation is a weapon which has to be used with great care and circumspection and the judiciary has to be extremely careful to see that behind the beautiful veil of public interest an ugly private malice, vested interest and/or publicity seeking is not lurking. It is to be used as an effective weapon in the armory of law for delivering social justice to the citizens. The attractive brand name of public interest litigation should not be used for suspicious products of mischief. It should be aimed at redressal of genuine public wrong or public injury and not publicity oriented or founded on personal vendetta. Court must be careful to see that a body of persons or member of public, who approaches the court is acting bona fide and not for personal gain or private motive or political motivation or other oblique consideration. The Court must not allow its process to be abused for oblique considerations. Some persons with vested interest indulge in the pastime of meddling with judicial process either by force of habit or from improper motives. Often they are actuated by a desire to win notoriety or cheap popularity. The petitions of such busy bodies deserve to be thrown out by rejection at the threshold, and in appropriate cases with exemplary costs[10].

10 **Meaning of Exemplary Costs:** Often called punitive damages, these are damages requested and/or awarded in a lawsuit when the defendant's willful acts were malicious, violent, oppressive, fraudulent, wanton, or grossly reckless. Examples of acts warranting exemplary damages: publishing that someone had committed murders when the publisher knew it was not true but hated the person; an ex-husband trashes his former wife's auto and threatens further property damage

The Council for Public Interest Law set up by the Ford Foundation in USA defined the "public interest litigation" in its report of Public Interest Law, USA, 1976 as follows:

"Public Interest Law is the name that has recently been given to efforts provide legal representation to previously unrepresented groups and interests. Such efforts have been undertaken in the recognition that ordinary market place for legal services fails to provide such services to significant segments of the population and to significant interests. Such groups and interests include the proper environmentalists, consumers, racial and ethnic minorities and others."

Cases on Public Interest Litigation:

In *State of H.P. v. A Parent of a Student of Medical College, Simla and Ors.*[11] , it has been said that public interest litigation is a weapon which has to be used with great care and circumspection.

In Chhetriya Pardushan Mukti Sangharsh Samiti v. State of U.P.[12], Sabyasachi Mukharji, C.J. observed:

"While it is the duty of Supreme Court to enforce fundamental rights, it is also the duty of Supreme Court to ensure that this weapon (PIL) under Article 32 should not be misused or permitted to be misused creating a bottleneck in the superior court preventing other genuine violation of fundamental rights[13] being considered by the court."

11 [1985]3SCR676

12 [1990]3SCR739

13 ***'Part III – Fundamental Rights'*** is a charter of rights contained in the Constitution of India. It guarantees civil liberties such that all Indians can lead their lives in peace and harmony as citizens of India. These include individual rights common to most liberal democracies, such asequality before law, freedom of speech and expression, and peaceful assembly, freedom to practice religion, and the right to constitutional remedies for the protection of civil rights by means of writs such as habeas corpus. Violation of these rights result in punishments as prescribed in the Indian Penal Code or other special laws, subject to discretion of the judiciary. The Fundamental Rights are defined as basichuman freedoms which every Indian citizen has the right to enjoy for a proper and harmonious development of personality. These rights universally apply to all citizens, irrespective of race, place of birth, religion, caste, creed, colour or gender. Aliens (persons who are not citizens) are also considered in matters like equality before law. They are enforceable by the courts, subject to certain restrictions. The Rights have their origins in many sources, including England's Bill of Rights, the United States Bill of Rights and France's Declaration of the Rights of Man.

In *Subhash Kumar v. State of* Bihar[14], it was observed as follows:

"Public interest litigation cannot be invoked by a person or body of persons to satisfy his or its personal grudge and enmity. If such petitions under Article 32, are entertained it would amount to abuse of process of the court, preventing speedy remedy to other genuine petitioners from Court. Personal interest cannot be enforced through the process of Court under Article 32 of the Constitution in the garb of a public interest litigation. Public interest litigation contemplates legal proceeding for vindication or enforcement of fundamental rights of a group of persons or community which are not able to enforce their fundamental rights on account of their incapacity, poverty or ignorance of law. A person invoking the jurisdiction of Court under Article 32 must approach Court for the vindication of the fundamental rights of affected persons and not for the purpose of vindication of his personal grudge or enmity. It is the duty of Court to discourage such petitions and to ensure that the course of justice is not obstructed or polluted by unscrupulous litigants by invoking the extraordinary jurisdiction of Court for personal matters under the garb of the public interest litigation".

Decision of Supreme Court:

Court dismissed the Petition.

14 [1991]1SCR5

37

Public interest litigation has been devised as a means to provide easy access to weaker sections of society[1]

Facts in Nutshell:

Writ petition[2] was filed by an Organization called the Madras Citizens Progressive Council, represented by its Chair Person one Kasturi Radhakrishnan, for a writ of mandamus[3] directing the first respondent[4], the Hon'ble the President of India, New Delhi, to forward the representations of the petitioner[5], dated 26-9-1993, 30-9-1993, 3-10-1993 and 9-10-1993, and obtain the opinion of the Election Commission in accordance with Article 103(2)[6] of the Constitution of India pertaining

1 Appellants: Madras **Citizens Progressive Council Vs.** Respondent: **Honourable President of India and others**
AIR1995Mad16
Hon'ble Judges/Coram: Raju, Judge

2 **Meaning of Writ Petition:** Under the Indian legal system, jurisdiction to issue 'prerogative writs' is given to the Supreme Court, and to the High Courts of Judicature of all Indian states. Parts of the law relating to writs are set forth in the Constitution of India. The Supreme Court, the highest in the country, may issue writs under Article 32 of the Constitution for enforcement of Fundamental Rights and under Articles 139 for enforcement of rights other than Fundamental Rights, while High Courts, the superior courts of the States, may issue writs under Articles 226. 'Writ' is eminently designed by the makers of the Constitution, and in the same way it is developed very widely and efficiently by the courts in India. The Constitution broadly provides for five kinds of "prerogative" writs, namely, Habeas Corpus, Certiorari, Mandamus, Quo Warranto and Prohibition.

3 **Mandamus** is a judicial remedy — in the form of an order from a superior court, to any government subordinate court, corporation, or public authority — to do (or forbear from doing) some specific act which that body is obliged under law to do (or refrain from doing) — and which is in the nature of public duty, and in certain cases one of a statutory duty. It cannot be issued to compel an authority to do something against statutory provision. For example, it cannot be used to force a lower court to reject or authorize applications that have been made, but if the court refuses to rule one way or the other then a mandamus can be used to order the court to rule on the applications.

4 **Meaning of Respondent:** A **respondent** is a person who is called upon to issue a response to a communication made by another. In legal usage, this specifically refers to the defendant in a legal proceeding commenced by a petition, or to an appellee, or the opposing party, in an appeal of a decision by an initial fact-finder.

5 **Meaning of Petitioner:** A person who presents a Petition. (**Meaning of Petition:** A formal message requesting something that is submitted to an authority)

6 **Article 103 in The Constitution Of India 1949**
103. Decision on questions as to disqualifications of members
(1) If any question arises as to whether a member of either House of Parliament has become

to the alleged disqualification against the fourth respondent, Dr. Manmohan Singh, a Member of the Parliament and the Minister for Finance, Government of India.

The move of the petitioner appeared to have been on an inspiration drawn from a publication of a news item in the Indian Express, English Daily, dated 26-9-1993, under a caption "Domicile Dilemma". The petitioner Institution attempts to activate the Hon'ble President of India to exercise his powers under Article 103(2) of the Constitution of India, on the allegation that the fourth respondent, who according to the petitioner, could not claim himself to be 'an ordinary resident' of Assam State, got himself enrolled as a voter at Gowhathi, in the State of Assam, and that he is not qualified to be so registered as a voter in the State of Assam, and consequently must be considered to have incurred a disqualification within the meaning of Article102(1)(e)[7] of the Constitution of India, which requires further action by the first respondent in terms of Article 103(2) of the Constitution of India. Claim of the petitioner was that the election of the fourth respondent to the Council of State is contrary to the rules and Regulations said to have been laid down by the Election Commission, and that on account of such an election, the State of Assam had lost an effective representative to voice the grievance of its people in the Elders Forum.

Question before the High Court:

Whether the petitioner could claim to have the locus[8] to maintain a writ

---

subject to any of the disqualifications mentioned in clause (1) of Article 102, the question shall be referred for the decision of the President and his decision shall be final

(2) Before giving any decision on any such question, the President shall obtain the opinion of the Election Commission and shall act according to such opinion

7 **Article 102 in The Constitution Of India 1949**

102. Disqualification s for membership

(1) A person shall be disqualified for being chosen as, and for being, a member of either House of Parliament

(a) if he holds any office of profit under the Government of India or the Government of any State, other than an office declared by Parliament by law not to disqualify its holder;

(b) if he is of unsound mind and stands so declared by a competent court;

(c) if he is an undischarged insolvent;

(d) if he is not a citizen of India, or has voluntarily acquired the citizenship of a foreign State, or is under any acknowledgement of allegiance or adherence to a foreign State;

(e) if he is so disqualified by or under any law made by Parliament Explanation For the purposes of this clause a person shall not be deemed to hold an office of profit under the Government of India or the Government of any State by reason only that he is a Minister either for the Union or for such State

8 **Meaning of Locus Standi:** The right of a party to appear and be heard before a court

petition even as a public interest litigation[9] as it is made to appear.

Immunity to President:

Article 361[10] of the Constitution of India has been held to extend immunity conferred on the President not only for acts of the President, which are done by him in the exercise of his functions, but also for acts 'purporting to be done' by the President in exercise of his powers.

Public Interest Litigation:

Public interest litigation has been devised as a means to provide easy access to weaker sections of society to combat exploitation and injustice, and in order to secure to the under-privileged segments of the society their social and economic entitlements and to rescue persons, who are unable to approach the Court on their own for justice and is not meant to be abused or misused for selfish ends. The claimant in the writ petition

9 **Public-Interest Litigation** is litigation for the protection of the public interest. In Indian law, **Article 32** of the Indian constitution contains a tool which directly joints the public with judiciary. PIL may be introduced in a court of law by the court itself (*suo motu*), rather than the aggrieved party or another third party. For the exercise of the court's jurisdiction, it is unnecessary for the victim of the violation of his or her rights to personally approach the court. In PIL, the right to file suit is given to a member of the public by the courts through judicial activism. The member of the public may be a non-governmental organization (NGO), an institution or an individual. The Supreme Court of India, rejecting the criticism of judicial activism, has stated that the judiciary has stepped in to give direction due to executive inaction; laws enacted by Parliament and the state legislatures for the poor since independence have not been properly implemented.

10 **Article 361 in The Constitution Of India 1949**

361. Protection of President and Governors and Rajpramukhs

(1) The President, or the Governor or Rajpramukh of a State, shall not be answerable to any court for the exercise and performance of the powers and duties of his office or for any act done or purporting to be done by him in the exercise and performance of those powers and duties: Provided that the conduct of the President may be brought under review by any court, tribunal or body appointed or designated by either House of Parliament for the investigation of a charge under Article 61: Provided further that nothing in this clause shall be construed as restricting the right of any person to bring appropriate proceedings against the Governor of India or the Government of a State

(2) No criminal proceedings whatsoever shall be instituted or continued against the President, or the Governor of a State, in any court during his term of office

(3) No process for the arrest or imprisonment of the President, or the Governor of a State, shall issue from any court during his term of office

(4) any civil proceedings in which relief is claimed against the President, or the Governor of a State, shall be instituted during his term of office in any court in respect of any act done or purporting to be done by him in his personal capacity, whether before or after he entered upon his office as President, or as Governor of such State, until the expiration of two months next after notice in writing has been delivered to the President or Governor, as the case may be, or left at his office stating the nature of the proceedings, the cause of action therefor, the name, description and place of residence of the party by whom such proceedings are to be instituted and the relief which he claims

must have some representative capacity at least, though not individual or personal grievance or interest. The opinion rendered by V. Khalid, Judge of the Supreme Court in the decision reported in *Shri Sechidanand Pandey v. State of W. B.*[11] may be usefully referred to in this regard (at p. 1136):

"It is only when Courts are apprised of gross violation of fundamental rights[12] by a group or a class action or when basic human rights are invaded or when there are complaints of such acts as shock the judicial conscience that the Courts, especially Supreme Court, should leave aside procedural shackles and hear such petitions and extend its jurisdiction under all available provisions for remedying the hardships and miseries of the needy, the underdog and the neglected. I will be second to none in extending help when such help is required. But this does not mean that the doors of this Court are always open for anyone to walk in. It is necessary to have some self imposed restraint, on public interest litigants. Otherwise, it would amount to permitting busy bodies masquerading in the role of Saviours indulge in actions besmirching the character of others creating unnecessary fuss more for the sake of publicity than in real public interest."

Decision of High Court:

Court held that the petitioner who claimed to be an Association of the Madras Citizens cannot claim to speak for or project the alleged grievance of the people of State of Assam, as if they are either disabled or unable to approach the Court. Thus court held that the writ petition appears to be a mere publicity oriented one rather than aimed at redressal of any genuine public wrong or any public injury. Court dismissed the petition.

---

11 [1987]2SCR223

12 *'Part III – Fundamental Rights'* is a charter of rights contained in the Constitution of India. It guarantees civil liberties such that all Indians can lead their lives in peace and harmony as citizens of India. These include individual rights common to most liberal democracies, such asequality before law, freedom of speech and expression, and peaceful assembly, freedom to practice religion, and the right to constitutional remedies for the protection of civil rights by means of writs such as habeas corpus. Violation of these rights result in punishments as prescribed in the Indian Penal Code or other special laws, subject to discretion of the judiciary. The Fundamental Rights are defined as basichuman freedoms which every Indian citizen has the right to enjoy for a proper and harmonious development of personality. These rights universally apply to all citizens, irrespective of race, place of birth, religion, caste, creed, colour or gender. Aliens (persons who are not citizens) are also considered in matters like equality before law. They are enforceable by the courts, subject to certain restrictions. The Rights have their origins in many sources, including England's Bill of Rights, the United States Bill of Rights and France's Declaration of the Rights of Man.

38

Public Interest Litigation for Pollution Free Environment[1]

Ratio Decidendi[2]: The "Polluter Pays" principle as interpreted by Supreme Court means that the absolute liability for harm to the environment extends not only to compensate the victims of pollution but also the cost of restoring the environmental degradation. Remediation of the damaged environment is part of the process of "Sustainable Development" and as such polluter is liable to pay the cost to the individual sufferers as well as the cost of reversing the damaged ecology.

Facts in Nutshell:

Public interest Petition[3] under Article 32[4] of the Constitution of India has been filed by Vellore Citizens Welfare Forum and is directed against the pollution which is being caused by enormous discharge of untreated effluent by the tanneries and other industries in the State of Tamil Nadu. It was stated that the tanneries are discharging untreated effluent into agricultural fields, road-sides, waterways and open lands. The untreated

---

1 Appellants: **Vellore Citizens Welfare Forum Vs.** Respondent: **Union of India and others** AIR1996SC2715
Hon'ble Judges: Kuldip Singh Singh, Faizan Uddin and K. Venkataswami, JJ.

2 **Meaning of Ration Decidendi:** ***Ratio decidendi*** is a Latin phrase meaning "the reason" or "the rationale for the decision." The *ratio decidendi* is "the point in a case which determines the judgment" or "the principle which the case establishes."

3 **Meaning of Petition:** A formal written application requesting a court for a specific judicial action

4 **Article 32 in The Constitution Of India 1949**
32. Remedies for enforcement of rights conferred by this Part
(1) The right to move the Supreme Court by appropriate proceedings for the enforcement of the rights conferred by this Part is guaranteed
(2) The Supreme Court shall have power to issue directions or orders or writs, including writs in the nature of habeas corpus, mandamus, prohibition, quo warranto and certiorari, whichever may be appropriate, for the enforcement of any of the rights conferred by this Part
(3) Without prejudice to the powers conferred on the Supreme Court by clause (1) and (2), Parliament may by law empower any other court to exercise within the local limits of its jurisdiction all or any of the powers exercisable by the Supreme Court under clause (2)
(4) The right guaranteed by this article shall not be suspended except as otherwise provided for by this Constitution

effluent was finally discharged in river Palar which is the main source of water supply to the residents of the area. According to the petitioner[5] the entire surface and sub-soil water of river Palar has been polluted resulting in non-availability of potable water to the residents of the area. It was stated that the tanneries in the State of Tamil Nadu have caused environmental degradation in the area. According to the preliminary survey made by the Tamil Nadu Agricultural University Research center Vellore nearly 35,000 hectares of agricultural land in the Tanneries Belt, has become either partially or totally unfit for cultivation. It has been further stated in the petition that the tanneries used about 170 types of chemicals in the chrome tanning processes. The said chemicals include sodium chloride, lime, sodium sulphate, chlorium sulphate, fat liquor Amonia and sulphuric acid besides dyes which are used in large quantities. Nearly 35 litres of water is used for processing one kilogram of finished leather, resulting in dangerously enormous quantities of toxic effluents being let out in the open by the tanning industry. These effluents have spoiled the physico-chemical properties of the soil, and have contaminated ground water by percolation.

Sustainable Development:

The traditional concept that development and ecology are opposed to each other, is no longer acceptable. "Sustainable Development" is the answer. In the International sphere "Sustainable Development" as a concept came to be known for the first time in the Stockholm Declaration of 1972. Thereafter, in 1987 the concept was given a definite shape by the World Commission on Environment and Development in its report called "Our Common Future". The Commission was chaired by the then Prime Minister of Norway Ms. G.N. Brundtland and as such the report is popularly known as "Brundtland Report". In 1991 the World Conservation Union, United Nations Environment Programme and World Wide Fund for Nature, jointly came out with a document called "Caring for the Earth" which is a strategy for sustainable living. Finally, came the Earth Summit held in June, 1992 at Rio which saw the largest gathering of world leaders ever in the history - deliberating and chalking out a blue print for the survival of the planet. Among the tangible achievements of the Rio Conference was the signing of two conventions, one on biological diversity and another on climate change. These conventions were signed by 153 nations. The delegates also approved by consensus three

5 **Meaning of Petitioner:** A person who presents a Petition. (**Meaning of Petition:** A formal message requesting something that is submitted to an authority)

non binding documents namely, a Statement on Forestry Principles, a declaration of principles on environmental policy and development initiatives and Agenda 21, a programme of action into the next century in areas like poverty, population and pollution. During the two decades from Stockholm to Rio "Sustainable Development" has come to be accepted as a viable concept to eradicate poverty and improve the quality of human life while living within the carrying capacity of the supporting eco-systems. "Sustainable Development" as defined by the Brundtland Report means "development that meets the needs of the present without compromising the ability of the future generations to meet their won needs". We have no hesitation in holding that "Sustainable Development' as a balancing concept between ecology and development has been accepted as a part of the Customary International Law though its salient features have yet to be finalised by the International Law jurists.

Some of the salient principles of "Sustainable Development", as culled-out from Brundtland Report and other international documents, are Inter-Generational Equity, Use and Conservation of Natural Resources, Environmental Protection, the Precautionary Principle, Polluter Pays pricniple, Obligation to assist and cooperate, Eradication of Poverty and Financial Assistance to the developing countries. "The Precautionary Principle" and "The Polluter Pays" principle are essential features of "Sustainable Development".

Precautionary Principle:

The "Precautionary Principle" - in the context of the municipal law - means :

(i) Environmental measures - by the State Government and the statutory authorities - must anticipate, prevent and attack the causes of environmental degradation.

(ii) Where there are threats of serious and irreversible damage, lack of scientific certainty should not be used as a reason for postponing measures to prevent environmental degradation.

(iii) The "Onus of proof is on the actor or the developer/industrialist to show that his action is environmentally benign.

Polluter Pays Principle:

The "Polluter Pays" principle has been held to be a sound principle by

Supreme Court in Indian Council for Enviro - Legal Action v. Union of India[6]. The Court observed, "We are of the opinion that any principle evolved in this behalf should be simple, practical and suited to the conditions obtaining in this country". The Court ruled that "Once the activity carried on is hazardous or inherently dangerous, the person carrying on such activity is liable to make good the loss caused to any other person by his activity irrespective of the fact whether he took reasonable care while carrying on his activity. The rule is premised upon the very nature of the activity carried on". Consequently the polluting industries are "absolutely liable to compensate for the harm caused by them to villagers in the affected area, to the soil and to the underground water and hence, they are bound to take all necessary measures to remove sludge and other pollutants lying in the affected areas". The "Polluter Pays" principle as interpreted by Supreme Court means that the absolute liability for harm to the environment extends not only to compensate the victims of pollution but also the cost of restoring the environmental degradation. Remediation of the damaged environment is part of the process of "Sustainable Development" and as such polluter is liable to pay the cost to the individual sufferers as well as the cost of reversing the damaged ecology.

The precautionary principle and the polluter pays principle have been accepted as part of the law of the land. Article 21[7] of the Constitution of India guarantees protection of life and personal liberty. Article47 48A and 51A(g) of the Constitutional are as under :

47. Duty of the State to raise the level of nutrition and the standard of living and to improve public health. - The State shall regard the raising of the level of nutrition and the standard of living of its people and the improvement of public health as among its primary duties and in particular, the State shall endeavour to bring about prohibition of the consumption except from medicinal purposes of intoxicating drinks and of drugs which are injurious to health.

48A. Protection and improvement of environment and safeguarding of forests and wild life. - The State shall endeavour to protect and improve the environment and to safeguard the forests and wild life of the country.

6 J.T. (1996) 2 196

7 **Article 21 in The Constitution Of India 1949**
21. Protection of life and personal liberty No person shall be deprived of his life or personal liberty except according to procedure established by law

51A(g). To protect and improve the natural environment including forests, lakes, rivers and wild life, and to have compassion for living creatures.

Apart from the constitutional mandate to protect and improve the environment there are plenty of post independence legislations on the subject but more relevant enactments for our purpose are : The Water (Prevention and Control of Pollution) Act, 1974 (the Water Act), The Air (Prevention and Control of Pollution) Act, 1981 (the Air Act) and the Environment Protection Act 1986 (the Environment Act). The Water Act provides for the Constitution of the Central Pollution Control Board by the Central Government and the Constitution of the State Pollution Control Boards by various State Governments in the country. The Boards function under the control of the Governments concerned. The Water Act prohibits the use of streams and wells for disposal of polluting matters. Also provides for restrictions on outlets and discharge of effluents without obtaining consent from the Board. Prosecution and penalties have been provided which include sentence of imprisonment. The Air Act provides that the Central Pollution Control Board and the State Pollution Control Boards constituted under the Water Act shall also perform the powers and functions under the Air Act. The main function of the Boards, under the Air Act, is to improve the quality of the air and to prevent, control and abate air pollution in the country.

Directions of the Supreme Court:

1. The Central Government shall constitute an authority under Section 3(3)[8] of the Environment (Protection) Act, 1986 and shall confer

8 **Section 3 (3) Environment Act, 1986**
Power of Central Government to take measures to protect and improve Environment:
(1) Subject to the provisions of this Act, the Central Government, shall have the power to take all such measures as it deems necessary or expedient for the purpose of protecting and improving the quality of the environment and preventing controlling and abating environmental pollution.
(2) In particular, and without prejudice to the generality of the provisions of sub-section (1), such measures may include measures with respect to all or any of the following matters, namely:--
(i) co-ordination of actions by the State Governments, officers and other authorities--
(a) under this Act, or the rules made thereunder, or
(b) under any other law for the time being in force which is relatable to the objects of this Act;
(ii) planning and execution of a nation-wide programme for the prevention, control and abatement of environmental pollution;
(iii) laying down standards for the quality of environment in its various aspects;
(iv) laying down standards for emission or discharge of environmental pollutants from various sources whatsoever:
Provided that different standards for emission or discharge may be laid down under this clause from different sources having regard to the quality or composition of the emission or discharge of environmental pollutants from such sources;
(v) restriction of areas in which any industries, operations or processes or class of industries,

on the said authority all the powers necessary to deal with the situation created by the tanneries and other polluting industries in the State of Tamil Nadu. The Authority shall be headed by a retired judge of the High Court and it may have other members - preferably with expertise in the field of pollution control and environment protection - to be appointed by the Central Government. The Central Government shall confer on the said authority the powers to issue directions under Section 5[9] of the Environment Act, 1986

---

operations or processes shall not be carried out or shall be carried out subject to certain safeguards;

(vi) laying down procedures and safeguards for the prevention of accidents which may cause environmental pollution and remedial measures for such accidents;

(vii) laying down procedures and safeguards for the handling of hazardous substances;

(viii) examination of such manufacturing processes, materials and substances as are likely to cause environmental pollution;

(ix) carrying out and sponsoring investigations and research relating to problems of environmental pollution;

(x) inspection of any premises, plant, equipment, machinery, manufacturing or other processes, materials or substances and giving, by order, of such directions to such authorities, officers or persons as it may consider necessary to take steps for the prevention, control and abatement of environmental pollution;

(xi) establishment or recognition of environmental laboratories and institutes to carry out the functions entrusted to such environmental laboratories and institutes under this Act;

(xii) collection and dissemination of information in respect of matters relating to environmental pollution;

(xiii) preparation of manuals, codes or guides relating to the prevention, control and abatement of environmental pollution;

(xiv) such other matters as the Central Government deems necessary or expedient for the purpose of securing the effective implementation of the provisions of this Act.

(3) The Central Government may, if it considers it necessary or expedient so to do for the purpose of this Act, by order, published in the Official Gazette, constitute an authority or authorities by such name or names as may be specified in the order for the purpose of exercising and performing such of the powers and functions (including the power to issue directions under section 5) of the Central Government under this Act and for taking measures with respect to such of the matters referred to in sub-section (2) as may be mentioned in the order and subject to the supervision and control of the Central Government and the provisions of such order, such authority or authorities may exercise and powers or perform the functions or take the measures so mentioned in the order as if such authority or authorities had been empowered by this Act to exercise those powers or perform those functions or take such measures.

9 **Section 5 Environment Act, 1986**
Power to Give Directions

Notwithstanding anything contained in any other law but subject to the provisions of this Act, the Central Government may, in the exercise of its powers and performance of its functions under this Act, issue directions in writing to any person, officer or any authority and such person, officer or authority shall be bound to comply with such directions.[3]

Explanation--For the avoidance of doubts, it is hereby declared that the power to issue directions under this section includes the power to direct--

(a) the closure, prohibition or regulation of any industry, operation or process; or

(b) stoppage or regulation of the supply of electricity or water or any other service.

2. The authority so constituted by the Central Government shall implement the "precautionary principle" and the "polluter pays" principle. The authority shall, with the help of expert opinion and after giving opportunity to the concerned polluters assess the loss to the ecology/environment in the affected areas and shall also identify the individuals/families who have suffered because of the pollution and shall assess the compensation to be paid to the said individuals/families. The authority shall further determine the compensation to be recovered from the polluters as cost of reversing the damaged environment. The authority shall lay down just and fair procedure for completing the exercise.

3. The authority shall compute the compensation under two heads namely, for reversing the ecology and for payment to individuals. A statement showing the total amount to be recovered, the names of the polluters from whom the amount is to be recovered, the amount to be recovered from each polluter, the persons to whom the compensation is to be paid and the amount payable to each of them shall be forwarded to the Collector/District Magistrate of the area concerned. The Collector/ District Magistrate shall recover the amount from the pollluters, if necessary, as arrears of land revenue. He shall disburse the compensation awarded by the authority to the affected persons/families.

4. The authority shall direct the closure of the industry owned/managed by a polluters in case he evades or refuse to pay the compensation awarded against him. This shall be in addition to the recovery from him as arrears of land revenue.

5. An industry may have set up the necessary pollution control device at present but it shall be liable to pay for the past pollution generated by the said industry which has resulted in the environmental degradation and suffering to the residents of the area.

6. Supreme Court imposed pollution fine of Rs. 10,000 each on all the tanneries in the districts of North Arcot Ambedkar, Erode periyar, Dindigul Anna, Trichi and Chengai M.G.R. The money shall be deposited, alongwith the compensation amount recovered from the polluters, under a separate head called "Environment protection Fund" and shall be utilised for compensating the affected persons as identified by the authorities and also for restoring the damaged environment. The pollution fine is liable to be recovered as arrears of land revenue. The tanneries which fail to deposit the amount shall be closed forthwith and shall also be liable under the Contempt of Courts Act.

Animal Rights

Why preservation of wild life is important for human society?

Preservation of wild life is important for maintaining the ecological balance in the environment and sustaining the ecological chain. It must be understood that there is inter-linking in nature. To give an example, snakes eat frogs, frogs eat insects and insects eat other insects and vegetation. If we kill all the snakes, the result will be that number of frogs will increase and this will result in the frogs eating more of the insects and when more insects are eaten, then the insects which are the prey of other insects will increase in number to a disproportionate extent, or the vegetation will increase to a disproportionate extent. This will upset the delicate ecological balance in nature. If we kill the frogs the insects will increase and this will require more insecticides. Use of much insecticide may create health problems. To give another example, destruction of dholes (wild dogs) in Bhutan was intended to protect livestock, but this led to greater number of wild bear and to resultant crop devastation causing several cases of abandonment by humans of agricultural fields. Destruction of carnivorous animals will result in increase of herbivorous animals, and this can result in serious loss of agricultural crops and other vegetation.

It must be realized that our scientific understanding of nature, and in particular of the ecological chain and the linkages therein is still very primitive, incomplete and fragmentary. Hence, it is all the more important today that we preserve the ecological balance because disturbing it may cause serious repercussions of which we may have no idea today. The wild life in India has already been considerably destroyed. At one time there were hundreds of thousands of tigers, leopards and other wild animals, but today there are only about 1400 tigers left, according to the Wildlife Institute. Until recently habitat loss was thought to be the largest threat to the future of tigers, leopards etc. However, it has now been established that illegal trade and commerce in skins and other body parts of tigers, leopards etc. has done even much greater decimation. Poaching of tigers for traditional Chinese medicine industry has been going on in India for several decades. Tigers and leopards are poached for their skins, bones and other constituent parts as these fetch high prices in countries such as China, where they are valued as symbols of power (aphrodisiacs) and ingredients of dubious traditional medicines.

Article 51A(g) of Constitution of India, 1950:

Article 51A(g)[1]of the Constitution of India, casts a fundamental duty on every citizen to have compassion for living creature. Article 51A(g) not only imposes a duty on every citizen to protect all animals on which unnecessary pain is being inflicted. Infliction of unnecessary pain, or suffering on animals is anti-thesis to compassion, the duty as imposed by Article 51A(g) of the Constitution of India. Nobody has a right to inflict pain or suffering to others inclusive of the animals and birds. Even birds can not be kept in cages by which they suffer a pain. To keep birds in cages would tantamount to illegal confinement of the birds which is in violation of right of the birds to live in free air/sky. For the aforesaid a specific law might not be required. It is the fundamental right of the bird to live freely in the open sky. It is the duty of every citizen to see that there is no unnecessary pain or suffering to any animal or bird.

---

1 **Article 51A in The Constitution Of India 1949**

51A. Fundamental duties It shall be the duty of every citizen of India (a) to abide by the Constitution and respect its ideals and institutions, the national Flag and the National Anthem;

(b) to cherish and follow the noble ideals which inspired our national struggle for freedom;

(c) to uphold and protect the sovereignty, unity and integrity of India;

(d) to defend the country and render national service when called upon to do so;

(e) to promote harmony and the spirit of common brotherhood amongst all the people of India transcending religious, linguistic and regional or sectional diversities; to renounce practices derogatory to the dignity of women;

(f) to value and preserve the rich heritage of our composite culture;

(g) to protect and improve the natural environment including forests, lakes, rivers and wild life, and to have compassion for living creatures;

(h) to develop the scientific temper, humanism and the spirit of inquiry and reform;

(i) to safeguard public property and to abjure violence;

(j) to strive towards excellence in all spheres of individual and collective activity so that the nation constantly rises to higher levels of endeavour and achievement

39

Fundamental right of birds to live freely in open sky[1]

Question before the Court:

Whether the birds have a right to live freely and/or Whether can birds be kept in illegal custody/cages and/or whether by keeping the birds in cages do their right to live freely is violated?

Facts in Nutshell:

Criminal complaint has been lodged against the Petitioner[2] for the offences punishable under Sections 11(1)(a)[3](e)[4](m)[5](k)[6] of Prevention of Cruelty to Animals Act, 1960 as well as under Section 12[7] of the

1 Appellants: **Abdulkadar Mohamad Azam Sheikh Vs.** Respondent: **State of Gujarat and 2 Ors.** MANU/GJ/0504/2011
Hon'ble Judges/Coram: Mukesh R. Shah, Judge

2 **Meaning of Petitioner:** A person who presents a Petition. (**Meaning of Petition:** A formal message requesting something that is submitted to an authority)

3 **Sections 11(1)(a) of Prevention of Cruelty to Animals Act, 1960**
11. Treating animals cruelly : (1) If any person (a) beats, kicks, over-rides, over-drives, over-loads, tortures or otherwise treats any animal so as to subject it to unnecessary pain or suffering or causes, or being the owner permits, any animal to be so treated

4 **Sections 11(1)(e) of Prevention of Cruelty to Animals Act, 1960**
11. Treating animals cruelly : (1) If any person (e) keeps or confines any animal in any -cage or other receptacle which does not measure sufficiently in height, length and breadth to permit the animal a reasonable opportunity for movement

5 **Sections 11(1)(m) of Prevention of Cruelty to Animals Act, 1960**
11. Treating animals cruelly : (1) If any person (m) solely with a view to providing entertainment

6 **Sections 11(1)(k) of Prevention of Cruelty to Animals Act, 1960**
11. Treating animals cruelly : (1) If any person (k) offers for sale or without reasonable cause, has in his possession any animal which is suffering pain by reason of mutilation, starvation, thirst, overcrowding or other illtreatment

7 **Section 12 of Wildlife Protection Act, 1972**
12. Grant of permit for special purposes. - Notwithstanding anything contained elsewhere in this Act, it shall be lawful for the Chief Wildlife Warden, to grant a permit, by an order in writing stating the reasons therefor, to any person, on payment of such fee as may be prescribed, which shall entitle the holder of such permit to hunt, subject to such conditions as may be specified therein, any wild animal specified in such permit, for the purpose of, –
(a) education;

Wildlife Protection Act, 1972 alleging inter-alia that 494 birds/animals have been found from the custody of the respective accused[8] which were kept in different small cages and that their wings were cut, their tails were cut and cello-tape was put on their wings, there were rings on their legs. Therefore, it was alleged that there was atrocity on the said birds. It was alleged that the respective accused are not having any licence or permit to keep the birds/animals and/or to sell them. That all 494 birds/animals were taken in the custody by the police and the same were sent to one Non-Governmental Organization ("NGO" for short) namely "Live and Let Live", Surat for their treatment. That from the different cages, number of parrots, pigeons, love birds, sparrows, rabbit, mouse, dog etc. were found and the Petitioners - accused were selling the said birds in the open market. That the Petitioners - accused from whose custody birds/animals were seized, submitted applications under Section 451[9] of the Code of Criminal Procedure for interim custody of the said birds/animals and the learned trial Court i.e. Third Additional Senior Civil Judge and Additional Chief Judicial Magistrate, Surat dismissed the said applications, after hearing the parties and considering the report of the Wildlife Protection Officer, and directed that the muddamal birds/animals be enlarged free in the air/sky. Being aggrieved by and dissatisfied with the orders passed by the learned trial Court in application under Section 451 of the Code of Criminal Procedure the Petitioner - accused from whom muddamal birds/ animals were seized preferred Revision Application before the learned

---

(b) scientific research;
(bb) scientific management;
Explanation:- for the purposes of Cl. (bb), the expression, "scientific management" means
(i) translocation of any wild animal to an alternative suitable habitat; or
(ii) population management of wildlife, without killing or poisoning or destroying any wild animals
(c) Collection of specimens
(i) for recognised zoos subject to the permission under section 38-1 or
(ii) for museums and similar institutions

8 **Meaning of Accused:** A person charged with a criminal offense, or the state of being so charged

9 **Section 451, CrPc, 1973:**
451. Order for custody and disposal of property pending trial in certain cases. When any property is produced before any Criminal Court during any inquiry or trial, the Court may make such order as it thinks fit for the proper custody of such property pending the conclusion of the inquiry or trial, and, if the property is subject to speedy and natural decay, or if it is otherwise expedient so to do, the Court may, after recording such evidence as it thinks necessary, order it to be sold or otherwise disposed of.
Explanation.-For the purposes of this section, "property" includes-
(a) property of any kind or document which is produced before the Court or which is in its custody,
(b) any property regarding which an offence appears to have been committed or which appears to have been used for the commission of any offence.

Sessions Court under Section 397[10] of the Code of Criminal Procedure and the learned 4th Additional Sessions Judge, Surat by the impugned orders partly allowed the said Revision Applications quashing and setting aside the order passed by the learned trial Court by which the learned trial Court directed that the birds be enlarged free in the air/sky, however, rejected the applications of the aforesaid revisionist - original accused of handing over the custody of the birds/animals to them and observed that it will be open for the learned trial Court to pass appropriate order to give custody of the birds to the voluntary organizations and pass appropriate order with respect to expenditure for maintaining them. Being aggrieved by and dissatisfied with the orders passed by the learned Additional Sessions Judge in Revision Application original accused/applicants preferred Special Criminal Application Numbers. The learned trial Court has passed further order directing the respective applicants - accused to deposit cost of Rs. 1,05,290 in the Court for payment to Beauty without Brutality Organization, Surat, with whom custody of the birds is". Being aggrieved by the order petitioner approached High Court.

Why preservation of wild life is important for human society?

Preservation of wild life is important for maintaining the ecological balance in the environment and sustaining the ecological chain. It must be understood that there is inter-linking in nature. To give an example, snakes eat frogs, frogs eat insects and insects eat other insects and vegetation. If we kill all the snakes, the result will be that number of frogs will increase and this will result in the frogs eating more of the insects and when more insects are eaten, then the insects which are the prey of other insects will increase in number to a disproportionate extent, or the vegetation will increase to a disproportionate extent. This will upset the delicate ecological balance in nature. If we kill the frogs the insects will increase

10 **Section 397, CrPc, 1973:**

397. Calling for records to exercise powers of revision.—

(1) The High Court or any Sessions Judge may call for and examine the record of any proceeding before any inferior Criminal Court situate within its or his local jurisdiction for the purpose of satisfying itself or himself as to the correctness, legality or propriety of any finding. Sentence or order, recorded or passed, and as to the regularity of any proceedings of such inferior Court, and may, when calling for such record, direct that the execution of any sentence or order be suspended, and if the accused is in confinement, that he be released on bail or on his own bond pending the examination of the record.

(2) The powers of revision conferred by sub-section (1) shall not be exercised in relation to any interlocutory order passed in any appeal, inquiry, trial or other proceeding.

(3) If an application under this section has been made by any person either to the High Court or to the Sessions Judge, no further application by the same person shall be entertained by the other of them.

and this will require more insecticides. Use of much insecticide may create health problems. To give another example, destruction of dholes (wild dogs) in Bhutan was intended to protect livestock, but this led to greater number of wild bear and to resultant crop devastation causing several cases of abandonment by humans of agricultural fields. Destruction of carnivorous animals will result in increase of herbivorous animals, and this can result in serious loss of agricultural crops and other vegetation.

It must be realized that our scientific understanding of nature, and in particular of the ecological chain and the linkages therein is still very primitive, incomplete and fragmentary. Hence, it is all the more important today that we preserve the ecological balance because disturbing it may cause serious repercussions of which we may have no idea today. The wild life in India has already been considerably destroyed. At one time there were hundreds of thousands of tigers, leopards and other wild animals, but today there are only about 1400 tigers left, according to the Wildlife Institute. Until recently habitat loss was thought to be the largest threat to the future of tigers, leopards etc. However, it has now been established that illegal trade and commerce in skins and other body parts of tigers, leopards etc. has done even much greater decimation. Poaching of tigers for traditional Chinese medicine industry has been going on in India for several decades. Tigers and leopards are poached for their skins, bones and other constituent parts as these fetch high prices in countries such as China, where they are valued as symbols of power (aphrodisiacs) and ingredients of dubious traditional medicines.

Article 51A(g) of Constitution of India, 1950:

Article 51A(g)[11]of the Constitution of India, casts a fundamental duty on

11 **Article 51A in The Constitution Of India 1949**

51A. Fundamental duties It shall be the duty of every citizen of India (a) to abide by the Constitution and respect its ideals and institutions, the national Flag and the National Anthem;

(b) to cherish and follow the noble ideals which inspired our national struggle for freedom;

(c) to uphold and protect the sovereignty, unity and integrity of India;

(d) to defend the country and render national service when called upon to do so;

(e) to promote harmony and the spirit of common brotherhood amongst all the people of India transcending religious, linguistic and regional or sectional diversities; to renounce practices derogatory to the dignity of women;

(f) to value and preserve the rich heritage of our composite culture;

(g) to protect and improve the natural environment including forests, lakes, rivers and wild life, and to have compassion for living creatures;

(h) to develop the scientific temper, humanism and the spirit of inquiry and reform;

(i) to safeguard public property and to abjure violence;

(j) to strive towards excellence in all spheres of individual and collective activity so that the nation constantly rises to higher levels of endeavour and achievement

every citizen to have compassion for living creature. Article 51A(g) not only imposes a duty on every citizen to protect all animals on which unnecessary pain is being inflicted. Infliction of unnecessary pain, or suffering on animals is anti-thesis to compassion, the duty as imposed by Article 51A(g) of the Constitution of India. Nobody has a right to inflict pain or suffering to others inclusive of the animals and birds. Even birds can not be kept in cages by which they suffer a pain. To keep birds in cages would tantamount to illegal confinement of the birds which is in violation of right of the birds to live in free air/sky. For the aforesaid a specific law might not be required. It is the fundamental right of the bird to live freely in the open sky. It is the duty of every citizen to see that there is no unnecessary pain or suffering to any animal or bird.

Decision of the High Court:

Court held hat the manner in which the birds are kept in the small cages, that too, when their wings are cut; their tails are cut; on their wings cello-tape is put and there are rings on their feet, nothing can be more heinous than such acts and there cannot be more glaring example of atrocity and inhumanity. Such an act cannot be tolerated and continued for a day. When everybody is talking about fundamental rights[12] of the citizen, such as, right to live freely, right to food, right to move freely etc. a day has come to think about the rights of the birds and animals, because of such act even the birds have vanished and their numbers are in decrease.

Every bird/animal has a right to move freely and it cannot be disputed that so far as the birds are concerned, they have right to move freely in the open sky/air and they cannot be kept in cages at all and that too with such a brutality. To keep the birds in the cages would be illegal confinement of such birds against their wish which would be against

12 ***'Part III – Fundamental Rights'*** is a charter of rights contained in the Constitution of India. It guarantees civil liberties such that all Indians can lead their lives in peace and harmony as citizens of India. These include individual rights common to most liberal democracies, such as equality before law, freedom of speech and expression, andpeaceful assembly, freedom to practice religion, and the right to constitutional remedies for the protection of civil rights by means of writs such as habeas corpus. Violation of these rights result in punishments as prescribed in the Indian Penal Code or other special laws, subject to discretion of the judiciary. The Fundamental Rights are defined as basic human freedoms which every Indian citizen has the right to enjoy for a proper and harmonious development of personality. These rights universally apply to all citizens, irrespective of race, place of birth, religion, caste, creed, colour or gender. Aliens (persons who are not citizens) are also considered in matters like equality before law. They are enforceable by the courts, subject to certain restrictions. The Rights have their origins in many sources, including England's Bill of Rights, the United States Bill of Rights and France's Declaration of the Rights of Man.

the fundamental right of the birds to move freely. Even practically and physically it is not possible to keep the custody of the birds even to the institutions/NGOs for long time, as it will be too expensive as well as nobody knows when the trial will take place. Even environmentally also it is not safe and/or in the interest of birds. Under the circumstances the court ordered to enlarge the birds/animals free in the open sky/air.

40

Bull fights are illegal and cannot be permitted to be organized[1]

Facts in Nutshell:

Petitioners[2] who claimed to be animal lovers and engaged in welfare of animals, in educating the general public concerning the necessity of treating all animals with compassion and to be the activist interested in ensuring that all laws concerning prevention of cruelty to the animals are enforced, have approached High Court of Bombay (Panaji Bench) with the complaint that the statutory authorities are either hesitant or negligent in taking appropriate steps to prevent the cruelty to the animals that is being inflicted in the course of the game of bull fights taking place in the State of Goa. According to the petitioners, bull fights are in contravention of section 11(1)[3] of the Prevention of Cruelty to Animals Act, 1968, hereinafter called as "the said Act'. It was the contention of the petitioners that inspite of their efforts to bring this fact to the notice of the authorities concerned, such illegalities are being committed in the State of Goa and further that inspite of requests to such authorities to take appropriate steps in the matter to prevent the same, no action was taken by the respondents[4] and thc bull fights continued tp take place in Goa. It was further contended by the petitioners that the immediate occasion for the

1 Appellants: **People for Animals through Mrs. Norma Alvares and Anr. Vs.** Respondent: **The State of Goa through its Chief Secretary and Ors.**
1997(4)BomCR271
Hon'ble Judges/Coram: R.K. Batta and R.M.S. Khandeparkar, JJ.

2 **Meaning of Petitioner:** A person who presents a Petition. (**Meaning of Petition:** A formal message requesting something that is submitted to an authority)

3 **Sections 11(1)(a) of Prevention of Cruelty to Animals Act, 1960**
11. Treating animals cruelly : (1) If any person (a) beats, kicks, over-rides, over-drives, over-loads, tortures or otherwise treats any animal so as to subject it to unnecessary pain or suffering or causes, or being the owner permits, any animal to be so treated

4 **Meaning of Respondent:** A **respondent** is a person who is called upon to issue a response to a communication made by another. In legal usage, this specifically refers to the defendant in a legal proceeding commenced by a petition, or to an appellee, or the opposing party, in an appeal of a decision by an initial fact-finder.

petitioners to approach High Court is the incident of killing of a person in a most brutal fashion by a violent bull at one of such bull fights organized at Fatorda near Margao on 17th September 1996.

The petitioners claimed that the bull fights are recent introduction in the State of Goa and though initially, no money or gambling was associated with it, in the recent times, due to the patronage of local politicians, the frequency of bull fights have increased enormously and they have become completely commercialised. Newspapers' advertisements of bull fights are openly published to attract more and more spectators. On any given day, there would be fights between 6 to 10 bulls and in the process, bulls get severely hurt and wounded and further they also become insane. Specific procedures are utilised by the bull owners to instigate[5] the bulls to fight with each other. Accordingly, two bulls or buffaloes specially trained and bred for this game only fight against each other, with their owner or trainer standing behind them goading them on. At regular intervals, either mud is rubbed on the back of the animal or water is poured on its back. This is done to agitate or cool down the animal as the need may be. It was further contended by the petitioners that several social evils have sprung up and are associated with events of bull fights and they include large scale of illegal betting relating to the fortunes and fate of the individual bull. It was stated that the situation gets worse when the defeated bull starts running away from the field and the victor charges him. Such bull fights are locally known as 'dhirio' and they are in direct contravention of the provisions contained in section 11(1)(m)[6] and section 11(1)(n)[7] of the Prevention of Cruelty to Animals Act, 1968 and that the authorities are duty-bound to take action against the said offenders.

The petitioners, therefore approached the High Court for necessary directions to the respondents (State Government) to take appropriate steps to stop the practice of bull fights in Goa.

5 **Meaning of Instigate:** To urge on to some drastic or inadvisable action

6 **Section 11(1)(m), Prevention of Cruelty to Animals Act, 1960:**
11. Treating animals cruelly : (1) If any person
(m)solely with a view to providing entertainment

7 **Section 11(1)(n), Prevention of Cruelty to Animals Act, 1960:**
(1) If any person
(n) organises, keeps uses or acts in the management or, any place for animal fighting or for the purpose of baiting any animal or permits or offers any place to be so used or receives money for the admission of any other person to any place kept or used for any such purposes

Bull Fight:

A bull fight consists of a fight between two bulls or two buffaloes or a bull and a buffalo. Such fights are organized in an open field and the same is witnessed by the crowd of spectators which spread all around the arena or the ground where such fights are arranged. The organizers of the bull fights collect fees from the spectators who witness such bull fights. The crowd of spectators range anywhere between 500 to 5000 depending upon the bulls and buffaloes arranged for such fights. The bulls or buffaloes are specially maintained for such fights by some of the people in the State of Goa. The fight begins when two bulls or buffaloes specially trained and bred for the fight are brought against each other with their owner or trainer standing behind them goading them on. At regular intervals, either mud is rubbed on the back of the animals or water is poured on its back. This is done either to agitate or to cool down the animal as the need may arise. In the process of such fight, the animals are goaded and incited not only by the owners or trainers who stand behind such bulls but almost the entire crowd participate in inciting the animals to fight. Before the actual fight begins, the bulls with their eyes turned red glare at each other and sometimes try to scare their opponent by scything their horns in the ground, flinging mud up into the air. Then suddenly they dash at each other, locking horns, pushing each other. They move back and forth intermittently charging and retreating. It all depends on the strength of the bull and its stamina. Pushing each other sometimes they even try their force on the spectators while the crowd scrambles for safety. The bull that gets pushed out of the arena first or turns and runs away, loses the fight. One fight could go on as long as an hour or get over within two or three minutes. On some occasions the bull runs away from the field without even locking horns. In the process the animals suffer injuries. At times, the bull can get gored and have to be put to sleep. Normally the defeated animal runs away from the field with the victor chasing it and on such occasions it can even run towards the spectators causing injuries to them.

In brief the bull fight involves fight between two bulls or buffaloes without any restrictions to be observed in such fights & without any control of human being as regards the nature of the fight which can take place between such bulls and in the result the animals are injured and at times go insane and also can inflict injuries to the spectators of such bull fights.

Decision of the High Court:

Court held that all animals are born with an equal claim for life without any cruelty to them. The bull fights or 'dhirios' are in contravention of the provisions of the Prevention of Cruelty to Animals Act, 1968 & therefore, illegal & cannot be permitted to be organized. Court directed the respondents (State Government) to take immediate steps to ban all types of animal fights including bull fights and 'dhirios' in the State of Goa and to see to it that the direction is fully complied with in letter and spirit which the Act seeks to achieve.

41

Positive action of Government Authorities and Police in preventing cruelty to animals required[1]

Ratio Decidendi[2]: ***"Cruelty to animals shall not be tolerable in name of religious festival."***

Facts in Nutshell:

Petitioner[3] seeks for a Writ of Mandamus[4] forbearing the Respondents[5] from interfering with the conducting of Bullock Cart Race in connection with the 'Maha Kumbhabishegam' Festival of Sree Nondi Karuppanasamy, Sree Ayyanar, Sree Peria Karuppanasamy, Sree Muneeswarar Kovil, Thaniankoottam Village, Kadaladi Taluk, Ramanathapuram District. The petitioner is the Vice President of Karisalkulam Panchayat in Ramanathapuram District. Village people are said to have arranged for a Bullock Cart Race (Rekla Race) in connection with the 'Maha Kumbhabishegam'. According to the petitioner, the Rekla Race is customary and hereditary function and has deep rooted religious sentiments. The Bullock Cart Owners from the Petitioner's village and neighbouring villages would participate in the rare and race is said to have

---

1 Appellants: **K. Munlasamythevar Vs.** Respondent: **Dy. Superintendent of Police and Anr.**
AIR2006Mad255
Hon'ble Judges/Coram: R. Banumathi, Judge

2 **Meaning of Ration Decidendi:** ***Ratio decidendi*** is a Latin phrase meaning "the reason" or "the rationale for the decision." The *ratio decidendi* is "the point in a case which determines the judgment" or "the principle which the case establishes."

3 **Meaning of Petitioner:** A person who presents a Petition. (**Meaning of Petition:** A formal message requesting something that is submitted to an authority)

4 **Mandamus** is a judicial remedy — in the form of an order from a superior court, to any government subordinate court, corporation, orpublic authority — to do (or forbear from doing) some specific act which that body is obliged under law to do (or refrain from doing) — and which is in the nature of public duty, and in certain cases one of a statutory duty. It cannot be issued to compel an authority to do something against statutory provision. For example, it cannot be used to force a lower court to reject or authorize applications that have been made, but if the court refuses to rule one way or the other then a mandamus can be used to order the court to rule on the applications.

5 **Meaning of Respondent:** A **respondent** is a person who is called upon to issue a response to a communication made by another. In legal usage, this specifically refers to the defendant in a legal proceeding commenced by a petition, or to an appellee, or the opposing party, in an appeal of a decision by an initial fact-finder.

been conducted in the village for more than 75 years. It was also stated that the bullocks participating in the race are given proper food and are capable of running effectively throughout the race. It was also alleged that the Respondent Police have no authority to stop or to interfere with the Temple festival and the Cart Race. The petitioner is said to have made representations on 20-3-2006 seeking the permission of the Respondents. But the Respondents did not pass any orders. Hence, the petitioner seeks for a Writ of Mandamus forbearing the Respondents from interfering with the conducting of the Bullock Cart Race in connection with 'Maha Kumbhabishegam' Festival.

Cruelty to Animals:

Whipping, beating kicking or otherwise treating any animal cruelly is punishable under the Prevention of Cruelty to Animals Act, 1960 (in short, PCA Act). Section 11 of the Prevention of Cruelty to Animals Act, 1960, deals with the offences for treating animals cruelly. Section 11(1)(a) reads:

11. Treating animals cruelly: (1) If any person -

(a) beats, kicks, over-rides, over-drives, over-loads, tortures or otherwise treats any animal so as to subject it to unnecessary pain or suffering or causes or, being the owner permits, any animals to be so treated ...shall be punishable.

If any person treats animals with cruelty he shall be punished for the first offence with fine up to fifty rupees and for the second or subsequent offence committed within three years of previous offence, with fine upto one thousand rupees or with imprisonment up to three months, or with both:

When the human beings are protected by the Fundamental Rights, why not such protection to the God's creations - dumb animals. The right to life and the habitat and the corresponding duty to protect it, is universal but limited, within the domain of the human species. The difficulty is that there is no such corresponding right to life and habitat acknowledged for the rest of the existing species. Hence, in the absence of such rights we are left only with duties of the human species towards the other species.

Article 51A[6] of the Constitution of India, it is the duty of every citizen of

6 **Article 51A in The Constitution Of India 1949**
51A. Fundamental duties It shall be the duty of every citizen of India (a) to abide by the Constitution and respect its ideals and institutions, the national Flag and the National Anthem;
(b) to cherish and follow the noble ideals which inspired our national struggle for freedom;
(c) to uphold and protect the sovereignty, unity and integrity of India;
(d) to defend the country and render national service when called upon to do so;

India to protect and improve the natural environment including forests, lakes, rivers and wild life and to have compassion for living creatures. Therefore, an individual who seeks to protect animals and their habitat is not exercising his right, but acting in furtherance of his duties, though on occasions, when this duty is pursued vigorously by an individual or a group of individuals, it is erroneously labelled as a right.

Law must respond to the needs of the changing society

In *National Textile Workers Union v. P.R. Ramakrishnan*[7], the Supreme Court has held as follows:

If the law fails to respond to the needs of the changing society, then either it will stifle the growth of the society and choke its progress or if the society is vigorous enough, it will cast away the law which stands in the way of its growth. Law must therefore constantly be on the move adopting itself to the fast changing society and not lag behind. It must shake off the inhibiting legacy of its colonial past and assume a dynamic role in the process of social transformation.

Direction of the High Court:

1. It is the duty of the State to see to it that the Prevention of Cruelty to Animals Act, 1960 is duly implemented in letter and spirit to fulfil the object with which the said Act has been enacted;

2. The State and the Authorities concerned were directed to take immediate steps to ban all types of Jallikattu, Rekla Race (Bullock Cart Race); Oxen Race or any other entertainment involving causing cruelty to animals in the State of Tamil Nadu and to see to it that the direction is fully complied with in letter and spirit which the Act seeks to achieve.

3. The Respondent Police and the State Police were directed to ensure prevention of cruelty to animals inflicted under the guise of Rekla Race or Oxen Race and Jallikattu or any other, entertainment causing cruelty to animals, and strictly implementing the provisions.

(e) to promote harmony and the spirit of common brotherhood amongst all the people of India transcending religious, linguistic and regional or sectional diversities; to renounce practices derogatory to the dignity of women;

(f) to value and preserve the rich heritage of our composite culture;

(g) to protect and improve the natural environment including forests, lakes, rivers and wild life, and to have compassion for living creatures;

(h) to develop the scientific temper, humanism and the spirit of inquiry and reform;

(i) to safeguard public property and to abjure violence;

(j) to strive towards excellence in all spheres of individual and collective activity so that the nation constantly rises to higher levels of endeavour and achievement

7 (1983)ILLJ45SC

Miscellaneous

Degree of Skill and Care Required by a Medical Practittioner:

In Halsbury's Laws of England the degree of skill and care required by a medical practitioner is stated as follows:

The practitioner must bring to his task a reasonable degree of skill and knowledge, and must exercise a reasonable degree of care. Neither the very highest nor a very low degree of care and competence, judged in the light of the particular circumstances of each case, is what the law requires, and a person is not liable in negligence because someone else of greater skill and knowledge would have prescribed different treatment or operated in a different way; nor is he guilty of negligence if he has acted in accordance with a practice accepted as proper by a responsible body of medical men skilled in that particular art, even though a body of adverse opinion also existed among medical men.

A medical practitioner is not liable to be held negligent simply because things went wrong from mischance or misadventure or through an error of judgment in choosing one reasonable course of treatment in preference to another. He would be liable only where his conduct fell below that of the standards of a reasonably competent practitioner in his field. For instance, he would be liable if he leaves a surgical gauze inside the patient after an operation[1] or operates on the wrong part of the body, and he would be also criminally liable if he operates on someone for removing an organ for illegitimate trade.

Protection to Doctors in Criminal Cases

In para 52 of ***Jacob Mathew** v. **State of Punjab and Anr.***[2] the Supreme Court realizing that doctors have to be protected from frivolous complaints of medical negligence, has laid down certain rules in this connection:

(i) A private complaint should not be entertained unless the complainant

1 *Achutrao Haribhau Khodwa and Ors. v. State of Maharashtra and Ors.* [1996]2SCR881

2 2005CriLJ3710

has produced prima facie evidence before the court in the form of a credible opinion given by another competent doctor to support the charge of rashness or negligence on the part of the accused doctor.

(ii) The investigating officer should, before proceeding against the doctor accused of rash or negligent act or omission, obtain an independent and competent medical opinion, preferably from a doctor in government service, qualified in that branch of medical practice who can normally be expected to give an impartial opinion.

(iii) A doctor accused[3] of negligence should not be arrested in a routine manner simply because a charge has been leveled against him. Unless his arrest is necessary for furthering the investigation or for collecting evidence or unless the investigating officer feels satisfied that the doctor proceeded against would not make himself available to face the prosecution unless arrested, the arrest should be withheld.

Rule of Law & Contempt of Court:

'Rule of Law' is the basic rule of governance of any civilised democratic policy. Our Constitutional scheme is based upon the concept of Rule of Law which we have adopted and given to ourselves. Everyone, whether individually or collectively is unquestionably under the supremacy of law. Whoever the person may be, however high he or she is, no-one is above the law notwithstanding how powerful and how rich he or she may be. For achieving the establishment of the rule of law, the Constitution has assigned the special task to the judiciary in the country. It is only through the courts that the rule of law unfolds its contents and establishes its concept. For the judiciary to perform its duties and functions effectively and true to the spirit with which it is sacredly entrusted, the dignity and authority of the courts have to be respected and protected at all costs. After more than half a century of independence, the judiciary in the country is under a constant threat and being endangered from within and without. The need of the time is of restoring confidence amongst the people for the independence of judiciary. Its impartiality and the glory of law has to be maintained, protected and strengthened. The confidence in the courts of justice, which the people possess, cannot, in any way, be allowed to be tarnished, diminished or wiped out by contumacious behavior of any person. The only weapon of protecting itself from the onslaught to the institution is the long hand of contempt of court left in

3 **Meaning of Accused:** A person charged with a criminal offense, or the state of being so charged

the armoury of judicial repository which, when needed, can reach any neck howsoever high or far away it may be.

In Re: Vinay Chandra Mishra (the alleged contemner)[4] Supreme Court reiterated the position of law relating to the powers of contempt and opined that the judiciary is not only the guardian of the rule of law and third pillar but in fact the central pillar of a democratic State. If the judiciary is to perform it duties and functions effectively and true to the spirit with which they are sacredly entrusted to it, the dignity and authority of the courts have to be respected and protected at all costs. Otherwise the very corner-stone of our constitutional scheme will give way and with it will disappear the rule of law and the civilized life in the society. It is for this purpose that the courts are entrusted with extraordinary powers of punishing those who indulge in acts, whether inside or outside the courts, which tend to undermine the authority of law and bring it in disrepute and disrespect by scandalizing it. When the court exercise this power, it does not do so to vindicate the dignity and honour of the individual judge who is personally attacked or scandalised, but to uphold the majesty of the law and of the administration of justice. The foundation of the judiciary is the trust and the confidence of the people in its ability to deliver fearless and impartial justice. When the foundation itself is shaken by acts which tend to create disaffection and disrespect for the authority of the court by creating distrust in its working, the edifice of the judicial system gets eroded.

No person can flout the mandate of law of respecting the courts for establishment of rule of law under the cloak of freedoms of speech and expression guaranteed by the Constitution. Such a freedom is subject to reasonable restrictions imposed by any law. Where a provision, in the law, relating to contempt imposes reasonable restrictions, no citizen can take the liberty of scandalizing the authority of the institution of judiciary. Freedom of speech and expression, so far as they do not contravene the statutory limits as contained in the Contempt of Courts Act, are to prevail without any hindrance. However, it must be remembered that the maintenance of dignity of courts is one of the cardinal principles of rule of law in a democratic set up and any criticism of the judicial institution couched in language that apparently appears to be mere criticism but ultimately results in undermining the dignity of the courts cannot be permitted when found crossed the limits and has to be punished.

4 1995CriLJ3994

Supreme Court in In Re: Harijai Singh and Anr.[5] has pointed out that a free and healthy Press is indispensable to the function of a true democracy but, at the same time, cautioned that the freedom of Press is not absolute, unlimited and unfettered at all times and in all circumstances. Lord Dening in his Book "Road to Justice" observed that Press is the watchdog to see that every trial is conducted fairly, openly and above broad but the watchdog may sometimes break loose and has to be punished for misbehavior. The law of contempt has been enacted to secure public respect and confidence in the judicial process. If such confidence is shaken or broken, the confidence of the common man in the institution of judiciary and democratic set up is likely to be eroded which, if not checked, is sure to be disastrous for the society itself.

Mental Cruelty:

Human mind is extremely complex and human behaviour is equally complicated. Similarly human ingenuity has no bound, therefore, to assimilate the entire human behaviour in one definition is almost impossible. What is cruelty in one case may not amount to cruelty in other case. The concept of cruelty differs from person to person depending upon his upbringing, level of sensitivity, educational, family and cultural background, financial position, social status, customs, traditions, religious beliefs, human values and their value system.

Apart from this, the concept of mental cruelty cannot remain static; it is bound to change with the passage of time, impact of modern culture through print and electronic media and value system, etc. etc. What may be mental cruelty now may not remain a mental cruelty after a passage of time or vice versa. There can never be any straitjacket formula or fixed parameters for determining mental cruelty in matrimonial matters. The prudent and appropriate way to adjudicate the case would be to evaluate it on its peculiar facts and circumstances while taking aforementioned factors in consideration.

Some instances of human behaviour which may be relevant in dealing with the cases of "mental cruelty". The instances indicated in the succeeding paragraphs are only illustrative and not exhaustive:

(i) On consideration of complete matrimonial life of the parties, acute mental pain, agony and suffering as would not make possible for the

5 1997CriLJ58

parties to live with each other could come within the broad parameters of mental cruelty.

(ii) On comprehensive appraisal of the entire matrimonial life of the parties, it becomes abundantly clear that situation is such that the wronged party cannot reasonably be asked to put up with such conduct and continue to live with other party.

(iii) Mere coldness or lack of affection cannot amount to cruelty, frequent rudeness of language, petulance of manner, indifference and neglect may reach such a degree that it makes the married life for the other spouse absolutely intolerable.

(iv) Mental cruelty is a state of mind. The feeling of deep anguish, disappointment, frustration in one spouse caused by the conduct of other for a long time may lead to mental cruelty.

(v) A sustained course of abusive and humiliating treatment calculated to torture, discommode or render miserable life of the spouse.

(vi) Sustained unjustifiable conduct and behaviour of one spouse actually affecting physical and mental health of the other spouse. The treatment complained of and the resultant danger or apprehension must be very grave, substantial and weighty.

(vii) Sustained reprehensible conduct, studied neglect, indifference or total departure from the normal standard of conjugal kindness causing injury to mental health or deriving sadistic pleasure can also amount to mental cruelty.

(viii) The conduct must be much more than jealousy, selfishness, possessiveness, which causes unhappiness and dissatisfaction and emotional upset may not be a ground for grant of divorce on the ground of mental cruelty.

(ix) Mere trivial irritations, quarrels, normal wear and tear of the married life which happens in day-to-day life would not be adequate for grant of divorce on the ground of mental cruelty.

(x) The married life should be reviewed as a whole and a few isolated instances over a period of years will not amount to cruelty. The ill conduct must be persistent for a fairly lengthy period, where the relationship has deteriorated to an extent that because of the acts and behaviour of a spouse, the wronged party finds it extremely difficult to live with the other party any longer, may amount to mental cruelty.

(xi) If a husband submits himself for an operation of sterilisation without medical reasons and without the consent or knowledge of his wife and similarly, if the wife undergoes vasectomy or abortion without medical reason or without the consent or knowledge of her husband, such an act of the spouse may lead to mental cruelty.

(xii) Unilateral decision of refusal to have intercourse for considerable period without there being any physical incapacity or valid reason may amount to mental cruelty.

(xiii) Unilateral decision of either husband or wife after marriage not to have child from the marriage may amount to cruelty.

(xiv) Where there has been a long period of continuous separation, it may fairly be concluded that the matrimonial bond is beyond repair. The marriage becomes a fiction though supported by a legal tie. By refusing to sever that tie, the law in such cases, does not serve the sanctity of marriage; on the contrary, it shows scant regard for the feelings and emotions of the parties. In such like situations, it may lead to mental cruelty.

A Hindu marriage solemnized under the Act can only be dissolved on any of the grounds specified therein.

Right to Privacy:

The right to privacy as an independent and distinctive concept originated in the field of Tort law, under which a new cause of action for damages resulting from unlawful invasion of privacy was recognised. This right has two aspects which are but two faces of the same coin: (1) the general law of privacy which affords a tort action for damages resulting from an unlawful invasion of privacy and (2) the constitutional recognition given to the right to privacy which protects personal privacy against unlawful governmental invasion. The first aspect of this right must be said to have been violated where, for example, a person's name or likeness is used, without his consent, for advertising - or non-advertising - purposes or for that matter, his life-story is written - whether laudatory or otherwise - and published without his consent as explained hereinafter. In recent times, however, this right has acquired a constitutional status. Right to privacy is not enumerated as a fundamental right[6] in our Constitution but has been inferred from Article 21[7].

Duty of Advocate:

The Supreme Court has time and again explained the role of the lawyers in the administration of justice and also their duties and obligations as officers of the Court. In *Lt. Col. S.J. Chaudhary Vs . State (Delhi Administration),*[8], the Supreme Court has held that it is the duty of every Advocate who accepts the brief in a criminal case to attend the trial from day-to-day and that, having accepted the brief, he will be committing a breach of his professional duty, if he so fails to attend.

In *Indian Council of Legal Aid and Advice & others Vs . Bar Council of India & another,*[9], the Supreme Court observed thus:

"It is generally believed that members of the legal profession have certain social obligations, e.g., to render "pro bono publico" service to the poor and the underprivileged. Since the duty of a lawyer is to assist the court in the administration of justice, the practice of law has a public utility flavour and, Therefore, he must strictly and scrupulously abide by the Code of Conduct behaving the noble profession and must not indulge in any activity which may tend to lower the image of the profession in society. That is why the functions of the Bar Council include the laying down of standards of professional conduct and etiquette which advocates must follow to maintain the dignity and purity of the profession."

6 ***'Part III – Fundamental Rights'*** is a charter of rights contained in the Constitution of India. It guarantees civil liberties such that all Indians can lead their lives in peace and harmony as citizens of India. These include individual rights common to most liberal democracies, such asequality before law, freedom of speech and expression, and peaceful assembly, freedom to practice religion, and the right to constitutional remedies for the protection of civil rights by means of writs such as habeas corpus. Violation of these rights result in punishments as prescribed in the Indian Penal Code or other special laws, subject to discretion of the judiciary. The Fundamental Rights are defined as basichuman freedoms which every Indian citizen has the right to enjoy for a proper and harmonious development of personality. These rights universally apply to all citizens, irrespective of race, place of birth, religion, caste, creed, colour or gender. Aliens (persons who are not citizens) are also considered in matters like equality before law. They are enforceable by the courts, subject to certain restrictions. The Rights have their origins in many sources, including England's Bill of Rights, the United States Bill of Rights and France's Declaration of the Rights of Man.

7 **Article 21 in The Constitution Of India 1949**
21. Protection of life and personal liberty No person shall be deprived of his life or personal liberty except according to procedure established by law

8 1984CriLJ340

9 [1995]1SCR304

In *RE Sanjeev Datta & others*[10], the Supreme Court has stated thus:

"The legal profession is a solemn and serious occupation. It is a noble calling and all those who belong to it are its honourable members. Although the entry to the profession can be had by acquiring merely the qualification of technical competence, the honour as a professional has to be maintained by its members by their exemplary conduct both in and outside the Court. The legal profession is different from other professions in that what the lawyers do, affects not only an individual but the administration of justice which is the foundation of the civilised society. Both as a leading member of the intelligentsia of the society and as a responsible citizen, the lawyer has to conduct himself as a model for others both in his professional and in his private and public life. The society has a right to expect of him such ideal behaviour. It must not be forgotten that the legal profession has always been held in high esteems and its members have played an enviable role in public life. The regard for the legal and judicial systems in this country is in no small measure due to the tireless role played by the stalwarts in the profession to strengthen them. They took their profession seriously and practiced it with dignity, deference and devotion. If the profession is to survive, the judicial system has to vitalised. No service will be too small in making the system efficient, effective and credible."

Active Euthanasia:

Active euthanasia is a crime all over the world except where permitted by legislation. In India active euthanasia is illegal and a crime under Section 302[11] or at least Section 304[12] IPC. Physician assisted suicide is a crime under Section 306[13] IPC (abetment to suicide). Active euthanasia

10 1995CriLJ2910

11 **Section 302, IPC 1860**
Punishment for murder
302. Punishment for murder.--Whoever commits murder shall be punished with death, or [imprisonment for life], and shall also be liable to fine

12 **Section 304 in The Indian Penal Code, 1860**
304. Punishment for culpable homicide not amounting to murder.-- Whoever commits culpable homicide not amounting to murder shall be punished with 1[imprisonment for life], or imprisonment of either description for a term which may extend to ten years, and shall also be liable to fine, if the act by which the death is caused is done with the intention of causing death. or of causing such bodily injury as is likely to cause death; or with imprisonment of either description for a term which may extend to ten years, or with fine, or with both, if the act is done with the knowledge that it is likely to cause death, but without any intention to cause death, or to cause such bodily injury as is likely to cause death.

13 **Section 306 in The Indian Penal Code, 1860**

is taking specific steps to cause the patient's death, such as injecting the patient with some lethal substance, e.g. sodium pentothal which causes a person deep sleep in a few seconds, and the person instantaneously and painlessly dies in this deep sleep. A distinction is sometimes drawn between euthanasia and physician assisted dying, the difference being in who administers the lethal medication. In euthanasia, a physician or third party administers it, while in physician assisted suicide it is the patient himself who does it, though on the advice of the doctor. In many countries/States the latter is legal while the former is not. **The difference between "active" and "passive" euthanasia is that in active euthanasia, something is done to end the patient's life' while in passive euthanasia, something is not done that would have preserved the patient's life.**

An important idea behind this distinction is that in "passive euthanasia" the doctors are not actively killing anyone; they are simply not saving him. While we usually applaud someone who saves another person's life, we do not normally condemn someone for failing to do so. If one rushes into a burning building and carries someone out to safety, he will probably be called a hero. But if one sees a burning building and people screaming for help, and he stands on the sidelines -- whether out of fear for his own safety, or the belief that an inexperienced and ill-equipped person like himself would only get in the way of the professional firefighters, or whatever -- if one does nothing, few would judge him for his inaction. One would surely not be prosecuted for homicide. (At least, not unless one started the fire in the first place.)

Thus, proponents of euthanasia say that while we can debate whether active euthanasia should be legal, there can be no debate about passive euthanasia: You cannot prosecute someone for failing to save a life. Even if you think it would be good for people to do X, you cannot make it illegal for people to not do X, or everyone in the country who did not do X today would have to be arrested.

---

306. Abetment of suicide.-- If any person commits suicide, whoever abets the commission of such suicide, shall be punished with imprisonment of either description for a term which may extend to ten years, and shall also be liable to fine.

42

Mentally retarded and orphan woman becoming pregnant in Welfare Institution[1]

Facts in Nutshell:

A Division Bench of the High Court of Punjab and Haryana by orders dated 9.6.2009 and 17.7.2009, ruled that it was in the best interests of a mentally retarded woman to undergo an abortion. The said woman (name withheld, hereinafter 'victim') had become pregnant as a result of an alleged rape that took place while she was an inmate at a government-run welfare institution located in Chandigarh. After the discovery of her pregnancy, the Chandigarh Administration, which is the respondent[2] in the case, had approached the High Court seeking approval for the termination of her pregnancy, keeping in mind that in addition to being mentally retarded she was also an orphan who did not have any parent or guardian to look after her or her prospective child. The High Court had the opportunity to peruse a preliminary medical opinion and chose to constitute an Expert Body consisting of medical experts and a judicial officer for the purpose of a more thorough inquiry into the facts. In its order dated 17.7.2009 the High Court directed the termination of the pregnancy in spite of the Expert Body's findings which show that the victim had expressed her willingness to bear a child.

Aggrieved by these orders, the appellants[3] moved Supreme Court and the second appellant - Ms. Tanu Bedi, Advocate appeared in person on and sought a hearing on an urgent basis because the woman in question had

1 Appellants: **Suchita Srivastava and Anr. Vs.** Respondent: **Chandigarh Administration** AIR2010SC235
Hon'ble Judges/Coram: K. G. Balakrishnan, C.J., P. Sathasivam and B. S. Chauhan, JJ.

2 **Meaning of Respondent:** A **respondent** is a person who is called upon to issue a response to a communication made by another. In legal usage, this specifically refers to the defendant in a legal proceeding commenced by a petition, or to an appellee, or the opposing party, in an appeal of a decision by an initial fact-finder.

3 **Meaning of Appellant:** A person who, dissatisfied with the judgment rendered in a lawsuit decided in a lower court or the findings from a proceeding before an Administrative Agency, asks a superior court to review the decision.

been pregnant for more than 19 weeks at that point of time. Court agreed to the same since the statutory limit for permitting the termination of a pregnancy, i.e. 20 weeks was fast approaching.

Medical Termination of Pregnancy Act:

Section 3 of the Medical Termination of Pregnancy Act, 1971 [Hereinafter also referred to as 'MTP Act'] which reads as follows:

3. When pregnancies may be terminated by registered medical practitioners.-(1) Notwithstanding anything contained in the Indian Penal Code [45 of 1860], a registered medical practitioner shall not be guilty of any offence under that Code or under any other law for the time being in force, if any, pregnancy is terminated by him in accordance with the provisions of this Act.

(2) Subject to the provisions of Sub-section (4), a pregnancy may be terminated by a registered medical practitioner:

(a) where the length of the pregnancy does not exceed twelve weeks, if such medical practitioner is, or

(b) where the length of the pregnancy exceeds twelve weeks but does not exceed twenty weeks, if not less than two registered medical practitioners are, of opinion, formed in good faith, that -

(i)the continuance of the pregnancy would involve a risk to the life of the pregnant woman or of grave injury to her physical or mental health; or

(ii)there is a substantial risk that if the child were born, it would suffer from such physical or mental abnormalities as to be seriously handicapped.

Explanation 1. - Where any pregnancy is alleged by the pregnant woman to have been caused by rape, the anguish caused by such pregnancy shall be presumed to constitute a grave injury to the mental health of the pregnant woman.

Explanation 2. - Where any pregnancy occurs as a result of failure of any device or method used by any married woman or her husband for the purpose of limiting the number of children, the anguish caused by such unwanted pregnancy may be presumed to constitute a grave injury to the mental health of the pregnant woman.

(3) In determining whether the continuance of a pregnancy would involve

such risk of injury to the health as is mentioned in Sub-section (2), account may be taken of the pregnant woman's actual or reasonable foreseeable environment.

(4) (a) No pregnancy of a woman who has not attained the age of eighteen years, or, who, having attained the age of eighteen years, is a mentally ill person, shall be terminated except with the consent in writing of her guardian.

(b) Save as otherwise provided in Clause (a), no pregnancy shall be terminated except with the consent of the pregnant woman.

A plain reading of the above-quoted provision makes it clear that Indian law allows for abortion only if the specified conditions are met. When the MTP Act was first enacted in 1971 it was largely modelled on the Abortion Act of 1967 which had been passed in the United Kingdom. The legislative intent was to provide a qualified 'right to abortion' and the termination of pregnancy has never been recognised as a normal recourse for expecting mothers. There is no doubt that a woman's right to make reproductive choices is also a dimension of 'personal liberty' as understood under Article 21[4] of the Constitution of India. It is important to recognise that reproductive choices can be exercised to procreate as well as to abstain from procreating. The crucial consideration is that a woman's right to privacy, dignity and bodily integrity should be respected. This means that there should be no restriction whatsoever on the exercise of reproductive choices such as a woman's right to refuse participation in sexual activity or alternatively the insistence on use of contraceptive methods. Furthermore, women are also free to choose birth-control methods such as undergoing sterilisation procedures. Taken to their logical conclusion, reproductive rights include a woman's entitlement to carry a pregnancy to its full term, to give birth and to subsequently raise children. However, in the case of pregnant women there is also a 'compelling state interest' in protecting the life of the prospective child. Therefore, the termination of a pregnancy is only permitted when the conditions specified in the applicable statute have been fulfilled. Hence, the provisions of the MTP Act, 1971 can also be viewed as reasonable restrictions that have been placed on the exercise of reproductive choices.

4 **Article 21 in The Constitution Of India 1949**
21. Protection of life and personal liberty No person shall be deprived of his life or personal liberty except according to procedure established by law

A perusal of the above mentioned provision makes it clear that ordinarily a pregnancy can be terminated only when a medical practitioner is satisfied that a 'continuance of the pregnancy would involve a risk to the life of the pregnant woman or of grave injury to her physical or mental health' [as per Section 3(2)(i)] or when 'there is a substantial risk that if the child were born, it would suffer from such physical or mental abnormalities as to be seriously handicapped' [as per Section 3(2)(ii)]. While the satisfaction of one medical practitioner is required for terminating a pregnancy within twelve weeks of the gestation period, two medical practitioners must be satisfied about either of these grounds in order to terminate a pregnancy between twelve to twenty weeks of the gestation period. The explanations to this provision have also contemplated the termination of pregnancy when the same is the result of a rape or a failure of birth-control methods since both of these eventualities have been equated with a 'grave injury to the mental health' of a woman. In all such circumstances, the consent of the pregnant woman is an essential requirement for proceeding with the termination of pregnancy. This position has been unambiguously stated in Section 3(4)(b) of the MTP Act, 1971. The exceptions to this rule of consent have been laid down in Section 3(4)(a) of the Act. Section 3(4)(a) lays down that when the pregnant woman is below eighteen years of age or is a 'mentally ill' person, the pregnancy can be terminated if the guardian of the pregnant woman gives consent for the same. The only other exception is found in Section 5(1) of the MTP Act which permits a registered medical practitioner to proceed with a termination of pregnancy when he/she is of an opinion formed in good faith that the same is 'immediately necessary to save the life of the pregnant woman'.

Principles contained in the *United Nations Declaration on the Rights of Mentally Retarded Persons, 1971* [G.A. Res. 2856 (XXVI) of 20 December, 1971] which have been reproduced below:

1. The mentally retarded person has, to the maximum degree of feasibility, the same rights as other human beings.

2. The mentally retarded person has a right to proper medical care and physical therapy and to such education, training, rehabilitation and guidance as will enable him to develop his ability and maximum potential.

3. The mentally retarded person has a right to economic security and to a decent standard of living. He has a right to perform productive work or to engage in any other meaningful occupation to the fullest possible extent of his capabilities.

4. Whenever possible, the mentally retarded person should live with his own family or with foster parents and participate in different forms of community life. The family with which he lives should receive assistance. If care in an institution becomes necessary, it should be provided in surroundings and other circumstances as close as possible to those of normal life.

5. The mentally retarded person has a right to a qualified guardian when this is required to protect his personal well-being and interests.

6. The mentally retarded person has a right to protection from exploitation, abuse and degrading treatment. If prosecuted for any offence, he shall have a right to due process of law with full recognition being given to his degree of mental responsibility.

7. Whenever mentally retarded persons are unable, because of the severity of their handicap, to exercise all their rights in a meaningful way or it should become necessary to restrict or deny some or all of these rights, the procedure used for that restriction or denial of rights must contain proper legal safeguards against every form of abuse. This procedure must be based on an evaluation of the social capability of the mentally retarded person by qualified experts and must be subject to periodic review and to the right of appeal to higher authorities.

Decision of the Supreme Court:

Court held that proceeding with an abortion at such a late stage (19-20 weeks of gestation period) poses significant risks to the physical health of the victim and abortion will not be in the best interest of the Victim. Court directed that the best medical facilities be made available so as to ensure proper care and supervision during the period of pregnancy as well as for post-natal care.

43

Medical Negligence[1]

Ratio Decidendi[2]: *"Whenever a complaint is received against a doctor or hospital by the Consumer Fora, then it should first refer the matter to a competent doctor or committee of doctors, specialized in the field and only on their report a prima facie case of medical negligence can be made out and a notice can be issued to the concerned doctor/hospital."*

Facts in Nutshell:

Appeal[3] against the judgment of the National Consumer Disputes Redressal Commission, New Delhi dated 22.3.2002 has been filed under Section 23[4] of the Consumer Protection Act, 1986 in Supreme Court. In March 1991, the respondent[5] who was suffering from chronic renal failure was referred by the Director, Health Services to the Nanavati Hospital, Mumbai for the purpose of a kidney transplant. On or about 24.4.1991,

---

1 Appellants: **Martin F. D'Souza Vs.** Respondent: **Mohd. Ishfaq**
AIR2009SC2049
Hon'ble Judges/Coram: Markandey Katju and G. S. Singhvi, JJ.

2 **Meaning of Ration Decidendi:** ***Ratio decidendi*** is a Latin phrase meaning "the reason" or "the rationale for the decision." The *ratio decidendi* is "the point in a case which determines the judgment" or "the principle which the case establishes."

3 **Meaning of Appeal:** In law, an **appeal** is a process for requesting a formal change to an official decision. Very broadly speaking there are appeals on the record and *de novo* appeals. In *de novo* appeals, a new decision maker re-hears the case without any reference to the prior decision maker. In appeals on the record, the decision of the prior decision maker is challenged by arguing that he or she misapplied the law, came to an incorrect factual finding, acted in excess of his jurisdiction, abused his powers, was biased, considered evidence which he should not have considered or failed to consider evidence that he should have considered.

4 **Section 23, Consumer Protection Act,1986**
Appeal
Any person aggrieved by an order made by the National Commission in exercise of its power conferred by sub-clause (i) of clause (a) of section 21, may prefer an appeal against such order to the Supreme Court within a period of thirty days from the date of the order :
Provided that the Supreme Court may entertain an appeal after the expiry of the said period of thirty days if it is satisfied that there was sufficient cause for not filing it within that period.

5 **Meaning of Respondent:** A **respondent** is a person who is called upon to issue a response to a communication made by another. In legal usage, this specifically refers to the defendant in a legal proceeding commenced by a petition, or to an appellee, or the opposing party, in an appeal of a decision by an initial fact-finder.

the respondent reached Nanavati Hospital, Bombay and was under the treatment of the appellant[6] Doctor. At that stage, the respondent was undergoing haemodialysis twice a week on account of chronic renal failure. Investigations were underway to find a suitable donor. The respondent wanted to be operated by Dr. Sonawala alone who was out of India from 1.6.1991 to 1.7.1991. On 20.5.1991, the respondent approached the appellant Doctor. At the time, the respondent, who was suffering from high fever, did not want to be admitted to the Hospital despite the advice of the appellant. Hence, a broad spectrum antibiotic was prescribed to him. From 20.5.1991 to 29.5.1991, the respondent attended the Haemodialysis Unit at Nanavati Hospital on three occasions. At that time, his fever remained between 1010-1040F. The appellant constantly requested the complainant to get admitted to hospital but the respondent refused. On 29.5.1991 the respondent who had high fever of 1040F finally agreed to get admitted to hospital due to his serious condition. On 30.5.1991 the respondent was investigated for renal package. The medical report showed high creatinine 13 mg., blood urea 180 mg. The Haemoglobin of the respondent was 4.3%.

On 8.6.1991, the respondent, despite the appellant's advice, got himself discharged from Nanavati Hospital. Since the respondent was suffering from blood and urinary infection and had refused to come for haemodialysis on alternate days, the appellant suggested Injection Amikacin (500 mg.) twice a day. Certain other drugs were also specified to be taken under the supervision of the appellant when he visited the Dialysis Unit.. On 11.6.1991, the respondent attended the Haemodialysis Unit and complained to the appellant that he had slight tinnitus (ringing in the ear). The appellant has alleged that he immediately told the respondent to stop taking the Amikacin and Augmentin and scored out the treatment on the discharge card. However, despite express instructions from the appellant, the respondent continued to take Amikacin till 17.6.1991. Thereafter, the appellant was not under the treatment of the appellant. On 7.7.1992, the respondent filed a complaint before the National Consumer Disputes Redressal Commission, New Delhi (being Original Petition No. 178 of 1992) claiming compensation of an amount of Rs. 12,00,000/- as his hearing had been affected. The appellant filed his reply stating, inter alia, that there was no material brought on record by the respondent to show any co- relationship between the drugs prescribed and the state of

6 **Meaning of Appellant:** A person who, dissatisfied with the judgment rendered in a lawsuit decided in a lower court or the findings from a proceeding before an Administrative Agency, asks a superior court to review the decision.

his health.

The case of the respondent, in brief, is that the appellant was negligent in prescribing Amikacin to the respondent of 500 mg twice a day for 14 days as such dosage was excessive and caused hearing impairment. It is also the case of the respondent that the infection he was suffering from was not of a nature as to warrant administration of Amikacin to him.

The National Consumer Disputes Redressal Commission (hereinafter referred to as `the Commission') allowed the complaint of the respondent by way of the impugned order dated 9.4.2002 and awarded Rs. 4 lakh with interest @ 12% from 1.8.1992 as well as Rs. 3 lakh as compensation as well as Rs. 5000/- as costs.

Degree of Skill and Care Required by a Medical Practtitioner:

In Halsbury's Laws of England the degree of skill and care required by a medical practitioner is stated as follows:

The practitioner must bring to his task a reasonable degree of skill and knowledge, and must exercise a reasonable degree of care. Neither the very highest nor a very low degree of care and competence, judged in the light of the particular circumstances of each case, is what the law requires, and a person is not liable in negligence because someone else of greater skill and knowledge would have prescribed different treatment or operated in a different way; nor is he guilty of negligence if he has acted in accordance with a practice accepted as proper by a responsible body of medical men skilled in that particular art, even though a body of adverse opinion also existed among medical men.

A medical practitioner is not liable to be held negligent simply because things went wrong from mischance or misadventure or through an error of judgment in choosing one reasonable course of treatment in preference to another. He would be liable only where his conduct fell below that of the standards of a reasonably competent practitioner in his field. For instance, he would be liable if he leaves a surgical gauze inside the patient after an operation[7] or operates on the wrong part of the body, and he would be also criminally liable if he operates on someone for removing an organ for illegitimate trade.

7 *Achutrao Haribhau Khodwa and Ors. v. State of Maharashtra and Ors.* [1996]2SCR881

Protection to Doctors in Criminal Cases

In para 52 of ***Jacob Mathew** v. **State of Punjab and Anr.***[8] the Supreme Court realizing that doctors have to be protected from frivolous complaints of medical negligence, has laid down certain rules in this connection:

(i) A private complaint should not be entertained unless the complainant has produced prima facie evidence before the court in the form of a credible opinion given by another competent doctor to support the charge of rashness or negligence on the part of the accused doctor.

(ii) The investigating officer should, before proceeding against the doctor accused of rash or negligent act or omission, obtain an independent and competent medical opinion, preferably from a doctor in government service, qualified in that branch of medical practice who can normally be expected to give an impartial opinion.

(iii) A doctor accused[9] of negligence should not be arrested in a routine manner simply because a charge has been leveled against him. Unless his arrest is necessary for furthering the investigation or for collecting evidence or unless the investigating officer feels satisfied that the doctor proceeded against would not make himself available to face the prosecution unless arrested, the arrest should be withheld.

Precautions which Doctor/Hospitals/Nursing Homes should take:

(a) No prescription should ordinarily be given without actual examination. The tendency to give prescription over the telephone, except in an acute emergency, should be avoided.

(b) A doctor should not merely go by the version of the patient regarding his symptoms, but should also make his own analysis including tests and investigations where necessary.

(c) A doctor should not experiment unless necessary and even then he should ordinarily get a written consent from the patient.

(d) An expert should be consulted in case of any doubt. Thus, in Smt. Indrani Bhattacharjee, Original Petition No. 233 of 1996 decided by the National Consumer Commission on 9.8.2007, the patient was diagnosed as having `Mild Lateral Wall Eschemia'. The doctor prescribed medicine for

8 2005CriLJ3710

9 **Meaning of Accused:** A person charged with a criminal offense, or the state of being so charged

gastro-entiritis, but he expired. It was held that the doctor was negligent as he should have advised consulting a Cardiologist in writing.

(e) Full record of the diagnosis, treatment, etc. should be maintained.

Duty of Doctor:

In ***Pt. Parmanand Katara*** *v.* ***Union of India and Ors.***, the petitioner referred to a report published in the newspaper "The Hindustan Times" in which it was mentioned that a scooterist was knocked down by a speeding car. Seeing the profusely bleeding scooterist, a person who was on the road, picked up the injured and took him to the nearest hospital. The doctors refused to attend and told the man that he should take the patient to another hospital located 20 kilometers away authorized to handle medico-legal cases. The injured was then taken to that hospital but by the time he could reach, the victim succumbed to his injuries. The Supreme Court referred to the Code of Medical Ethics drawn up with the approval of the Central Government under Section 33 of the Indian Council Medical Act and observed "Every doctor whether at a Government Hospital or otherwise has the professional obligation to extend his services for protecting life. The obligation being total, absolute and paramount, laws of procedure whether in statutes or otherwise cannot be sustained and, therefore, must give way." The Supreme Court held that it is the duty of the doctor in an emergency to begin treatment of the patient and he should not await the arrival of the police or to complete the legal formalities. The life of a person is far more important than legal formalities. This view is in accordance with the Hippocratic oath of doctors. Although this decision has laid down that it is the duty of a doctor to attend to a patient who is brought to him in an emergency, it does not state what penalty will be imposed on a doctor who refuses to attend the said patient. Consequently it will depend on the fact and circumstances of the case.

In *Paschim Banga Khet Mazdoor Samity and Ors. v. State of West Bengal and Anr.*[10], the Supreme Court held that the denial of emergency aid to the petitioner due to the non availability of bed in the Government Hospital amounts to the violation of the right to life under Article 21[11] of the Constitution of India. The Court went on to say that the Constitutional

---

10 AIR1996SC2426

11 **Article 21 in The Constitution Of India 1949**
21. Protection of life and personal liberty No person shall be deprived of his life or personal liberty except according to procedure established by law

obligation imposed on the State by Article 21 cannot be abdicated on the ground of financial constraint.

In ***Md. Suleman Ansari (D.M.S.)*** *v.* ***Shankar Bhandari***[12] the respondent suffered a fracture of his hand. He went to the appellant who held himself out to be a qualified medical practitioner. The appellant bandaged the respondent's hand and prescribed certain medicines. He was ultimately taken to another doctor but by this time the damage to his hand was permanent. It was found that the appellant was not a qualified doctor to give treatment to the respondent. The Supreme Court had directed him to pay Rs. 80,000 as compensation to the respondent.

In ***Spring Medows Hospital and Anr.*** *v.* ***Harjol Ahluwalia thr' K.S. Ahluwalia and Anr.***[13], a minor child was admitted by his parents to a nursing home as he was suffering fever. The patient was admitted and the doctor diagnosed typhoid and gave medicines for typhoid fever. A nurse asked the father of the patient to get an injection Lariago which was administered by the nurse to the patient who immediately collapsed. The doctor was examined and testified that the child suffered a cardiac arrest on account of the medicine having being injected which led to brain damage. The National Commission held that the cause of cardiac arrest was intravenous injection of Lariago of such a high dose. The doctor was negligent in performing his duty because instead of administering the injection himself he permitted the nurse to give the injection. There was clear dereliction of duty on the part of the nurse who was not even a qualified nurse and was not registered with any nursing council of any State. Both the doctor and nurse and the hospital were found liable and Rs. 12.5 lakhs was awarded as compensation to the parents.

Decision of the Supreme Court:

Court directed that whenever a complaint is received against a doctor or hospital by the Consumer Fora (whether District, State or National) or by the Criminal Court then before issuing notice to the doctor or hospital against whom the complaint was made the Consumer Forum or Criminal Court should first refer the matter to a competent doctor or committee of doctors, specialized in the field relating to which the medical negligence is attributed, and only after that doctor or committee reports that there is a prima facie case of medical negligence should notice be then issued to

12 (2005) 12 SCC 430

13 [1998]2SCR428

the concerned doctor/hospital. This is necessary to avoid harassment to doctors who may not be ultimately found to be negligent.

In the present case the appellant was faced with an extremely serious situation. Had the appellant been only suffering from renal failure it is possible that a view could be taken that the dose prescribed for the appellant was excessive. However, the respondent was not only suffering from renal failure but he was also suffering from urinary tract infection and also blood infection i.e Septicaemia which is blood poisoning caused by bacteria or a toxin. He had also extremely high urea. In this extremely serious situation, the appellant had naturally to take a drastic measure to attempt to save the life of the respondent. The situation was aggravated by the non-cooperation of the respondent who seems to be of an assertive nature as deposed by the witnesses. Extraordinary situations require extraordinary remedies. Even assuming that such a high dose of Amikacin would ordinarily lead to hearing impairment, the appellant was faced with a situation between the devil and the deep sea. If he chose to save the life of the patient rather than his hearing surely he cannot faulted.

In the present case the blood urea of the respondent was found to be 180 mgs.% whereas normally it should not exceed 10-50 mgs.%. This shows that very serious infection in the kidney of the respondent was taking place which required drastic measures.

The allegation against the appellant is that he gave overdose of the antibiotic. In this connection it may be mentioned that antibiotics are usually given for a minimum of five days, but there is no upper limit to the number of days for which they should continue, and it all depends on the condition of the patient. Giving lesser dose of antibiotic may create other complications because it can cause resistance in the bacteria to the drug, and then it will be more difficult to treat.

As regards the impairment of hearing of the respondent it may be mentioned that there is no known antibiotic drug which has no side effect. Hence merely because there was impairment in the hearing of the respondent that does not mean that the appellant was negligent. The appellant was desperately trying to save the life of the respondent, which he succeeded in doing. Life is surely more important than side effects.

For example many Anti Tubercular drugs (e.g. Streptomycin) can cause impairment of hearing. Does this mean that TB patients should be allowed to die and not be given the Anti Tubercular drug because it impairs the hearing? Surely the answer will be in the negative.

The courts and Consumer Fora are not experts in medical science, and must not substitute their own views over that of specialists. It is true that the medical profession has to an extent become commercialized and there are many doctors who depart from their Hippocratic oath for their selfish ends of making money. However, the entire medical fraternity cannot be blamed or branded as lacking in integrity or competence just because of some bad apples. It must be remembered that sometimes despite their best efforts the treatment of a doctor fails. For instance, sometimes despite the best effort of a surgeon, the patient dies. That does not mean that the doctor or the surgeon must be held to be guilty of medical negligence, unless there is some strong evidence to suggest that he is.

Court further held that the appellant was not guilty of medical negligence. Court set aside the impugned judgment and order of the National Commission.

44

Contempt of Court[1]

Rule of Law & Contempt of Court:

'Rule of Law' is the basic rule of governance of any civilised democratic policy. Our Constitutional scheme is based upon the concept of Rule of Law which we have adopted and given to ourselves. Everyone, whether individually or collectively is unquestionably under the supremacy of law. Whoever the person may be, however high he or she is, no-one is above the law notwithstanding how powerful and how rich he or she may be. For achieving the establishment of the rule of law, the Constitution has assigned the special task to the judiciary in the country. It is only through the courts that the rule of law unfolds its contents and establishes its concept. For the judiciary to perform its duties and functions effectively and true to the spirit with which it is sacredly entrusted, the dignity and authority of the courts have to be respected and protected at all costs. After more than half a century of independence, the judiciary in the country is under a constant threat and being endangered from within and without. The need of the time is of restoring confidence amongst the people for the independence of judiciary. Its impartiality and the glory of law has to be maintained, protected and strengthened. The confidence in the courts of justice, which the people possess, cannot, in any way, be allowed to be tarnished, diminished or wiped out by contumacious behavior of any person. The only weapon of protecting itself from the onslaught to the institution is the long hand of contempt of court left in the armoury of judicial repository which, when needed, can reach any neck howsoever high or far away it may be.

In Re: Vinay Chandra Mishra (the alleged contemner)[2] Supreme Court reiterated the position of law relating to the powers of contempt and opined that the judiciary is not only the guardian of the rule of law and

1 Appellants: **In Re: Arundhati Roy**
AIR2002SC1375
Hon'ble Judges/Coram: G. B. Pattanaik and R. P. Sethi, JJ.

2 1995CriLJ3994

third pillar but in fact the central pillar of a democratic State. If the judiciary is to perform it duties and functions effectively and true to the spirit with which they are sacredly entrusted to it, the dignity and authority of the courts have to be respected and protected at all costs. Otherwise the very corner-stone of our constitutional scheme will give way and with it will disappear the rule of law and the civilized life in the society. It is for this purpose that the courts are entrusted with extraordinary powers of punishing those who indulge in acts, whether inside or outside the courts, which tend to undermine the authority of law and bring it in disrepute and disrespect by scandalizing it. When the court exercise this power, it does not do so to vindicate the dignity and honour of the individual judge who is personally attacked or scandalised, but to uphold the majesty of the law and of the administration of justice. The foundation of the judiciary is the trust and the confidence of the people in its ability to deliver fearless and impartial justice. When the foundation itself is shaken by acts which tend to create disaffection and disrespect for the authority of the court by creating distrust in its working, the edifice of the judicial system gets eroded.

No person can flout the mandate of law of respecting the courts for establishment of rule of law under the cloak of freedoms of speech and expression guaranteed by the Constitution. Such a freedom is subject to reasonable restrictions imposed by any law. Where a provision, in the law, relating to contempt imposes reasonable restrictions, no citizen can take the liberty of scandalizing the authority of the institution of judiciary. Freedom of speech and expression, so far as they do not contravene the statutory limits as contained in the Contempt of Courts Act, are to prevail without any hindrance. However, it must be remembered that the maintenance of dignity of courts is one of the cardinal principles of rule of law in a democratic set up and any criticism of the judicial institution couched in language that apparently appears to be mere criticism but ultimately results in undermining the dignity of the courts cannot be permitted when found crossed the limits and has to be punished.

Supreme Court in In Re: Harijai Singh and Anr.[3] has pointed out that a free and healthy Press is indispensable to the function of a true democracy but, at the same time, cautioned that the freedom of Press is not absolute, unlimited and unfettered at all times and in all circumstances. Lord Dening in his Book "Road to Justice" observed that Press is the watchdog to see that every trial is conducted fairly, openly

3 1997CriLJ58

and above broad but the watchdog may sometimes break loose and has to be punished for misbehavior. The law of contempt has been enacted to secure public respect and confidence in the judicial process. If such confidence is shaken or broken, the confidence of the common man in the institution of judiciary and democratic set up is likely to be eroded which, if not checked, is sure to be disastrous for the society itself.

Facts in Nutshell:

Case of the respondent[4] against whom suo motu[5] contempt proceedings have been initiated by Supreme Court. The respondent[6], who is stated to be an author of name and fame, has landed herself in the dock of the court, apparently by drifting away from the path on which she was traversing by contributing to the art and literature. During whole of the proceeding she has not shown any repentance or remorse and persistently and consistently tried to justify her action which, prima facie, was found to be contemptuous. To frustrate the proceedings, the respondent has resorted to all legal tactics and pretences.

The facts of the case, which are not seriously disputed, are that an organisation, namely, Narmada Bachao Andolan filed a petition under Article 32[7] of the Constitution of India being Writ Petition[8] No. 319

4 **Meaning of Respondent:** A **respondent** is a person who is called upon to issue a response to a communication made by another. In legal usage, this specifically refers to the defendant in a legal proceeding commenced by a petition, or to an appellee, or the opposing party, in an appeal of a decision by an initial fact-finder.

5 Suo motu, meaning "on its own motion," is a Latin legal term, approximately equivalent to the English term sua sponte. It is used, for example, where a government agency acts on its own cognizance, as in "the Commission took suo motu control over the matter."

6 **Meaning of Respondent:** A **respondent** is a person who is called upon to issue a response to a communication made by another. In legal usage, this specifically refers to the defendant in a legal proceeding commenced by a petition, or to an appellee, or the opposing party, in an appeal of a decision by an initial fact-finder.

7 **Article 32 in The Constitution Of India 1949**
32. Remedies for enforcement of rights conferred by this Part
(1) The right to move the Supreme Court by appropriate proceedings for the enforcement of the rights conferred by this Part is guaranteed
(2) The Supreme Court shall have power to issue directions or orders or writs, including writs in the nature of habeas corpus, mandamus, prohibition, quo warranto and certiorari, whichever may be appropriate, for the enforcement of any of the rights conferred by this Part
(3) Without prejudice to the powers conferred on the Supreme Court by clause (1) and (2), Parliament may by law empower any other court to exercise within the local limits of its jurisdiction all or any of the powers exercisable by the Supreme Court under clause (2)
(4) The right guaranteed by this article shall not be suspended except as otherwise provided for by this Constitution

8 **Writ Petition:** Under the Indian legal system, jurisdiction to issue 'prerogative writs' is given to

of 1994 in Supreme Court. The petitioner was a movement or andolan, whose leaders and members were concerned about the alleged adverse environmental impact of the construction of the sardar Sarovar Reservoir Dam in Gujarat and the far-reaching and tragic consequences of the displacement of hundreds of thousands of people from their ancestral homes that would result from the submerging of vast extents of land, to make up the reservoir. During the pendency of the writ petition court passed various order. By one of the order, the Court permitted to increase the height of the dam to RL 85 meters which was resented to and protested by the writ petitioners[9] and others including the respondent. The respondent Arundhati Roy, who was not a party to the writ proceedings, published an article entitled "The Greater Common Good" which was published in Outlook Magazine and in some portion of a book written by her. Two judges of Supreme Court, forming the three-judge Bench felt that the comments made by her were, prima facie, a misrepresentation of the proceedings of the court. It was observed that judicial process and institution cannot be permitted to be scandalised or subjected to contumacious violation in such a blatant manner, it had been done by her. The action of the respondent had caused the court much anguish and when the court expressed its displeasure on the action of the respondent in making distorted writing or manner in which leaders of the petitioner Ms. Medha Patkar and one Dharmadikhari despite giving assurance to the court acted in breach of the injunction[10], the Court observed:

"We are unhappy at the way the leaders of NBA and Ms. Arundhati Roy have attempted to undermine the dignity of the Court. We expected better behavior from them.

However, after the judgment was pronounced in case, an incident was stated to have taken place on 30th December, 2000 regarding which

---

the Supreme Court, and to the High Courts of Judicature of all Indian states. Parts of the law relating to writs are set forth in the Constitution of India. The Supreme Court, the highest in the country, may issue writs under Article 32 of the Constitution for enforcement of Fundamental Rights and under Articles 139 for enforcement of rights other than Fundamental Rights, while High Courts, the superior courts of the States, may issue writs under Articles 226. 'Writ' is eminently designed by the makers of the Constitution, and in the same way it is developed very widely and efficiently by the courts in India. The Constitution broadly provides for five kinds of "prerogative" writs, namely, Habeas Corpus, Certiorari, Mandamus, Quo Warranto and Prohibition.

9 **Meaning of Petitioner:** A person who presents a Petition. (**Meaning of Petition:** A formal message requesting something that is submitted to an authority)

10 **Meaning of Injunction:** A court order by which an individual is required to perform, or is restrained from performing, a particular act.

Contempt Petition was filed by J.R. Parashar, Advocate and others (Petitioners). According to the appellations made in that petition, the respondents named therein, led a huge crowd and held a Dharna in front of Supreme Court and shouted abusive slogans against the court including slogans ascribing lack of integrity and dishonesty to his institution. It was alleged that when the petitioners therein protested, they were attacked and assaulted by the respondents. In the evening on the same day, the respondents are stated to have attacked, abused and assaulted the petitioners. A complaint was stated to have been lodged with the Tilak Marg Police Station on the next day. In for aforesaid contempt proceeding notices were issued to the respondents in response to which they filed separate affidavits[11]. All the three respondents (Arundhati Roy, Ms. Medha Patkar and Dharmadhikari) therein admitted that there was a Dharna outside the gates of Supreme Court on 30th December, 2000 which was organised by Narmada Bachao Andolan and the gathered crowd were persons who lived in the Narmada Valley and were aggrieved by the majority judgment of Supreme Court relating to the building of the dam on the Narmada River.

Contempt of Court Act, 1971:

The Act, which was enacted in the year 1971, much after the adoption of the Constitution by the People of India, defined criminal contempt under Section 2(c) to mean:

"Criminal contempt" means the publication (whether by words, spoken or written or by signs, or by visible representation, or otherwise) of any matter or the doing of nay other act whatsoever which

i) scandalises or tends to scandalise, or lowers or tends to lower the authority of, any court, or

ii) prejudices, or interferes or tends to interfere with, the due course of any judicial proceeding; or

iii) interferes or tends to interfere with, or obstructs or tends to obstruct, the administration of justice in any other manner."

11 **Meaning of Affidavit:** An **affidavit** is a written sworn statement of fact voluntarily made by an *affiant* or *deponent* under an oath or affirmation administered by a person authorized to do so by law. Such statement is witnessed as to the authenticity of the affiant's signature by a taker of oaths, such as a notary public or commissioner of oaths.

Freedom of Speech and Expression:

The Constitution of India has guaranteed freedom of speech and expression to every citizen as a fundamental right. While guaranteeing such freedom, it has also provided under Article 129[12] that the Supreme Court shall be a Court of Record and shall have all the powers of such a Court including the power to punish for contempt of itself. Similar power has been conferred on the High Courts of the States under Article 215[13]. Under the Constitution, there is no separate guarantee of the freedom of the press and it is the same freedom of expression, which is conferred on all citizens under Article 19(1)[14]. Any expression of opinion would, therefore, be not immune from the liability for exceeding the limits, either under the law of defamation or contempt of Court or the other constitutional limitations under Article 19(2)[15]. If a citizen, therefore, in the grab of exercising right of free expression under Article 19(1), tries to scandalise the court or undermines the dignity of the court, then the court would be entitled to exercise power under Article 129 or Article 215, as the case may be.

Decision of the Supreme Court:

Court held that the respondent is proved to have shot the arrow, intended

12 **Article 129 in The Constitution Of India 1949**
129. Supreme Court to be a court of record The Supreme Court shall be a court of record and shall have all the powers of such a court including the power to punish for contempt of itself

13 **Article 215 in The Constitution Of India 1949**
215. High Courts to be courts of record Every High Court shall be a court of record and shall have all the powers of such a court including the power to punish for contempt of itself

14 **Article 19(1) in The Constitution Of India 1949**
(1) All citizens shall have the right
(a) to freedom of speech and expression

15 **Article 19(2)in The Constitution Of India 1949**
19. Protection of certain rights regarding freedom of speech etc
(1) All citizens shall have the right
(a) to freedom of speech and expression;
(b) to assemble peaceably and without arms;
(c) to form associations or unions;
(d) to move freely throughout the territory of India;
(e) to reside and settle in any part of the territory of India; and
(f) omitted
(g) to practise any profession, or to carry on any occupation, trade or business
(2) Nothing in sub clause (a) of clause (1) shall affect the operation of any existing law, or prevent the State from making any law, in so far as such law imposes reasonable restrictions on the exercise of the right conferred by the said sub clause in the interests of the sovereignty and integrity of India, the security of the State, friendly relations with foreign States, public order, decency or morality or in relation to contempt of court, defamation or incitement to an offence

to damage the institution of the judiciary and thereby weaken the faith of the public in general and if such an attempt is not prevented, disastrous consequences are likely to follow resulting in the destruction of rule of law, the expected norm of any civilised society. Court further held that respondent has committed the criminal contempt of Supreme Court by scandalizing its authority with malafide intentions[16]. The respondent was therefore, held guilty for the contempt of court punishable under Section 12[17] of the Contempt of Courts Act, 1971. Court sentenced respondent to simple imprisonment for one day and to pay a fine of Rs. 2,000/-.

---

16 **Meaning of Malafide Intention:** The expression comes from Latin; 'mal' means 'bad' and 'fide' means 'faith'. 'Mala fide' means in bad faith. A mala fide action is one that is performed with dishonest intent; a person purposely attempts to cheat or deceive you. The opposite of 'mala fide' is 'bona fide' meaning 'in good faith'.

17 **Section 12 in The Contempt Of Courts Act, 1971**

12. Punishment for contempt of court

(1) Save as otherwise expressly provided in this Act or in any other law, a contempt of court may be punished with simple imprisonment for a term which may extend to six months, or with fine which may extend to two thousand rupees, or with both.: Provided that the accused may be discharged or the punishment awarded may be remitted on apology being made to the satisfaction of the court. Explanation.- An apology shall not be rejected merely on the ground that it is qualified or conditional if the accused makes it bona fide.

(2) Notwithstanding anything contained in any law for the time being in force, no court shall impose a sentence in excess of that specified in sub- section (1) for any contempt either in respect of itself or of a court subordinate to it.

(3) Notwithstanding anything contained in this section, where a person is found guilty of a civil contempt, the court, if it considers that a fine Will not meet the ends of justice and that a sentence of imprisonment is necessary shall, instead of sentencing him to simple imprisonment, direct that he be detained in a civil prison for such period not exceeding six months as it may think fit.

(4) Where the person found guilty of contempt of court in respect of any undertaking given to a court is a company, every person who, at the time the contempt was committed, was in charge of, and was responsible to, the company for the conduct of the business of the company, as well as the company, shall be deemed to be guilty of the contempt and the punishment may be enforced, with the leave of the court, by the detention in civil prison of each such person: Provided that nothing contained in this sub- section shall render any such person liable to such punishment if he proves that the contempt was committed without his knowledge or that he exercised all due diligence to prevent its commission.

(5) Notwithstanding anything contained in sub- section (4), where the contempt of court referred to therein has been committed by a company and it is proved that the contempt has been committed with the consent or connivance of, or is attributable to any neglect on the part of, any director, manager, secretary or other officer of the com- pany, such director, manager, secretary or other officer shall also be deemed to be guilty of the contempt and the punishment may be enforced. with the leave of the court, by the detention in civil prison of such director, manager, secretary or other officer. Explanation.- For the purpose of sub- sections (4) and (5),-

(a) " company" means any body corporate and includes a firm or other association of individuals; and

(b) " director", in relation to a firm, means a partner in the firm.

45

'Personal Liberty' includes a right to travel abroad[1]

Facts in Nutshell:

Appeal[2] raised an important question as to the interpretation of Article 21[3] of the Constitution, and the question raised is whether the expression "personal liberty" occurring in the said Article includes the right to travel abroad. The second important question that arises is whether the refusal of a passport to the respondent[4] by appellant[5] No. 1 has resulted in the contravention[6] of Articles 21 and 14[7] of the Constitution of India.

Respondent a citizen of India who is a partner of a firm in Bombay which carries on business of Bankers (Exporters and Importers). He is also a partner of a firm doing business at Dubai in Persian Gulf, which carries on the business of Indent Agents and Importers. According to the respondent

---

1 Appellants: **A.G. Kazi and Ors. Vs.** Respondent: **C.V. Jethwani**
AIR1967Bom235
Hon'ble Judges/Coram: Tambe, C.J. and Bal, Judge

2 **Meaning of Appeal:** In law, an **appeal** is a process for requesting a formal change to an official decision. Very broadly speaking there are appeals on the record and *de novo* appeals. In *de novo* appeals, a new decision maker re-hears the case without any reference to the prior decision maker. In appeals on the record, the decision of the prior decision maker is challenged by arguing that he or she misapplied the law, came to an incorrect factual finding, acted in excess of his jurisdiction, abused his powers, was biased, considered evidence which he should not have considered or failed to consider evidence that he should have considered.

3 **Article 21 in The Constitution Of India 1949**
21. Protection of life and personal liberty No person shall be deprived of his life or personal liberty except according to procedure established by law

4 **Meaning of Respondent:** A **respondent** is a person who is called upon to issue a response to a communication made by another. In legal usage, this specifically refers to the defendant in a legal proceeding commenced by a petition, or to an appellee, or the opposing party, in an appeal of a decision by an initial fact-finder.

5 **Meaning of Appellant:** A person who, dissatisfied with the judgment rendered in a lawsuit decided in a lower court or the findings from a proceeding before an Administrative Agency, asks a superior court to review the decision.

6 **Meaning of Contravention:** A term of French law meaning an act violative of a law

7 **Article 14 in The Constitution Of India 1949**
14. Equality before law The State shall not deny to any person equality before the law or the equal protection of the laws within the territory of India Prohibition of discrimination on grounds of religion, race, caste, sex or place of birth

passports were granted to him during the period from October 1952 to October 1962 to enable him to make trips to Dubai and certain other ports in the Persian Gulf. The passport that had been granted, expired on 28th October 1962. On 10th January 1963, the respondent applied to the Regional Passport Officer (second appellant) for the grant of a new passport for a period of three years. That application was rejected by the Assistant Passport Officer, (first appellant). There was certain correspondence between the respondent and appellants Nos. 1 and 2, but ultimately by a further letter of date 27th June 1963 he was informed that the passport authorities had nothing to add to their previous letter date 24th May 1963. The respondent then filed a writ petition[8] under Article 226[9] of the Constitution for an appropriate writ or direction to quash the order refusing to grant him a passport and for a direction

8 **Writ Petition:** Under the Indian legal system, jurisdiction to issue 'prerogative writs' is given to the Supreme Court, and to the High Courts of Judicature of all Indian states. Parts of the law relating to writs are set forth in the Constitution of India. The Supreme Court, the highest in the country, may issue writs under Article 32 of the Constitution for enforcement of Fundamental Rights and under Articles 139 for enforcement of rights other than Fundamental Rights, while High Courts, the superior courts of the States, may issue writs under Articles 226. ⍰Writ⍰ is eminently designed by the makers of the Constitution, and in the same way it is developed very widely and efficiently by the courts in India. The Constitution broadly provides for five kinds of "prerogative" writs, namely, Habeas Corpus, Certiorari, Mandamus, Quo Warranto and Prohibition.

9 **Article 226 in The Constitution Of India 1949**

226. Power of High Courts to issue certain writs

(1) Notwithstanding anything in Article 32 every High Court shall have powers, throughout the territories in relation to which it exercise jurisdiction, to issue to any person or authority, including in appropriate cases, any Government, within those territories directions, orders or writs, including writs in the nature of habeas corpus, mandamus, prohibitions, quo warranto and certiorari, or any of them, for the enforcement of any of the rights conferred by Part III and for any other purpose

(2) The power conferred by clause (1) to issue directions, orders or writs to any Government, authority or person may also be exercised by any High Court exercising jurisdiction in relation to the territories within which the cause of action, wholly or in part, arises for the exercise of such power, notwithstanding that the seat of such Government or authority or the residence of such person is not within those territories

(3) Where any party against whom an interim order, whether by way of injunction or stay or in any other manner, is made on, or in any proceedings relating to, a petition under clause (1), without

(a) furnishing to such party copies of such petition and all documents in support of the plea for such interim order; and

(b) giving such party an opportunity of being heard, makes an application to the High Court for the vacation of such order and furnishes a copy of such application to the party in whose favour such order has been made or the counsel of such party, the High Court shall dispose of the application within a period of two weeks from the date on which it is received or from the date on which the copy of such application is so furnished, whichever is later, or where the High Court is closed on the last day of that period, before the expiry of the next day afterwards on which the High Court is open; and if the application is not so disposed of, the interim order shall, on the expiry of that period, or, as the case may be, the expiry of the aid next day, stand vacated

(4) The power conferred on a High Court by this article shall not be in derogation of the power conferred on the Supreme court by clause (2) of Article 32

against the appellants requiring them to grant and issue to him a passport as applied for by him. The respondent founded his petition principally on three grounds. According to him, the refusal of the passport was violative of his fundamental rights[10] conferred on him by Article 19(1)(d)[11] to (g) and Article 21 and Article 14 of the Constitution. According to the respondent it was not possible for him to leave India without a passport. Government having issued instructions to the shipping companies and Airlines not to take on board passengers leaving India unless they possess a valid passport. It was therefore impossible for him to leave India without a valid passport. Secondly it was alleged that the passport is necessary for reentry into India, and on this ground also it was claimed that possession of a valid passport is absolutely essential for going abroad both because without a passport no shipping company or an Airline would book a passage for him, and secondly because it would not be possible for him to return to his country. He further alleged that it was absolutely necessary for the purposes of his business to go to Dubai and to return to India as he had been doing for so many years. The right to travel abroad and return to India, according to the respondent, is a part of his "personal liberty" assured to him under Article 21 of the Constitution. He could be deprived of that liberty only "according to the procedure established by law" as provided in the said Article. There is no procedure prescribed by any law regulating the grant or refusal of a passport.

10 ***'Part III – Fundamental Rights'*** is a charter of rights contained in the Constitution of India. It guarantees civil liberties such that all Indians can lead their lives in peace and harmony as citizens of India. These include individual rights common to most liberal democracies, such asequality before law, freedom of speech and expression, and peaceful assembly, freedom to practice religion, and the right to constitutional remedies for the protection of civil rights by means of writs such as habeas corpus. Violation of these rights result in punishments as prescribed in the Indian Penal Code or other special laws, subject to discretion of the judiciary. The Fundamental Rights are defined as basichuman freedoms which every Indian citizen has the right to enjoy for a proper and harmonious development of personality. These rights universally apply to all citizens, irrespective of race, place of birth, religion, caste, creed, colour or gender. Aliens (persons who are not citizens) are also considered in matters like equality before law. They are enforceable by the courts, subject to certain restrictions. The Rights have their origins in many sources, including England's Bill of Rights, the United States Bill of Rights and France's Declaration of the Rights of Man.

11 **Article 19 in The Constitution Of India 1949**

19. Protection of certain rights regarding freedom of speech etc

(1) All citizens shall have the right

(a) to freedom of speech and expression;

(b) to assemble peaceably and without arms;

(c) to form associations or unions;

(d) to move freely throughout the territory of India;

(e) to reside and settle in any part of the territory of India; and

(f) omitted

(g) to practise any profession, or to carry on any occupation, trade or business

Decision of Learned Single Judge:

The learned Judge held that the compendious expression "personal liberty" used in Article 21 includes in its ambit the right to go abroad, and that a person cannot be deprived of this right "except according to procedure established by law" as laid down in Article 21. The issue of passport is not regulated by any statute. Every citizen of India, therefore, as a right, entitled to have a passport issued to him. In absence of a law regulating the grant or refusal of a passport, the right to equal protection contained in Airlines 14 is available both against legislative as well as executive acts.

In view of the matter the learned Judge quashed the order of refusing passport facilities to the respondent, and the appellants were directed to grant and issue to the respondent a passport as applied by him by his application dated 10th January 1963. Against the judgment of the learned Judge appeal has was filed in High Court.

Right to Go Abroad:

The right to go abroad was recognized as early as in the year 1215 in Article 42 of the Magna Carta[12] which reads:

"It shall be lawful to any person for the future to go out of Kingdom, and to return, safely and securely, by land or by water, saving his allegiance to use unless it be in time of war, for some short space, for the common good of the Kingdom; excepting prisoners and outlaws, according to the laws of land, and of the people of the nation at war against us, and Merchants who shall be treated as it is said above"

On 10th December, 1948, the General Assembly of the United Nations proclaimed the "Universal Declaration of Human Rights", and the preamble indicates that this declaration of human rights has been made with a view that they should be recognised as inalienable rights[13] of all human beings inasmuch as experience has shown that the disregard of these rights has compelled men to have recourse as the last resort to

---

12 **Magna Carta** (Latin for **Great Charter**), also called **Magna Carta Libertatum** or **The Great Charter of the Liberties of England**, is an Angevin charter originally issued in Latin in the year 1215.
Magna Carta was the first document forced onto a King of England by a group of his subjects, the feudal barons, in an attempt to limit his powers by law and protect their privileges.

13 **Meaning of Inalienable Right:**
A right according to natural law, a right that cannot be taken away, denied, or transferred

rebellion against tyranny and oppression. It was, therefore considered essential that these human rights should be protected by the rule of law. Article 13 of UDHR, 1948 thereof provided:

"1. Everyone has the right to freedom of movement and residence within the borders of each State.

2. Everyone has the right to leave any country, including his own, and to return to his country."

Judgments Referred:

In *Dr. S. S. Sadashiva Rao v. Union of India* [14] the petitioners[15] were medical graduates. They were desirous of having higher studies, some in U. S. A. and some in U. K. for that purpose, each of them submitted an application to the Regional Passport Officer for a passport. The request was not complied with. Each of the petitioners, therefore, filed a writ application under Art. 226 praying for a writ of mandamus[16] or order or direction requiring the passport officer Madras, to issue a passport. One of the questions that fell for consideration was whether the right to go abroad was included in Art. 21. It has been held:

"The right of a citizen to go abroad must be held to fall within Art. 21 of the Constitution. Thus a citizen has a fundamental right under Art. 21 to go abroad and also a fundamental right to come back to this country."

The freedom of movement of a citizen has three aspects[17]-

(a) the right to move from any part of his country to any other part;

(b) the right to move out of his country;

(c) the right to return to his country from abroad .

14 1965 (44) M LJ 605

15 **Meaning of Petitioner:** A person who presents a Petition. (**Meaning of Petition:** A formal message requesting something that is submitted to an authority)

16 **Mandamus** is a judicial remedy — in the form of an order from a superior court, to any government subordinate court, corporation, or public authority — to do (or forbear from doing) some specific act which that body is obliged under law to do (or refrain from doing) — and which is in the nature of public duty, and in certain cases one of a statutory duty. It cannot be issued to compel an authority to do something against statutory provision. For example, it cannot be used to force a lower court to reject or authorize applications that have been made, but if the court refuses to rule one way or the other then a mandamus can be used to order the court to rule on the applications.

17 Page 714 of Basu's Commentary on the Constitution of India, 5th Ed. (Vol. I):

Decision of the High Court:

Court held that the case of the respondent in brief was that in absence of any law regulating the grant of refusal to grant a passport, it was left to the whim and pleasure and arbitrary decision of the passport authorities to give passports. A number of passports have been given to various persons who were similarly situated to him. The refusal to grant renewal of the passport to the respondent contravenes Article 14 inasmuch as it has resulted in arbitrarily discriminating him against the other persons similarly situated and who have been granted passports to go to Dubai.

The functions of the State have been divided into legislative, judicial and executive . There is no fourth category. It is an admitted position that there is no law regulating the grant or refusal of a passport. It is clear that arbitrary and uncontrolled powers have been conferred on the passport authorities in the matter of grant or refusal of the passports. No guidance has been given to them in this respect and the conferral of such arbitrary and uncontrolled powers is by itself violative of Article 14 of the Constitution. High Court further directed the appellants to grant and issue to the respondent a passport as applied by him by his application dated 10th January 1963.

46

Marriage and Mental Cruelty[1]

Ratio Decidendi[2]: ***"The married life should be assessed as a whole and a few isolated instances over certain period will not amount to cruelty."***

Facts in Nutshell:

The appellant[3], a Principal in ITI College, Sirhali, Amritsar, has approached Supreme Court against the judgment and final order of the High Court of Punjab & Haryana at Chandigarh whereby the learned single Judge dismissed the appeal[4] filed by him against the judgment and order of the Additional District Judge (Ad hoc), Amritsar, dismissing the petition[5] filed under Section 13[6] of the Hindu Marriage Act, 1955 (hereinafter referred

---

1 Appellants: **Gurbux Singh Vs.** Respondent: **Harminder Kaur**
AIR2011SC114
Hon'ble Judges/Coram: P. Sathasivam and B. S. Chauhan, JJ.

2 **Meaning of Ration Decidendi:** ***Ratio decidendi*** is a Latin phrase meaning "the reason" or "the rationale for the decision." The *ratio decidendi* is "the point in a case which determines the judgment" or "the principle which the case establishes."

3 **Meaning of Appellant:** A person who, dissatisfied with the judgment rendered in a lawsuit decided in a lower court or the findings from a proceeding before an Administrative Agency, asks a superior court to review the decision.

4 **Meaning of Appeal:** In law, an **appeal** is a process for requesting a formal change to an official decision. Very broadly speaking there are appeals on the record and *de novo* appeals. In *de novo* appeals, a new decision maker re-hears the case without any reference to the prior decision maker. In appeals on the record, the decision of the prior decision maker is challenged by arguing that he or she misapplied the law, came to an incorrect factual finding, acted in excess of his jurisdiction, abused his powers, was biased, considered evidence which he should not have considered or failed to consider evidence that he should have considered.

5 **Meaning of Petition:** A formal written application requesting a court for a specific judicial action

6 **Section 13 in The Hindu Marriage Act, 1955**
13. Divorce.
(1) Any marriage solemnized, whether before or after the commencement of this Act, may, on a petition presented by either the
husband or the wife, be dissolved by a decree of divorce on the ground that the other party-
(i) has, after the solemnization of the marriage, had voluntary, sexual intercourse with any person other than his or her spouse; or
(ia) has, after the solemnization of the marriage, treated the petitioner with cruelty; or
(ib) has deserted the petitioner for a continuous period of not less than two years immediately preceding the presentation of the petition; or]
(ii) has ceased to be a Hindu by conversion to another religion; or

to as "the Act") for a decree of divorce against the respondent[7]-wife, who was working as a Librarian in Government Institute DIET at Verka, Amritsar on the ground of 'cruelty'. Both the courts have rejected the claim of the appellant on the ground that he has failed to prove 'cruelty' sufficient for grant of a decree of divorce.

On 23.11.1997, the appellant got married with the respondent at Amritsar according to Sikh rites and customs. Even on the date of marriage, the respondent had been working as a Librarian in a Government Institute DIET at Verka, Amristar. From the very beginning, the respondent expressed her dislike towards the appellant and his family and gradually started misbehaving with them. She started exhibiting short-tempered behaviour and treated the parents of the appellant with cruelty and disrespect. The father of the appellant aged about 80 years and his mother more than 75 years. In the month of January 1998, on the first Lohri festival after their marriage, the respondent being annoyed with the appellant on a trivial issue, abused his mother in filthy language in the presence of their relatives and neighbours causing immense pain to the entire family. Since then, the respondent started insisting that

---

(iii) has been incurably of unsound mind, or has been suffering continuously or intermittently from mental disorder of such a kind and to such an extent that the petitioner cannot reasonably be expected to live with the respondent. Explanation.- In this clause,-

(a) the expression" mental disorder" means mental illness, arrested or incomplete development of mind, psychopathic disorder or any other disorder or disability of mind and includes schizophrenia;

(b) the expression" psychopathic disorder" means a persistent disorder or disability of mind (whether or not including sub- normality of intelligence) which results in abnormally aggressive or seriously irresponsible conduct on the part of the other party, and whether or not it require or is susceptible to medical treatment; or

(iv) been suffering from a virulent and incurable from of leprosy; or

(v) been suffering from venereal disease in a communicable from; or

(vi) has renounced the world by entering any religious order; or

(vii) has not been heard of as being alive for a period of seven years or more by those persons who would naturally have heard of it, had that party been alive.

(2) A wife may also present a petition for the dissolution of her marriage by a decree of divorce on the ground,-

(i) in the case of any marriage solemnized before the commencement of this Act, that the husband had married again before such commencement or that any other wife of the husband married before such commencement was alive at the time of the solemnization of the marriage of the petitioner: Provided that in either case the other wife is alive at the time of the presentation of the petition; or

(ii) that the husband has, since the solemnization of the marriage, been guilty of rape, sodomy or bestiality

7 **Meaning of Respondent:** A **respondent** is a person who is called upon to issue a response to a communication made by another. In legal usage, this specifically refers to the defendant in a legal proceeding commenced by a petition, or to an appellee, or the opposing party, in an appeal of a decision by an initial fact-finder.

she cannot live with the parents of the appellant who are mental and nuisance in her life and pressed upon the appellant to have a separate abode from his parents. On 15.05.1999, a male child was born out of the wedlock. Even after the birth of the child, there was no improvement in the behaviour of the respondent. She always insisted that she being financially independent is not in need of the appellant and his family. Just five days before the third birthday of their child i.e. on 10.05.2002, the respondent, without any justifiable reason left the matrimonial home leaving the child unattended and went to her parents house and staying there since then. The appellant having failed in his efforts to bring back the respondent to the matrimonial home and in view of the consistent cruelty filed HMA Case before the Addl. District Judge, Amritsar, praying for a decree of divorce under Section 13 of the Hindu Marriage Act, 1955.

Decision of the District Court and High Court:

The Additional District Judge, Amritsar, after analyzing the plea of both the parties, oral and documentary evidence concluded that the appellant-husband failed to substantiate the allegations of 'cruelty' and dismissed his divorce petition. Aggrieved by the same, the appellant approached the High Court. The learned single Judge of the High Court while agreeing with the conclusion of the Additional District Judge dismissed the appeal filed by the appellant. Questioning the above said orders, the appellant filed the appeal by way of special leave petition[8] in Supreme Court.

Question before the Supreme Court:

The only question for consideration was whether the appellant-husband has made out a case for divorce on the ground of 'cruelty' by the respondent-wife.

Mental Cruelty:

In *Samar Ghosh v. Jaya Ghosh*[9], a three-Judge Bench of Supreme Court while considering Section 13(1)(ia) of the Hindu Marriage Act laid down

8 **Article 136 in The Constitution Of India 1949**
136. Special leave to appeal by the Supreme Court
(1) Notwithstanding anything in this Chapter, the Supreme Court may, in its discretion, grant special leave to appeal from any judgment, decree, determination, sentence or order in any cause or matter passed or made by any court or tribunal in the territory of India
(2) Nothing in clause (1) shall apply to any judgment, determination, sentence or order passed or made by any court or tribunal constituted by or under any law relating to the Armed Forces

9 (2007) 4 SCC 511

certain guidelines.

The analysis and ultimate conclusion are relevant which reads as under:

There cannot be any comprehensive definition of the concept of "mental cruelty" within which all kinds of cases of mental cruelty can be covered. No court in our considered view should even attempt to give a comprehensive definition of mental cruelty.

Human mind is extremely complex and human behaviour is equally complicated. Similarly human ingenuity has no bound, therefore, to assimilate the entire human behaviour in one definition is almost impossible. What is cruelty in one case may not amount to cruelty in other case. The concept of cruelty differs from person to person depending upon his upbringing, level of sensitivity, educational, family and cultural background, financial position, social status, customs, traditions, religious beliefs, human values and their value system.

Apart from this, the concept of mental cruelty cannot remain static; it is bound to change with the passage of time, impact of modern culture through print and electronic media and value system, etc. etc. What may be mental cruelty now may not remain a mental cruelty after a passage of time or vice versa. There can never be any straitjacket formula or fixed parameters for determining mental cruelty in matrimonial matters. The prudent and appropriate way to adjudicate the case would be to evaluate it on its peculiar facts and circumstances while taking aforementioned factors in consideration.

Some instances of human behaviour which may be relevant in dealing with the cases of "mental cruelty". The instances indicated in the succeeding paragraphs are only illustrative and not exhaustive:

(i) On consideration of complete matrimonial life of the parties, acute mental pain, agony and suffering as would not make possible for the parties to live with each other could come within the broad parameters of mental cruelty.

(ii) On comprehensive appraisal of the entire matrimonial life of the parties, it becomes abundantly clear that situation is such that the wronged party cannot reasonably be asked to put up with such conduct and continue to live with other party.

(iii) Mere coldness or lack of affection cannot amount to cruelty, frequent rudeness of language, petulance of manner, indifference and neglect may reach such a degree that it makes the married life for the other spouse absolutely intolerable.

(iv) Mental cruelty is a state of mind. The feeling of deep anguish, disappointment, frustration in one spouse caused by the conduct of other for a long time may lead to mental cruelty.

(v) A sustained course of abusive and humiliating treatment calculated to torture, discommode or render miserable life of the spouse.

(vi) Sustained unjustifiable conduct and behaviour of one spouse actually affecting physical and mental health of the other spouse. The treatment complained of and the resultant danger or apprehension must be very grave, substantial and weighty.

(vii) Sustained reprehensible conduct, studied neglect, indifference or total departure from the normal standard of conjugal kindness causing injury to mental health or deriving sadistic pleasure can also amount to mental cruelty.

(viii) The conduct must be much more than jealousy, selfishness, possessiveness, which causes unhappiness and dissatisfaction and emotional upset may not be a ground for grant of divorce on the ground of mental cruelty.

(ix) Mere trivial irritations, quarrels, normal wear and tear of the married life which happens in day-to-day life would not be adequate for grant of divorce on the ground of mental cruelty.

(x) The married life should be reviewed as a whole and a few isolated instances over a period of years will not amount to cruelty. The ill conduct must be persistent for a fairly lengthy period, where the relationship has deteriorated to an extent that because of the acts and behaviour of a spouse, the wronged party finds it extremely difficult to live with the other party any longer, may amount to mental cruelty.

(xi) If a husband submits himself for an operation of sterilisation without medical reasons and without the consent or knowledge of his wife and similarly, if the wife undergoes vasectomy or abortion without medical reason or without the consent or knowledge of her husband, such an act of the spouse may lead to mental cruelty.

(xii) Unilateral decision of refusal to have intercourse for considerable period without there being any physical incapacity or valid reason may amount to mental cruelty.

(xiii) Unilateral decision of either husband or wife after marriage not to have child from the marriage may amount to cruelty.

(xiv) Where there has been a long period of continuous separation, it may fairly be concluded that the matrimonial bond is beyond repair. The marriage becomes a fiction though supported by a legal tie. By refusing to sever that tie, the law in such cases, does not serve the sanctity of marriage; on the contrary, it shows scant regard for the feelings and emotions of the parties. In such like situations, it may lead to mental cruelty.

A Hindu marriage solemnized under the Act can only be dissolved on any of the grounds specified therein.

Decision of the Supreme Court:

The married life should be assessed as a whole and a few isolated instances over certain period will not amount to cruelty. The ill-conduct must be precedent for a fairly lengthy period where the relationship has deteriorated to an extent that because of the acts and behaviour of a spouse, one party finds it extremely difficult to live with the other party no longer may amount to mental cruelty. Making certain statements on the spur of the moment and expressing certain displeasure about the behaviour of elders may not be characterized as cruelty. Mere trivial irritations, quarrels, normal wear and tear of married life which happens in day to day life in all families would not be adequate for grant of divorce on the ground of cruelty. Sustained unjustifiable and reprehensible conduct affecting physical and mental health of the other spouse may lead to mental cruelty.

The appellant and respondent were living separately from 2002 and it would be impossible for their re-union, hence Supreme Court exercising its jurisdiction under Article 142[10] of the Constitution held that their marriage may be dissolved in the interest of both parties.

10 **Article 142 in The Constitution Of India 1949**

142. Enforcement of decrees and orders of Supreme Court and unless as to discovery, etc (1) The Supreme Court in the exercise of its jurisdiction may pass such decree or make such order as is necessary for doing complete justice in any cause or matter pending before it, and any decree so passed or orders so made shall be enforceable throughout the territory of India in such manner as may be prescribed by or under any law made by Parliament and, until provision in that behalf is so made, in such manner as the President may by order prescribe

(2) Subject to the provisions of any law made in this behalf by Parliament, the Supreme Court shall, as respects the whole of the territory of India, have all and every power to make any order for the purpose of securing the attendance of any person, the discovery or production of any documents, or the investigation or punishment of any contempt of itself

47

Right to Privacy[1]

Facts in Nutshell:

The first petitioner[2] the editor, printer and publisher of a Tamil weekly magazine 'Nakkheeran', published from Madras. The second petitioner, the associate editor of the magazine. They seek issuance of an appropriate, writ[3], order or direction under Article 32[4] of the Constitution, restraining the respondents[5], viz., (1) State of Tamil Nadu represented by the Secretary, Home Department, (2) Inspector General of Prisons, Madras and (3) Superintendent of Prisons (Central Prison), Salem, Tamil Nadu from interfering with the publication of the autobiography of the condemned prisoner, Auto Shankar, in their magazine.

Shankar @ Gauri Shankar @ Auto Shankar was charged and tried for as many as six murders. He was convicted and sentenced to death by the learned Sessions Judge, Chenglepat on May 31, 1991 which was confirmed by the Madras High Court on July 17,1992. His appeal to Supreme Court

1 Appellants:**R. Rajagopal alias R.R. Gopal and Another Vs.**Respondent: **State of Tamil Nadu and Others**
AIR1995SC264
Hon'ble Judges/Coram: B.P. Jeevan Reddy and S. C. Sen, JJ.

2 **Meaning of Petitioner:** A person who presents a Petition. (**Meaning of Petition:** A formal message requesting something that is submitted to an authority)

3 **Meaning of Writ:** A written order issued by a court, commanding the party to whom it is addressed to perform or cease performing a specified act.

4 **Article 32 in The Constitution Of India 1949**
32. Remedies for enforcement of rights conferred by this Part
(1) The right to move the Supreme Court by appropriate proceedings for the enforcement of the rights conferred by this Part is guaranteed
(2) The Supreme Court shall have power to issue directions or orders or writs, including writs in the nature of habeas corpus, mandamus, prohibition, quo warranto and certiorari, whichever may be appropriate, for the enforcement of any of the rights conferred by this Part
(3) Without prejudice to the powers conferred on the Supreme Court by clause (1) and (2), Parliament may by law empower any other court to exercise within the local limits of its jurisdiction all or any of the powers exercisable by the Supreme Court under clause (2)
(4) The right guaranteed by this article shall not be suspended except as otherwise provided for by this Constitution

5 **Meaning of Respondent:** A **respondent** is a person who is called upon to issue a response to a communication made by another. In legal usage, this specifically refers to the defendant in a legal proceeding commenced by a petition, or to an appellee, or the opposing party, in an appeal of a decision by an initial fact-finder.

was dismissed on April 5, 1994.

Auto Shankar wrote his autobiography running into 300 pages while confined in Chenglepat sub-jail during the year, 1991. The autobiography was handed over by him to his wife, Smt. Jagdishwari, with the knowledge and approval of the jail authorities, for being delivered to his advocate, Sri Chandrasekharan. The prisoner requested his advocate to ensure that his autobiography is published in the petitioners' magazine, 'Nakkheeran'. The petitioners agreed to the same. Auto Shankar affirmed this desire in several letters written to his advocate. The autobiography sets out the close nexus between the prisoner and several LAS, and other officers, some of whom where indeed his partners in several crimes. The presence of several such officers at the house warming ceremony of Auto Shankar's house is proved by the video cassette and several photographs taken on the occasion. Before commencing the serial publication of the autobiography in their magazine, the petitioner announced in the Issue dated May 21, 1994 that very soon the magazine would be coming out with the sensational life history of Auto Shankar. This announcement sent shock waves among several police and prison officials who were afraid that their links with the condemned prisoner would be exposed. They forced the said prisoner, by applying third degree methods, to write letters addressed to the second respondent (Inspector General of Prisons) and the first petitioner requesting that his life-story should not be published in the magazine. Ultimately, the Inspector General of Prisons (R-2) wrote the letter dated June 15, 1994 to the first petitioner. The letter states that the petitioner's assertion that Auto Shankar had written his autobiography while confined in jail in the year 1991 is false. It is equally false that the said autobiography was handed over by the said prisoner to his wife with the knowledge and approval of the prison authorities. The prisoner has himself denied the writing of any such book. It is equally false that any power of attorney was executed by the said prisoner in favour of his advocate, Sri Chandrasekharan in connection with the publication of the alleged book. If a prisoner has to execute a power of attorney in favour of another, it has to be done in the presence of the prison officials as required by the prison Rules.

The petitioners asserted the freedom of press guaranteed by Article 19(1)(a)[6], which, according to them, entitles them to publish the said

6 **Article 19(1) in The Constitution Of India 1949**
(1) All citizens shall have the right
(a) to freedom of speech and expression

autobiography. It was submitted that the condemned prisoner has also the undoubted right to have his life-story published and that he cannot be prevented from doing so.

Question before the Supreme Court:

(1) Whether a citizen of this country can prevent another person from writing his life-story or biography? Does such unauthorised writing infringe the citizen's right to privacy? Whether the freedom of press guaranteed by Article 19(1)(a) entitle the press to publish such unauthorised account of a citizen's life and activities and if so to what extent and in what circumstances? What are the remedies open to a citizen of this country in case of infringement of his right to privacy and further in case such writing amounts to defamation?

(2)(a) Whether the government can maintain an action for its defamation?

(b) Whether the government has any legal authority to impose prior restraint on the press to prevent publication of material defamatory of its officials? and

(c) Whether the public officials, who apprehend that they or their colleagues may be defamed, can impose a prior restraint upon the press to prevent such publication?

Right to Privacy:

The right to privacy as an independent and distinctive concept originated in the field of Tort law, under which a new cause of action for damages resulting from unlawful invasion of privacy was recognised. This right has two aspects which are but two faces of the same coin: (1) the general law of privacy which affords a tort action for damages resulting from an unlawful invasion of privacy and (2) the constitutional recognition given to the right to privacy which protects personal privacy against unlawful governmental invasion. The first aspect of this right must be said to have been violated where, for example, a person's name or likeness is used, without his consent, for advertising - or non-advertising - purposes or for that matter, his life-story is written - whether laudatory or otherwise - and published without his consent as explained hereinafter. In recent times, however, this right has acquired a constitutional status. Right to privacy is not enumerated as a fundamental right[7] in our Constitution but has been

7 ***'Part III – Fundamental Rights'*** is a charter of rights contained in the Constitution of India. It

inferred from Article 21[8].

Supreme Court summarized the broad Principles:

(1) The right to privacy is implicit in the right to life and liberty guaranteed to the citizens of this country by Article 21. It is a "right to be let alone". A citizen has a right to safeguard the privacy of his own, his family, marriage, procreation, motherhood, child bearing and education among other matters. None can publish anything concerning the above matters without his consent - whether truthful or otherwise and whether laudatory or critical. If he does so, he would be violating the right to privacy of the person concerned and would be liable in an action for damages. Position may, however, be different, if a person voluntarily thrusts himself into controversy or voluntarily invites or raises a controversy.

(2) The rule aforesaid is subject to the exception, that any publication concerning the aforesaid aspects becomes unobjectionable if such publication is based upon public records including court records. This is for the reason that once a matter becomes a matter of public record, the right to privacy no longer subsists and it becomes a legitimate subject for comment by press and media among others. In the interest of decency [Article 19(2)[9]] an exception must be carved out to this rule, viz., a

---

guarantees civil liberties such that all Indians can lead their lives in peace and harmony as citizens of India. These include individual rights common to most liberal democracies, such asequality before law, freedom of speech and expression, and peaceful assembly, freedom to practice religion, and the right to constitutional remedies for the protection of civil rights by means of writs such as habeas corpus. Violation of these rights result in punishments as prescribed in the Indian Penal Code or other special laws, subject to discretion of the judiciary. The Fundamental Rights are defined as basichuman freedoms which every Indian citizen has the right to enjoy for a proper and harmonious development of personality. These rights universally apply to all citizens, irrespective of race, place of birth, religion, caste, creed, colour or gender. Aliens (persons who are not citizens) are also considered in matters like equality before law. They are enforceable by the courts, subject to certain restrictions. The Rights have their origins in many sources, including England's Bill of Rights, the United States Bill of Rights and France's Declaration of the Rights of Man.

8 **Article 21 in The Constitution Of India 1949**
21. Protection of life and personal liberty No person shall be deprived of his life or personal liberty except according to procedure established by law

9 **Article 19 in The Constitution Of India 1949**
19. Protection of certain rights regarding freedom of speech etc
(1) All citizens shall have the right
(a) to freedom of speech and expression;
(b) to assemble peaceably and without arms;
(c) to form associations or unions;
(d) to move freely throughout the territory of India;
(e) to reside and settle in any part of the territory of India; and
(f) omitted
(g) to practise any profession, or to carry on any occupation, trade or business

female who is the victim of a sexual assault, kidnap, abduction[10] or a like offence should not further be subjected to the indignity of her name and the incident being publicised in press/media.

(3) There is no law empowering the State or its officials to prohibit, or to impose a prior restraint upon the press/media.

Decision of the Supreme Court:

Court held that the petitioners have a right to publish, what they allege to be the life-story/autobiography of Auto Shankar insofar as it appears from the public records, even without his consent or authorisation. But if they go beyond that and publish his life-story, they may be invading his right to privacy and will be liable for the consequences in accordance with law. Similarly, the State or its officials cannot prevent or restrain the said publication.

(2) Nothing in sub clause (a) of clause (1) shall affect the operation of any existing law, or prevent the State from making any law, in so far as such law imposes reasonable restrictions on the exercise of the right conferred by the said sub clause in the interests of the sovereignty and integrity of India, the security of the State, friendly relations with foreign States, public order, decency or morality or in relation to contempt of court, defamation or incitement to an offence

10 **Section 362 in The Indian Penal Code, 1860**
362. Abduction.-- Whoever by force compels, or by any deceitful means induces any person to go from any place, is said to abduct that person.

48

Noise is injurious to human health[1]

Question before the Supreme Court:

Whether musical functions in an open theatre being Rang Bhavan should be allowed to be carried on or not despite the fact that it is situated within 100 meters of an educational institution and a hospital, is the question involved in the appeal[2].

Facts in Nutshell:

Rang Bhavan is an institution owned and run by the State of Maharashtra. It is the only open theatre in the city of Mumbai. It is let out on hire for the purpose of holding music and cultural programmes. It charges a meagre amount for allowing private parties to hold functions. It has a sitting capacity of 4000 persons. It is stated that the world's greatest artists, both Western and Indian, have performed therein. Dr. Yeshwant Trimbak Oke & Ors. filed a public interest litigation[3] for a direction to the State to curb noise pollution in general in the city of Mumbai and particularly during the festive season of Navratri and Ganesh Utsav.

The Noise Pollution (Regulation and Control) Rules, 2000 (for short "the Rules") have been framed by the Central Government

---

1 Appellants: **Farhd K. Wadia Vs.** Respondent: **Union of India (UOI) and Ors.** (2009)2SCC442
Hon'ble Judges/Coram: S. B. Sinha and Cyriac Joseph, JJ.

2 **Meaning of Appeal:** In law, an **appeal** is a process for requesting a formal change to an official decision. Very broadly speaking there are appeals on the record and *de novo* appeals. In *de novo* appeals, a new decision maker re-hears the case without any reference to the prior decision maker. In appeals on the record, the decision of the prior decision maker is challenged by arguing that he or she misapplied the law, came to an incorrect factual finding, acted in excess of his jurisdiction, abused his powers, was biased, considered evidence which he should not have considered or failed to consider evidence that he should have considered.

3 **Public-Interest Litigation** is litigation for the protection of the public interest. In Indian law, **Article 32** of the Indian constitution contains a tool which directly joints the public with judiciary. PIL may be introduced in a court of law by the court itself (*suo motu*), rather than the aggrieved party or another third party. For the exercise of the court's jurisdiction, it is unnecessary for the victim of the violation of his or her rights to personally approach the court. In PIL, the right to file suit is given to a member of the public by the courts through judicial activism. The member of the public may be a non-governmental organization (NGO), an institution or an individual.

"Educational institution" and "hospital" have been defined in Rules 2 (e) and 2(f) of the Rules in the following terms:

(e) "educational institution" means a school, seminary, college, university, professional academies, training institutes or other educational establishment, not necessarily a chartered institution and includes not only buildings, but also all grounds necessary for the accomplishment of the full scope of educational instruction, including those things essential to mental, moral and physical development;

(f) "hospital" means an institution for the reception and care of sick, wounded, infirm or aged persons, and includes government or private hospitals, nursing homes and clinics.

Sub-rule (5) of Rule 3 of the Rules reads as under:

(5) An area comprising not less than 100 meters around hospitals, educational institutions and courts may be declared as silence area/zone for the purpose of these rules.

Rule 5 of the Rules reads as under:

5. Restrictions on the use of loudspeakers/public address system.--(1) A loudspeaker or a public address system shall not be used except after obtaining written permission from the authority.

(2) A loudspeaker or a public address system shall not be used at night (between 10.00 p.m. to 6.00 a.m.) except in closed premises for communication within, e.g. auditoria, conference rooms, community halls and banquet halls.

(3) Notwithstanding anything contained in sub- rule (2), the State Government may, subject to such terms and conditions as are necessary to reduce noise pollution, permit use of loudspeakers or public address systems during night hours (between 10.00 p.m. to 12.00 midnight) on or during any cultural or religious festive occasion of a limited duration not exceeding fifteen days in all during a calendar year.

Silence Zone:

Silence Zone is an area comprising not less than 100 metres around hospitals, educational institutions, courts, religious places or any other area which is declared as such by the competent authority.

Judgment Referred:

The Calcutta High Court in *Om Birangana Religious Society v. State of West Bengal*[4] issued various directions regarding noise pollution; some of them being:

(a) there will be complete ban on the use of horn type loud-speakers within city residential areas and also prohibit the use of play back of pre-recorded music etc. through such horn type loud- speakers unless used with sound-limiter.

(b) In cultural functions which are live functions, use of such pre-recorded music should not be used excepting for the purpose of announcement and/ or actual performance and placement of speaker boxes should be restricted within the area of performance facing the audience. No sound generating devise should be placed outside the main area of performance.

(c) Cultural programmes in open air may be held excepting at least before three days of holding Board/ Council Examinations to till examinations are completed in residential areas or areas where educational institutions are situated.

(d) The distance of holding such functions from the silence zones should be 100 meters and in so far as Schools, Colleges, Universities, Courts are concerned, it will be treated as silence zones till the end of the office hours and/ or the teaching hours. Hospitals and some renowned and important Nursing Homes will be treated as silence zones round the clock[5].

As regards loudspeakers and amplifiers, it was directed:

Loudspeakers and amplifiers or other equipment or gadgets which produce offending noise once detected as violating the law, should be liable to be seized and confiscated by making provision in the law in that behalf.

Decision of the Supreme Court:

Supreme Court dismissed the appeal filed by Dr. Yeshwant Trimbak Oke & Ors.

4 Decided on 11th August, 1998, (1996) 100 CWN 617

5 See Noise Pollution, Laws & Remedies by Justice Bhagabati Prosad Banerjee, pages 327-328

49

Lawyers have no right to strike[1]

Facts in Nutshell:

Petitioner[2] Dr. B.L. Wadehra, a practicing advocate. He filed petition[3] under Article 226[4] of the Constitution of India in public interest. The provocation for filing petition is the situation arising out of the lawyer's strike which has been going on for more than one month demanding an

1 Appellants: **B.L. Wadehra (Dr.) Vs.** Respondent: **State (NCT of Delhi) & Ors.** AIR2000Delhi266
Hon'ble Judge: Devinder Gupta, ACJ., Cyriac Joseph, Judge

2 **Meaning of Petitioner:** A person who presents a Petition. (**Meaning of Petition:** A formal message requesting something that is submitted to an authority)

3 **Meaning of Petition:** A formal message requesting something that is submitted to an authority

4 **Article 226 in The Constitution Of India 1949**
226. Power of High Courts to issue certain writs
(1) Notwithstanding anything in Article 32 every High Court shall have powers, throughout the territories in relation to which it exercise jurisdiction, to issue to any person or authority, including in appropriate cases, any Government, within those territories directions, orders or writs, including writs in the nature of habeas corpus, mandamus, prohibitions, quo warranto and certiorari, or any of them, for the enforcement of any of the rights conferred by Part III and for any other purpose
(2) The power conferred by clause (1) to issue directions, orders or writs to any Government, authority or person may also be exercised by any High Court exercising jurisdiction in relation to the territories within which the cause of action, wholly or in part, arises for the exercise of such power, notwithstanding that the seat of such Government or authority or the residence of such person is not within those territories
(3) Where any party against whom an interim order, whether by way of injunction or stay or in any other manner, is made on, or in any proceedings relating to, a petition under clause (1), without
(a) furnishing to such party copies of such petition and all documents in support of the plea for such interim order; and
(b) giving such party an opportunity of being heard, makes an application to the High Court for the vacation of such order and furnishes a copy of such application to the party in whose favour such order has been made or the counsel of such party, the High Court shall dispose of the application within a period of two weeks from the date on which it is received or from the date on which the copy of such application is so furnished, whichever is later, or where the High Court is closed on the last day of that period, before the expiry of the next day afterwards on which the High Court is open; and if the application is not so disposed of, the interim order shall, on the expiry of that period, or, as the case may be, the expiry of the aid next day, stand vacated
(4) The power conferred on a High Court by this article shall not be in derogation of the power conferred on the Supreme court by clause (2) of Article 32

enquiry by a Sitting Judge of the Supreme Court into the circumstances leading to the use of force and the 'lathi-charge' by the police on the lawyers during their 'Parliament March' on 24th February, 2000 and also the immediate suspension of the police officials responsible for the lathi charge. The petitioner stated that though he is a part of the lawyers' fraternity and is a participant in the strike, he has approached the Court with a disturbed feeling that the continued stalemate can lead to further unhealthy developments. According to him, in order to avoid further complications and to ensure resolution of the disputes in an orderly, civilised and constitutional manner the problem needs to be tackled at this stage, instead of allowing the parties to continue their fight with hardened and inflexible attitudes. The petitioner feels that the best course to be adopted by the disputing parties is to articulate the disputed issues and to leave them for determination by Court and that in the meanwhile the Government should be directed by Court to suspend the police officials responsible for the 'lathi-charge' and simultaneously the lawyers also should be directed by Court to suspend their strike and agitation.

The State (NCT of Delhi); the Commissioner of Police, Delhi; the President, Delhi High Court Bar Association; the Secretary, Ministry of Law, Justice and Company Affairs, Govt. of India; the Secretary, Ministry of Home Affairs, Govt. of India and the Chairman, Delhi Bar Council are the respondents[5] in the petition. The petitioner prayed that in the meanwhile the Government authorities concerned may be directed to suspend from service the police officials for the alleged excesses committed by police on the lawyers on 24th February, 2000. The petitioner has further prayed that simultaneously the striking lawyers may be directed to suspend their strike and agitation till the disputed matters are decided by Court.

In Short Controversy arises when Lawyers from all over India were protesting against the Civil Procedure Code Amendment Act, 1999 and certain changes in the Advocates Act suggested by the Law Commission and the apprehended entry of foreign lawyers to practice in Indian Courts. The issues raised by the lawyers were directly connected with the legal profession and the administration of justice. Whatever be the merits and demerits of their objections, the lawyers had a right to protest and they

5 **Meaning of Respondent:** A **respondent** is a person who is called upon to issue a response to a communication made by another. In legal usage, this specifically refers to the defendant in a legal proceeding commenced by a petition, or to an appellee, or the opposing party, in an appeal of a decision by an initial fact-finder.

decided to hold a Parliament March on 24.2.2000 to lodge their protest. Thousands of lawyers from different parts of India assembled in Delhi and marched to the Parliament House shouting slogans and holding placards and banners. The programme was pre-arranged and police authorities were informed of it in advance. However, the lawyers were denied permission to hold the demonstration in the vicinity of the Parliament House. A prohibitory order under Section 144[6] of the Criminal Procedure Code was already in force in the localities surrounding the Parliament House. In such circumstances the police stopped the demonstrators at Parliament Street and prevented them from proceeding to the Parliament House. The police directed the demonstrators to disperse on the ground that the assembly had been declared an unlawful assembly. When some of the lawyers crossed over the barricades put up by the police and tried to march forward, the police used tear gas, water cannone and ultimately

---

6 **Section 144 CrPc, 1973:**

144. Power to issue order in urgent cases of nuisance or apprehended danger

(1) In cases where, in the opinion of a District Magistrate, a Sub-divisional Magistrate or any other Executive Magistrate specially empowered by the State Government in this behalf, there is sufficient ground for proceeding under this section and immediate prevention or speedy remedy is desirable, such Magistrate may, by a written order stating the material facts of the case and served in the manner provided by section 134, direct any person to abstain from a certain act or to take certain order with respect to certain property in his possession or under his management,

if such Magistrate considers that such direction is likely to prevent, or tends to prevent, obstruction, annoyance or injury to any person lawfully employed, or danger to human life, health or safety, or a disturbance of the public tranquillity, or a riot, or an affray

(2) An order under this section may, in cases of emergency or in cases where the circumstances do not admit of the serving in due time of a notice upon the person against whom the order is directed, be passed ex parte

(3) An order under this section may be directed to a particular individual, or to persons residing in a particular place or area, or to the public generally when frequenting or visiting a particular place or area

(4) No order under this section shall remain in force for more than two months from the making thereof:

Provided that, if the State Government considers it necessary so to do for preventing danger to human life, health or safety or for preventing a riot or any affray, it may, by notification, direct that an order made by a Magistrate under this section shall remain in force for such further period not exceeding six months from the date on which the order made by the Magistrate would have, but for such order, expired, as it may specify in the said notification

(5) Any Magistrate may, either on his own motion or on the application of any person aggrieved, rescind or alter any order made under this section, by himself or any Magistrate subordinate to him or by his predecessor-in-office

(6) The State Government may, either on its own motion or on the application of any person aggrieved, rescind or alter any order made by it under the proviso to sub- section (4)

(7) Where an application under sub-section (5), or sub-section (6) is received, the Magistrate, or the State Government, as the case may be, shall afford to the applicant an early opportunity of appearing before him or it, either in person or by pleader and showing cause against the order, and if the Magistrate or the State Government, as the case may be, rejects the application wholly or in part, he or it shall record in writing the reasons for so doing

lathi-charge to disperse the unlawful assembly. In this process about 135 lawyers got injured and many of them sustained grievous injuries. Some of the injured lawyers had to be admitted and treated in the different hospitals.

Freedom of Speech and Expression:

Supreme Court in *LIC of India Vs . Prof. Manubhai D. Shah*[7] freedom of speech and expression is a natural right which a human being acquires on birth and therefore it is a basic human right. This basic human right has been recognised by the Universal Declaration of Human Rights (1948). In the Preamble of the Constitution of India, the People of India declared their solemn resolve to secures to all its citizen liberty of thought and expression. This resolve is reflected in Article 19(1)(a)[8] of the Constitution which guarantees to all citizens the fundamental right to freedom of speech and expression. In *Kameshwar Prasad and Ors. Vs . State of Bihar*[9] the Supreme Court considered the question whether the right to make a "demonstration" is covered by either or both of the two freedoms guaranteed by Article 19(1)(a) or 19(1)(b)[10] of the Constitution i.e. the freedom of speech and expression and the right to assemble peaceably and without arms. The Supreme Court has held in the said case that a "demonstration" is a visible manifestation of the feelings or sentiments of an individual or a group and thus a communication of one's ideas to others to whom it is intended to be conveyed. It has also been held that "demonstration" is in effect a form of speech or of expression and that it might also take the form of an assembly and even then the intention is to convey to the person or authority to whom the communication is intended, the feelings of the group which assembles. There are forms of demonstration which would fall within the freedoms guaranteed by Article 19(1)(a) and 19[11]. A demonstration may take various forms such as

7 [1992]3SCR595

8 **Article 19 in The Constitution Of India 1949**
19. Protection of certain rights regarding freedom of speech etc
(1) All citizens shall have the right
(a) to freedom of speech and expression

9 (1962)ILLJ294SC

10 **Article 19 in The Constitution Of India 1949**
19. Protection of certain rights regarding freedom of speech etc
(1) All citizens shall have the right
(a) to freedom of speech and expression;
(b) to assemble peaceably and without arms

11 **Article 19 in The Constitution Of India 1949**
19. Protection of certain rights regarding freedom of speech etc

noisy and disorderly or peaceful and orderly. But the Supreme Court has clarified that a violent and disorderly demonstration would not fall within Article 19(1)(a) or 19.

Duty of Advocate:

The Supreme Court has time and again explained the role of the lawyers in the administration of justice and also their duties and obligations as officers of the Court. In *Lt. Col. S.J. Chaudhary Vs . State (Delhi Administration),*[12], the Supreme Court has held that it is the duty of every Advocate who accepts the brief in a criminal case to attend the trial from day-to-day and that, having accepted the brief, he will be committing a breach of his professional duty, if he so fails to attend.

---

(1) All citizens shall have the right
(a) to freedom of speech and expression;
(b) to assemble peaceably and without arms;
(c) to form associations or unions;
(d) to move freely throughout the territory of India;
(e) to reside and settle in any part of the territory of India; and
(f) omitted
(g) to practise any profession, or to carry on any occupation, trade or business
(2) Nothing in sub clause (a) of clause (1) shall affect the operation of any existing law, or prevent the State from making any law, in so far as such law imposes reasonable restrictions on the exercise of the right conferred by the said sub clause in the interests of the sovereignty and integrity of India, the security of the State, friendly relations with foreign States, public order, decency or morality or in relation to contempt of court, defamation or incitement to an offence
(3) Nothing in sub clause (b) of the said clause shall affect the operation of any existing law in so far as it imposes, or prevent the State from making any law imposing, in the interests of the sovereignty and integrity of India or public order, reasonable restrictions on the exercise of the right conferred by the said sub clause
(4) Nothing in sub clause (c) of the said clause shall affect the operation of any existing law in so far as it imposes, or prevent the State from making any law imposing, in the interests of the sovereignty and integrity of India or public order or morality, reasonable restrictions on the exercise of the right conferred by the said sub clause
(5) Nothing in sub clauses (d) and (e) of the said clause shall affect the operation of any existing law in so far as it imposes, or prevent the State from making any law imposing, reasonable restrictions on the exercise of any of the rights conferred by the said sub clauses either in the interests of the general public or for the protection of the interests of any Scheduled Tribe
(6) Nothing in sub clause (g) of the said clause shall affect the operation of any existing law in so far as it imposes, or prevent the State from making any law imposing, in the interests of the general public, reasonable restrictions on the exercise of the right conferred by the said sub clause, and, in particular, nothing in the said sub clause shall affect the operation of any existing law in so far as it relates to, or prevent the State from making any law relating to,
(i) the professional or technical qualifications necessary for practising any profession or carrying on any occupation, trade or business, or
(ii) the carrying on by the State, or by a corporation owned or controlled by the State, of any trade, business, industry or service, whether to the exclusion, complete or partial, of citizens or otherwise

12 1984CriLJ340

In *Indian Council of Legal Aid and Advice & others Vs . Bar Council of India & another,*[13], the Supreme Court observed thus:

"It is generally believed that members of the legal profession have certain social obligations, e.g., to render "pro bono publico" service to the poor and the underprivileged. Since the duty of a lawyer is to assist the court in the administration of justice, the practice of law has a public utility flavour and, Therefore, he must strictly and scrupulously abide by the Code of Conduct behaving the noble profession and must not indulge in any activity which may tend to lower the image of the profession in society. That is why the functions of the Bar Council include the laying down of standards of professional conduct and etiquette which advocates must follow to maintain the dignity and purity of the profession."

In *RE Sanjeev Datta & others*[14], the Supreme Court has stated thus:

"The legal profession is a solemn and serious occupation. It is a noble calling and all those who belong to it are its honourable members. Although the entry to the profession can be had by acquiring merely the qualification of technical competence, the honour as a professional has to be maintained by its members by their exemplary conduct both in and outside the Court. The legal profession is different from other professions in that what the lawyers do, affects not only an individual but the administration of justice which is the foundation of the civilised society. Both as a leading member of the intelligentsia of the society and as a responsible citizen, the lawyer has to conduct himself as a model for others both in his professional and in his private and public life. The society has a right to expect of him such ideal behaviour. It must not be forgotten that the legal profession has always been held in high esteems and its members have played an enviable role in public life. The regard for the legal and judicial systems in this country is in no small measure due to the tireless role played by the stalwarts in the profession to strengthen them. They took their profession seriously and practiced it with dignity, deference and devotion. If the profession is to survive, the judicial system has to vitalised. No service will be too small in making the system efficient, effective and credible."

13 [1995]1SCR304

14 1995CriLJ2910

Decision of the High Court:

High Court held that in exercise of the right to protest, a lawyer may refuse to accept new engagements and may even refuse to appear in a case in which he had already been engaged, if he has been duly discharged from the case. But so long as a lawyer holds the vakalat for his client and has not been duly discharged, he has no right to abstain from appearing in Court even on the ground of a strike called by the Bar Association or any other body of lawyers. If he so abstains, he commits a professional misconduct, a breach of professional duty, a breach of contract and also a breach of trust and he will be liable to suffer all the consequences thereof. There is no fundamental right, either under Article 19 or under Article 21[15] of the Constitution, which permits or authorises a lawyer to abstain from appearing in Court in a case in which he holds the vakalat for a party in that case. On the other hand a litigant has a fundamental right for speedy trial of his case, because, speedy trial, as held by the Supreme Court in *Hussainara Khatoon & others Vs . Home Secretary, State of Bihar*[16], is an integral and essential part of the fundamental right to life and liberty enshrined in Article 21 of the Constitution. Strike by lawyers will infringe the above-mentioned fundamental right of the litigants and such infringement cannot be permitted. Assuming that the lawyers are trying to convey their feelings or sentiments and ideas through the strike in exercise of their fundamental right to freedom of speech and expression guaranteed by Article 19(1)(a) of the Constitution, Court was of the view that the exercise of the right under Article19(1)(a) will come to an end when such exercise threatens to infringe the fundamental right of another. Hence the lawyers cannot go on strike infringing the fundamental right of the litigants for speedy trial. The right to practice any profession or to carry on any occupation guaranteed by Article 19(1)(g) may include the right to discontinue such profession or occupation but it will not include any right to abstain from appearing in Court while holding a vakalat in the case. The lawyer has a duty and obligation to co-operate with the Court in the orderly and pure administration of justice.

Either in the name of a strike or otherwise, no lawyer has any right to obstruct or prevent another lawyer from discharging his professional duty of appearing in Court. If anyone does it, he commits a criminal offence

15 **Article 21 in The Constitution Of India 1949**
21. Protection of life and personal liberty No person shall be deprived of his life or personal liberty except according to procedure established by law

16 1979CriLJ1036

and interferes with the administration of justice and commits contempt of court and he is liable to be proceeded against on all these counts.

Court further held that strike by lawyers is illegal and unethical.

Directions of High Court :

(a) Lawyers have no right to strike. Strike by lawyers is illegal and unethical.

(b) If, on the ground of strike, a lawyer abstains from appearing in court in a case in which he holds the vakalat for the client, he is committing a professional misconduct, a breach of contract, a breach of trust and a breach of professional duty.

(c) If, in the name of strike, anyone obstructs or prevents a lawyer from discharging his professional duty of appearing in court, he is committing a criminal offence and is interfering with the administration of justice and is committing contempt of court.

(d) There is absolutely no justification for the continuance of the ongoing strike by lawyers and we expect them to recall it immediately.

50

Euthanasia[1]

Facts in Nutshell:

Euthanasia is one of the most perplexing issues which the courts and legislatures all over the world are facing today. A writ petition[2] under Article 32of the Constitution[3], and has been filed on behalf of the Petitioner[4] Aruna Ramachandra Shanbaug by one Ms. Pinki Virani of Mumbai, claiming to be a next friend in Supreme Court of India.

It was stated in the writ petition that the Petitioner Aruna Ramachandra Shanbaug was a staff Nurse working in King Edward Memorial Hospital, Parel, Mumbai. On the evening of 27th November, 1973 she was attacked by a sweeper in the hospital who wrapped a dog chain around her neck

---

1 Appellants: **Aruna Ramchandra Shanbaug Vs.** Respondent: **Union of India (UOI) and Ors.** AIR2011SC1290
Hon'ble Judges/Coram: Markandey Katju and Gyan Sudha Mishra, JJ.

2 **Writ Petition:** Under the Indian legal system, jurisdiction to issue ?prerogative writs? is given to the SupremeCourt, and to the High Courts of Judicature of all Indian states. Parts of the law relating to writs are set forth in the Constitution of India. The Supreme Court, the highest in the country, may issue writs under Article 32 of the Constitution for enforcement of Fundamental Rights and under Articles 139 for enforcement of rights other than Fundamental Rights, while High Courts, the superior courts of the States, may issue writs under Articles 226. ?Writ? is eminently designed by the makers of the Constitution, and in the same way it is developed very widely and efficiently by the courts in India. The Constitution broadly provides for five kinds of "prerogative" writs, namely, Habeas Corpus, Certiorari, Mandamus, Quo Warranto and Prohibition.

3 **Article 32 in The Constitution Of India 1949**
32. Remedies for enforcement of rights conferred by this Part
(1) The right to move the Supreme Court by appropriate proceedings for the enforcement of the rights conferred by this Part is guaranteed
(2) The Supreme Court shall have power to issue directions or orders or writs, including writs in the nature of habeas corpus, mandamus, prohibition, quo warranto and certiorari, whichever may be appropriate, for the enforcement of any of the rights conferred by this Part
(3) Without prejudice to the powers conferred on the Supreme Court by clause (1) and (2), Parliament may by law empower any other court to exercise within the local limits of its jurisdiction all or any of the powers exercisable by the Supreme Court under clause (2)
(4) The right guaranteed by this article shall not be suspended except as otherwise provided for by this Constitution

4 **Meaning of Petitioner:** A person who presents a Petition. (**Meaning of Petition:** A formal message requesting something that is submitted to an authority)

and yanked her back with it. He tried to rape her but finding that she was menstruating, he sodomized her. To immobilize her during this act he twisted the chain around her neck. The next day on 28th November, 1973 at 7.45 a.m. a cleaner found her lying on the floor with blood all over in an unconscious condition. It was alleged that due to strangulation by the dog chain the supply of oxygen to the brain stopped and the brain got damaged. It was alleged that the Neurologist in the Hospital found that she had plantars' extensor, which indicates damage to the cortex or some other part of the brain. She also had brain stem contusion injury with associated cervical cord injury. It was alleged that 36 years have expired since the incident and now Aruna Ramachandra Shanbaug is about 60 years of age. She is featherweight, and her brittle bones could break if her hand or leg are awkwardly caught, even accidentally, under her lighter body. She has stopped menstruating and her skin is now like papier mache' stretched over a skeleton. She is prone to bed sores. Her wrists are twisted inwards. Her teeth had decayed causing her immense pain. She can only be given mashed food, on which she survives. It was alleged that Aruna Ramachandra Shanbaug is in a persistent negetative state (p.v.s.) and virtually a dead person and has no state of awareness, and her brain is virtually dead. She can neither see, nor hear anything nor can she express herself or communicate, in any manner whatsoever. Mashed food is put in her mouth, she is not able to chew or taste any food. She is not even aware that food has been put in her mouth. She is not able to swallow any liquid food, which shows that the food goes down on its own and not because of any effort on her part. The process of digestion goes on in this way as the mashed food passes through her system. However, Aruna is virtually a skeleton. Her excreta and the urine is discharged on the bed itself. Once in a while she is cleaned up but in a short while again she goes back into the same sub-human condition. Judged by any parameter, Aruna cannot be said to be a living person and it is only on account of mashed food which is put into her mouth that there is a facade of life which is totally devoid of any human element. It was alleged that there is not the slightest possibility of any improvement in her condition and her body lies on the bed in the KEM Hospital, Mumbai like a dead animal, and this has been the position for the last 36 years. The prayer of the Petitioner was that the Respondents[5] be directed to stop feeding Aruna, and let her die peacefully.

5 Respondent Nos. 3 and 4, the Mumbai Municipal Corporation and the Dean, KEM Hospital by Dr. Amar Ramaji Pazare, Professor and Head in the said hospital

Active Euthanasia:

Active euthanasia is a crime all over the world except where permitted by legislation. In India active euthanasia is illegal and a crime under Section 302[6] or at least Section 304[7] IPC. Physician assisted suicide is a crime under Section 306[8] IPC (abetment to suicide). Active euthanasia is taking specific steps to cause the patient's death, such as injecting the patient with some lethal substance, e.g. sodium pentothal which causes a person deep sleep in a few seconds, and the person instantaneously and painlessly dies in this deep sleep. A distinction is sometimes drawn between euthanasia and physician assisted dying, the difference being in who administers the lethal medication. In euthanasia, a physician or third party administers it, while in physician assisted suicide it is the patient himself who does it, though on the advice of the doctor. In many countries/States the latter is legal while the former is not. **The difference between "active" and "passive" euthanasia is that in active euthanasia, something is done to end the patient's life' while in passive euthanasia, something is not done that would have preserved the patient's life.**

An important idea behind this distinction is that in "passive euthanasia" the doctors are not actively killing anyone; they are simply not saving him. While we usually applaud someone who saves another person's life, we do not normally condemn someone for failing to do so. If one rushes into a burning building and carries someone out to safety, he will probably be called a hero. But if one sees a burning building and people screaming for help, and he stands on the sidelines -- whether out of fear for his own safety, or the belief that an inexperienced and ill-equipped person

6 **Section 302, IPC 1860**
Punishment for murder
302. Punishment for murder.--Whoever commits murder shall be punished with death, or [imprisonment for life], and shall also be liable to fine

7 **Section 304 in The Indian Penal Code, 1860**
304. Punishment for culpable homicide not amounting to murder.-- Whoever commits culpable homicide not amounting to murder shall be punished with 1[imprisonment for life], or imprisonment of either description for a term which may extend to ten years, and shall also be liable to fine, if the act by which the death is caused is done with the intention of causing death. or of causing such bodily injury as is likely to cause death; or with imprisonment of either description for a term which may extend to ten years, or with fine, or with both, if the act is done with the knowledge that it is likely to cause death, but without any intention to cause death, or to cause such bodily injury as is likely to cause death.

8 **Section 306 in The Indian Penal Code, 1860**
306. Abetment of suicide.-- If any person commits suicide, whoever abets the commission of such suicide, shall be punished with imprisonment of either description for a term which may extend to ten years, and shall also be liable to fine.

like himself would only get in the way of the professional firefighters, or whatever -- if one does nothing, few would judge him for his inaction. One would surely not be prosecuted for homicide. (At least, not unless one started the fire in the first place.)

Thus, proponents of euthanasia say that while we can debate whether active euthanasia should be legal, there can be no debate about passive euthanasia: You cannot prosecute someone for failing to save a life. Even if you think it would be good for people to do X, you cannot make it illegal for people to not do X, or everyone in the country who did not do X today would have to be arrested.

Legislation in some countries relating to Euthanasia or Physician Assisted Death:

Netherlands:

Euthanasia in the Netherlands is regulated by the "Termination of Life on Request and Assisted Suicide (Review Procedures) Act", 2002. It states that euthanasia and physician-assisted suicide are not punishable if the attending physician acts in accordance with the criteria of due care. These criteria concern the patient's request, the patient's suffering (unbearable and hopeless), the information provided to the patient, the presence of reasonable alternatives, consultation of another physician and the applied method of ending life. To demonstrate their compliance, the Act requires physicians to report euthanasia to a review committee.

The legal debate concerning euthanasia in the Netherlands took off with the "Postma case" in 1973, concerning a physician who had facilitated the death of her mother following repeated explicit requests for euthanasia. While the physician was convicted, the court's judgment set out criteria when a doctor would not be required to keep a patient alive contrary to his will. This set of criteria was formalized in the course of a number of court cases during the 1980s.

Termination of Life on Request and Assisted Suicide (Review Procedures) Act took effect on April 1, 2002. It legalizes euthanasia and physician assisted suicide in very specific cases, under very specific circumstances. The law was proposed by Els Borst, the minister of Health. The procedures codified in the law had been a convention of the Dutch medical community for over twenty years.

The law allows a medical review board to suspend prosecution of doctors who performed euthanasia when each of the following conditions is fulfilled:

• the patient's suffering is unbearable with no prospect of improvement

• the patient's request for euthanasia must be voluntary and persist over time (the request cannot be granted when under the influence of others, psychological illness, or drugs)

• the patient must be fully aware of his/her condition, prospects and options

• there must be consultation with at least one other independent doctor who needs to confirm the conditions mentioned above

• the death must be carried out in a medically appropriate fashion by the doctor or patient, in which case the doctor must be present

• the patient is at least 12 years old (patients between 12 and 16 years of age require the consent of their parents)

The doctor must also report the cause of death to the municipal coroner in accordance with the relevant provisions of the Burial and Cremation Act. A regional review committee assesses whether a case of termination of life on request or assisted suicide complies with the due care criteria. Depending on its findings, the case will either be closed or, if the conditions are not met, brought to the attention of the Public Prosecutor. Finally, the legislation offers an explicit recognition of the validity of a written declaration of the will of the patient regarding euthanasia (a "euthanasia directive"). Such declarations can be used when a patient is in a coma or otherwise unable to state if they wish to be euthanized.

Euthanasia remains a criminal offense in cases not meeting the law's specific conditions, with the exception of several situations that are not subject to the restrictions of the law at all, because they are considered normal medical practice. These are:

• stopping or not starting a medically useless (futile) treatment

• stopping or not starting a treatment at the patient's request

• speeding up death as a side-effect of treatment necessary for alleviating serious suffering Euthanasia of children under the age of 12 remains technically illegal; however, Dr. Eduard Verhagen has documented several cases and, together with colleagues and prosecutors, has developed a protocol to be followed in those cases. Prosecutors will refrain from pressing charges if this Groningen Protocol is followed.

Switzerland:

Switzerland has an unusual position on assisted suicide: it is legally permitted and can be performed by non-physicians. However, euthanasia is illegal, the difference between assisted suicide and euthanasia being that while in the former the patient administers the lethal injection himself, in the latter a doctor or some other person administers it.

Article 115 of the Swiss penal code, which came into effect in 1942 (having been approved in 1937), considers assisting suicide a crime if, and only if, the motive is selfish. The code does not give physicians a special status in assisting suicide; although, they are most likely to have access to suitable drugs. Ethical guidelines have cautioned physicians against prescribing deadly drugs.

Switzerland seems to be the only country in which the law limits the circumstances in which assisted suicide is a crime, thereby decriminalising it in other cases, without requiring the involvement of a physician. Consequently, non-physicians have participated in assisted suicide. However, legally, active euthanasia e.g. administering a lethal injection by a doctor or some other person to a patient is illegal in Switzerland (unlike in Holland where it is legal under certain conditions).

The Swiss law is unique because (1) the recipient need not be a Swiss national, and (2) a physician need not be involved. Many persons from other countries, especially Germany, go to Switzerland to undergo euthanasia.

Belgium:

Belgium became the second country in Europe after Netherlands to legalize the practice of euthanasia in September 2002. The Belgian law sets out conditions under which suicide can be practised without giving doctors a licence to kill. Patients wishing to end their own lives must be conscious when the demand is made and repeat their request for euthanasia. They have to be under "constant and unbearable physical or psychological pain" resulting from an accident or incurable illness.

The law gives patients the right to receive ongoing treatment with painkillers -- the authorities have to pay to ensure that poor or isolated patients do not ask to die because they do not have money for such treatment. Unlike the Dutch legislation, minors cannot seek assistance to die. In the case of someone who is not in the terminal stages of illness, a third medical opinion must be sought. Every mercy killing case will have to be filed at a special commission to decide if the doctors in charge are following the regulations.

U.K., Spain, Austria, Italy, Germany, France, etc.

In none of these countries is euthanasia or physician assisted death legal. In January 2011 the French Senate defeated by a 170-142 vote a bill seeking to legalize euthanasia. In England, in May 2006 a bill allowing physician assisted suicide, was blocked, and never became law.

United States of America:

Active Euthanasia is illegal in all states in U.S.A., but physician assisted dying is legal in the states of Oregon, Washington and Montana. As already pointed out above, the difference between euthanasia and physician assisted suicide lies in who administers the lethal medication. In the former, the physician or someone else administers it, while in the latter the patient himself does so, though on the advice of the doctor.

Oregon:

Oregon was the first state in U.S.A. to legalize physician assisted death.

The Oregon legislature enacted the Oregon Death with Dignity Act, in 1997. Under the Death With Dignity Act, a person who sought physician assisted suicide would have to meet certain criteria:

- He must be an Oregon resident, at least 18 years old, and must have decision making capacity.

- The person must be terminally ill, having six months or less to live.

- The person must make one written and two oral requests for medication to end his/her life, the written one substantially in the form provided in the Act, signed, dated, witnessed by two persons in the presence of the patient who attest that the person is capable, acting voluntarily and not being coerced to sign the request. There are stringent qualifications as to who may act as a witness.

• The patient's decision must be an 'informed' one, and the attending physician is obligated to provide the patient with information about the diagnosis, prognosis, potential risks, and probable consequences of taking the prescribed medication, and alternatives, including, but not limited to comfort care, hospice care and pain control. Another physician must confirm the diagnosis, the patient's decision making capacity, and voluntariness of the patient's decisions.

• Counselling has to be provided if the patient is suffering from depression or a mental disorder which may impact his judgment.

• There has to be a waiting period of 15 days, next of kin have to be notified, and State authorities have to be informed.

• The patient can rescind his decision at any time In response to concerns that patients with depression may seek to end their lives, the 1999 amendment provides that the attending physician must determine that the patient does not have 'depression causing impaired judgment' before prescribing the medication. Under the law, a person who met all requirements could receive a prescription of a barbiturate that would be sufficient to cause death. However, the lethal injection must be administered by the patient himself, and physicians are prohibited from administering it. The landmark case to declare that the practice of euthanasia by doctors to help their patients shall not be taken into cognizance was ***Gonzalez** v. **Oregon*** decided in 2006. After the Oregon Law was enacted about 200 persons have had euthanasia in Oregon.

Washington:

Washington was the second state in U.S.A. which allowed the practice of physician assisted death in the year 2008 by passing the Washington Death with Dignity Act, 2008.

Montana:

Montana was the third state (after Oregon and Washington) in U.S.A. to legalize physician assisted deaths, but this was done by the State judiciary and not the legislature. On December 31, 2009, the Montana Supreme Court delivered its verdict in the case of *Baxter v. Montana* permitting physicians to prescribe lethal indication. The court held that there was "nothing in Montana Supreme Court precedent or Montana statutes indicating that physician aid 66 in dying is against public policy.

Other States in U.S.A.:

In no other State in U.S.A. is euthanasia or physician assisted death legal. Michigan banned euthanasia and assisted suicide in 1993, after Dr. Kevorkian (who became known as 'doctor death') began encouraging and assisting in suicides. He was convicted in 1999 for an assisted suicide displayed on television, his medical licence cancelled, and he spent 8 years in jail.

In 1999 the State of Texas enacted the Texas Futile Care Law which entitles Texas hospitals and doctors, in some situations, to withdraw life support measures, such as mechanical respiration, from terminally ill patient when such treatment is considered futile and inappropriate. However, Texas has not legalized euthanasia or physician assisted death. In California, though 75 of people support physician assisted death, the issue is highly controversial in the State legislature. Forty States in USA have enacted laws which explicitly make it a crime to provide another with the means of taking his or her life.

In 1977 California legalized living wills, and other States soon followed suit. A living will (also known as advance directive or advance decision) is an instruction given by an individual while conscious specifying what action should be taken in the event he/she is unable to make a decision due to illness or incapacity, and appoints a person to take such decisions on his/her behalf. It may include a directive to withdraw life support on certain eventualities.

Canada:

In Canada, physician assisted suicide is illegal vide Section 241(b) of the Code of Criminal Procedure of Canada.

The leading decision of the Canadian Supreme Court in this connection is ***Sue Rodriguez** v. **British Columbia (Attorney General)***[9]. Rodriguez, a woman of 43, was diagnosed with Amyotrophic Lateral Sclerosis (ALS), and requested the Canadian Supreme Court to allow someone to aid her in ending her life. Her condition was deteriorating rapidly, and the doctors told her that she would soon lose the ability to swallow, speak, walk, and move her body without assistance. Thereafter she would lose

9 (1993) 3 SCR 519

her capacity to breathe without a respirator, to eat without a gastrotomy, and would eventually be confined to bed. Her life expectancy was 2 to 14 months.

The Canadian Supreme Court was deeply divided. By a 5 to majority her plea was rejected. Justice Sopinka, speaking for the majority (which included Justices La Forest, Gonthier, Iacobucci and Major) observed:

Sanctity of life has been understood historically as excluding freedom of choice in the self infliction of death, and certainly in the involvement of others in carrying out that choice. At the very least, no new consensus has emerged in society opposing the right of the State to regulate the involvement of others in exercising power over individuals ending their lives.

The minority, consisting of Chief Justice Lamer and Justices L'Heureux-Dube, Cory and McLachlin, dissented.

Passive Euthanasia:

Passive euthanasia is usually defined as withdrawing medical treatment with a deliberate intention of causing the patient's death. For example, if a patient requires kidney dialysis to survive, not giving dialysis although the machine is available, is passive euthanasia. Similarly, if a patient is in coma or on a heart lung machine, withdrawing of the machine will ordinarily result in passive euthanasia. Similarly not giving life saving medicines like antibiotics in certain situations may result in passive euthanasia. Denying food to a person in coma or PVS (Permanent Vegetative State) may also amount to passive euthanasia.

Euthanasia can be both voluntary or non voluntary. In voluntary passive euthanasia a person who is capable of deciding for himself decides that he would prefer to die (which may be for various reasons e.g., that he is in great pain or that the money being spent on his treatment should instead be given to his family who are in greater need, etc.), and for this purpose he consciously and of his own free will refuses to take life saving medicines. In India, if a person consciously and voluntarily refuses to take life saving medical treatment it is not a crime. Non voluntary passive euthanasia implies that the person is not in a position to decide for himself e.g., if he is in coma or PVS.

Question before Supreme Court of India:

Whether not taking food consciously and voluntarily with the aim of ending one's life is a crime under section 309[10] IPC (attempt to commit suicide). Whether to allow a person to die who is not in a position to give his/her consent.

Abetment of Suicide and Attempt to Commit Suicide:

In India abetment of suicide (Section 306 Indian Penal Code) and attempt to suicide (Section 309 of Indian Penal Code) are both criminal offences. This is in contrast to many countries such as USA where attempt to suicide is not a crime.

The Constitution Bench of the Indian Supreme Court in ***Gian Kaur** v. **State of Punjab***[11] held that both euthanasia and assisted suicide are not lawful in India.

Sections 306 and 309 IPC read as under:

306. Abetment of suicide -If any person commits suicide, whoever abets the commission of such suicide, shall be punished with imprisonment of either description for a term which may extend to ten years, and shall also be liable to fine.

309. Attempt to commit suicide - Whoever attempts to commit suicide and does any act towards the commission of such offence, shall be punished with simple imprisonment for a term which may extend to one year or with fine, or with both.

When can a Person is said to be Dead:

A person's most important organ is his/her brain. This organ cannot be replaced. Other body parts can be replaced e.g. if a person's hand or leg is amputed, he can get an artificial limb. Similarly, we can transplant a kidney, a heart or a liver when the original one has failed. However, we cannot transplant a brain. If someone else's brain is transplanted into one's body, then in fact, it will be that other person living in one's body.

10 **Section 309 in The Indian Penal Code, 1860**
309. Attempt to commit suicide.-- Whoever attempts to commit suicide and does any act towards the commission of such offence, shall be punished with simple imprisonment for a term which may extend to one year [or with fine, or with both.]

11 1996 (2) SCC 648

The entire mind, including one's personality, cognition, memory, capacity of receiving signals from the five senses and capacity of giving commands to the other parts of the body, etc. are the functions of the brain. Hence one is one's brain. It follows that one is dead when one's brain is dead.

As is well-known, the brain cells normally do not multiply after the early years of childhood (except in the region called hippocampus), unlike other cells like skin cells, which are regularly dying and being replaced by new cells produced by multiplying of the old cells. This is probably because brain cells are too highly specialized to multiply. Hence if the brain cells die, they usually cannot be replaced (though sometimes one part of the brain can take over the function of another part in certain situations where the other part has been irreversibly damaged).

Brain cells require regular supply of oxygen which comes through the red cells in the blood. If oxygen supply is cut off for more than six minutes, the brain cells die and this condition is known as anoxia. Hence, if the brain is dead a person is said to be dead.

Decision of the Supreme Court:

Court held that there is no statutory provision in our country as to the legal procedure for withdrawing life support to a person in PVS (Permanent Vegetative State) or who is otherwise incompetent to take a decision in this connection. Court dismissed the petition of Ms. Pinki Virani.

Directions of the Court:

(i) A decision has to be taken to discontinue life support either by the parents or the spouse or other close relatives, or in the absence of any of them, such a decision can be taken even by a person or a body of persons acting as a next friend. It can also be taken by the doctors attending the patient. However, the decision should be taken bona fide in the best interest of the patient.

In the present case, Aruna Shanbaug's parents are dead and other close relatives are not interested in her ever since she had the unfortunate assault on her. It is the KEM hospital staff, who have been amazingly caring for her day and night for so many long years, who really are her next friends, and not Ms. Pinky Virani who has only visited her on few occasions and written a book on her. Hence it is for the KEM hospital staff to take that decision. The KEM hospital staff have clearly expressed their wish that Aruna Shanbaug should be allowed to live.

(ii) Hence, even if a decision is taken by the near relatives or doctors or next friend to withdraw life support, such a decision requires approval from the High Court concerned. In Court opinion, this is even more necessary in our country as we cannot rule out the possibility of mischief being done by relatives or others for inheriting the property of the patient.

In Courts opinion, if it is left solely to the patient's relatives or to the doctors or next friend to decide whether to withdraw the life support of an incompetent person there is always a risk in our country that this may be misused by some unscrupulous persons who wish to inherit or otherwise grab the property of the patient. Considering the low ethical levels prevailing in our society today and the rampant commercialization and corruption, we cannot rule out the possibility that unscrupulous persons with the help of some unscrupulous doctors may fabricate material to show that it is a terminal case with no chance of recovery. There are doctors and doctors. While many doctors are upright, there are others who can do anything for money.[12] The commercialization of our society has crossed all limits.

12 See George Bernard Shaw's play 'The Doctors Dilemma'.

51

Premises ruined due to natural causes - Landlord and tenant relationship came to an end[1]

Question before the High Court:

Whether the tenancy[2] extinguishes after collapse of tenement whatever the reasons may be for the collapse?

Facts in Nutshell:

The Plaintiff[3] was the tenant of the respondent[4] in respect of a tenement bearing House No. 83 situated at Comba, Margao admeasuring 23.45 sq. meters on payment of monthly rent of Rs. 15/-. The plaintiff alleging that on or about 24-9-1979 the defendants[5] had damaged the said tenement and further alleging that the tenement was demolished by the defendants on 22-7-1979, filed the suit[6] for recovery of possession of the land where the tenement was situated and for restoration of the said tenement. The suit was resisted by the defendants stating that the tenement/suit structure was an old crumbling structure and although the defendants had requested the plaintiff to vacate the same in order to enable them to carry out the repairs the plaintiff had refused to vacate the same and had

1 Appellants: **Shivram Ladu Nitardekar Vs. Respondent: Alex Fernandes and Ors.** 2006(1)BomCR846
Hon'ble Judges/Coram: Britto N.A., Judge

2 **Meaning of Tenancy:** The temporary possession or holding by a tenant of lands or property owned by another

3 **Meaning of Plaintiff:** The party that institutes a suit in a court.

4 **Meaning of Respondent:** A **respondent** is a person who is called upon to issue a response to a communication made by another. In legal usage, this specifically refers to the defendant in a legal proceeding commenced by a petition, or to an appellee, or the opposing party, in an appeal of a decision by an initial fact-finder.

5 **Meaning of Defendant:** The party against which an action is brought.

6 **Meaning of Suit:** Generic term for any filing of a complaint (or petition) asking for legal redress by judicial action, often called a "lawsuit." In common parlance a suit asking for a court order for action rather than a money judgment is often called a "petition," but technically it is a "suit in equity.

allowed by his own negligence and acquiescence the said tenement to deteriorate further and on account of the heavy rains the said structure became dangerous for occupation and in the month of July, 1979 part of the said structure collapsed. Plaintiff had vacated the tenement/structure prior to its demolition/collapse.

Decision of the Civil Judge and first Appellate Court:

The learned Civil Judge came to the conclusion that the tenement/ structure had collapsed due to the rains and since the subject matter was not in existence and the plaintiff was not in occupation of the land on which it existed the plaintiff could not succeed in the suit. The first Appellate Court concluded that tenement/hut/structure had collapsed due to very heavy rains and since the tenanted premises were not in existence the plaintiffs tenancy ended there and the plaintiff could not go either beyond or beneath it.

Tenanted Premises (Hon'ble Supreme Court Judgments):

Hon'ble Supreme Court in the case of *Vannattankandy Ibrayi v. Kunhabdulla Hajee*[7] held that if the tenanted premises are destroyed due to natural causes or due to acts of negligence attributable to the tenant, the relationship between the plaintiff as tenant and the defendants as landlords would certainly come to an end and the tenant would not be entitled to insist that the landlord re-erects the said premises and gives to the tenant for his occupation.

In *Hind Rubber Industries (P) Ltd. v. Tayebhai Mohammedbhai Bagasarwalla*[8] court come to the conclusion that in cases where tenancy is created in respect of a building standing on the land, it is the building and the land which are both components and the destruction of the building alone does not determine the tenancy when the land which was the site of the building continues to exist; more so when the building has been destroyed or demolished neither by the landlord nor by the act of nature but solely by the act of the tenant or the person claiming under him.

Decision of the High court:

Court held that Tenancy is a relationship between a landlord and a tenant

7 2001(1) C.C.C. 55 (S.C.)

8 1996(4) Bom. C.R. 414 : A.I.R. 1996 Bombay 389

and that relationship is in respect of a subject-matter and in the present case it was in respect of a hut/ structure which the plaintiff fearing its collapse, abandoned and thereafter it collapsed on account of natural causes. The interest of the tenant in the land on which the premises existed was only incidental. The plaintiff was not in possession of the land on which the premises stood before they had collapsed after the plaintiff abandoned the same fearing their collapse. Court further held that a tenancy of residential premises will extinguish if the tenanted premises collapse either to acts attributable to the tenant or on account of natural causes.

Glossary Of Common Legal Terms

Advocate

A person authorized to appear in a litigation on behalf of a party. An advocate possesses a law degree and is enrolled with a Bar Council, as prescribed by the Advocates Act, 1961. Advocates are the only class of persons legally entitled to practise law. They provide legal advice. After being authorized to appear in a case by a client who has signed a vakalat, advocates prepare cases and argue them in Court. In the Bombay and Calcutta High Courts there is a separate class of legal practitioners, known as solicitors, who prepare the case, but do not argue in Court. When appearing in a courtroom, an advocate usually dresses in black and white, and wears a band and gown. Any complaint against an advocate is made to the Bar Council of India. See junior advocate, advocate-on-record, senior advocate, amicus curiae, vakalath.

Advocate-on-record (AOR)

An advocate who has passed a qualifying examination conducted by the Supreme Court. The examination is taken by an advocate who has been enrolled with a Bar Council for at least five years and has completed one year''s training with an AOR of not less than five years standing. Only an AOR can file a vakalath, a petition, an affidavit or any other application on behalf of a party in the Supreme Court. All the procedural aspects of a case are dealt with by the AOR, with the assistance of a registered clerk. It is the AOR''s name that appears on the cause list. The AOR is held accountable, by the Court, for the conduct of the case. Any notices and correspondence from the Court are sent to the AOR, and not to the party.

Advocate's fees

There are no standardized fees charged for the various tasks performed by an advocate. Some advocates charge a lump sum amount for dealing with an entire case, others charge separate fees for each task - e.g., drafting, filing, legal advice, arguing. Senior advocates generally charge a separate fee for every hearing. In the majority of PIL cases, these fees have been waived by the advocates. When appearing on behalf of a legal aid committee, an advocate receives expenses and nominal fees, at no cost to the party. In some PIL cases the Court has awarded costs to the party.

Affidavit

This is a sworn statement made by a party, in writing, made in the presence of an oath commissioner or a notary public which is used either in support of applications to the Court or as evidence in court proceedings. In writ jurisdiction, cases are generally disposed of on the basis of affidavits. An affidavit in reply to a petition, filed by a respondent, is called a counter affidavit. The petitioner's response to this counter, is called a rejoinder affidavit. All affidavits are verified as to the truth of their contents.

Amicus curiae

Translated from the Latin as 'friend of the Court'. An advocate appears in this capacity when asked to help with the case by the Court or on volunteering services to the Court.

Appeal

The correctness of the decision of a lower court or tribunal is questioned by way of an appeal in a higher court.

Cognizable offence

An offence in which arrest can be made without a warrant.

Commission

A commission is appointed by a court to ascertain or investigate facts needed to decide a case. A commission is usually given specific terms of reference. Members of a commission have been chosen from amongst experts, academics, social activists/workers, advocates, judges and others. Costs of the commission are usually borne by the State. Such commissions have often been appointed in PILs.

Court Fees

These are mandatory charges payable by affixing judicial stamps on petitions, applications and various kinds of documents before they are filed in a court. It is only in legal aid matters that the petitioners are exempt from paying these fees.

Court Master

An officer of the court who occupies a seat just below the judges' dias and assists in the conduct of proceedings.

Decree

The formal expression of an adjudication which, so far as regards the Court expressing it, conclusively determines the rights of the parties with regard to all or any of the matters in controversy in the suit and may be either preliminary or final.

Decree –holder

A person in whose favour a decree has been passed or an order capable of execution has been made.

High Court

Article 214 of the Constitution provides that each state shall have a High Court. This is the highest court in a state and is subordinate only to the Supreme Court of India. The powers of the High Court are broadly categorized as judicial and administrative. In its judicial function the High Court can be approached directly (eg. writ petitions), or in appeals or revisions—both civil and criminal. In its administrative function the High Court supervises the functioning of the lower judiciary in the State. In the civil side, in an ascending order of hierarchy, is the Civil Judge (Junior Division), Civil Judge (Senior Division), the Additional District Judge and the District Judge; the criminal side includes Metropolitan Magistrates, Chief Metropolitan Magistrates, Additional Sessions Judges and the Sessions Judge. The powers of a High Court do not extend beyond the territory of the State. While every decision of the Supreme Court is binding on the High Courts, the decisions of one High Court is not binding on the other. The High Court is a court of record.

Legal Aid

A system by which legal services are rendered at government cost to those in financial need and who cannot afford the cost of litigation. This is mandated by Article 39A of the Constitution. In Delhi, the Delhi High Court Legal Services Committee (DHCLSC) and the Delhi Legal Services Authority (DLSA) provide legal aid on behalf of the State.

Legal Representative

A person who in law represents the estate of a deceased person, and includes any person who intermeddles with the estate of the deceased and where a party sues or is sued in a representative character the person on whom the estate devolves on the death of the party so suing or sued

Locus Standi

Translated from Latin as 'place of standing', locus standi gives the right to pursue a litigation. Under this rule, only a person or group of persons affected by the issue may petition the Court. A petition may be dismissed on the preliminary ground that the petitioner lacks locus standi. However, in PIL, the locus standi of public spirited persons to petition on behalf of others has been recognized. This relaxation of the rule of standing is an important feature of PIL—for instance, journalists, lawyers, politicians, social activists, students, or any 'concerned individual' not acting for personal interest or gain, and not as a 'busy body', have been given standing.

Mesne-profits

Those profits which the person in wrongful possession of such property actually received or might with ordinary diligence have received therefrom, together with interest on such profits, but shall not include profits due to improvements made by the person in wrongful possession

Notification

Notice, information or announcement published in the official gazette notifying, for instance, the coming into effect of a changed law.

Obiter dicta

Remarks of a judge, which are said by the way and are not directly relevant to the case at hand.

Ratio decidendi

The reason behind or crux of a judicial decision.

Res Judicata

A legal principle which prevents a party to a case which has been finally decided from bringing an action on the same issue. For example, a case is barred by res judicata if an earlier case between the same parties has decided upon the same points. This is embodied in Section 11 of the Code of Civil Procedure, 1908.

Respondent

A party against whom a petition is filed. A proforma respondent is a party against whom no relief is sought.

Review

A court has the power to review its orders on specified grounds, as provided by law. Generally the same court which passed the order or judgement in a case reviews its decision. There is, however, no inherent power in a court to review its decisions. The power has to be given by statute or be found in the Constitution.

Revision

Orders that cannot be appealed against can be revised by the High Court on specific grounds, as provided in S 115 of the Code of Civil Procedure, 1908 and Ss. 397 and 401 of the Code of Criminal Procedure, 1973.

Supreme Court

The highest court in the country constituted under Article 124 of the Constitution. Its decisions are law under Article 141 and are binding on all lower courts. It has unlimited powers to do complete justice. It exercises original as well as appellate jurisdiction. Under Article 143 the President of India can ask the Supreme Court for an opinion on questions of law or fact. States can file suits against each other or against the Union of India under Article 131. The Supreme Court can transfer cases to itself from the High Courts or from one High Court to another under Article 139A of the Constitution. It can also transfer civil cases from one Court to another under S 25 of the Code of Civil Procedure, 1908, and likewise criminal cases under S 406 of the Code of Criminal Procedure, 1973. Apart from special leave petitions, in certain instances, appeals can be filed directly against the judgments of lower courts and tribunals. Petitions challenging the election of the President or Vice-President of India are also filed directly in the Supreme Court. The chairperson of a public service commission may be removed only after an inquiry by the Supreme Court. The Supreme Court has a sanctioned strength of 31 judges, headed by the Chief Justice of India. The seat of the Supreme Court is New Delhi and its language is English.

Void

One that law regards as never having taken place.

Writ

A writ is a direction that the Court issues, which is to be obeyed by the authority/person to whom it is issued.

Writ Petition

A petition seeking issuance of a writ is a writ petition. Pits in the first instance in the High Courts and the Supreme Court are writ petitions.

A writ of habeas corpus is issued to an authority or person to produce in court a person who is either missing or kept in illegal custody. Where the detention is found to be without authority of law, the Court may order compensation to the person illegally detained.

A writ of mandamus is a direction to an authority to either do or refrain from doing a particular act. For instance, a writ to the Pollution Control Board to strictly enforce the Pollution Control Acts. For a mandamus to be issued, it must be shown:

a) That the authority was under obligation, statutory or otherwise to act in a particular manner;

b) that the said authority failed in performing such obligation;

c) that such failure has resulted in some specific violation of a fundamental right of either the petitioner or an indeterminate class of persons.

A writ of certiorari is a direction to an authority to produce before the Court the records on the basis of which a decision under challenge in the writ petition has been taken. By looking into those records, the Court will examine whether the authority applied its mind to the relevant materials before it took the decision. If the Court finds that no reasonable person could come to the decision in question, it will set aside (quash) that decision and give a further direction to the authority to consider the matter afresh.

For instance, the permission given by an authority to operate a distillery next to a school can be challenged by filing a petition asking for a writ of certiorari.

A writ of prohibition issues to prevent a judicial authority subordinate to the High Court from exercising jurisdiction over a matter pending before it. This could be on the ground that the authority lacks jurisdiction and further that prejudice would be caused if the authority proceeds to decide the matter. Where the authority is found to be biased and refuses to rescue, a writ of prohibition may issue.

A petition seeking a writ of quo warranto questions the legal basis and authority of a person appointed to public office. For instance, the appointment of a member of a Public Service Commission not qualified to hold the post can be questioned by a writ of quo warranto and appointment nullified if found to be illegal.

A writ of declaration issues to declare an executive, legislative or quasi-judicial act to be invalid in law. For instance, a court could declare S. 81 of the Mental Health Act, 1987 that permits use of mentally ill patients for experimentation to be violative of the fundamental rights of the mentally ill and therefore illegal and void. A petition seeking such declaratory relief must also necessarily seek certain consequential reliefs. For instance, immediate discontinuance of the illegal practice and appropriate remedial compensation.

These apart, a writ petition could seek other writs, orders and directions which the Court may fashion in response to the facts placed before it.

IF YOU THINK[9]

If you think you are beaten, you are
If you think you dare not, you don't!
If you like to win, but think you can't,
It's almost a cinch you won't
If you think you'll lose, you're lost;
For out in the world we find
Success begins with a fellow's will;
It's all in the state of mind.

If you think you are outclassed, you are,
You've got to think high to rise;
You've got to be sure of yourself before
You can ever win a prize
Life's battles don't always go
To the stronger and faster man,
But sooner or later the man who wins
Is the man who thinks he can.

9 You Can Win, Page 55-56